Cultures at War

CULTURES

Moral Conflicts in

Western Democracies

T. ALEXANDER SMITH & RAYMOND TATALOVICH

 broadview press

NATIONAL LIBRARY OF CANADA CATALOGUING IN PUBLICATION

Smith, T. Alexander, 1936–
    Cultures at war : moral conflicts in western democracies /
by T. Alexander Smith and Raymond Tatalovich.

Includes bibliographical references and index.
ISBN 1-55111-334-1

    1. Social values — Political aspects.   2. Social policy.
I. Tatalovich, Raymond II. Title.

JA79.S597 2002   361.6'1   C2002-905114-2

Broadview Press, Ltd. is an independent, international publishing house, incorporated in 1985. Broadview believes in shared ownership, both with its employees and with the general public; since the year 2000 Broadview shares have traded publicly on the Toronto Venture Exchange under the symbol BDP.

We welcome any comments and suggestions regarding any aspect of our publications — please fee free to contact us at the addresses below, or at broadview@broadviewpress.com

North America
Post Office Box 1243,
Peterborough, Ontario,
Canada K9J 7H5
Tel: (705) 743-8990
Fax: (705) 743-8353

3576 California Road,
Orchard Park, New York
USA 14127

customerservice@broadviewpress.com
www.broadviewpress.com

United Kingdom
Thomas Lister, Ltd.
Unit 3 & 4A
Old Boundary Way,
Burscough Rd.
Ormskirk, Lancashire L39
2YW
Tel: (01695) 575112
Fax: (01695) 570120
books@tlyster.co.uk

Australia
UNIREPS
University of
New South Wales
Sydney, NSW, 2052
Tel: + 61 2 96640999
Fax: + 61 2 96645420
info.press@unsw.edu.au

Broadview Press Ltd. gratefully acknowledges the financial support of the Government of Canada through the Book Publishing Industry Development Program for our publishing activities.

Cover design by Liz Broes, Black Eye Design, Inc.
Typeset by Zack Taylor.

Printed in Canada

Contents

Acknowledgements   9

1   Introduction: A New Politics for a New Century   11

PART ONE   *Raw Material for a Politics and Policy of Moral Conflict*

2   Status Anxiety and Political Ideology   25
3   Cultural Theory and Warring Cultures   47

PART TWO   *Morality Politics by Unconventional Means*

4   Breaking Into or Breaking Apart the Political System   65
5   Politicians Strike Back: Legislative Restraints on
      Morality Policy   107
6   The Juridicization of the Morality Policy Process   137
7   Bypassing Elites: Morality Policy by Plebiscite   173

PART THREE   *Uncompromising Ends of Morality Policy*

8   Building Political Consensus and the Public Peace   201
9   Conclusion: Morality Policy and Democratic Governance   239

APPENDIX

A.1   Attitudes Toward Capital Punishment in Five Western
       Democracies   253
A.2   Attitudes Toward Abortion in Five Western Democracies   259
A.3   Attitudes Toward Homosexuality in Five Western
       Democracies   267

Selected Bibliography   275

Index   297

For Alex and Graham

T.A.S.

To Anne,
and Our Legacy of Bassethounds:

Sir Hugo of Baskerville
Sir Beauregard of Brighton-Downs
Sir Boswell of Phillips-Glen
Lady Beatrice of Sussex-on-Lake
Sir Frederic of Nottingham Lane

R.T.

Acknowledgements

A project that seeks to discuss the range of moral conflicts in Canada, the United States, the United Kingdom, France, and Germany is too ambitious not to cause the authors moments of self-doubt. A project of this scope needs nurturing, learned counsel, and reality-checking. We are so thankful that Michael Harrison, vice-president at Broadview Press, saw promise despite our very tentative beginnings. Thanks, Michael, for being there when we needed you.

We worked and reworked each chapter. Though we both are policy analysts, our range of knowledge does not encompass the politics of all five countries, nor the fields of public law, critical social philosophy, and sociology of religion which proved to be critically important to our analysis. It was not until we submitted a first draft and received the reviews which Broadview had commissioned that we knew we were on solid intellectual ground. Not only were those reviews insightful and candid but—above all—they excited our creative energies. Their enthusiasm validated that we were on the cusp of producing a significant work of scholarship. For that, we are eternally grateful to Professor Leslie Pal of Carleton University, Canada, and Professor Philip Cowley of the University of Nottingham, United Kingdom. Professors Pal and Cowley: we owe you an intellectual and emotional debt.

Yet significant scholarship unread or incomprehensible is hardly an achievement. The purpose of our academic enterprise is to share knowledge and, more importantly insights, with our colleagues, students, and, hopefully, the general reader. Because Broadview Press has offices in Canada, the United States, and the United Kingdom, our hope is to reach a worldwide audience, because moral conflicts—as shown by 9/11/01—have gone global. They are going to pose threats to civil society for years and decades to come, so we must understand them in hopes of reworking our political institutions in ways that civil society can tame them. Was it the luck of the draw, or Michael Harrison's good sense, that Broadview Press assigned our manuscript for copyediting to Betsy Struthers, herself the author of six books of poetry and three murder mysteries? She is an immensely talented person, and she applied those talents to making sense of our, at times, convoluted writings. The result is a book written in a prose immediately accessible to all.

Along the way Tatalovich made desperate phone calls and e-mails to scholars who are more expert than he on the variety of approaches and topics included in this book. They mailed him articles and papers, or clarified citations, or offered referrals to other specialists. There were many, including Ted Jelen (University of Nevada-Las Vegas), Dorothy Stetson (Florida Atlantic University), Kenneth Holland (University of Memphis), Susan Mezey (Loyola University Chicago), Donley T. Studlar (West Virginia University), Byron D'Andra Orey (University of Nebraska), Gary Mauser (Simon Fraser University, British Columbia), Tom Flanagan (University of Calgary, Alberta), David Conradt (East Carolina University, North Carolina), Stewart Hyson (University of New Brunswick), Melissa Haussman (Suffolk University, Massachusetts), Michael MacMillan (Mount Saint Vincent University, Nova Scotia), James Guth (Furman University, South Carolina), Fred Kniss (Loyola University Chicago), Dennis Hoover (Trinity College, Connecticut), Richard Braunstein (University of South Dakota), Suzanne Staggenborg (McGill University, Quebec), David Ingram (Loyola University Chicago), Timothy Newman (Kent State University, Ohio), David Rayside (University of Toronto), and Mildred Schwartz (University of Illinois at Chicago and New York University). A special thank-you goes to Jason Azmier at Canada West Foundation, for supplying us with referendum results on video lottery terminals. To any other colleagues to whom I availed myself but have not acknowledged, forgive me, and blame the aging process!

Without doubt the unsung heroes of academic research are librarians, but Ursula Scholz and Jennifer Stegen shall remain anonymous no longer. They are the professional staff charged with inter-library loan services at Loyola University Chicago. In doing this research Tatalovich ordered books and articles on occasions too numerous to count. Making use of those sources was easy after Ursula and Jennifer had acted expeditiously to get them.

I

Introduction:
A New Politics for a New Century

Why did the United States constitutionalize abortion on demand when most Americans were opposed? How could Canada abolish capital punishment despite overwhelming opposition by the Canadian people? What would inspire Catholic France to legalize same-sex unions against the preferences of most French Catholics? Surely it is not because morality policies are too trivial or routine to be recognized by ordinary citizens since, all observers agree, these conflicts are highly visible, intense, and contagious. *It is because morality policy is rule by elites—not the people.* And this is happening *not* in authoritarian regimes but in Western nations that proudly proclaim themselves to be representative governments. The contradiction between democratic politics and elitist policies is the most compelling normative and empirical lesson of this project.

Cultures At War brings together two policy analysts, one educated in comparative European politics and the other an Americanist, who draw upon a relatively new approach in political science—"cultural theory"—as well as rich sociological and social psychological literatures to explain the rise of moral conflicts in the mature democracies of North America and Europe. The recent increase of morality policies and politics has stimulated the research interests of political scientists but, while morally charged political conflicts in themselves are hardly novel, students of public policy generally have not appreciated the extent to which the advent of the postindustrial or postmaterialist age is rapidly transforming the mix of policy issues that matter most to ordinary citizens.[1]

Conflicts over bread-and-butter issues, so dominant in the industrial era and readily reinforced by a mass of industrial workers, cohesive working-class neighbourhoods, and strong trade union membership, have been eroded by unparalleled income growth, mass consumption, and increasing demands for white collar occupations. At a time when consumption goods have become more plentiful than ever, it may seem strange that moral controversies are assuming more importance in public life. In fact, the contradiction is more apparent than real. The salience of moral conflicts are caused less by a decline in the relative importance of material goods than by the social strains created by rapid social and geographic mobility, a general delegitimization of elites, and growing demands for equality in many areas of social life.

The profound changes in the way we live make the individual far less dependent today upon family, group, neighbourhood, and church. This "individualization" and the emotional loss entailed by the decline of those traditional social supports, when combined with the growth in education and leisure, have unleashed competitive struggles over *status*—who among us ought to be esteemed and why.[2] Liberated from the tyranny of tradition and custom, the individual is freer than ever to fashion his or her own way of life. It is not that we value material goods less but that social activists are focusing on the moral aspects of politics as a vehicle either to claim new status or to defend old status from attack. Anybody who lived in the rigid status and class societies of the nineteenth and early twentieth centuries undoubtedly would find all these pretensions of status rivalries difficult to fathom.

These status frustrations are manifested in politics.[3] The stresses of modern life cause us to identify political issues and public policies that support our own cultural ways of life. The growing moralization of issues is largely stimulated by the growth of fundamentally different cultural values, "egalitarianism" and "individualism" on the one hand, and "hierarchism" on the other. What fuels moral controversies are the many threats posed to the individual's status and identity and, assuming that aggregate wealth continues rising in the future, it is probable that demands for *status recognition* will so accelerate that they may pose periodic threats to the stability of political institutions no less dangerous than the class conflicts of the past century.

In the remainder of this chapter, we first offer a brief overview of this subfield of policy studies. Second, we consider the essential qualities of moral controversies and why they produce political processes different from other types of public policy. Third, we suggest why morality issues have surfaced in this particular historical era. Relatedly, we must consider whether such stable democracies as Canada, the United Kingdom, Germany, France, and the United States possess the necessary institutional resources to manage these explosive kinds of issues. If the answer is no, then these developed democracies may be faced with even more intractable policy disputes in the future. What the rise of multiple episodes of moral controversy portend for democratic politics is the ultimate concern of this book.

The Study of Morality Policy

If one had to date the beginnings of this subfield of policy analysis, the honours likely would go to the late Professor James B. Christoph of Indiana University, who observed parliamentary irregularities when the UK debated the abolishment of capital punishment. In parliamentary systems like Britain, the government ordinarily presents legislation to Parliament. Since the political party of the government of the day holds the majority of legislative seats, Parliament typically rubber-stamps its proposals. This was not true, however, for capital punishment; according to Christoph, "because of the high moral and emotional content of the dispute, government leaders often viewed it as a matter of private conscience and treated it as an instance of that limited category of issues which, peripheral to the main business of government (and to the class differences that separate the parties), can be freed from the ordinary claims of party cohesion and discipline."[4] Moreover these attributes, Christoph noted, were typical of other issues, notably birth control, homosexuality, and prostitution, that also "plumb deep-seated moral codes."[5] Thus, Christoph's assessment of capital punishment showed a pattern of policymaking which deviated sharply from the parliamentary norm.

The voluminous case-study literature written in the 1950s and 1960s was devoted primarily to economic issues and the role of interest groups. But those studies left many political scientists troubled that the sheer accumulation of information was not being matched by the development of sound theory.[6] It was this intellectual vacuum that Theodore J. Lowi filled in 1964 with the publication of a widely-acclaimed article.[7] Lowi made sense of the mountain of case studies by classifying policies according to the particular attributes they had in common. In his formulation of policymaking processes, Lowi stood the cause-and-effect relationship ordinarily applied to group polities on its head. Whereas political scientists generally sought to explain policy outcomes as a result of political conflict among interest groups, Lowi contended that "policy determines politics," meaning that public policy shapes the political process. He argued that three types of public policies—distributive, regulatory, and redistributive—each produces different political patterns.[8] Although his typology directly involved the United States, Lowi's insight soon was applied to comparative public policy analysis.[9]

Missing from Lowi's typology, however, were those policy disputes that involved Christoph's "deep-seated moral codes." To resolve this problem, an "emotive symbolic" policy type was added by T. Alexander Smith to Lowi's original typology. Emotive symbolic policies "generate emotional support for deeply held values, but unlike the other [public policy] types ... the values sought are essentially noneconomic."[10] Typical examples include not only capital punishment but school prayer, abortion, homosexuality, racial segregation, flag disputes, and racial or ethnic conflicts. In the 1970s case-studies of morality issues by comparative scholars began to appear on such diverse subjects as racial immigration in Britain and daylight savings time in New South Wales.[11]

Similar concerns were voiced by American political scientists who, though otherwise sympathetic to Lowi's approach, were convinced that morality issues were substantively different from distribution, regulation, or redistribution. In a study of American abortion policy, Tatalovich and Daynes concluded that an additional type of policy was necessary to round out the Lowi paradigm.[12] While agreeing that issues of morality were also regulatory, the nature of this kind of regulation is very different from economic regulation. As Tatalovich and Daynes later argued. "what is being regulated is not an economic transaction but a social relationship," whether it be gay rights, church-state relations, gun control, pornography, or official English (language) laws.[13] Moreover social regulations are much more likely to find their way into the courts, and single-issue groups also tended to play a dominant political role. Thus, the politics and processes surrounding social and economic regulation bear scant resemblance to one another.

There are other scholars who conceptualize a relationship between morality policy and Lowi's redistributive policy. Moral controversies are said to resemble redistribution in all respects save one—the values involved are non-economic—so these scholars draw a distinction between the redistribution of economic *goods* and the redistribution of social *values*. Their intellectual leader, Kenneth J. Meier, is an important policy analyst, whose many works include a book on illicit drugs and alcohol. Morality politics, says Meier, occur when "one segment of society attempts by government fiat to impose their values on the rest of society" and "[a]s such they are a form of redistributive policy that is rarely viewed as redistributive because the policies redistribute values rather than income." Yet even Meier seemingly agrees that government policies also attempt to regulate behaviour (prevent the use of drugs or driving while intoxicated).[14] The claim that morality policies redistribute values, a view initially put forth by Ripley and Franklin, has wide currency among quantitative analysts of morality policy who follow Meier's lead.[15]

The source of this intellectual debate lies in Lowi's seminal 1964 article, in which he said that redistributive policies were characterized by large-scale *class* conflicts, strong ideological debate, and the dominant role of huge coalitions representing labour versus management. At that stage of his career Lowi was strongly influenced by E.E. Schattschneider, the pluralist theorist who had argued that politics was basically a struggle between those who hoped to "privatize" politics and those who wished to "socialize" political issues.[16]

Thus, redistributive policies were characterized by broad scopes and intensities of conflict between bourgeoisie and proletariat, Left and Right, haves and have-nots, or employers and employees in which *class* tensions were clearly evident. For those analysts of morality policy with empirical data in search of a theory, the obvious answer was to eliminate economics from Lowi's formulation; the resulting political process looks like what is exhibited by moral controversies.

Analysts of abortion policy in Europe are inclined to believe that regulation, not value redistribution, best explains morality politics.[17] Elaine Sharp, the leading American urbanist who studies "culture wars" in American cities, seemingly agrees.[18] Lowi's typology inspired Paul Peterson to classify urban policy "arenas" based on government outputs—developmental, allocational, or redistributional—but Sharp counters that "[c]ulture war issues do not comfortably fit within any of these arenas," and "[i]t takes a conceptual stretching to fit culture wars into Peterson's redistribution area" since "moral values rather than material resources are at stake" and because the economic repercussions are "not as clear" as in cases of "targeted programs for the poor." Thus Sharp joins the policy perspective that "[c]ulture wars therefore may be viewed more properly as constituting a distinctive, fourth arena of city politics."[19] We shall have more to say about this intellectual debate in subsequent chapters. For now, let us suggest that, while governments can redistribute wealth by compulsion, they most assuredly cannot redistribute personal values. The imposition of government edicts by no means guarantees that citizens have changed their attitudes, certainly not in the short run.

The Nature of Moral Controversies

Moral controversies are essentially cultural disputes, affirming certain cultural values while rejecting others. They bear little upon material self-interest, because whatever material gain is derived from either side is likely to be negligible as compared to other-directed ends. On capital punishment, abortion, or gay rights, the political incentive depends upon the depth of cultural animosity and philosophical argument since, statistically speaking, relatively few individuals have a friend or acquaintance on death row, a pregnant but unmarried daughter, or a son or daughter who has "come out of the closet." The dispute over fox-hunting in the UK in the late 1990s, for example, brought crowds into the streets once the Labour government of Prime Minister Tony Blair sought elimination of the practice. No major economic group seemed to care in the least, but there was a sharp division between Left and Right, town and country, Labour and Tory, and environmentalist versus anti-environmentalist.

The vast majority of participants will be moved to action by principled arguments about equality and liberty, although self-interest may be a motivation for certain policies targeted to beneficiary groups, like affirmative action. Struggles over the regulation of property that pit environmentalists against real estate owners may impose substantial economic costs on the latter group, but the environmentalists do not necessarily enjoy any more of the "collective good" that results from purer water or cleaner air as compared to the vast majority of "free riders" who stand on the side-lines. These activists are willing to invest substantial political commitment because the environmentalism debate is grounded more in cultural values than in economic attitudes.[20]

The levels of political participation in policy disputes vary enormously, and Meier argues that the political forces surrounding morality policies are either entirely quiescent or extremely volatile. Meier is drawing an important distinction between two-sided and one-sided morality policy. Two-sided disputes (what Meier terms "redistributive" morality policy) like abortion, school prayer, and gay rights provoke deep conflict between divergent constituencies and interest groups. Unlike those controversies, one-sided morality policies represent what Meier calls the "politics of sin," which, for example, include drunk driving, drug abuse, and murder. "Everybody is opposed to sin," says Meier, since the "only opposition to this type of morality policy is clearly the work of Satan."[21]

An absence of conflict with regard to a particular issue in any particular nation-state at any one time does not foreclose conflict over the same issue at a future date. A pertinent illustration is capital punishment. In the United States, for example, capital punishment has been sanctioned by 38 states and the federal government, upheld as constitutional by the Supreme Court, and has nearly reached its high-water mark in the level of support it receives from the American people. While arguments for and against the death penalty are primarily grounded in morals and ethics rather than material concerns, there is so far no serious opposition to its continuation. On the other hand, any serious effort to resurrect the death penalty in Canada, the UK, or France would undoubtedly precipitate serious political resistance. All morality policy, rest assured, does not necessarily involve moral conflict.[22] However, one can say that what, at one moment in time, is one-sided morality policy could, with a bit of political agitation, become quite two-sided. While ideologically committed individuals will become politically engaged, direct political agitation by the public at large is more problematic. Arousing the public to action may depend more upon unique triggering events, such as an unjust execution, that dramatize how an issue cuts to the heart of our core values.

Given the tendency of the public to draw a line in the sand, the rigidity of public opinion leaves elected officials in a quandary. Since these issues arouse deep controversy but also encourage activists on both sides to resist compromise, they can erode the democratic "rules of the game" and lead to political volatility. Political elites are often not eager to address such issues, as they would prefer to bargain quietly behind the closed doors of government. A study of "culture wars" in American cities led Elaine Sharp to conclude that "local officials do indeed play this role of *evasion*" insofar as "they attempt to defuse culture wars by delaying or deferring action on the demands of activists, making symbolic gestures to appease one side without activating the other, or otherwise diverting attention from what could be a heated and full-blown controversy."[23] However this covert strategy is not always an option for political leaders. When emotions are sufficiently aroused, when information can be simplified, and when advocates are clearly polarized along an issue divide, negotiation of differences is exceedingly difficult and costly in political and electoral terms, especially for those officials whose political parties and constituents are deeply divided.

Moral Conflicts as Status Struggles

Firmly held beliefs do not exist in a social vacuum. When social roles are clearly defined and custom reigns supreme, moral controversies are less likely to surface in the political life of a community. Under those conditions the individual is more secure in knowing that his or her expectations will generally match the expectations of others. In postmaterialist society, however, one's status is often in dispute. Disagreements continually arise about how basic values ought to be ranked and how merit should be determined. Social roles can be contradictory, overlapping, or confused, with the result that mutually shared expectations about social roles and status gradations are much more difficult to establish. The resulting psychological and social tensions undoubtedly provide fodder for the growth in the number and variety of social and political demands for recognition based on race, ethnicity, gender, or any alternative lifestyle.

The political significance of status frustration for democratic societies was clearly appreciated by Alexis de Tocqueville, the French observer of American life during the 1830s. He wrote: "One must not blind oneself to the fact that democratic institutions most successfully develop sentiments of envy in the human heart. This is not because they provide the means for everybody to rise to the level of everybody else but because these means are constantly proving inadequate in the hands of those using them. Democratic institutions awaken and flatter the passion for equality without ever being able to satisfy it entirely"[24] At the turn of the nineteenth century it was Max Weber, the German sociologist, whose reaction to Marxism gave the concept "status" greater sociological precision. By status groups Weber meant "communities based upon the sharing of similar claims to social honor and prestige" as contrasted with social classes that reflected "similar economic capacity to command scarce resources and life chances."[25] Weber thought that Marx's emphasis on class was excessive and that Marxian social conflict had unduly neglected the role of both political power and social status in generating societal conflict. In drawing a sharp distinction between the concepts of *status* and *class*, Weber felt that status was no less significant for social relationships than class was to the means of economic production.

Weber's conceptualization of status would eventually prove more influential in America than in Europe. While European scholars placed relatively more emphasis on the role of class as opposed to status in their research, their American counterparts gave more weight to status. We should not be surprised by this difference in emphasis, because the extensive labour-management disputes, the close allegiance between trade unions and socialist or communist parties, and the greater class voting in Europe as compared with the United States meant that class conflict has provided the fundamental orientation for most European social scientists.[26]

Yet it would be unfair to conclude that European scholars totally neglected the problem of status. The growth of fascism after World War I led various scholars to focus on the political effects of status frustration. The mass appeal of fascist parties called for an explanation. The effort by rigid Marxist scholars to conceptualize fascism as the "last stage of capitalism" was an inadequate reading of historical events given that, throughout Italy, Spain, and Germany, fascist parties had gained electoral support among various social groups, even the working class, though its greatest strength came from the "petty bourgeoisie." Fascism was generally more populist than was the membership of the bourgeois and rightist parties of the 1930s.

A more important scholarly argument was that many individuals attracted to fascism had relatively few attachments to established groups or classes. Small merchants apparently felt trapped between the great industrial conglomerates and the giant unions, and white-collar workers on the lowest rungs of the middle class felt pressure from well-paid skilled blue-collar labourers. Moreover, the growth of huge public and private bureaucracies, the social and economic dislocations from rapid industrialization, the centralized power of party machines, the concentration of media control, and the massive inflation of the 1920s coupled with the worldwide Depression of the 1930s converged to create what sociologists came to call "mass society." The mass society was depicted as an impersonal social order where the family, neighbourhood, trade unions, professional associations, and other groups—all of which had traditionally mediated between the individual and the state—no longer could provide sufficient psychological support for what were increasingly alienated and isolated individuals.[27]

Organization of the Book

Chapter 2 deals with the ideological manifestations of status politics. Five decades ago American sociologists viewed "status anxiety" as endemic to right-wing causes, but that diagnosis was time-bound as well as culture-bound. Today the concept of status has been resurrected by the political left to promote "identity politics" to remedy the inferior status of disadvantaged social groups. The justification for giving preferences and political recognition to women, gays, minorities, and indigenous peoples is grounded in multiculturalism, for which there is no better contemporary example of cultural egalitarianism. The postmaterialists envision a political backlash to this social agenda coming from the New Right, and in the United States (and to a lesser degree in Canada) it has surfaced as a coalition of fundamentalists and evangelicals known as the Christian Right. The literature on the sociology of religion addresses what has been popularized as "culture wars" in American politics. Morality politics implies that values will displace economics as the mainstay of politics, an interpretation consistent with the postmaterialist thesis. We discuss postmaterialism towards understanding how the Left-Right ideological axis is becoming politically realigned. We conclude this chapter by introducing the reader to cultural theory, which we think is a superior framework for assessing status conflict in modern society.

Chapter 3 details the basics of cultural theory and explains how social structure provokes the emergence of cultural hierarchs, cultural individualists, and cultural egalitarians. From the perspective of cultural theory, moral conflicts are fundamentally disputes between the forces of *status-differentiation* and *status-equalization*.

Chapter 4 turns to the political system. Ideas that germinate in a society will not have much public impact until they influence decision-makers in government. To do so, new ideas must gain wide currency in society by influencing the mass media and ultimately shaping public opinion. In many instances this stage is a precondition before morality policy finds its way onto the policy agenda. Anything as traumatic as threats to the normative order will face obstacles in trying to reach the agenda of government. Thus, identity politics relies upon a variety of agenda-setting approaches, including "new" social movements, to gain political redress.

As explained in Chapter 5, however, political elites may not be willing to risk their standing with the electorate by fully embracing these new demands for social egalitarianism. Especially in the parliamentary regimes of Canada, the UK, Germany, and France, an array of legislative devices are available to politicians to deflect, delay, or defeat highly controversial issues. But times are changing, and the legislative arena no longer may be the preferred institutional venue for resolving these morally charged issues.

Chapter 6 discusses judicial activism as an alternative policymaking venue. This we call the "juridicization" of the morality policy process. The United States has been the leading indicator of what is now happening in other Western democracies. The American Bill of Rights was established in 1791, and in 1982 Canada entrenched a Charter of Rights and Freedoms in its repatriated Constitution. The UK, France, and Germany are signatories to the European Human Rights Convention which authorizes a supra-national European Court of Human Rights to decide cases against those sovereign nations, including such issues as abortion, homosexuality, and language rights. Another policy alternative, the subject of Chapter 7, is quite common in the American states and has been used frequently in Ireland, Italy, Australia, and notably Switzerland. It resolves morality policy questions by voter referendum or plebiscite.

Chapter 8 revisits the question of morality policy as "redistribution of values" by focusing on public opinion and the consensus-building effects of law. The question is whether the majority is supportive of changing morality policy *before* those laws are enacted. If not, then the relevant question is whether the general public will come to accept new proscriptions on their personal behaviour. This issue of compliance is central to morality policy implementation, which we conceptualize as a mixture of regulatory and redistributive processes.

Chapter 9 summarizes our analytical findings towards one unmistakable conclusion: morality policy is both anti-majoritarian and politically unaccountable. Whether the decision-makers are judicial or parliamentary, the process is elitist because across Europe, Canada, and (at the national level) in the United States, cases of morality policy by direct democracy are few and far between. We end on a prescriptive note, by endorsing "postmaterialist shift" as the optimal way of bringing about value change through consensus-building, as is evidenced by one last case study: legalized euthanasia in The Netherlands.

Notes

1. Ronald Inglehart, *Culture Shift in Advanced Industrial Society* (Princeton, NJ: Princeton University Press, 1990).

2. Ulrich Beck, "Beyond Status and Class: Will There Be an Individualized Class Society?," *Modern German Sociology*, ed. Volker Meja, Dieter Misgeld, and Nico Stehr (New York: Columbia University Press, 1987) 340-55.

3. See Arnold Gehlen, *Man in the Age of Technology* (New York: Columbia University Press, 1980); Zygmunt Bauman, *Freedom* (Minneapolis, MN: University of Minnesota Press, 1988); and Seymour Martin Lipset, *Political Man* (Garden City, NY: Doubleday, 1960).

4. James B. Christoph, "Capital Punishment and British Party Responsibility," *Political Science Quarterly* 77 (March 1962): 32.

5. James B. Christoph, *Capital Punishment and British Politics* (Chicago: University of Chicago Press, 1962) 173.

6. Consider, for instance, that there are literally thousands of domestic public policies, from public works to social welfare to taxation, and then add others which mainly affect a nation's foreign affairs, and then multiply that total by the 20 or so developed countries of the Western world, and the resulting multitude of policies would do more than strain our imaginations—they would render impossible any meaningful scholarly analysis of public policy, specifically how they arose and what impacts they have on society.

7. Theodore J. Lowi, "American Business, Public Policy, Case Studies, and Political Theory," *World Politics* 16 (July 1964): 677-715.

8. The meaning of regulatory policy is apparent from our discussion. Distributive policy involves the allocation of government largess, mainly funding, to a large number of recipients, for example highway construction money, or college student loans, or research grants to universities, or even homeowners' tax exemptions for mortgage interest paid. Redistributive policy involves the reallocation of wealth between economic classes, usually from the more affluent to the less affluent, through the use of progressive taxes and welfare programs.

9. T. Alexander Smith, "A Phenomenology of the Policy Process," *International Journal of Comparative Sociology* 23 (1969): 1-16.

10. T. Alexander Smith, *The Comparative Policy Process* (Santa Barbara, CA: CLIO Press, 1975) 90.

11. Donley T. Studlar, "Elite Responsiveness or Elite Autonomy: British Immigration Policy Reconsidered," *Ethnic and Racial Studies* 3 (April 1980): 207-23; Keith Richmond, "Daylight Savings in New South Wales: A Case of Emotive Symbolic Politics," *Australian Journal of Public Administration* 37 (1978): 374-85.

12. Raymond Tatalovich and Byron W. Daynes, *The Politics of Abortion* (New York: Praeger, 1981) 221-28.

13. Raymond Tatalovich and Byron W. Daynes, "Introduction," *Moral Controversies in American Politics* (Armonk, NY: M.E. Sharpe, 1998) xxx.

14. Kenneth J. Meier, *The Politics of Sin* (Armonk, NY: M.E. Sharpe, 1994) 246-47. Note also p. 4.

15. Randall B. Ripley and Grace A. Franklin, *Congress, the Bureaucracy, and Public Policy* (Pacific Grove, CA: Brooks/Cole, 1991) 16. A close reading (16-17) of Ripley and Franklin, however, shows that they do not believe that all morality policies are redistributive but that some may be regulatory. Looking at school prayer, pornography, crime, gun control, affirma-

tive action, and abortion, they wrote: "The most important issue in that set is affirmative action. It fits our scheme very well as a redistributive issue and generates that kind of politics. Abortion is, for the most part, a redistributive issue. Well-off women can afford safe abortions, short of a complete national ban that is effectively enforced. Poor women are the first to be denied access to safe abortions. To the extent that gun control and pornography are linked to attempts to reduce crime, a form of protective regulation is involved, as are federal crime measures in general. Only school prayer is not accounted for. However, school prayer is dealt with almost exclusively in rhetorical terms, so federal policy is not really formulated." Empirical applications of Meier's formulation can be found in Christopher Z. Mooney, ed., *The Public Clash of Private Values: The Politics of Morality Policy* (New York: Chatham House Publishers, 2001).

16. E.E. Schattschneider, *The Semi-Sovereign People* (New York: Holt, Rinehart and Winston, 1960) 7.

17. Joni Lovenduski and Joyce Outshoorn, eds., *The New Politics of Abortion* (London: SAGE Publications, 1986) 9-11.

18. Elaine B. Sharp, "Introduction," *Culture Wars and Local Politics*, ed. Elaine B. Sharp (Lawrence, KS: University Press of Kansas, 1999) 3.

19. Sharp, "Introduction" 8. She debunks this conceptualization of culture wars as redistributional after saying: "Perhaps the closest fit is with the redistributional arena, in that culture war issues typically involve conflicts between the community's status quo with respect to the legitimacy of various ways of life or acceptable standards of behaviour and the demands of challenging groups for a share of the community's stock of legitimacy. But in order to accommodate the values and morality standards of these new claimants, there would be encroachments on the values and morality standards of dominant groups."

20. Gunnar Grendstad and Per Selle, "Cultural Theory, Postmaterialism, and Environmental Attitudes," Ellis and Thompson, *Culture Matters* 151-68.

21. Meier 247.

22. See Christopher Z. Mooney and Mei-Hsien Lee, "The Influence of Values on Consensus and the Contentious Morality Policy: U.S. Death Penalty Reform, 1956-1982," *Journal of Politics* 62 (February 2000): 223-39.

23. Sharp, "Introduction" 5. Also see Elaine B. Sharp, "Culture Wars and City Politics: Local Government's Role in Social Conflict," *Urban Affairs Review* 31 (July 1996): 738-58.

24. Alexis de Tocqueville, *Democracy in America*, Vol. 1, ed. J.P. Mayer, trans. George Lawrence (c1969; New York, Perennial Library, Harper and Row, 1988) 198.

25. Max Weber, *Economy and Society* (New York: Bedminister, 1968) 302-07, 901-40.

26. Maurice Duverger, *Political Parties* (New York: John Wiley and Sons, 1963) 419. The UK and Northern Europe, including West Germany, had class-based party alignments.

27. Emil Lederer, *State of the Masses* (New York: W.W. Norton, 1940); Erich Fromm, *Escape from Freedom* (New York: Farrar and Rinehart, 1941); Hanna Arendt, *The Origins of Totalitarianism* (New York: Harcourt, Brace, 1951); and William Kornhauser, *The Politics of Mass Society* (Glencoe, IL: The Free Press, 1959).

PART ONE

Raw Material for a Politics and Policy of Moral Conflict

2

Status Anxiety and
Political Ideology

Status anxiety in postmaterialist societies knows no ideological boundaries. If status anxiety leads to preservationist politics on the Right, then most assuredly status anxiety excites political demands for equalization on the Left. What is commonly understood as "identity politics" are essentially campaigns by "victim" groups—women, racial and ethnic minorities, homosexuals, and indigenous peoples—to elevate their social status by gaining political recognition and legal rights as members of groups, not as autonomous individuals. Obviously it matters whether a group is super-ordinate or subordinate in the social hierarchy of a nation. We begin with the social psychological theory of how the status of individuals or groups are ordered in Western democracies. The modern view is that status is socially constructed through interpersonal relationships.

The Importance of "Status Identity"

Once traditional social and economic restraints on individuals are relaxed, there is a tendency for competitive claims for status to expand. This increased demand for social esteem, in turn, is accompanied by a growth in individualism and equality of treatment as criteria which test social conventions. In more affluent and mobile societies, the quest for status prestige is mainly confined to those people for whom time, education, and money are not barriers to the creation of unique lifestyles. Under these conditions, what we may call a "paradox of progress" emerges, in which rising incomes, social mobility, and mass consumption have the effect of not so much eliminating social and political tensions as shifting them more and more to issues of lifestyle and culture. Indeed, material progress may breed both optimism about what the future ought to bring and a gnawing dissatisfaction with existing social arrangements and political institutions.[1] In this milieu, we suggest, status frustrations and

25

cultural disagreements are powerful stimuli for a growing concern with morality policies. Broadly construed, these new forms of political conflict reflect cultural and status disputes between those individuals and groups determined to make social statuses more equal and other forces that wish to retain the traditional status ordering or to make them even more unequal.

Imagine a traditional society in which general economic scarcity is the norm, and where class and status patterns sharply differentiate the aristocracy, bourgeoisie, and peasantry. Social mobility between these three social rankings is extremely rare, if not impossible, because each status group is identified by distinctive education, speech, manners, and consumption habits. People generally do not question the existing inequalities and either enforce or passively obey a plethora of social conventions ascribed to each group from the moment of birth.

Now imagine a modern economic and political system characterized by sustained economic growth, steady capital accumulation, an intricate division of labour, and a very large and diverse middle class. Social mobility—upward and downward—is not unusual. Only at the very top or very bottom of the social hierarchy do both economic class and social status merge neatly. Also affluence, education, leisure, and geographical mobility are widespread, all of which encourages a rich diversity of opinion—a "pluralism of life-worlds."[2] Understandably, conventional standards and traditional values will come under pressure in a modern society. With a rich variety of consumer goods to put on display, many individuals are able to develop unique and diverse lifestyles as one method of gaining respect and deference.[3]

What is usually understood to be status identification, according to sociologist C. Wright Mills, depends upon *claims* to honour and standing from one side and the *bestowal* of honour and standing from the other.[4] Status identification, therefore, is a two-way street of communicated values. Undoubtedly modern conditions in numerous ways make social agreement over status positions more difficult. Should money determine status? Family background? Education? Race? Ethnicity? Occupation? In what particular combinations? When individuals profoundly disagree about what values ought to be given priority, or which types of conduct and manners ought to be accepted, a social consensus is unlikely to emerge.[5]

If we humans are competitive creatures, we are also social animals in continual need of companionship, approval, and material assistance from other human beings. When we learn that some types of conduct are acceptable to our associates and friends, even strangers, but other kinds of behaviour are frowned upon, we are often willing to alter our behaviour in order to gain the approval of others. In other words, we become role-takers by "taking the attitudes" of others.[6] By imagining how others will respond to our own actions under similar conditions, we try to anticipate their reactions and thus arrive at a mutual understanding of how we ought to behave.[7] Every day in multiple ways we internalize norms and values that become part of our habitual behaviour. As mutually shared expectations, the social roles we adopt become the means by which we navigate the treacherous waters of human relations. Roles introduce an element of predictability into our social relationships. If challenged or violated, established roles are likely to be vigorously defended. Gender "rights" or same-sex marriage, for example, not only represent the quest by women or gays for an alternative identity but are also viewed, by men and heterosexuals, as serious attacks on traditional social roles.

Let us be more precise. *Identity* establishes *what* the person is and *where* he or she is *situated* in terms of others. According to social psychologist Gregory Stone, each individual possesses an identity "when others PLACE him as a social object by assigning him the same words of identity that he appropriates for himself or ANNOUNCES. It is the coincidence of placements and announcements that identity becomes a meaning of the self."[8] Note the implication: a good sense of "who I am"—the bedrock of a secure "self"—requires that there be a meaningful correspondence between *how we wish to be seen*, on the one hand, and *how others actually see us*. The "inner" subjective world of the individual and his or her interpretation of the "outer" world (family, friends, peers) must be seen as "meaningful." It must make "sense."

The principal means by which identity is established, says Stone, are *discourse* and *appearance*.[9] Discourse extends to ordinary conversation and gestures, while appearance can include dress, body, carriage, and manners as well as more general qualities related to image, reputation, or style. Discourse and appearance are crucial to one's "placement" by others. The short-hand term "identity" implies some kind of identification *with other people*, and the range of possible reactions run the gamut of emotions from strong sympathy to boredom to intense hostility.

Unlike traditional societies, the socio-psychological "fit" between "announcements" and "placements" in modern or postmodern societies is very weak. For example, economic class and social status are more likely to diverge in important ways and, as a consequence, disagreements over definitions of status become more salient. Traditional social roles become unclear or confusing and, therefore, are challenged. Given the proliferation and diversity of lifestyles, it is a price paid for the benefits of modern existence. Complex bureaucracies with their divisions of labour, multiplication of tasks, and highly paid experts and middle-class professionals leave the average person confused.[10] In other words, the incredible diversity of the modern workplace means that the traditional norms and roles no longer signal whether one's status is being recognized, let alone appreciated, by others in society.

The effort to create a secure status identity, and hence a meaningful self, through occupation or consumption is harmless enough in individual cases. But if the competition over alternative lifestyles stimulates the formation of organized interests, whose disagreements are transformed into political conflicts revolving around such explosive issues as race, ethnicity, or gender, then a very different situation arises. Status will not entirely displace class as we march into the future, although many observers anticipate that status will become more significant in the "political systems of late capitalism" by being essential to the "process of political mobilization, whereby groups, enjoying relative levels of privilege or disprivilege, constantly organize in the interests of maintaining or improving their position within society."[11] Why so? Because implicit in advanced capitalistic democracies is a strong principle of *equality* which fosters the growth of status groups that make demands on government for special recognition and exclusive benefits.

The political demands of these groups may vary from society to society. One profound historical difference is the feudalistic legacy of Europe and the non-feudal traditions of the United States, Canada, Australia, and New Zealand. Its historical significance is that those white colonial settler societies were "inevitably bound up with racial conflict, ethnic differences, and the problem of national identity" and, therefore, "the problem of order was debated in the context of the problems associated with the melting pot, the notion of a mosaic society, and the issue of multi-culturalism."[12] Sociologists in the 1950s associated the American melting pot with right-wing status politics.

Extremism as Status Politics on the Right

Once Italian fascism and German national socialism were demolished by the Allied armies, it did not take long before scholars began to extend the concepts of "mass man" and status anxiety to the analysis of extremist movements in the United States. The catalyst was the rise of Senator Joseph McCarthy (Republican-Wisconsin) to political prominence. The anti-communist crusade known as McCarthyism encouraged academics to look to Europe for clues to this home-grown extremism.

McCarthy's sudden rise to popularity was read as confirmation of a "massification" tendency in segments of the population, a warning that even the United States was not completely immune to the fascist virus. Pessimists could also find similarities in the kinds of social support received by McCarthy's legions and European fascists in the pre- and postwar periods. That the German Nazis, Italian fascists, and the Poujadists of the French Fourth Republic received support, as did McCarthy, from similar demographic groups—small businessmen, portions of the working class, and the less educated—was offered as evidence that not all was well with American democracy.[13]

Publication of the *New American Right*, edited by Daniel Bell with chapters by several academic luminaries was an important event in this intellectual history. Its underlying theme was the danger the New or Radical Right posed for individual liberty. To his credit, Bell did not ignore the vast differences between the social conditions of prewar Europe and postwar United States. Unlike Europe, the political turmoil in America resulting from McCarthyism happened in the midst of prosperity rather than depression.[14]

Students of the New Right assumed that the popularity of McCarthy reflected a dislocation in the social system and an outburst of populism, both presumably caused by the "massification" of individuals whose social ties and institutional loyalties were extremely tenuous.[15] American political culture, it was argued, was unable to provide governing elites with sufficient political insulation from the demands of populist agitators and mass movements. Observers pointed out that the UK produced no McCarthy, and their explanation was the traditional deference of the British people coupled with the relative secrecy and autonomy enjoyed by British governing institutions.[16]

Historian Richard Hofstadter condemned the New Right as being a revolt of rootless, paranoid "pseudo-conservatives" involved in a "peculiar scramble for status and its peculiar search for secure identity."[17] According to Hofstadter, status resentments stemmed from a number of quarters but particularly from the large influx of East European immigrants earlier in the century. Their different languages, religious traditions, and social behaviours aroused fears among the predominant White Anglo-Saxon Protestant (WASP) groups that their cultural way of life was threatened, a concern that made some WASPs highly receptive to demagogues like McCarthy. Increasingly fearful of Communism from abroad and subversion at home, these members of the social establishment were portrayed by Hofstadter and others as alienated and paranoid misfits. Ironically, the WASPs were joined in supporting McCarthyism by various immigrant groups, especially Germans and Irish, usually Catholics and urban. What made this strange political alliance possible? Again the sociological answer was status frustration and the search for identity. Whereas the WASPs were preoccupied with preserving their dominant status position, the newer immigrants were obsessed with improving their status within American society. Craving acceptance as (not hyphenated) Americans, white ethnics wanted to prove themselves every bit as patriotic as the WASPs.[18]

Perhaps the most systematic effort to link status frustration and the politics of resentment to the political Right was published by Lipset and Rabb some 15 years after the *New American Right* appeared.[19] Lipset and Rabb equated right-wing status with "preservation" in terms of "maintaining or narrowing lines of power and privilege," whereas the left-wing was equated with "innovation" for its "broadening lines of power and privilege." They knew that another "ideological axis" in American history positioned the "antistatist [conservatives] at one pole and statist [liberals] at the other," but they believed that this Left-Right economic dimension was secondary because "[i]t is the axis of preservation which most essentially and invariably distinguishes 'Left Wing' from 'Right Wing.'"[20] That viewpoint is held by contemporary sociologists, for whom "right-wing movements" are conceptualized as "social movements whose stated goals are to maintain structures of order, status, honor, or traditional social differences or values" as compared to left-wing movements which seek "greater equality or political participation."[21] In other words, the sociological perspective sees preservationist politics as a right-wing attempt to defend privilege within the *social hierarchy*.

Right-wing preservationists were essentially stereotyped as exhibiting status anxiety. However, this provocative sociological interpretation was time-bound since relatively few scholars have pursued that paradigm. Historian John Higham linked nativist outbursts in the United States to "status rivalries," and sociologists applied "status anxiety" to explain such counter-movements as the Women's Christian Temperance Union, anti-pornography campaigns, and opposition to the proposed women's Equal Rights Amendment and secularized education, as well as support for prayer in public schools.[22] Sociologist Kristin Luker argued that abortion is "*a referendum on the place and meaning of motherhood*" that involves fundamentally unlike pro-choice or pro-life "world views," and that for pro-life women "to accept contraception or abortion would devalue the one secure resource left to these women: the private world of home and hearth."[23] In explaining the rise of the Christian Right in contemporary American politics, "status discontent proved to be a significant predictor of orientation to the Christian Right," concluded Wald, Owen, and Hill.[24]

IDENTITY AS STATUS POLITICS ON THE LEFT

Identity politics has its roots in the writings of German philosopher Hegel, whose conception of a "struggle for recognition" inspires contemporary theorists.[25] To make his point, Hegel employed a dialectic between master and servant to show that "self-consciousness" depends, as explained by Herbert Marcuse, on "association with other individuals." This relationship is not a harmonious one "between essentially unequal individuals, the one a 'master' and the other a 'servant.' Fighting out the battle is the only way man can come to self-consciousness, that is, to the knowledge of his potentialities and to the freedom of their realization.'"[26] To restate this thesis in lay terms, no person's identity is inherent but rather is defined by his or her relationships in society. There can be no master without a servant; there can be no servant without a master. Karl Marx came to view this Hegelian struggle between master and servant in economic terms, as people who represented "class" interests in terms of the ownership of property, but what motivates the contemporary understanding of Hegel by critical social philosophers is the "status" relations between people in higher or lower social positions.

Amy Guttman explains that during the "ancien regime" only a minority was honoured as "'Ladies' and 'Lords,' whereas the majority had no aspirations to public recognition."[27] Critical social philosophy thus argues that social justice demands more than a fair distribution of material goods. According to political theorist Charles Taylor, "misrecognition shows not just a lack of due respect. It can inflict a grievous wound, saddling its victims with a crippling self-hatred. Due recognition is not just a courtesy we owe people. It is a vital human need." The irreducible philosophical principle of *universal dignity* drives his argument as Taylor believes that "this concept of dignity is the only one compatible with a democratic society" and, as such, replaces the premodern concept of "honor" in hierarchical societies.[28]

Class requires distributive justice based on the wide availability of social entitlements "that protect against disadvantages born of hunger, homelessness, and other forms of deprivation," whereas status based on "race ... ethnicity, religious orientation, gender, sexuality, and disability call for recognition rights that protect against domination."[29] In this context, the word domination has a vitally different meaning than the term oppression for critical social theorists. *Oppression* indicates a subordinate class position within the economic system whereas *domination* "involves hierarchies of decision-making and power that prevent some persons from exercising control over their lives."[30] Feminist theorist Kate Millett argues that gender "is a status category" which qualifies as "a relationship of dominance and subordination" because what is "unexamined" and "unacknowledged" in our social order "is the birthright priority whereby males rule females." Even today, "sexual dominion obtains nevertheless as perhaps the most pervasive ideology of our culture and provides its most fundamental concept of power." It exists "because our society, like all other historical civilizations, is a patriarchy," meaning that "every avenue of power within the society, including the coercive force of the police, is entirely in male hands."[31]

Where conventional liberals would oppose any discrimination by government and prefer state neutrality with respect to minorities (their analogy would be church-state separation), the politics of identity *requires* public policies that recognize differences among individuals *as* groups. "The demand for recognition, animated by the ideal of human dignity," Guttman claims, "points ... both to the protection of the basic rights of individuals as human beings and to the acknowledgment of the particular needs of individuals as members of specific cultural groups."[32] Given the powerful norm of cultural individualism in the United States (see Chapter 3), most Americans would take issue with that argument, but citizens of more communitarian societies may not. Take Canada, for example, where political theorist Charles Taylor agrees that "[w]here the politics of universal dignity fought for forms of nondiscrimination that were quite 'blind' to the ways which citizens differ, the politics of difference often redefines nondiscrimination as requiring that we make these distinctions the basis of preferential treatment," which is why Taylor recommends a "deep diversity" for Canada based on granting "special status" to Francophones (French-speakers).[33] Fellow Canadian philosopher Will Kymlicka also justifies granting collective rights to the Aboriginal peoples (or First Nations) to guarantee that these disadvantaged cultural groups are able to sustain their way of life.[34] Joseph Raz is another philosopher for whom "multiculturalism requires a political society to recognize the equal standing of all the stable and viable cultural communities existing in that society."[35]

The Francophones of Quebec are more important politically (if not philosophically) than the Aboriginal peoples of Canada, but what other victimized groups are worthy of recognition? They are not the garden variety of interest group but rather "affinity" groups whose members have a unique "perspective" not experienced by any other social group. Says Iris Marion Young, an American feminist, they are "[g]roups experiencing cultural imperialism [that] have found themselves objectified and marked with a devalued essence from the outside, by a dominant culture they are excluded from making" or shaping.[36] American philosopher David Ingram agrees that "unlike any belief, interest, and value, an experience cannot be consciously rejected; it forever remains as memory trace and habitual affect, tacitly shaping one's perspective on life."[37]

Similar assumptions guided three researchers who studied gay rights in the United States insofar as "[i]dentity politics is rooted in groups based on 'race, ethnicity, gender and sexuality' rather than the traditional group divisions associated with politics—economic classes, interest groups, industries, labor unions, and the like."[38] This distinction between identity politics and economics is applicable to ethnicity, since H.D. Forbes concluded that "the most typical ethnic conflicts seem to have remarkably little to do with clashing material or economic interests ... [but rather] more intangible goods such as power, respect, or social status."[39] And race. Dollard's sociological classic on racism in America pointed out that the divide between poor blacks and poor whites in the South was based on "caste," not class,[40] and his 1949 insight remains telling. A 1996 study found that white racial attitudes are grounded less in personal self-interest than in perceptions of group-interest, and this racial divide "is not a mask for class differences" but "is rooted in race itself" and "widens when whites talk with whites and blacks talk with blacks, itself a sign of the tensions associated with race in American life."[41]

English feminist Anne Phillips rejects the liberal orthodoxy that political representation involves communications between the governed and the governors. That is insufficient for identity politics because, in effect, no white can "represent" a black, nor can a woman be "represented" by a man. To quote Phillips: "Many of the current arguments over democracy revolve around what we might call demands for political presence: demands for the equal representation of women with men; demands for a more even-handed balance between the different ethnic groups that make up each society; demands for the political inclusion of groups that have come to see themselves as marginalized or silenced or excluded. In this major reframing of the problems of democratic equality ... [t]he politics of ideas is being challenged by an alternative *politics of presence*" (italics added).[42]

Not many American academics embrace group entitlements because they are unable to betray the classical liberal principles of individual rights and non-discrimination. Charles Taylor calls the United States the "source" of this "liberal perspective" and, as examples, unapprovingly points to John Rawls, Ronald Dworkin, and Bruce Ackerman.[43] This contentious issue made the front pages when Lani Guinier, an African-American legal scholar, was nominated by President Clinton to be Assistant Attorney General for Civil Rights (later Clinton withdrew his support). Guinier alleged that white majorities are tyrannical, and "[b]lacks cannot enjoy equal dignity and political status until black representatives join the council of government," but that they are foiled from doing so because the election system preserves white power. Thus, she advocated such devices as "cumulative" voting to facilitate minority voter coalitions and "supermajority" requirements for legislation to give the minority more political leverage.[44]

While some liberals willingly accept affirmative action programs for minorities and women, few conservatives would agree, though there are exceptions. Nathan Glazer is a neo-conservative thinker who favours affirmative action for African-Americans, who represent the "one great failure of assimilation in American life," a "failure that has led in its turn to a more general counterattack on the ideology of assimilation." The fact that the black experience has been so profoundly different from that of all other immigrant groups, says Glazer, "is the most powerful force arguing for multiculturalism and for resistance to the assimilatory trends of American education and of American society."[45]

In sum, multiculturalists who advocate group recognition and the "politics of presence" are not thinking about pro-lifers, hunters, or male-chauvinists. This literature abounds with concern for those "victims" denied their social worth: people of colour, indigenous or colonized populations, ethnic minorities, gays, and women. As one commentator put it, "[r]egularly, members of marginalized and subaltern groups have been systematically denied recognition for the worth of their culture or way of life, the dignity of their status as persons, and the inviolability of their physical integrity. Most strikingly in the politics of identity, their struggles for recognition have come to dominate the political landscape."[46]

The United States Congress enacted the Hate Crime Statistics Act of 1990 (HCSA) and the Hate Crimes Sentencing Enhancement Act of 1994. Although acts of bigotry against various minorities are manifested throughout American history, such incidents were not deemed unique until HCSA "gave national recognition to hate crimes as a bona fide category of crime." These new enactments by the federal government and the majority of states since the mid-1980s "extend identity politics to the domain of crime and punishment," argue Jacobs and Potter, because they were prompted "not by an epidemic of unprecedented bigotry but by heightened sensitivity to prejudice and, more important, by our society's emphasis on identity politics." Advocacy groups for "gays and lesbians, Jews, blacks, women, Asian Americans, and disabled persons have all claimed that recent unprecedented violence against their members" required those enactments, though Jacobs and Potter suggest that their alleged "epidemic" of hate crimes was more myth than fact since "[i]n contemporary American society there is less prejudice-motivated violence against minority groups than in many earlier periods of American history." The sad political effect from hate crime demagoguery is that "[i]t distorts the discourse about crime in America, turning a social problem that used to unite Americans into one that divides us." By that, Jacobs and Potter mean that "[b]reaking down generic criminal law into new crimes and punishment hierarchies depending on the prejudices of offenders and the demographic identities of victims may exacerbate rather than ameliorate social schisms and conflicts."[47]

HCSA directed the attorney general to collect data on crimes showing "manifest evidence of prejudice based on race, religion, sexual orientation, or ethnicity," but hopefully the law enforcement community will be as even-handed in prosecuting hate crimes against whites. For the multiculturalists, however, it should go without saying that (male) whites are never victims. According to Ingram, "Because white racial affinity is not grounded in a genuine experience of oppression, it cannot be the legitimate locus of even a nonracist identity."[48] Nor does it make any difference if a white (male) is impoverished. Identity trumps class!

Status Extremism on the Left

What about animal rights? Not just laboratory monkeys but also the minuscule snail darter, whose existence was threatened by a dam construction in Tennessee? The snail darter is named on the list of endangered species by the United States Department of the Interior and, as such, its survival can be safeguarded by somebody suing in court on its behalf.

Talk to any animal rights lawyer and he or she will tell you that no dog or cat can be considered simply property for you to treat as you see fit, like a table or chair. Activists disavow the anthropocentric perspective that human beings are superior to all other living beings in favour of the biocentric or anthropomorphic perspective that affirms the *inherent* value of all life forms. Animal rights activists basically want to elevate the moral status of animals vis-à-vis human beings and, as such, they refer to "companion animals" instead of pets to imply "a relationship based more on friendship and equality than on domination and obedience." Moreover they "believe that animals share traits such as the ability to plan a life, to have intentions, and to carry them out, or to be loyal and loving" and go so far as to argue that "the life of a healthy chimpanzee must be granted a greater value than the life of a human who is a hopelessly retarded infant orphan."[49] To their mind, "speciesism [the bias that humans are superior] is no more morally defensible than racism, sexism, or other forms of discrimination that arbitrarily exclude some humans from the scope of moral concern."[50]

If philosophical arguments can be rallied to advance status claims for animals, surely this kind of thinking can do the same for the disabled. A modest example is the personal crusade by American billionaire Charles Schwab (who owns a chain of brokerage firms) to have Americans with "learning disabilities" referred to as having "learning differences." "What you're trying to do with all this definitional stuff is to make sure you don't beat the kids down and make them think they're fully defective," said Schwab.[51] More extreme is the contemporary debate on whether American Sign Language (ASL) is a disability or a linguistic culture.

Those who believe that ASL represents the "deaf culture" are opposed to technological advances (like cochlear implants) which can restore hearing to the children of deaf parents. Consider the views of Roslyn Rosen, ex-president of the National Association of the Deaf whose parents were deaf and whose children are deaf: "I'm happy with who I am," she said, "and I don't want to be 'fixed.' Would an Italian-American rather be a WASP? In our society everyone agrees that whites have an easier time than blacks. But do you think a black person would undergo operations to become white?" ASL is the everyday language of perhaps a half-million Americans, and, because the "deaf culture" militants view cochlear implants as posing a threat to family bonding, this issue not only divides the deaf community from the medical establishment but also from those advocates for the disabled who long have fought to "mainstream" the mentally and physically challenged.[52]

Postmaterialism and Ideological Realignment

Students of morality policy owe a huge debt to those scholars in comparative politics who posit a New Political Culture (NPC) or "postmaterialist" thesis, notably Ronald Inglehart and Terry Nichols Clark. They make the argument that political values in Western democracies are undergoing profound change, with postmaterialist values gradually supplanting the materialist values forged during the industrial era. According to Inglehart, "[m]aterialist/ Postmaterialist values seem to be part of a broader syndrome of orientations involving motivation to work, political outlook, attitudes toward the environment and nuclear power, the role of religion in people's lives, the likelihood of getting married or having children, an attitude toward the role of women, homosexuality, divorce, abortion, and numerous other topics."[53] The postmaterialist society anticipates that moral and ethical issues will rise front and centre on the political stage.[54]

Cross-national research on Canada, the United States, and ten European nations found that they all more or less experienced postmaterialist value shifting during the 1990s. Neil Nevitte concludes, "publics in at least twothirds of the twelve nations moved in the same direction on twenty-one of the twenty-four value dimensions considered. Equally striking is the *breadth* of the changes. These dynamics are plainly *not* limited to the political domain; significant shifts are taking place across a whole range of economic and social values as well and, indeed, the shifts in social values are the most consistent of all."[55]

The old ideological labels no longer apply. The Old Left was represented by organized labour, academics, and the working class who favoured the welfare state and government intervention in private enterprise, or socialism at the extreme, in order to promote economic equality. The Old Right was comprised of financiers, capitalists, farmers, merchants, and the growing middle class whose belief in *laissez-faire* economics made them individualists (libertarians) fearful of state threats to private property and the free market. All this is changing. Terry Clark asserts that "NPC [New Political Culture] leaders disagree as much with the views of Ronald Reagan and Margaret Thatcher as they do with Karl Marx and Franklin Roosevelt" because the "main conflicts today are not about socialism versus capitalism or more versus less government, but about *hierarchy versus egalitarianism*" (emphasis added).[56]

While true that a growth of postmaterialist values has taken place in postmodern societies, the increase is probably not as great or as *uniform* as Inglehart and Clark might imply. There are pockets of resistance. An analysis by Savage shows that, although postmaterialists "do usually support leftist ideologies," there are "a sizeable number" of postmaterialists who "identify with the political right," which leads him to speculate that future cleavages may not be "simply postmaterialist versus materialist as Inglehart predicts" but a "four-way split" consisting of "right and left postmaterialists and right and left materialists."[57]

But the most prominent dissenter to Inglehart's thesis is comparativist Scott Flanagan, who anticipates that postmaterialism may yet fuel another political cleavage between "the New Left issue agenda, including liberalizing abortion, women's lib[eration], gay rights and other new morality issues; protecting the environment, antinuclear weapons, and other quality-of-life issues; and support for protest activities, more direct forms of participation, and minority rights ... [and] the new Right issue agenda, which includes right-to-life, anti-women's lib[eration], creationism, antipornography, and support for traditional moral and religious values; a strong defense, patriotism, law and order, opposition to immigration and minority rights, and respect for the traditional symbols and offices of authority." In other words, both Flanagan and Inglehart agree on the distinction between Old Politics (class) and New Politics (values), but *within* New Politics Flanagan conceptualizes an "authoritarian" New Right opposing a "libertarian" New Left. Yet Flanagan suggests that his perspective and Inglehart's may not be so far apart, since Inglehart (in an article co-authored with Rabier) now acknowledges that what "define[s] Left and Right for Western publics today are not class conflict [issues], so much as a polarization between the goals emphasized by post-materialists, and the *traditional social and religious values* emphasized by materialists" (emphasis added by Flanagan).[58] In other words, by 1986 Inglehart and Rabier agreed that the terms Left and Right, "like a universal solvent, tend to absorb whatever major conflicts are present in the political system," when the political reality today across Europe is that the "strongest indicators" of one's ideological position are "the New Politics issues" which include support for abortion and the peace movement on the Left and support for nuclear power plans, a belief in God, and patriotism on the Right.[59]

Key to Flanagan's New Left-New Right cleavage is the degree of realignment within the working class. Originally Inglehart had suggested an "*em-*

bourgeoisiement thesis" which presumed that workers with a much improved economic position will remain materialistic but, to protect their newfound bounty, will become attracted to political parties on the Right. Flanagan sees workers as "cross-pressured voters, who ... may fall on the Left side on the Old Politics cleavage because of their working-class occupations and union memberships but on the Right side of the New Politics cleavage because of their authoritarian values." However he does agree with Inglehart's prognosis of a middle-class realignment, insofar as a "younger generation of highly educated, middle-class respondents, whose families have traditionally supported the Right for economic reasons, may now be induced to vote Left as a result of their socialization into libertarian-postmaterialist values."[60]

Postmaterialists lump together economic libertarians and social libertarians because "[b]oth [market and social] individualisms foster skepticism toward traditional left policies, such as nationalization of industry and welfare state growth"; for that reason, the New Political Culture merges the "market liberalism" previously identified with the right with "social progressiveness" previously associated with the left to produce a "new *combination of policy preferences* [that] leads NPCs to support new programs, and follow new rules of the game."[61] Thus, Flanagan agrees with Inglehart that only one kind of libertarianism really matters today—a *social* libertarianism that is conflated with economic libertarianism. A good test of this thesis is environmentalism.

Inglehart now believes that environmentalism is a core value of postmaterialism, just as other observers judge the "Green" movement across Europe to be "the archetypical example of postmaterialist politics."[62] Researchers have derived a "New Environmental Paradigm" to tap "antianthropocentrism, a belief that there are limits to growth, a view of nature as fragile, an awareness of the imminent possibility of ecological catastrophe, and a belief in the need for a basic transformation in the way we live our lives."[63] One analysis of environmental extremism concluded that "[e]galitarianism ... is very much at the heart of today's environmental movement," so much so that "environmentalism has become enmeshed in a culture war between individualists and egalitarians. For competitive individualists, environmentalism is seen as a Trojan horse used by egalitarians to cripple markets and restrict the use of private property. For egalitarians, unregulated markets are the source of both unconscionable inequalities and environmental destruction."[64]

Religion and the Culture Wars

One of the strongest forces in society that affirms traditional values is organized religion, in particular the fundamentalist churches, so it is no coincidence that sociologists of religion are devoting more attention to the "culture wars" in North American politics. In the United States this subject was inspired by the rise of the Moral Majority that supported the presidency of Ronald Reagan.[65] Best known is sociologist James Davison Hunter, who coined the phrase "culture wars" to describe the battles over abortion, child care, government funding for the arts, affirmative action and quotas, gay rights, and secularism in public education, as well as multiculturalism, all of which he traces to divergent views of "moral authority" or "the basis by which people determine whether something is good or bad, right or wrong, acceptable or unacceptable, and so on."[66]

Culture wars divide "*the impulse toward orthodoxy*" from "*the impulse toward progressivism*" and emerge from a "fundamental disagreement" over the sources of moral truth. Hunter says "we can label those on one side cultural conservatives or moral traditionalists, and those on the other side liberals or cultural progressives." At its heart "*cultural conflict is ultimately about the struggle for domination,*" about raw force in "a struggle to achieve or maintain the power to define reality."[67]

What brought about the culture wars? Hunter cites many social developments, but perhaps the "central factor" was the "transformation of our economy from an industry-oriented to an information-oriented system" with a "huge expansion in the number of people who derive their livelihoods from the economics of knowledge, information, ideas," as well as an "expansion of higher education," which, in turn, led to "the economic and political empowerment of women" and, in totality, "contributed to the undermining of previous agreements about how Americans should order our lives together." Hunter foresees a religious realignment where "the progressive alliances tend to draw popular support from among the highly educated, professionally committed, *upper* middle classes, while the orthodox alliances tend to draw from the *lower* middle and working classes." Moreover "[t]his is not a struggle over scarce economic resources, nor is the exploitation of the working classes even an issue." Rather it is a struggle to "define the meaning of America."[68]

The culture wars reflect clashing public philosophies. Orthodox believers hold certain "non-negotiable moral 'truths,'" of which those most relevant for our purposes "are that the world, and all of the life within it, was created by God, and that human life begins at conception ... .[and] the belief that the natural and divinely mandated sexual relationship among humans is between male and female and this relationship is legitimate only under one social arrangement, marriage between one male and one female. Homosexuality, therefore, is a perversion of the natural or created order." The progressive religious creed sees all this very differently, namely, "that personhood begins at or close to the moment of birth ... [and] male and female are differentiated solely by biology; other differences are probably human constructions imposed … by powerful and sometimes oppressive institutions. So too, human sexuality is based in biological need. The forms in which those needs are met are historically and culturally variable and completely legitimate so long as those forms reflect a positive and caring relationship. Homosexuality, then, does not represent an absolute and fundamental perversion of nature but simply one way in which nature can evolve and be expressed."[69] Later Hunter raised the stakes. He argued that culture wars are destabilizing because political rhetoric is the primary weapon in this ideological warfare. Its discourse "is very much a war to impose a new consensus by virtually any political and rhetorical means possible."[70]

The Hunter thesis has been criticized on conceptual and empirical grounds, one being Hunter's presumption that our whole society is cleaved by one huge cultural divide. According to Williams, Hunter's "all-encompassing bipolar ideological axis is overly simplistic and masks as much variance as it illuminates," given that there is empirical evidence showing that no unidimensional "culture war" has polarized American public opinion.[71] For example, one 20-year study found "no support for the proposition that the United States has experienced dramatic polarization in public opinion on social issues since the 1970s"—with the notable exception of abortion attitudes.[72] Also, critics like Davis and Robinson found that the religious divide "is primarily on gender and family-related issues of children, sexuality, reproductive rights, and women's involvement in the family and workplace" but "does not extend to issues of racial and economic inequality."[73] Hunter retorts that simply revealing the nature of public opinion does not carry much political weight. More important are the views of political activists and opinion leaders, because regarding "public discourse, any reasoned and substantive center that may exist is certainly eclipsed by the polarizing rhetoric produced by the gatekeeping institutions of public culture."[74]

In sum, the "common wisdom" about "a" culture war sociologist Fred Kniss finds "too simplistic" because "[s]ome issues … are crosscutting and may produce attenuation rather than intensification of conflict. Different issues have different histories, different ideological components, and different constituencies."[75] Kniss is right on target, we believe, which is why we chose to title our book *Cultures at War* to signify that there are *many* culture wars, in different places, over different issues, involving different social groups (though some, like abortion, surface repeatedly).

For most of their political history, conservative Christians were apolitical, not only in the United States but also in Canada. Simpson and MacLeod argue that denominationally a "significantly higher proportion" of Americans than Canadians are "oriented in the direction of Moral Majority-type politics," in addition to the "deep structure" of the Canadian regime that "imposes limits upon the possibility" that a version of Moral Majority will surface there.[76] But that may be changing. A 1996 survey indicated that 18 per cent of Canadians but 34 per cent of Americans feel somewhat or very close to the "Christian Right," which suggests that the American Christian Right is twice the size of the Canadian Christian Right although the United States is ten times larger than Canada.[77] Also, Hoover reports that "the past fifteen years have witnessed a remarkable upturn in conservative Christian advocacy in Canada" to the point where, although the Christian Right "has far fewer sympathizers" in Canada, "it has achieved a level of mobilization that ... is more than proportionate" to the United States.[78] Many evangelical Protestants favour the recently organized (in 1987) Reform Party (since renamed the Canadian Alliance Party), whose programmatic agenda, candidates, and party staff are decidedly conservative and Christian (see Chapter 4).[79] The Christian Right also is increasingly involved in litigation to defend and promote their objectives (see Chapter 6). In sum, "Canadian politics barely registered the existence of conservative Christians in the early 1980s," observe Hoover and den Dulk, but today the "Canadian interest group system is developing in an American direction, with a Canadian-style complement of 'culture warriors' whose tactical arsenal includes legal mobilization."[80]

The recognition that the Christian Right is a political force for the normative status quo has lead the quantitative analysts of morality policy to include some religious variable(s) in their statistical models to measure its impact. As Mooney explains, given that "the United States is perhaps the most religious Western democracy today" and "[w]ith so many people holding authoritative religious values, the chances for a fundamental clash of first principles increase."[81] The presence of conservative Christians helps to explain why certain American states do not adopt lotteries as a revenue source and why others do enforce anti-obscenity laws.[82] But Catholics were not necessarily opposed to state-sponsored lotteries, nor does a Catholic presence have any effect on anti-pornography enforcement. Those findings support our position that Catholics and the Christian Right are not allies on every morality policy.

In other words, as noted by Kniss above, our dissent from the Hunter thesis rests on pluralist grounds,[83] not on ideological grounds since we agree that moral conflicts do involve a Left-Right cleavage. However, we doubt that only one *social* cleavage divides the entire array of social groups in fixed political coalitions. Rather, we are impressed with the multitude of social groups in Western democracies and the ever-changing politics of their coalition-building, depending on the issue. The abortion issue may provoke the Roman Catholics but not the environmentalists, as illustrated by the Green Party in Germany, nor are Anglophones exercised about language policy in France the way they are in Quebec. "Location, location, location" may be the marketing slogan that drives real estate; for policy studies, the analogue is "issue, issue, issue."

Concluding Observations

The historic Left-Right cleavage based on class politics once cleanly defined economic libertarians as "conservatives" because economic liberals favoured state intervention in business affairs. With the rise of postmaterialist values and the shift towards social egalitarianism, however, postmaterialist scholars tend to conflate economic libertarians with social libertarians. They justify this ideological packaging by attributing to both types of libertarians such post-materialist qualities as self-actualization. But is it not more logical that social libertarians and economic libertarians would part company depending upon whether the political issue is social or economic? Surely what motivates economic libertarians is *not* status anxiety but a *cultural* way of life, one that puts a premium on their ability to transact freely with others in a marketplace.

Status in 1950s sociology and today in multiculturalism has been viewed through the prism of ideology. Sociologists used status to *explain* right-wing behaviour, and critical social philosophers now use status to *promote* a left-wing moral imperative. Both these approaches pose difficulty for anybody seeking an analytically neutral tool for studying morality policy in a dispassionate manner. What is needed is a framework that focuses scholarly research on status without any ideological baggage, a theory that more cleanly differentiates economic life from social life so that status becomes the pivot on which postmaterialist conflict erupts. Our preference is to apply "cultural theory" to the study of morality policy, the subject of Chapter 3.

Notes

1. See Fred Hirsch, *The Social Limits of Growth* (Cambridge, MA: Harvard University Press, 1978) 15-54, 102-14.

2. Peter Berger, Brigitte Berger, and Hansfried Kellner, *The Homeless Mind: Modernization and Consciousness* (New York: Random House, 1973), chapter 4.

3. Bauman 60, 62-64; also see Ulrich Beck, *Risk Society: Towards a New Modernity* (London: Sage, 1992) 121-50.

4. C. Wright Mills, "The Sociology of Stratification," *Power, Politics, and People: The Collected Essays of C. Wright Mills*, ed. Irving Louis Horowitz (New York: Ballantine, 1963) 305-23.

5. Peter Berger and Thomas Luckmann, "Social Mobility and Personal Identity," *Life-World and Social Realities*, ed. Thomas Luckmann (London: Heinemann Educational Books, 1983) 110-23.

6. George Herbert Mead, *Mind, Self and Society: From the Standpoint of a Social Behavioralist* (Chicago: University of Chicago Press, 1934).

7. Peter Berger, "Identity as a Problem in the Sociology of Knowledge," *European Journal of Sociology* 7 (1966): 105-15.

8. Gregory P. Stone, "Appearance and the Self," *Human Behavior and Social Processes*, ed. Arnold M. Rose (Boston: Houghton Mifflin, 1962) 87-95. Also T. Alexander Smith and Lenahan O'Connell, *Black Anxiety, White Guilt, and the Politics of Status Frustration* (Westport, CT: Praeger, 1997), chapter 1.

9. Stone 87-95.

10. Peter Berger, *The Human Shape of Work* (New York: Macmillan, 1964).

11. Robert J. Holton and Bryan S. Turner, *Max Weber on Economy and Society* (London: Routledge, 1989) 145-46.

12. Holton and Turner 158.

13. Kornhauser 66, 181, 205-07.

14. Daniel Bell, "Interpretations of American Politics," *The New American Right*, ed. Daniel Bell (New York: Criterion Books, 1955) 4.

15. Kornhauser; Seymour Martin Lipset and Earl Rabb, *The Politics of Unreason: Right-Wing Extremism in America, 1790-1970* (New York: Harper and Row, 1970).

16. Edward A. Shils, *The Torment of Secrecy* (Glencoe, IL: The Free Press, 1956).

17. Richard Hofstadter, "The Pseudo-Conservative Revolt," Bell 39, 41-42.

18. Hofstadter 33-37, 44.

19. Lipset and Rabb.

20. Lipset and Rabb 19-20.

21. Clarence Y.H. Lo, "Countermovements and Conservative Movements in the Contemporary US," *American Review of Sociology* 8 (1982): 111-12.

22. John Higham, "Another Look at Nativism," *Catholic Historical Review* 44 (July 1958): 151-52; Joseph R. Gusfield, *Symbolic Crusade: Status Politics and the American Temperance Movement* (Urbana, IL: University of Illinois Press, 1963); Louis A. Zurker, Jr. and R. George Kirkpatrick, *Citizens for Decency: Antipornography Crusades as Status Defense* (Austin, TX: University of Texas Press, 1976); Louis A. Zurcher, Jr., R. George Kirkpatrick, Robert G. Cushing, and Charles K. Bowman, "The Anti-Pornography Campaign: A Symbolic Crusade," *Social Problems* 19 (Fall 1971): 217-38; Wilbur J. Scott, "The Equal Rights Amendment as Status Politics," *Social Forces* 64 (December 1985): 499-506; Ann L. Page and Donald Clelland, "The Kanawha County Textbook Controversy: A Study of the Politics of Life Style Concern," *Social Forces* 57 (September 1978): 265-81; Matthew C. Moen, "School Prayer and the Politics of Life-Style Concern," *Social Science Quarterly* (December 1984): 1065-71.

23. Kristin Luker, *Abortion and the Politics of Motherhood* (Berkeley, CA: University of California Press, 1984) 193, 214.

24. Kenneth D. Wald, Dennis E. Owen, and Samuel S. Hill, Jr., "Evangelical Politics and Status Issues," *Journal for the Scientific Study of Religion* 28 (1989): 13.

25. Hegel, *The Phenomenology of Spirit*, trans. A.V. Miller (Oxford: Oxford University Press, 1977), chapter 4; Axel Honneth, *The Struggle for Recognition: The Moral Grammar of Social Conflicts*, trans. Joel Anderson (Cambridge, UK: Polity Press, 1995) xi.

26. Herbert Marcuse, *Reason and Revolution: Hegel and the Rise of Social Theory* (New York: The Humanities Press, 1954) 114-15.

27. Amy Guttman, "Introduction," *Multiculturalism and "The Politics of Recognition:" An Essay by Charles Taylor*, Charles Taylor (Princeton, NJ: Princeton University Press, 1992) 6.

28. Charles Taylor, *Multiculturalism and "The Politics of Recognition:" An Essay by Charles Taylor* (Princeton, NJ: Princeton University Press, 1992) 26, 27. Also see David Ingram, *Group Rights: Reconciling Equality and Difference* (Lawrence, KS: University Press of Kansas, 2000) 13.

29. Ingram 14.

30. Ingram, *Group Rights* 36.

31. Kate Millett, *Sexual Politics* (Garden City, NY: Doubleday and Company, 1970) 24-25.

32. Guttman 8.

33. Taylor 39.

34. Will Kymlicka, *Liberalism, Community and Culture* (Oxford: Clarendon Press, 1989); Will Kymlicka, *Multicultural Citizenship: A Liberal Theory of Minority Rights* (Oxford: Clarendon Press, 1995).

35. Joseph Raz, "Multiculturalism: A Liberal Perspective," *Dissent* 41 (Winter 1994): 69.

36. Iris M. Young, *Justice and the Politics of Difference* (Princeton, NJ: Princeton University Press, 1990) 172.

37. Ingram 58.

38. James W. Button, Barbara A. Rienzo, and Kenneth D. Wald, *Private Lives, Public Conflicts: Battles over Gay Rights in American Communities* (Washington, DC: CQ Press, 1997) 5.

39. H.D. Forbes, *Ethnic Conflict: Commerce, Culture, and the Contact Hypothesis* (New Haven, CT: Yale University Press, 1997) 14.

40. John Dollard, *Caste and Class in a Southern Town* (New York: Harper, 1949).

41. Donald R. Kinder and Lynn M. Sanders, *Divided by Color: Racial Politics and Democratic Ideals* (Chicago: University of Chicago Press, 1996) 287-88.

42. Anne Phillips, *The Politics of Presence* (Oxford: Clarendon Press, 1995) 5. The classic statement of liberalism on representation which Phillips criticizes is Hanna Pitkin, *The Concept of Representation* (Berkeley, CA: University of California Press, 1967). Also see Young 184.

43. Taylor 56. Those liberal theorists Taylor mentioned are John Rawls, *A Theory of Justice* (Cambridge, MA: Harvard University Press, 1971); John Rawls, "Justice as Fairness: Political Not Metaphysical," *Philosophy and Public Affairs* 14 (1985): 223-51; Ronald Dworkin, *Taking Rights Seriously* (London: Duckworth, 1977); Bruce Ackerman, *Social Justice in the Liberal State* (New Haven, CT: Yale University Press, 1980).

44. Lani Guinier, "Keeping the Faith: Black Voters in the Post-Reagan Era," *Harvard Civil Rights-Civil Liberties Law Review* 24 (1989): 421; Lani Guinier, *The Tyranny of the Majority: Fundamental Fairness in Representative Democracy* (New York: The Free Press, 1994) 14-17.

45. Nathan Glazer, "Is Assimilation Dead?," *Multiculturalism and American Democracy*, ed. Arthur M. Melzer, Jerry Weinberger, and M. Richard Zinman (Lawrence, KS: University Press of Kansas, 1998) 16 and 34.

46. Joel Anderson, "Translator's Introduction," Honneth x.

47. James B. Jacobs and Kimberly Potter, *Hate Crimes: Criminal Law and Identity Politics* (New York: Oxford University Press, 1998) 4-6, 63-64, 144.

48. Ingram 70.

49. James M. Jasper and Dorothy Nelkin, *The Animal Rights Crusade: The Growth of a Moral Protest* (New York: The Free Press, 1992) 11-12.

50. Gary L. Francione, *Rain Without Thunder: The Ideology of the Animal Rights Movement* (Philadelphia, PA: Temple University Press, 1996) 13.

51. Kruti Trivedi, "The Big Push for Learning 'Differences,' Not Disabilities," *New York Times* 8 August 2000: A18.

52. Edward Dolnick, "Deafness as Culture," *Atlantic Monthly* 272 (September 1993): 38. Dolnick calls linguist Harlan L. Lane of Northeastern University "the chief theoretician of the deaf-culture movement," who authored *The Mask of Benevolence: Disabling the Deaf*

Community (New York: Vintage Books, 1992). Also see Maria Arana-Ward, "As Technology Advances, a Bitter Debate Divides the Deaf," *Washington Post* 11 May 1997: A1, A20-A21.

53. Inglehart 423.

54. Terry Nichols Clark and Vincent Hoffmann-Martinot, eds., *The New Political Culture* (Boulder, CO: Westview Press, 1998).

55. Neil Nevitte, *The Decline of Deference* (Peterborough, Ontario: Broadview Press, 1996) 288.

56. Terry Nichols Clark, "Preface," Clark and Hoffmann-Martinot ix.

57. James Savage, "Postmaterialism of the Left and Right: Political Conflict in Postindustrial Society," *Comparative Political Studies* 17 (January 1985): 433.

58. Scott C. Flanagan, "Value Change in Industrial Societies," *American Political Science Review* 81(December 1987): 1319, 1306, 1308. The article that Flanagan quotes from is Ronald Inglehart and Jacques-René Rabier, "Political Realignment in Advanced Industrial Society: From Class-Based Politics to Quality of Life Politics," *Government and Opposition* 21(1986): 456-79.

59. Inglehart and Rabier 470-71.

60. Flanagan 1305, 1307.

61. Terry Nichols Clark and Ronald Inglehart, "The New Political Culture: Changing Dynamics of Support for the Welfare State and other Policies in Postindustrial Societies," Clark and Hoffmann-Martinot 11-12.

62. See Grendstad and Selle 158; also Russell J. Dalton, *The Green Rainbow: Environmental Groups in Western Europe* (New Haven, CT: Yale University Press, 1994) xiii.

63. Riley E. Dunlap and Kent D. Van Liere, "The 'New Environmental Paradigm,'" *Journal of Environmental Education* 9 (1978): 10-19; Richard J. Ellis and Fred Thompson, "Seeing Green: Cultural Biases and Environmental Preferences," Ellis and Michael Thompson, *Culture Matters* 172.

64. Ellis and Thompson, "Seeing Green" 183-84.

65. Wade Clark Roof, *Community and Commitment: Religious Plausibility in a Liberal Protestant Church* (New York: Elsevier, 1978); Dean R. Hoge and David A. Roozen, "Some Sociological Conclusions about Church Trends," *Understanding Church Growth and Decline: 1950-1978*, ed. Dean R. Hoge and David A. Roozen (New York: Pilgrim, 1979) 315-33; Robert Wuthnow, *The Restructuring of American Religion: Society and Faith Since World War II* (Berkeley, CA: University of California Press, 1988); Mark Gerson, *The Neoconservative Vision: From the Cold War to the Culture Wars* (Lanham, MD: Madison, 1996).

66. James Davison Hunter, *Culture Wars* (New York: Basic Books, 1991) 42.

67. Hunter, *Culture Wars* 43, 46, 52.

68. Hunter, *Culture Wars* 62-63, 63-64.

69. Hunter, *Culture Wars* 122, 126.

70. James Davison Hunter, *Before the Shooting Begins: Searching for Democracy in America's Culture War* (New York: The Free Press, 1994) 10.

71. Rhys H. Williams, "Introduction," *Cultural Wars in American Politics: Critical Reviews of a Popular Myth*, ed. Rhys H. Williams (New York: Aldine De Gruyter, 1997) 3.

72. Paul DiMaggio, John Evans, and Bethany Bryson, "Have American's Social Attitudes Become More Polarized?," *American Journal of Sociology* 102 (November 1996): 738.

73. Nancy J. Davis and Robert V. Robinson, "Are the Rumors of War Exaggerated? Religious Orthodoxy and Moral Progressivism in America," *American Journal of Sociology* 102 (November 1996): 758.

74. James Davison Hunter, "Reflections on the Culture War Hypothesis," *The American Culture Wars: Current Contests and Future Protests*, ed. James L. Nolan (Charlottesville, VA: University Press of Virginia, 1996) 247. Also see James Davison Hunter, "Response to Davis and Robinson: Remembering Durkeim," *Journal for the Scientific Study of Religion* 35 (1996): 246-48.

75. Fred Kniss, "Culture Wars (?): Remapping the Battleground," Williams, *Culture Wars in American Politics* 259, 277.

76. John H. Simpson and Henry G. MacLeod, "The Politics of Morality in Canada," *Religious Movements*, ed. Rodney Stark (New York: Paragon, 1985) 226, 235.

77. This 1996 survey of Americans and Canadians by the Angus Reid Research Group is reported in Dennis R. Hoover, "The Christian Right Under Old Glory and the Maple Leaf," *Sojourners in the Wilderness: The Christian Right in Comparative Perspective*, ed. Corwin E. Smidt and James M. Penning (Lanham, MD: Rowman and Littlefield, 1997) 195.

78. Hoover 199, 210.

79. James L. Guth and Cleveland Fraser, "Religion and Partisan Preference in Canada," *Journal for the Scientific Study of Religion* 40 (March 2001): 51-64.

80. Dennis R. Hoover and Kevin den Dulk, "Christian Conservatives Go to Court: Religion and Legal Mobilization in the United States and Canada," *International Political Science Review* (forthcoming).

81. Christopher Z. Mooney, "The Public Clash of Private Values," Mooney, *The Public Clash of Private Values* 16.

82. Patrick A. Pierce and Donald E. Miller, "Variations in the Diffusion of State Lottery Adoptions: How Revenue Dedication Changes Morality Policy," *Symposium: The Politics of Morality Policy*, ed. Christopher Z. Mooney *Policy Studies Journal* 27/4 (1999): 696-706; Kevin B. Smith, "Clean Thoughts and Dirty Minds: The Politics of Porn," Mooney, "Symposium" 723-34.

83. The foundations of pluralism date back to James Madison and his *Federalist* #10 essay on factions, but was formalized as a theory at the turn of the last century by Arthur Bentley and sustained by later generations of pluralist thinkers like David Truman. See Arthur F. Bentley, *The Process of Government* (Chicago: University of Chicago Press, 1908); David B. Truman, *The Governmental Process* (New York: Alfred A. Knopf, 1960).

3

Cultural Theory and
Warring Cultures

To stand back and compare the social and political institutions of Europe and North America at the dawn of the new millennium with those at the end of the nineteenth century makes us keenly aware of the profound social changes experienced by that generation. In traditional societies, where rigid barriers divide established groups and outsiders, class and status systems were mutually reinforcing. Class and status tended to *overlap* as high class and high status almost always involved the same groups. "Consumption in the upper class or aristocracy," observes Featherstone, "tends more towards the reproduction of a stable status system ... [insofar as] the fashion code was restricted ... and the courtier had to conform to strict rules of dress, manners and deportment."[1] In other words, control over material resources and the distribution of honour and prestige tend to be monopolized by the same individuals and social groups.

If the nineteenth century can be characterized by a struggle for personal rights, for security of private property, and for extension of the franchise to the masses, the twentieth century may be characterized by the extension of social rights through the modern welfare state. At the same time there has been a quickening shift in the balance of social and political power between established ruling groups and outsiders.[2] By 1900 serious cracks began to appear in the wall of separation erected by the nobility to maintain its exclusive status in European social systems. Financiers, industrialists, and wealthy merchants occasionally entered its ranks, though elevation to the aristocracy was the exception rather than the rule. Far removed from Europe, the social climate of the United States proved more favourable to the growth of democratic values. The United States extended the suffrage earlier and more broadly than most European nations, and, without forgetting the painful exception of slavery in America, both the United States and Canada were governed from the beginning by a rising middle class. In North America there was no hereditary aristocracy, although Canadian political and social life was relatively more hierarchical in tone—more like the UK—than the United States. Thus, democratization proceeded more rapidly in the New World than in Europe.

The incredible growth in the accumulation of capital goods over the past century has resulted in a standard of living for the masses that our forefathers would have believed impossible to achieve.[3] The unprecedented rise in aggregate income has unleashed insatiable demands by the public for an incredible quantity and variety of consumption goods.[4] With rising incomes, not only do competitive pressures accelerate as entrepreneurs pursue consumers' dollars, pounds, or euros, but the stable consumption patterns, upon which the traditionally dominant classes had depended, eventually deteriorated. Increased social mobility meant that positions within the social hierarchy could be threatened by parvenus whose own property and income were sufficiently great to challenge the "old money" of the dominant groups. "Inequalities have diminished without losing importance, and ranking criteria like individual merit and achievement, [and] lifestyle ... have gained in importance," a Dutch scholar informs us, "whereas traditional status criteria like 'birth' and wealth have lost some weight, without becoming unimportant."[5] In sum, with the increase in aggregate wealth and the rise of mass education, the democratization of credit availability, rapid social mobility, and more plentiful consumer goods, the competition for social status will accelerate, and lifestyles as a means of self-expression will proliferate in Western societies.[6] In modern economies the *source* of income recedes in importance as a "marker" of social status while the *amount* of income and education becomes more significant.[7]

One significant contribution of Western civilization has been the increased emphasis on the individual *as* an individual. But the shift in the balance of social power from established groups toward outsider groups has introduced dysfunctional social consequences for the "modern" individual, who finds that his or her choices for self-expression have expanded enormously.[8] The decline of traditional status hierarchies, where social roles were generally respected, left a socio-psychological void in which not only individual but especially "group" demands for respect and esteem have become democratized throughout society.

A "New" Individualism

What distinguished the emerging bourgeoisie was its role in developing capitalism and its demand for equality before the law—the ideal that economic, social, and political advancement ought to depend upon *merit* rather than accident of birth. Since the bourgeoisie played a dominant role in finance, banking, and other sectors of economic life, above all else it opposed any legal and political privileges for the hereditary nobility so that the middle class could achieve important positions in society irrespective of birthright or other ascribed status.[9] "Succeeding waves of democratization and the redistribution of economic surpluses according to welfare state principles," it is said, "have resulted in the depletion or disappearance of the groups at either end of the social ladder, with a sharp increase of the jostling and status struggle in the middle."[10]

There has been a proliferation of white-collar occupations, where advanced degrees and other credentials are major requirements for promotion. The fact that so much employment within bureaucracies is hidden from public view means that this segment of the middle class seeking "recognition" may be inclined to emphasize the accumulation of credentials as status symbols.[11] According to Ulrich Beck, a German sociologist, the most important attribute of the modern bourgeoisie is the "acquisition, proffering, and application of a variety of work skills."[12] In this world résumés are pitted against résumés in an ongoing struggle for income, self-esteem, and status.[13] No doubt the scope for individual freedom and self-actualization for the modern middle class dwarfs those experienced by the emerging bourgeoisie of the nineteenth century.[14] In a sense, therefore, the modern middle class may be viewed as a product of *individualization*, namely, a social process whereby traditional institutions and values that "defined" the individual within society have crumbled under the weight of industrialization, free markets, and greater social mobility. With marketable skills and comfortable incomes more widely available, the pathway to new neighbourhoods, new friends, new cities, and new lifestyles can be forged more easily than ever. All these changes toward social equality and variety provide grist for competitive display in a world where status and identity are no longer fixed but are perpetually under threat. Because one's "place" in society is constantly being questioned, and because he or she seeks the approval of others, the modern individual is receptive to all manner of novelty, fashion, and lifestyle.[15] People in the service sectors in government and private industry—teachers, psychologists, welfare workers—no less than globe-trotting entrepreneurs, advertising experts, and international corporate executives are prone to these forces of individualized cultural influences.[16]

Even more dramatic, the increasing demand for skilled workers has given rise to differences in outlook between skilled and unskilled workers.[17] Traditional working-class culture has been losing its hold on the loyalties of its rank and file, which also gives way to individualization. Sociologist Ulrich Beck, for example, depicts the German working class as increasingly "individualized in relation to family, neighborhood, and occupational ties." Not only has collective action by labour against the market been undermined, Beck laments, but individualization tends to "*dissolve* the shared life-worlds and the shared cultural certainties of class and status groups" (his emphasis).[18] If Beck's assessment of individualization in Germany is correct, imagine how much more valid his observations would be for societies like the United States and Canada, where class consciousness was never as strong as in Germany or even the present-day United Kingdom.

In our age of economic affluence, objects of consumption are significant identifiers of status and, hence, identity. Because the quality of our goods provides information by which others judge us,[19] consumption patterns draw distinctions between class and status groups.[20] The upper classes have long employed "high" culture to distance themselves from the "low" culture of popular taste. "The constant supply of new, fashionably desirable goods, or the usurpation of existing marker goods by lower groups," says Featherstone, "produces a paperchase effect in which those above have to invest in new (informational) goods to re-establish the original social distance."[21] The older socialization process by which family, peer groups, and neighbourhood groups facilitated the basic learning pattern has given way to what sociologist Peter Berger calls, "[a]nticipatory socialization"—a personal experience by which the individual draws his preferred models for emulation from the world of national television and celebrity figures.[22]

In politics, with the decline in class politics came weakened legitimacy for those traditional agencies most crucial to political socialization—trade unions, employer associations, and political parties.[23] One consequence has been an upsurge of demands and political causes linked less to economics and class than to the lifestyle and social "identity" in which different groups seek to legitimize the cultural values they hold dear.

A "Postmodern" Era?

There has been much discussion in popular and literary circles about the meaning of postmodernism. Today it is an outdated and quaint notion to believe that social roles define the meaning of our life-experiences.[24] Instead, postmodernists believe that identities in our world are increasingly "decentred," meaning that one's sense of identity—"who I am"— "give[s] way to fragmentation" and "erode[s] all sense of continuity between past, present and future."[25] According to Bernstein, two different types of decentred identities are characteristic of postmodern societies.[26]

The first is based on *consumerism*. Here the individual may construct his or her identity by projecting upon consumer goods. One need not entirely agree with the postmodern argument, of course, to appreciate that consumerism has exerted a profound influence over and above its ability to deliver a high standard of living.[27] The proliferation of consumer goods has contributed to the status struggle and the quest for status identity in advanced societies. The second is based on *self-therapy*, where one seeks to construct an identity through introjection upon the self.[28] Here the self is regarded as a special project for personal therapy. Some people go to extremes in seeking new identities. A veritable army of ministers, psychologists, physical fitness and sports enthusiasts, health counselors, etiquette advisers, and sex experts are available to craft a new self-image.[29] "If the market identity is dependent upon the segmentation of the shopping mall," says Bernstein, "then the therapeutic [identity] is dependent upon internal making-sense procedures of the external segmentation."[30]

Whether by *projection* or *introjection*, both these decentred identities are constructed from resources so immediate and transient that they provide little guidance for the future. They are so engulfed in the present-day, so self-absorbed, and so easily influenced by fleeting social phenomena that they are psychologically incapable of thinking in terms of creating large-scale political organizations and collective movements.[31] Decentred identities imply a psycho-social personality type dedicated to highly individualized modes of living, whether through consumer goods or self-therapy. These identities may well be the quintessentially postmodern types: localistic, insecure, open to new ideas, but resistant to collective action.

Other identities, however, are more firmly anchored either in the past or the future. Bernstein argues that these "retrospective" and "prospective" identities are much more stable and less affected by temporary social phenomena.[32] Identities that reflect the past are constructed from historical narratives and grounded in texts and folklore, whereas futuristic identities may draw upon sources from the past no less than the present but with a significant difference: the information these people collect is used to fashion an identity grounded in a different—and ideally better—future.

Unlike the decentred identities, prospective and retrospective identities offer a psychological basis for the growth of social movements. "Whereas decentred identities announce distance from the collective," concludes Bernstein, "prospective identities point to a new basis for solidarity for those entitled to be recognized. In this respect prospective identities may be said to be recentring."[33] Hence, prospective or retrospective identities are inclined to value the "self" through large-scale collective projects, whereas individuals who construct an identity from consumables or self-therapy are more likely to remain indifferent or even hostile to political mobilization aimed at decisive changes in the status quo. Social movements based on *gender, race*, and *ethnicity* are often fuelled by prospective identities.

Essentials of Cultural Theory

To conceptualize the status anxieties that individuals face in post-modern society, we borrow the term "cultural theory" as pioneered by English anthropologist Mary Douglas and subsequently introduced into American political science by the late Aaron Wildavsky.[34] Most important are three concepts: (1) *cultural bias*, (2) *social relations*, and (3) *cultural way of life*. The third—cultural way of life—is derived by integrating cultural bias with social relations, to suggest that beliefs are not free-floating, somehow adrift from our occupational lives, families, peer groups, and other influences. By demonstrating the relationship between the manner in which beliefs are framed within particular social contexts and the strategies by which individuals use their beliefs to hold other people accountable, cultural theory offers a powerful intellectual tool for the study of social conflict and change as well as consensus and stability.[35]

CULTURAL BIAS

A "cultural bias," says Mary Douglas, is a "point of view, with its own framing assumptions and readily available solutions for standardized problems."[36] It is a continuing "dialogue" about how life *ought* to be lived. Because people constantly disagree about how life ought to be lived, the ongoing dialogue is largely one of blaming and holding others accountable. Cultural bias, therefore, is as much about what we dislike as what we like. Moreover, cultural bias is an "attitude to power and authority." There are two fundamental ways by which power and authority may be *exercised*. One is by bureaucratic and *hierarchical* means; the other is by *bargaining* and exchange. There are also two basic ways to *resist* the exercise of power—either by *active criticism* or by *withdrawal*.[37] Thus, we can derive four types of cultural bias—hierarchies, markets, critical activists, and isolates—each with its own attitude toward power and authority.

Consider the exercise of power. Two cultural biases determine how power will be exercised: competitive individualism or hierarchical collectivism. Where power is exercised hierarchically, all parts of organizational, or social, life must be related to the collective. This relationship implies a division of functions, specialization, respect for expertise and social roles, deference to authority, and a sacrificial ethic by which the individual is deemed less important than the welfare of the whole group, organization, or community. One consequence is a tendency toward large-scale organization. On the other hand, if authority and power are exercised by people who desire a life of bidding and bargaining, a very different set of institutional arrangements are required, namely, competitive markets. In this instance, power must be limited to a few clear rules designed to keep the competition fair. A prime objective is the enforcement of contractual obligations and property rights. Other than that, individuals are left free to pursue their interests in the marketplace.

Now consider the resistance to power. Two other cultural biases—the isolates and the critical activists or egalitarians—resist the power exercised by competitive individualists or hierarchical collectivists. Unless one is willing to resort to physical force, the best resistance to hierarchical organizations or competitive markets is to expose, and thus undermine, the inequalities they create and the unfair advantages they favour. From the standpoint of critical activists, what hierarchies and markets have in common is their tolerance for inequality, whether of income, property, or political power. Unlike the critical activists, isolates refuse to engage in the political struggle, either because they think it a useless endeavour or fear retribution from the powerful.

SOCIAL RELATIONS

The institutional constraints imposed on us by our social relationships are conceptualized in cultural theory by what is called "grid-group" analysis. Although these terms may seem strange at first glance, the idea has long interested social scientists. Grid may be conceptualized as the dimension of "individuation," whereas group is one of "social incorporation."[38] Grid includes those systems of rules, regulations, and classifications that to varying degrees and in various ways restrict or enhance our ability to *transact* or network with other individuals. These "prescriptions"—to employ Wildavsky's terminology—on individuals may be numerous and varied or few and simple.[39] They may be explicit, formal, and externally imposed on us by others, or they may be implicit, informal, and internal to each individual. For example, the various social roles we occupy are one aspect of grid. When a widespread assumption exists that a particular role ought to be performed, a refusal to act accordingly may carry a high social or material cost. Thus, individuals compelled to follow a large number and variety of prescriptions are characterized as being in a "strong grid" because their ability to transact with other people is greatly circumscribed. Any number of social, economic, and legal barriers to transactions by people of different statuses may be regarded as oppressive, particularly when the status roles are sharply delineated according to such ascriptive criteria as race, religion, ethnicity, gender, and class.

On the other hand, when social roles are not so closely scripted and transactions between individuals are subject to very few obstacles, individuals have much more freedom of action to negotiate their social environments. In this case, personal rights are upheld, and the rules and regulations—normative, social, or political—are few. Such individuals in "weak grid" are highly disposed to test traditional restraints, to wheel and deal by cutting through the normal barriers of status, class, or other prescribed roles.

What about "group" in grid-group analysis? "The group," says Mary Douglas, "is defined in terms of the claims it makes over its constituent members, the boundary it draws around them, the rights it confers on them to use its name and other protections, and the levies and constraints it applies." In order to play a meaningful role in the life of the individual, the group must obviously determine the terms of admission into and exit from its ranks by establishing boundary lines that separate outsiders from insiders. At one extreme is the "strong group," in which the individual's life is absorbed. As Douglas puts it, face-to-face contacts are possible and members of the group "draw the same boundaries and accept the alignment of insiders and outsiders." [40] At the other extreme is the "weak group," meaning that one can move easily between various groups and, if need arises, ignore them. Hence, organizational loyalty will be weak and relatively unimportant to the individual's social and psychological well-being.

When the four cultural biases are interrelated with the four patterns of grid-group relations, the result is a typology of cultures (see Figure 3.1). The "weak grid/weak group" represents *competitive individualists* (quadrant A); "strong grid/weak group" represents *isolates* (quadrant B); "strong grid/ strong group" represents *hierarchical collectivists* (quadrant C); and "weak grid/strong group" represents *egalitarians* (quadrant D).

FIGURE 3.1

Grid-Group Analysis of Social Relations and Four Cultural Ways of Life

	weak group	*strong group*
strong grid	*B* (strong grid, weak group) ISOLATES	*C* (strong grid, strong group) HIERARCHICAL COLLECTIVISTS
weak grid	*A* (weak grid, weak group) COMPETITIVE INDIVIDUALISTS	*D* (weak grid, strong group) EGALITARIANS

"Weak grid, weak group" is peopled by free-wheeling entrepreneurs, small businessmen constantly in search of a deal, even government bureaucrats on the lookout for more money and new programs. In "strong grid, weak group," we expect to find poorly paid tenant farmers, the urban poor, and others whose lives are controlled by landlords, planters, banks, or welfare agencies, as well as the lonely elderly whose net worth may be entirely adequate but who nonetheless feel lost, neglected, and unable to cope with daily life because their lives are devoid of close social relationships. Typical of "strong grid, strong group" is the government careerist, the loyal executive in a large corporation, and the devoted member of a hierarchical church, temple, or mosque. Each of these individuals is likely to have a strong idea of what his or her place within the larger collective ought to be. In "weak grid, strong group," finally, we may find a hippie in a commune, a radical environmentalist, a life-long member of a left-wing socialist group, or a member of a small religious sect like the Shakers, all of whom are likely to value a simple life among equals.

Three Cultural Ways of Life

With respect to our four cultural types, it is their *differences*, their relative *importance* in various societies, and their *imposition* of distinctive lifestyles that provide an explanation for the increasing importance of morality politics today. However, only three cultures are relevant for our purposes. Since the isolates are passive, they are not major players in the cultural wars. Rather, it is the hierarchists and individualists who tend to be culturally and politically dominant. Because egalitarians reject authority, and because their primary function is to criticize, their dominance over an extended period of time would probably lead to political instability.[41]

COMPETITIVE INDIVIDUALISM

Individualists desire a lifestyle conducive to bidding and bargaining. Status, rank, class, role, or other social classifications—if viewed as barriers to the pursuit of their self-interest—will be resisted if possible. Property rights and freedom of contract are their watchwords, and individualists who refuse to follow these rules are sanctioned. Beyond these limits, however, individualists are not generally prepared to go: people ought to be free from social and political coercion, and opportunities to transact freely should be exploited. Achievement is generally defined by outcomes in the marketplace, and merit is a willingness to compete and succeed on an equal basis with others. Even if substantial class and status inequalities do result from competition, individualists will not object so long as the rules of the game are duly observed. If markets are free, individualists contend, competition will make everyone better off in the long run.[42]

A world in which transactions between people are unencumbered is, therefore, the preferred way of life for competitive individualists. In fact, economic and social freedom fosters positive attitudes toward scientific inquiry and tolerance. Since experimentation abounds, there will be resistance to regulating public morality too closely. "Moral and social deviance can barely be defined," asserts Mary Douglas. That which is considered sacred will be scrutinized and challenged, and the emphasis on living according to one's own lights can justify what other cultures may regard as indecent or immoral behaviour. Because transactions among individuals are so free and theoretically equal, interpersonal relations are often ambiguous and instrumental.[43]

EGALITARIANISM

Egalitarians want a way of life in which people live as equals. As Wildavsky put it, egalitarians "prefer reduction of differences—between races, or income levels, or sexes, or parents and children, teachers and students, authorities and citizens."[44] If the individualist thinks that social distinctions ought to grow on their own and the hierarchist believes that they ought to be reinforced at every turn, the egalitarian counters that they ought to be diminished. The relative absence of scripted roles by which power and authority can be delegated, expertise acknowledged, and roles segregated from one another means that leadership in egalitarian cultures is almost never considered quite legitimate. Indeed, since egalitarians do not readily accept, much less evolve stable and organized leadership, they are continually subject to quarrels, schisms, and expulsions. In sum, their obsession with reducing differences and their alertness to violations of the principle of equality lead egalitarians to oppose the necessary distinctions in statuses and roles so essential for sustained leadership.

Where individualists thrive with a minimum of impediments to transaction on any number of fronts, egalitarians claim to see a perpetual threat to society from what they judge ruthless marketplace competition and dominance by large-scale organizations. The ultimate irony, perhaps, is that egalitarians often utilize the most powerful of all hierarchies—the bureaucratic state—to mandate greater equality. The old-fashioned notion of *formal* equality before the law, or equality of opportunity, leaves egalitarians cold. Their preference is equality of *result*, which may require using the coercive power of the state.[45] In general, cultural egalitarians are drawn from cosmopolitan commercial sectors, intellectuals, journalists, academics, feminists, gays, environmentalists, and the liberal membership of mainstream Protestant churches.

HIERARCHICAL COLLECTIVISM

Egalitarians would destroy social distinctions, and individualists would allow them to grow, whereas hierarchical cultures can justify differences based on status, rank, role, expertise, or specialization. Because hierarchists value role and status distinctions, they willingly accept the inequalities of income and privilege attached to various social ranks. However, they are also more likely than individualists to tolerate some redistribution of wealth if they believe the welfare of the collective is threatened. "Hierarchies," Wildavsky points out, "are rationalized by a sacrificial ethic: the parts are supposed to sacrifice for the whole."[46] The inequalities of income and rank that bedevil other cultures, leading to resentment and envy, are more easily managed within hierarchical cultures. Moreover, their propensity to defer to statuses and roles means that leaders gain more autonomy in decision-making as compared to other cultures. If competitive individualists generally take a pragmatic view of public authority, and egalitarians find many reasons to castigate the system, the hierarchists may be relied upon to defend it. In general, hierarchists are typically found in government bureaucracies, "traditional" churches, the military, and established trade unions, as well as among small business and farming communities untouched by metropolitanism and globalization.

Moral Conflicts as Culture Wars: Equality vs. Hierarchy

Historical forces and structural changes are undoubtedly responsible for the development of weak grid, propelling modern societies along paths conducive to both the growth of competitive individualism and egalitarianism. We observed that weak grid has positive economic advantages, but it also has a less appealing side. "As a cultural type," writes Mary Douglas, "low grid goes with eclecticism, fashion-ridden openness to any new gimmick; then pragmatism, secularity, the privateness of access to spiritual powers; each man claiming his own secret resources, hereditary, unique and personal to himself." It therefore tends to exert a radicalizing and relativizing influence upon morals and customs. In societies where conspicuous consumption, moral relativism, experimentation, obsession with novelty and fashion, and skepticism toward public authority are present, its members may become so individualized and alienated as to undermine their own social and political unity.[47]

In this respect, weak grid mirrors postmaterialism. Thus, we hypothesize an affinity between certain postmodern identities, as defined previously by Bernstein, and Mary Douglas's cultural ways of life. Bernstein's "decentred" identities, which are grounded in consumerism, will be attracted to *cultural individualism*, whereas "recentred retrospective" identities will tend toward *cultural hierarchism*, and "recentred prospective" identities will be attracted to cultural egalitarianism. To take this logic one more step, it is hypothesized that prospective identities will be inclined toward *status equalization* as a deeply-felt need, whereas retrospective identities will favour *status differentiation* as an antidote to the moral relativism and excessive individualism they find in unstructured postmodern life.

The popular term "culture wars" lacks theoretical clarity for public policy analysis. In terms of cultural theory, therefore, culture wars are a struggle between the forces of *status differentiation* and *status equalization*.[48] "The dismantling of classifications proceeds in the name of the unique value of the individual, so it is a constant justifying point of reference," says Mary Douglas. "Equality is the most acceptable principle of low grid since it is the only one that does not call for explicit reclassification."[49] From the perspective of the hierarchist, because moral codes of conduct are essential to social order, clear lines ought to be drawn between what is legal and illegal, right and wrong, appropriate and inappropriate. But the opposition to the cultural hierarchist—egalitarian and individualist—is typically in the business of re-classifying and blurring distinctions. As the postmoderns would say, they both "transgress" social boundaries, reclassifying them for the sake of individual freedom and/or equality. In the Western democracies, therefore, hierarchists are painted as opponents of change—judgmental, old-fashioned, and out-of-date—who obstruct the course of human history, democracy, and economic progress. One does not have to fully embrace culture theory to see that status-equalization forces have grown over the past decades.

Historical sociologist Norbert Elias has detected similar trends, for example, by observing a general increase in the ratio of "informal" to "formal" standards of behaviour in society.[50] The informalization of manners and conduct over the past several decades has wrought profound changes in dress, manners, and rapport, which allow people of various social rankings to relate to one another. Indeed, today any overt display of superiority is suspect. Formal language usage is also less apparent, as the more informal French "tu" and German "du" have been extended to wider circles of acquaintances. These changes in social etiquette reflect the diminished status relations between men and women, old and young, parents and children, teachers and students, and employers and employees. Consumerism obviously has helped to reduce status and class distinctions in Western societies but, in the process, has unleashed what a Dutch sociologist termed "style competition."[51]

Weak-grid social relations are the breeding ground for moral conflicts, because the root cause of the present "culture wars" is the "cultural shift" from premodernity to postmodernity.[52] When economic change and social mobility are widespread and most people have the resources to play the status game, confusion and disagreements arise about what statuses ought to be valued.[53] This logic of postmaterialism is incompatible with the cultural assumptions of hierarchists.[54] If hierarchical structures, like the family, church, and government, are weakened in postmodern societies, individualism and egalitarianism must necessarily be gaining in strength. The family, in particular, seems vulnerable to these status-equalization forces.

Evidence is provided in a cross-national study of 12 Western democracies by Neil Nevitte, who found that "[b]etween 1981 and 1990 publics became *increasingly* inclined to see egalitarianism in spousal relations as important to a successful marriage," and, similarly, "on parent-child relations in 1981 and 1990 … all publics became more egalitarian during the course of the decade."[55] In compromising the traditional roles within the family, thus making it easier for all family members to act more or less as status equals, both cultural egalitarianism and cultural individualism have an impact on fragmenting the traditional family—the first by equalizing statuses, the second by individualizing them.

The fundamental political consequence for societies with weakened social hierarchies and growing status demands is that "culture wars" will be defined primarily by *cultural hierarchists* versus *cultural egalitarians*. Cultural egalitarians are opposed to any status inequalities.[56] And their search for injustice through inequality can be unrelenting: humans against animals and nature; corporations against the environment; men against women; adults against children; First World Nations against Third World Nations; whites against blacks and other people of colour; heterosexuals against homosexuals; rich against poor. Especially tempting targets—because they are so hierarchical—are established churches, the military, government agencies, and multinational corporations. Whether the issue is fox-hunting in England, abortion rights in the United States, redefining farming or commercial property as wetlands, logging trees in the American Northwest, saving the whales, or same-sex marriage, there is a sharp divide between cultural egalitarians versus status quo hierarchists and individualists, with some exceptions.

How exactly do individualists fit into this cultural struggle between the egalitarians and hierarchists? Hierarchists are principled opponents to egalitarianism, but the weak-grid position that egalitarianism shares with individualism makes the competitive individualist a less reliable foe. Sometimes, individualists are opponents when their freedom to compete in the marketplace is threatened, which explains why individualists and egalitarians may agree on issues of personal liberty. But they will diverge sharply if freedom and equality cannot be easily reconciled, which is precisely the case when economics surface. While each culture accepts equality as a starting point, individualists prefer equality of opportunity but resist equality of outcome, at which point the egalitarians would likely abandon that political coalition.

The ideological divide over abortion, or gay rights, or school prayer is commonly viewed by public opinion and the news media as Left versus Right. And it is, but this ideological terrain is cultural, not the politics of economic class. Where (re)distributional politics seeks to widen the horizontal playing field by assuring everybody the economic necessities of life, morality politics is a battle over reducing the *vertical distance between social groups and social roles*. It is for that reason that the New Left talks about victimization, the oppressed, and subordination. Since much law embodies the Judeo-Christian ethic, morality policy both in Canada and, especially, in the United States provokes liberal versus conservative churches, giving the culture wars a distinctly religious cast in North America. But a purely sectarian view of the culture wars is too limiting for Europe, whose political and social life is far less influenced by organized religion. There other forces of tradition are aligned against change agents, as illustrated by the recent debate over fox-hunting in the UK. To capture the infinite variety of morality policies, researchers need a framework that casts a wider theoretical net. For that reason, our choice is cultural theory.

The profound institutional, social, and psychological changes in postmodern society must inevitably have an impact on political life and public policy. If the old class-based politics are in decline, our New Politics is being fuelled by the perpetual quest for status and identity. Moral conflict in the postmodern age is a struggle between the forces of *status differentiation* and the forces of *status equalization*. As we begin the twenty-first century, however, there are serious implications for political systems that historically have been shaped to cope with bread-and-butter economic issues. Conventional political processes will be subjected to unusual pressures, and such durable political institutions as political parties may have to be reconfigured if not bypassed and ignored. How status claims are forced into the political system is the subject of our next chapter.

Notes

1. Mike Featherstone, *Undoing Culture: Globalization, Postmodernism and Identity* (London: Sage, 1995) 25.

2. Norbert Elias and John L. Scotson, *The Established and the Outsiders: A Sociological Enquiry into Community Problems* (London: Frank Cass, 1965).

3. For example, see Ludwig von Mises, *Human Action: A Treatise on Economics* (Chicago: Regnery, 1966) 479-523.

4. Bauman 57-63.

5. Cas Wouters, "On Status Competition and Emotion Management," *Journal of Social History* 24 (1991): 699.

6. Norbert Elias, *The Germans: Power Struggles and the Development of Habitus in the Nineteenth and Twentieth Centuries* (New York: Columbia University Press, 1996) 25-27; Beck, *Risk Society* 121-50; Bauman 63-64.

7. For example see C. Wright Mills, "Sociology of Stratification," Horowitz 305-23.

8. Elias 25-28; Bauman 57-62.

9. Edmond Goblot, "Class and Occupation," *Theories of Society: Foundations of Modern Sociological Theory*, ed. Talcott Parsons, Edward Shils, Kasper D. Naegele, and Jesse R. Pitts (Glencoe, IL: Free Press, 1961) 535-40. Bauman 30-33.

10. Wouters 699.

11. Berger, Berger, and Kellner chapters 1, 4.

12. Ulrich Beck, "Beyond Status and Class" 344; Beck, *Risk Society* 121-50.

13. Beck, "Beyond Status and Class" 344-45.

14. Beck, *Risk Society* 103-38; Beck, "Beyond Status and Class" 340-55.

15. Beck, *Risk Society* 103-21; Bauman 57-63; Gehlen51-52, 107-08.

16. Scott Lash and Scott Urry, *The End of Organized Capitalism* (Madison, WI: University of Wisconsin Press, 1987) 296-300.

17. Rene Koenig, "West Germany," *Contemporary Europe: Class, Status, and Power*, ed. Margaret S. Archer and Salvador Giner (London: Weidenfeld and Nicholson, 1971) 279-96.

18. Beck, "Beyond Status and Class" 342.

19. Mary Douglas and Baron Isherwood, *The World of Goods* (New York: Basic Books, 1979) 74-90, 111-16.

20. Pierre Bourdieu, *Distinction: A Social Critique of the Judgment of Taste* (Cambridge, MA: Harvard University Press, 1984).

21. Featherstone 22.

22. Berger and Luckmann 110-23.

23. Beck, "Beyond Status and Class" 343-45.

24. Featherstone 43-48; Lash and Urry 296-300.

25. Featherstone 44.

26. Basil Bernstein, *Pedagogy, Symbolic Control and Identity: Theory, Research, Critique* (London: Taylor and Francis, 1996) 76-78.

27. For different approaches to the problem of excess consumption at the expense of production, see Wilhelm Roepke, *Welfare, Freedom and Inflation* (Tuscaloosa, AL: University of Alabama Press, 1960) 37-48, and T. Alexander Smith, *Time and Public Policy* (Knoxville, TN: University of Tennessee Press, 1988) 25-50, 182-98.

28. Bernstein 77-78.

29. Bauman 62-64.

30. Bernstein 78.

31. Bernstein 76-78.

32. Bernstein 78-79.

33. Bernstein 79.

34. Various approaches used by students of "political culture" have significantly contributed to our knowledge of politics and policy. The works of Almond and Verba, Inglehart, Eckstein, and Clark and Hoffmann-Martinot have enriched our understanding of this phenomenon, but we believe that "cultural theory" provides a better approach to understanding morality policy, both theoretically and empirically. See Gabriel A. Almond and Sidney Verba, *The Civic Culture: Political Attitudes and Democracy in Five Nations* (Boston: Little, Brown and

Company); Clark and Hoffmann-Martinot; Harry Eckstein, "A Culturalist Theory of Political Change," *American Political Science Review* 82 (1988): 789-804; Inglehart.

35. Michael Thompson and Richard J. Ellis, "Introduction," Ellis and Thompson, *Culture Matters* 1-10.

36. Mary Douglas, "The Depoliticization of Risk," Ellis and Thompson, *Culture Matters* 128.

37. Douglas, "The Depoliticization of Risk" 129.

38. Mary Douglas, "Cultural Bias," *Occasional Paper* 34 (London: Royal Anthropological Institute of Great Britain and Ireland, 1978) 7.

39. Aaron Wildavsky, "A Cultural Theory of Preference Formation," *American Political Science Review* 81 (March 1987): 7-21.

40. Mary Douglas, "Cultural Bias" 7-8, 15.

41. Aaron Wildavsky, *The Rise of Radical Egalitarianism* (Washington, DC: The American University Press, 1991) 6.

42. Regarding the economic aspects of cultural individualism, see various essays in Shaun Hargreaves Heap and Angus Ross, eds., *Understanding the Enterprise Culture: Themes in the Work of Mary Douglas* (Edinburgh: Edinburgh University Press, 1992).

43. Douglas, "Cultural Bias" 10, 21.

44. Wildavsky, *The Rise of Radical Egalitarianism* 6.

45. Wildavsky, *The Rise of Radical Egalitarianism*.

46. Wildavsky, *The Rise of Radical Egalitarianism*.

47. Douglas, "Cultural Bias" 46-53.

48. This notion is derived from Michael Thompson, "The Dynamics of Cultural Theory and their Implications for the Enterprise Culture," Heap and Ross 185-89.

49. Douglas, "Cultural Bias" 46-47.

50. Elias 25-43.

51. Wouters 699-717.

52. In general, see Thompson, "The Dynamics of Cultural Theory " 182-202.

53. Bauman 63-64.

54. Thompson, "The Dynamics of Cultural Theory " 188.

55. Nevitte 246, 263.

56. For example see Wildavsky, *The Rise of Radical Egalitarianism* 9-12.

PART TWO

Morality Politics by Unconventional Means

4

Breaking Into
or Breaking Apart
the Political System

Our discussion turns to the agenda-setting process of "how issues are created and why some controversies or incipient issues come to command the attention and concern of the formal centers of decision-making, while others fail."[1] Policy analysts differentiate between the *systemic* (or popular) agenda, which includes all the myriad problems identified in society by the public, mass media, and interest groups, and the *institutional* (or governmental) agenda where public authorities enact policies to redress specific problems. The systemic agenda is much broader and varied, whereas the institutional policy agenda is more focused.

Many analysts utilize a stages model of the policy process, and, though there are variations on this theme, scholars generally agree that *agenda-setting* precedes the *adoption* stage when a new law, regulation, or judicial ruling results.[2] We begin with theories of agenda-setting and then proceed to discuss how and why the various political venues for building public awareness—political parties, social movements, interest groups, triggering events, and the mass media—operate differently when moral conflicts are at stake. To illustrate, we offer case studies on abortion, capital punishment, and gay rights, as well as vignettes of other morality policies.

We anticipate that agenda-setting for moral conflicts is more ad hoc and less dependent on established institutions than economic disputes of whatever variety. Non-conventional political activism is the hallmark of agenda-setting via moral conflicts, simply because the political organizations heretofore perfected by decades of economic conflict are geared to defending the economic self-interests of their constituents, not promoting causes that benefit others.

Avenues to the Policy Agenda

How do issues reach the attention of policymakers? An important article by Cobb, Ross, and Ross points to three routes for gaining access to the institutional agenda.[3] First, the "outside-initiative" model presumes that an issue is lifted from the systemic agenda, where it begins, to the institutional agenda. Public opinion and the mass media are critical, particularly where policymakers are responsive to the views of the general public or media elites.[4] Second, the "inside-access" model finds decision-makers trying to confine an issue to the institutional agenda and not involve the mass public. The process of regulating strip-mining in the United States shows that state legislatures, the Congress, and the presidency were more important to initiating this policy agenda than the media or interest groups.[5] Third, the "mobilization" model shifts an issue from the institutional agenda down to the systemic agenda because political elites need to win public support. For example, an election campaign is a top-down interactive process by which political elites articulate a policy platform with the purpose of mobilizing electoral support.

Taking these models as a beginning point, let us ponder their implications for morality policy. But first, political context is needed, and, for that, we return to Meier's insight that morality policy may be one-sided or two-sided. Meier is especially troubled by one-sided or consensual morality policy because it seems immune from "rational" planning. Since the public has a fixed mind-set on such issues, policy entrepreneurs have a free hand to advocate stronger programs which, Meier feels, will be ultimately dysfunctional for society. To quote Meier:

> One-sided morality issues tend to be dominated by entrepreneurs without the restraints of opposition. Individual politicians compete to be the most aggressive morality advocates.... Morality policies pertaining to one-sided issues are rarely subjected to the expertise of bureaucrats; assessments of these morality policies are generally found only in academic journals, which no self-respecting politician would read.... Such a policy process is much more likely to generate policies that will not work because the policy proposals have not been tempered by informed debate....[6]

This point has immediate relevance to agenda-setting because policy entrepreneurs are a very important feature of the inside-access model, and they play a role in the mobilization model as well. In contrast, the policy entrepreneurial role is limited when a two-sided morality policy is involved. The electoral survival instinct will cause most politicians to try to avoid or deflect moral conflicts, given their highly charged debate over non-negotiable principles. For this reason it seems unlikely that the inside-access model applies. Surely there are policy entrepreneurs within the government who may want to promote a controversial morality policy, but the odds are great that the scope of two-sided morality policy cannot be confined to the institutional agenda for very long. The opposition, the mass media, and eventually the public would learn about political elites who covertly promote such a policy.

Evidence from Canada and the United States suggests that the inside-access model has applicability to environmentalism, an issue with both economic and normative overtones. Radical activists, says Lowi, "see environmental issues as highly morally charged" to the degree that "small is beautiful" or "capitalism is immoral," and "economic development has replaced infectious disease as the primary health problem" for society.[7] Policy elites are key to environmental agenda-setting in Canada. On the issue of acid rain, for example, the coverage in the media has had no relationship to governmental decision-making, and Howlett concludes that "there is as much evidence ... that the government agenda drives the public as there is for the reverse situation." This he attributes to "the institutional structure of parliamentary regimes, which deliver extensive agenda-setting powers to governments by ... curtailing public and media access to information."[8] In looking at why Canada and the United States both responded to the problem of dioxin emissions but, unlike the United States, Canada did not address the issue of indoor air pollution from radon, Harrison and Hoberg also point to regime differences. "The parliamentary system in Canada makes it easier to control the scope of conflict, whereas the US system of checks and balances leads more naturally to a much broader scope of conflict."[9] In other words, there are limited opportunities for policy entrepreneurship in Canada.

In the United States the initial 1960s environmental impulse occurred at a time "when media exposure and public opinion were just beginning to coalesce behind environmental goals, and the environmental issue networks were not fully institutionalized."[10] Indeed, the first Earth Day of 1970, viewed by many as the high-water mark of the burgeoning American environmental movement, was organized by Senator Gaylord Nelson (Democrat-Wisconsin), to show how environmentalism had captured the attention of key legislators. Another well-known environmental leader during the 1960s was Senator Edmund Muskie (Democrat-Maine), but also important were President "Kennedy and then President Johnson [who] sent messages to Congress each year during the 1960s increasingly highlighting values and concerns which were to become identified in the press as those of the environmental movement."[11]

The advocacy of environmentalism by political elites during its formative years parallels the experience of the American women's movement, because "[a]lthough organizational strength, collective consciousness, and political opportunities all increased for women in the early 1960s, the most decisive change seemed to involve government's willingness to act. At the presidential, congressional, and executive agency levels, new initiatives were offered with little tangible evidence that women were yet ready to organize and press their concerns."[12]

The general inappropriateness of the inside-access strategy for two-sided morality policy needs qualification in two respects. First, there is a variety of policy leadership in parliamentary regimes that resembles the inside-access model: the private member's bill. As will be discussed (Chapter 5), many issues of conscience are sponsored in Parliament not by the government of the day, which may fear that it would be politically embarrassed by a losing vote, but by individual members of Parliament (MPs) who do so with the tacit understanding of the governing party. These attempts will fail unless there is sentiment within the parliamentary majority to consider them. Then again, if public opinion is supportive, there is less need to rely upon private member's bills as the legislative vehicle for reform. On its face, therefore, the private member's bill seemingly reflects the inside-access model, since its introduction to the policy agenda requires behind-the-scenes support from the governing party leadership.

Ultimately we will argue that Canada is a maverick among our five western democracies, one reason being its unusual reliance on the insider mode of agenda-setting. Specifically, until 1968 Canada had highly restrictive policies on abortion, divorce, homosexuality, and even gambling. What propelled legal reforms in all these areas was an omnibus bill to modernize the Criminal Code, which was introduced by Pierre Trudeau, when he was minister of justice, and shepherded by him through Parliament when he became the new Liberal prime minister. Also included was a provision for legalized gambling which, when enacted in May 1969, "represented a major policy shift for the country, away from the mainly prohibitory orientation of the past to a system of state operation and regulation."[13] It was also under the Liberal government that capital punishment was partially suspended and eventually abolished. Therefore, unlike the tentative role played by the Labour government in the UK during the late 1960s (see Chapter 5), the Canadian Liberal government set the parliamentary agenda by introducing this package of high-profile morality policies.

A similar process of agenda-setting from the top affects Germany. One study of 150 key enactments from 1949 to 1994 concluded that, "[d]espite exaggerations of media power, the legislative processes show that the media on the whole is reactive rather than active—in agenda-setting as well as in the pressuring for the carrying of a bill."[14] Dramatic reforms in morality policy were unlikely so long as the Christian Democrats—the Christian Democratic Union (CDU) and its Bavarian affiliate the Christian Social Union (CSU)—dominated postwar Germany through the 1960s, because the CDU/CSU had strong ties to the Roman Catholic Church. During the Grand Coalition government of 1966-69, when a weakened CDU was forced to accept the leftist Social Democratic Party (SPD) into its governing coalition in order to maintain power, "criminal penalties for homosexual relations between consenting adults, blasphemy, and adultery were removed." Actually, decriminalization was a "one-party" proposal from the "mini-opposition" liberals (the FDP, or Free Democratic Party), although "many Social Democrats sympathized with the 'homosexuality' bill from the outset" but "did not dare to antagonize the conservative wing of their Christian Democratic coalition partner."[15] After the SPD joined forces with the FDP to oust the CDU/CSU from 1969 to 1982, the Social-Liberal government ignored strong Catholic opposition and proceeded to liberalize the divorce and pornography laws.[16]

Secondly, policy literature focused on legislative elites, ignoring the role of the courts. Thus, because activists often turn to the judiciary to avoid the time-consuming process of lobbying the legislature, morality policy offers a new twist to the inside-access model. Judges are not policy entrepreneurs like MPs or members of Congress (MCs), however, since they cannot initiate policy; they must wait for cases that afford the opportunity to rule on moral controversies in ways that will establish policy. Lawsuits are the vehicle for such a litigation strategy, and bringing "test cases" requires substantial financial and legal resources provided to plaintiffs by interest groups. In Canada, Morton and Knopff label these litigation activists "the Court Party."[17] Thus, a variant of the inside-access approach—judges abetted by group activists—may be characterized as a litigation strategy (see Chapter 6).

When would political elites openly politicize morality policy through a mobilization strategy in order to cultivate public opinion? To actively engage the public seems a risky option for politicians on two-sided issues but political leaders can operate indirectly, if not directly, through party platforms and election campaigns. One might think that campaigns can experiment with any issue, including moral ones, to test public reaction, but parties prefer to ensure a win by promoting safe (one-sided morality) issues rather than polarizing the electorate with hard-and-fast positions on controversial ones. One "safe" issue in the United States is drug abuse. The recent history of anti-drug policy led Sharp to conclude that "[n]o instances of the outside-initiative model [of agenda-setting] emerge. Despite the common assumption that public fears about drugs propel politicians to action, this analysis shows that politicians lead rather than follow on this issue."[18] With the 1986 War on Drugs, for example, "public concern over the drug issue, as measured in opinion polls, escalated after politicians promoted it," despite the fact that trends actually showed "an overall decline" in the use of illicit drugs from the late 1970s into the 1980s.[19] By the mid-1980s, says Sharp, partisanship over the drug issue was "thoroughly institutionalized," which explains why "each of the major pieces of drug-related legislation in the 1980s was passed in an election year."[20]

A study of recent American presidential elections found that, although party elites gave increased attention to environmentalism, "the saliency of their environmental agenda did not yield a commensurate response within the electorate."[21] In contrast, the mobilization model does apply to economic issues because party platforms reinforced by campaign rhetoric yielded a sizeable segment of the electorate who mentioned economic concerns. Thus, environmental agenda-setting was more akin to the inside-access model because "presidents exhibit leadership on environmentalism *once elected* rather than widely broadcasting their views on environmentalism during the political campaign."[22] Abortion is the most contentious two-sided moral conflict in North America, yet it seems not to have mobilized the electorate, except at the edges. Studies of abortion attitudes on voting behaviour have found little or no impact on the American electorate, and the same pertains to elections for Congress and state-wide offices. Nor has the abortion debate surfaced with any impact in recent Canadian national elections.[23]

Political Parties

Historical experiences in European nations have yielded party systems that reflect deep-seated social cleavages, identified in a classic article by Lipset and Rokkan: centre vs. periphery, state vs. church, land vs. industry, and owner vs. worker. The last—class conflict—flowered in virtually every society after the Russian Revolution of 1917,[24] although all four types of social cleavages have persisted in various European nations into the 1960s.

Can the matrix of class-based political parties accommodate the new morality politics? Class politics has been weakened in the decades since Lipset and Rokkan wrote, but the major European parties have not been fully realigned to reflect postmaterialist cleavages. Says Dalton, "Most of the established political parties are still oriented to traditional social divisions, and they have repeatedly resisted attempts to incorporate postmaterial issues into a partisan framework."[25] A time lag between the emergence of postmaterialist forces and the ideological realignment of the political parties suggests that party organizations, with exceptions, have not been the institutional vehicles for bringing identity politics to the policy agenda of government.[26] Dalton agrees that "[a] major factor in the destabilization of modern party systems was the initial inability or unwillingness of the major parties to respond fully to the new [postmaterialist] demands," with the consequence that "several new parties formed specifically to represent the new political perspectives." He points to "the green parties in Germany and France or Left-libertarian parties" which, in turn, "stimulated a counter wave of New Right parties, such as the National Front in France or the Republikaner in Germany."[27]

There is evidence that the share of the American population that subscribes to postmaterialist values has markedly increased and, concurrently, that class cleavages have weakened. Yet researchers have not conclusively pointed to the materialist-postmaterialist divide as having much power in explaining contemporary American politics.[28] For example, voting tendencies in the United States are paradoxical according to the 1990 World Values Survey. Among our five nations, Dalton determined that class voting is strongest in the UK, slightly higher in France than in East/West Germany within the moderate range, and weakest in the United States and Canada. Yet values voting was *also* weakest in the United States, mid-range for Canada and East Germany, and much higher in France, though especially high in the UK and West Germany.[29]

Layman and Carmines suggest that "American politics *has* become more culturally based but that Inglehart's value priorities thesis is inadequate for explaining these developments because it does not take into account the unique features of the American political context and of cultural conflict in the United States." The missing ingredient, they say, is religion because "while religion has become a much less important part of politics and society in most advanced industrial democracies, it continues to play an important role in the United States." They agree with Inglehart's critics (see Chapter 2) that his dichotomy is flawed insofar as the "Postmaterialist category contains both social liberals and social conservatives" and the "Materialist category contains both economic conservatives and economic liberals," and, in fact, any "conception of cultural orientations that does differentiate between traditionalists and progressives on the cultural axis of political conflict performs better than Inglehart's value priorities in explaining American political behavior." Contrary to what Inglehart would anticipate, continue Layman and Carmines, the main opposition to "cultural progressivism" is not the working class but "religious conservatives seeking to maintain the role of traditional moral values in American culture."[30]

Recent American elections signal that cultural forces are paving the way for some partisan realignment. The class-based cleavage that allowed the Democratic Party to emerge and remain dominant since the Depression-fueled presidential election of 1932 (when Franklin D. Roosevelt was elected) has yielded to a Republican resurgence. The reason often given for this partisan shift, especially in the South, is race relations, although others point to a host of social issues that have assisted the Republican's rise in presidential and, now, congressional politics. One development that facilitates partisan realignment is issue polarization among party activists, and there is substantial evidence that Republican and Democratic elites diverge sharply on such issues as abortion, school prayer, and gun control. Also during the 1980s the proportion of committed religious conservatives among Republican activists increased concurrently with a rise in the number of religious liberals and secularists among Democratic activists. This cultural divide between party elites has also reached downward to the parties' rank and file.[31] The parties also express diametrically opposing views in their platforms, which can influence presidential decisions. One study found that Democratic presidents act more liberally on affirmative action, abortion, and gun control—but avoid dealing with pornography or school prayer—whereas Republican presidents redeemed their platform pledges on pornography, school prayer, abortion, and gun control. The abortion issue seems especially potent to reshaping the partisan electoral alignment.[32]

The relationship between the Christian Right and the Canadian party system is "more complex," says Hoover, though "[m]ore recently, Christian Right activists have established connections to sympathetic elements of the new Reform Party." Based in western Canada, Reform—renamed the Canadian Alliance Party in 2000—"eschews any explicit religious identity, and instructs its MPs to follow a strictly 'populist' ... decision procedure regarding moral issues in the House of Commons," namely that "they are instructed to vote the 'consensus' of their riding (constituency)" and to rely on their own judgment only when that consensus is lacking. In 1996 the American Christian Right favoured Republican Bob Dole, while the majority of Americans re-elected Democratic President Bill Clinton; that same year, 52 per cent of the Canadian Christian Right sympathizers favoured the Liberal Party, whereas the Progressive Conservatives and Reform Party together drew only 39 per cent of their vote. This outcome suggests to Hoover "that conservative Christians in Canada do not lean as consistently to the partisan 'right' as their American counterparts."[33]

In France, the Socialists under François Mitterrand advocated the abolition of capital punishment; they ended the use of the guillotine in 1982 when they were in power. Also, although the most permissive abortion reforms in Europe had been enacted in France under the centre-right coalition government of Valéry Giscard d'Estaing, as early as 1965 Mitterrand's Socialists demanded repeal of the restrictive 1920 abortion law. In 1971 the Communist Party also favoured "the repeal of all repressive measures concerning abortion" as well as increased sex education and contraceptive services. Elections for the National Assembly in March 1973, therefore, "gave the [abortion] issue its final boost to the public agenda," but initial parliamentary efforts stalled, to be resurrected upon the death of President Pompidou in April, 1974 and a new election for president during which "[a]ll [candidates] responded to the policy deadlock on abortion."[34]

On the other hand, the French Green Party's strategy of "non-alignment" with the major political parties—including their rejection of overtures from the French Socialists—precluded them from political power. Given the ecologists' disappointing performance in the 1993 parliamentary elections, Szarka wonders "whether the Greens can maintain unity within their own ranks yet achieve sufficient convergence with fellow-travelers on the Left to allow the substantial restructuring of party politics in France that the implementation of their policies require."[35]

In the UK, due to ongoing public debate during the early 1960s, the issue of capital punishment had "remarkable salience to the public," according to one election analysis, with 70 per cent in 1964 and 77 per cent in 1966 favouring the hangman. Nonetheless, the British were unable to "sharply differentiate the parties on the question since the parties took no official stand in Parliament" but allowed MPs a "free vote" (see Chapter 5). Thus, capital punishment "never became a major basis for appraising the parties and exerted no real influence on their relative strength" within the electorate.[36]

British electoral behaviour over the 1970s and 1980s indicates to Studlar and McAllister that "the most substantial changes in party support have been on the economic dimension, not the noneconomic one," which is not unexpected since party leaders used "economic issues to unite their followers, while generally ignoring or downplaying the potentially divisive noneconomic issues like race or abortion." The fact that "traditional morality" had "no discernible effect in any of the four [national] elections" suggests that the continued saliency of economic issues "may owe more to the behaviour of political parties rather than the preferences of voters. Class-based voting may have declined, but political leaders still feel more comfortable in making appeals on economic issues." Also, "the majority of the electorate displays social conservatism or moderation," whereas "political elites are generally more socially liberal than the masses."[37]

Nor has a Canadian election in recent decades engaged morality policy, since usually economic conditions, American-Canadian trade relations, federal-provincial relations, and the perennial issue of national unity (Quebec) have dominated its national political campaigns.[38] Arguably one exception occurred during the early 1960s as a prelude to the flag debate (see Chapter 5) when, at the insistence of Prime Minister Lester Pearson, the Liberal Party platform of 1961 pledged to establish a uniquely Canadian flag to replace the British Union Jack or Red Ensign (which combined the Union Jack with the Canadian coat-of-arms). The Liberals under Pearson were victorious in 1963, and the pledge to redesign the Canadian flag was redeemed in December 1964.

Because no majority party in Canada has advocated capital punishment (despite opinion polls; see Chapter 8), those wanting to restore the death penalty face obstacles to promoting that issue in election campaigns. The same applies to abortion, where both sides find Canadian election campaigns devoid of outward party appeals. One exception is the firm pro-choice stance taken by the New Democratic Party (NDP) after feminist activist Judy Rebick pressured the NDP leadership in Ontario and British Columbia in the early 1980s to formally endorse abortion decriminalization and the establishment of free-standing abortion clinics in their party platforms.[39]

Unlike European environmentalists, who avoided entanglements with the major parties, North American feminists were eager to engage the established parties. Party responsiveness can be judged in terms of personnel or policy and, according to Lisa Young, the Progressive Conservatives of Canada were decidedly moderate as compared to the anti-feminist Reform/Alliance Party and, even more so, the Republican Party, whereas the Democratic Party was more pro-feminist than the Canadian Liberal Party, although neither were as solidly committed to the women's movement as the New Democratic Party. Because feminists in the United States "tended towards a partisan relationship with the Democratic party, while the Canadian women's movement has remained multipartisan, with strong apartisan tendencies growing since the mid-1980s," the political consequence has been to polarize the American party system but *not* Canada's. This unexpected finding, given that in both countries "the bulk of voters espouse moderate positions" on feminist goals, led Young to conclude that Republican opposition is rooted in those anti-feminist and Christian Right groups which are "an extremely influential constituency," whereas "the absence of a thriving organized anti-feminist movement in Canada combined with the more ambiguous partisan cues of the Canadian women's movement to make the Progressive Conservatives far less hostile to feminism than their American counterparts."[40]

A notable departure in the failure of debates over morality policy to intrude on Canadian political campaigns was the 1997 national election. The major parties took divergent stands on the 1995 Firearms Act requiring licensing of gun-owners and registration of firearms, and it has been alleged that the governing Liberal Party deliberately exploited this issue to mobilize urban voters in central Canada, fearing the growing electoral power of the (conservative) Canadian Alliance in western Canada.[41] As Canada prepared for new elections in 2000, policy declarations by both the Progressive Conservatives (PC) and Canadian Alliance pledged to abolish the firearms registration system. The PC platform upheld "the individual rights of law-abiding gun owners," and the Alliance promised to "replace" the current law with one that "respects the rights of Canadians to own and use firearms responsibly." On another contemporary issue facing Canada, the Alliance's 2000 platform pledged legislation and programs "to strength and protect the family" and specifically defined marriage "as the union of a man and a woman."

Mass Mobilization

Frontally assaulting long-standing values that define the hierarchy of social relationships between men and women, gays and straights, parents and children, or human and nonhumans requires social mobilization on a broad scale. As illustrated by *Animal Liberation*, the "bible" for animal rights activists, popular exposés are often the intellectual springboards for new social movements. Rachel Carson's *The Silent Spring* was the intellectual genesis of the environmental movement. Ralph Nader's *Unsafe at Any Speed* energized the consumer movement in the United States. The feminist movement was stimulated by several best-sellers including Betty Friedan's *The Feminine Mystique* (1963) and Kate Millet's *Sexual Politics* (1970).[42] The consciousness-raising impact on women that resulted after a magazine excerpted Friedan's book prompted her to establish the National Organization for Women (NOW), the leading American feminist advocacy group.

The "New" Social Movements

The parallel experiences of working-class mobilization in the United States and Europe[43] prompted three American sociologists to make this telling observation: "'Old movements' coalesced around shared grievances and perceptions of injustice" so their "[p]rograms for amelioration of these grievances and attribution of cause constituted the ideological base for mobilization." At base, the link between grievance and ideology was strong insofar as working-class "[p]eople participated massively in collective action because they were hungry and without jobs." But the "status movements" of today are more "closely linked with identity issues" since "grievances are actuated by perceived threats to how one defines oneself," not their impact on one's life. For "new" social movements, the "very nature of grievances ... merges ... closely with the concept of identity," and, even where actual grievances exist, the "identity quest" is a "fundamental raison d'être of group formation." Regarding the environmental movement, for example, the question is whether ᴗuch environmental grievances "as threats to the ozone level, nuclear prolif-eration, or saving whales are so distant from everyday life that they can only remain immediate through their ongoing social construction and reassertion in the group context."[44] In other words, what makes ecological grievances seem so compelling to ecological activists are the interpersonal dynamics that give meaning to their movement, not because ecological damage poses any greater threat to the everyday lives of its membership.

Theories of collective behaviour seem inadequate to explain the rise of peace movements, student movements, anti-nuclear energy protests, ethnic nationalism, gay or women's rights, animal rights, and the ecology move-ment. According to sociologist Joseph Gusfield, their "[s]uccess is measured not only by victory or defeat in legislative, bargaining or legal arenas but also in how the movement has changed the rules that are admissible in public are-nas." Thus, "[t]he struggle over abortion in the United States is symbolically a struggle about the place of women relative to men" just as "efforts to change street names ... to one honoring Martin Luther King ... symbolize the relative place of blacks in the American social order." In short, these social movements "can create the recognition that some accepted pattern of social life is now in contention; it has become an issue."[45]

SINGLE-ISSUE GROUPS

While all pluralists assume that group conflict is endemic to democratic politics, the more compelling question is the magnitude of group conflict over morality policy, which is directly related to the issue of what motivates politi-cal activism. This discussion revisits the methodological debate over whether morality policy is more analogous to "redistribution of values" or "social regulation," or perhaps an amalgam of both types (Chapter 1). Here the issue is joined in terms of group mobilization; later (Chapter 8) it is evaluated in terms of public opinion.

For a long time a cardinal principle of pluralist theory was that economic self-interest motivates political behaviour. A seminal work by Mancur Olson claimed that the most effective interest groups must offer tangible benefits to members as an incentive for them to coalesce around collective objectives. Olson acknowledged that there were deviant cases of groups that pursue non-economic objectives—philanthropic organizations, religious lobbies, and people committed to "lost causes"—but such activism he viewed as "nonrational" or "irrational" behaviour.[46] Olson was much influenced by economics, but there are political scientists who take other-directed motiva-tions more seriously. A study of agenda-setting by Cobb and Elder argued that "do-gooders" are activists "who have no positions or resources to gain for themselves" but "merely acquire a psychological sense of well-being for doing what they believe is in the public interest."[47] Clark and Wilson identified three incentives—material, solidarity, purposive—for joining groups, and today's social scientists are beginning to appreciate that purposive incentives, other-directed goals, and even altruism can be powerful forces undergirding political activism; for instance, the rescuers of Jews from the Nazis have been credited with acting from altruism.[48] Militant anti-abortionists also invoke the higher authority of the Lord to justify their activism: "For many rescuers spiritual growth and activism were linked in their own particular 'walk with God' ... [insofar as] rescue satisfied specific needs more pressing than the risks rescue entailed. In this sense, rescue was more than a logical response to abortion disapproval ... [but] was also a response to God and to oneself—to one's own needs."[49]

LOWI AND WEBER

Theodore Lowi argued that each type of public policy is enacted by a uniquely configured "arena of power," and, for that reason, groups that influence dis-tributive policy tend to be the clientele or beneficiaries who directly obtain public grants, subsidies, or tax rebates. Trade associations angered over gov-ernment regulations generally represent the precise *sector* of the economy directly affected. Lowi saw the widest array of interest groups mobilizing around redistributive policies designed to reallocate wealth. Though both regulation and redistribution involve an ideological battle between the Left and Right, Lowi anticipated a huge difference in their scope of conflict, be-cause regulation affected only *sectors* of the economy, whereas redistribution impacted entire economic *classes*. To assess the scope of conflict over morality policy involves determining whether group mobilization is limited to "sec-tors" of society, or not.

The logic of Lowi's typology is that different political *processes* result because there are unlike *types* of public policies. It is relevant, therefore, that economic goals as opposed to moral objectives are fundamentally different. Surely the *perceptions* of political actors are influenced by whether econom-ics or morality is at stake. And they are. Local political elites draw a distinc-tion between distributional questions and moral regulation. In assessing the perspectives of local officials regarding "culture wars" in American cities, Schumaker calls attention to two "distinct moral questions": what restrictions should government impose on the pursuit of the good life by self-regarding individuals, and how should social goods be distributed? Though related, the first embodies the culture wars by dealing "with 'good' or 'virtuous' human behavior and the kinds of social policies that are required to promote such behavior and curtail 'bad' or 'sinful' acts."[50]

Sociologist Max Weber was alert to these dynamics of social action, and Miller integrated Weber's insights into Lowi's typology to more fully describe the policy process. Weber classified human action in terms of motivation. He believed that people are motivated by *traditional, affective, value-rational,* and *instrumentally rational* goals. Traditional behaviour is determined by habit, re-action, and imitation, whereas affective action is motivated by feelings—fear, joy, hurt, anger, wanting, guilt, or whatever. More relevant to morality policy is "value-rational" action, which, says Miller, is "a value which manifests its worthiness in and of itself, determined by a conscious belief in the value for its own sake, without regard for the likelihood of the eventual success," meaning that "persons who practice their *convictions* as required by duty, honor, pursuit of beauty, loyalty, or *righteousness* are oriented toward value-rational action" (italics added). This kind of motivation is unlike "instrumentally rational" actions which are utilitarian, a means-ends orientation by people who pursue "one's own rationally calculated ends." [51]

The rational-actor model of human action underlies much social science research, especially in economics. We already noted that most scholars believe that political activists are typically motivated by instrumentally rational goals. But Miller agrees with Tatalovich and Daynes that "examples abound which indicate that Americans do orient policy action toward absolute end values" like anti-abortion, school prayer, freedom of expression, anti-pornography, and civil rights. Moreover "symbols such as the flag, country, states' rights, and liberty are readily available to leaders who seek to stir the passions of their followers." Lowi's distributive policy "is dominated by actors who possess an instrumentally rational outlook" and thus pursue "self-interest and material accumulation." The same applies to regulatory policy, but here self-interested actors "are confronted by other actors whose interests conflict," although the regulatory policy debate may blend both value-rational and instrumental-rational arguments. The redistributive arena "is a debate over values" that emphasizes "broad-based social change in opposition to the privileged *class*" (italics added).[52]

Morality policy mobilizes people mainly through value-rational actions, though Miller also believes that symbols like the flag can activate "affective" motivations. The truth of that observation was shown by the flag debate in the Canadian Parliament during 1964, which "symbolized in a most dramatic manner the problem of Canadian identity"[53] (see Chapter 5). However, the usual political battleground is the regulatory arena, as Miller agrees with Tatalovich and Daynes that "[a]t some point, individual incentives—whether economic, social, or psychological—do not account for events which take place in the regulatory arena. Environmental policy, anti-abortion protest, and consumer protection policy do not require the rational self-interest assumption to account for the behavior of the protagonists."[54] This is precisely why Theodore Lowi reformulated his original policy typology to underscore the fundamental distinction between "mainstream" politics based on utilitarian (what Weber called "instrumentally rational") assumptions and "radical" politics based on moral zealotry (see Introduction).[55]

Since economics plays little or no role in socializing moral conflict, citizens have no material reason to become involved in issues like abortion or gay rights. This begs the question of whether other-directed goals are a sufficient motivation for widespread citizen participation in morality policy. We are dubious, yet happily (for democratic politics) there may be a double-edged quality to the debate over values and morals. Many observers worry about the down-side—that single-minded zealots are disposed never to say die—but there may be an up-side to these disputes. The vast majority of citizens may not be so fixated in their normative commitments that they will expend time, money, and energy on such causes. Our presumption is that there are organizational limits to the scope of conflict over morality policy, and, because the primary motivation is other-directed rather than self-interested behaviour, the public at large may often be a passive force in the political drama.

Single-issue groups are key players in morality politics. The political debate over gun ownership and registration in the United States pits the pro-gun National Rifle Association (NRA) with its nearly 4-million members against the smaller anti-gun organization, Handgun Control, Inc. Virtually every American organization within the animal rights movement is a single-issue group: Animal Legal Defense Fund, Animal Liberation Front, Animal Rights Mobilization, In Defense of Animals, and People for the Ethical Treatment of Animals (PETA), among others. Those committed to the "right to die" for the terminally ill have organized in Canada as Dying with Dignity and the Right to Die Society and, in the United States, as the Hemlock Society. Abortion legalization in Canada was a personal campaign by Dr. Henry Morgentaler; he was charged several times (but acquitted by juries) for opening illegal clinics in Quebec, and his appeal to the Supreme Court of Canada eventually led to ending criminal bans on abortion. The Canadian pro-life crusade was personified by former Manitoba politician Joe Borowski, who was so angered by Morgentaler's activities that he litigated before the Supreme Court of Canada (unsuccessfully) on behalf of the unborn.[56]

In Germany, so-called "civic initiative groups" are characterized by Burkett as "'one-issue' groups" that "used 'an action repertory which had been mainly borrowed from the student movement'" in order to press their policy agendas. The major parties "had cause to see the rise of these groups as more than a threat to their monopoly" because they represented "a new phenomenon within the political system whose demands—in the environmental field—ran counter to the parties' consensus on economic growth, a consensus to which powerful economic groups are subscribers."[57] In other words, a new vehicle for political action was invented in Germany to promote various policies, notably environmentalism, at odds with the economic game plan of established party elites.

In France, adds Stetson, the demand for legalized abortion "came from 'cause' groups outside the government" that were effective in "expanding the conflict to other groups in the population." As early as 1956 the *Mouvement Français pour le planning familial* (MFPF) campaigned to legalize contraception and to repeal the 1920 anti-abortion law. After enactment of the 1967 contraceptive reform law, Dr. Marie-Andrée Weill-Hallé, founder of MFPF, established an organization to focus specifically on liberalizing the 1920 abortion law. The next year the "first new feminist group," *Mouvement de libération des femmes* (MLF), demanded free contraceptives and abortion on demand. Later some MLF activists formed pro-abortion groups, and by 1971 *Choisir*, founded by "lawyer Gisèle Halimi and author Simone de Beauvoir, had become the most well organized feminist cause group for abortion reform" and for securing guaranteed funding for abortions under the French health services.[58]

Historic efforts to end capital punishment in the UK involved several minor groups, one being the National Council for the Abolition of the Death Penalty, which judged the extreme penalty to be immoral, ineffectual, and unnecessary. At the forefront of a partially successful 1950s crusade to reform the British death statute was the newly organized National Campaign for the Abolition of Capital Punishment. These abolitionists gained from intensity what they lacked in numbers, though the scope of group mobilization was not that extensive. Opposing abolitionism was the Home Office, party associations, and some fundamentalist religious groups which "never welded together into a formal retentionist pressure group, [but] nevertheless acted in a manner quite similar to one." During that period "the group struggle was between a passionate and organized minority on the one side and a less organized, less dedicated, but more numerous coalition of official groups, heavily reinforced by majority opinion and control of Parliamentary institutions, on the other."[59]

Liberalization of abortion in the UK was the single-issue concern of the Abortion Law Reform Association (ALRA) from its founding in 1936 until victory was achieved in 1967. With barely 1,000 members, ALRA nonetheless "had excellent contacts within Parliament, where its main efforts were focused, and a solid knowledge of the procedure. However, it might be argued its greatest success was in getting the issue of abortion reform onto the political agenda."[60]

If abortion is the consummate moral controversy in the United States, taking a closer look at its scope of conflict may give hints about the range of interest group mobilization. Abortion spawned an outpouring of single-issue organizations, representing 69 per cent of all groups giving testimony before Congress and 53 per cent of all *amici* before the Supreme Court of the United States.[61] Most prominent were the National Right to Life Committee, Americans United for Life, and the Legal Defense Fund for Unborn Children. A unique single-issue coalition was the Religious Coalition for Abortion Rights (RCAR), representing 28 groups from 14 denominations, which formed in 1973, the year of *Roe v. Wade*, to prevent an anti-abortion constitutional amendment which, RCAR believed, "would enact into civil law one particular theology—a theology that is not shared by a majority of Western denominations."[62] Single-issue groups are the mainstay of the American pro-life movement, whereas they are more prominent within the Canadian pro-choice coalition. Alliance for Life exemplifies single-issue activism in Canada, others including Canadian Physicians for Life and the Campaign Life Coalition. In both Canada and the United States pro-lifers are aligned with Catholic, Mormon, Fundamentalist, and Evangelical denominations. While the pro-choice coalition has more established interest groups, there are definite sectoral boundaries. "In the United States, the mainstays of the pro-choice coalition are women's groups, health care associations, organized religion, and family planning organizations," the best-known single-issue group being the National Abortion Rights Action League. In Canada, women's organizations and single-issue pro-choice groups together accounted for 66 per cent of those that lobbied Parliament, and "[m]ore than half of the eighty-five member groups in CARAL [the Canadian Abortion Rights Action League] represent women's interests of one kind of another."[63]

In both the United States and Canada there was an outpouring from feminist groups when the state seemed ready to recriminalize abortion. For American feminists, the occasion was the Supreme Court ruling in *Webster v. Reproductive Health Services* (1989) and the prospect that the conservative majority led by Chief Justice William Rehnquist would reverse the landmark precedent in *Roe v. Wade*. That activated 88 women's groups (82 per cent of the 107 groups filing briefs) that "had not been involved as *amici* in any previous Supreme Court abortion case."[64] In Canada the threat came from the Mulroney government. In 1988 the Supreme Court of Canada in *Morgentaler v. The Queen* nullified the highly restrictive abortion law of 1969, but afterwards the Progressive Conservatives tried to re-enact regulations on abortions. Most interest groups have little to no influence on the Canadian legislative process,

Les Pal found, but not so with abortion bill c-43, which feminists "saw as absolutely fundamental to their agenda" and which died in the Canadian Senate
in no small measure because "[a]dvocacy lobbying, grounded in the Charter,
had changed the balance of power in the legislative process."[65]

Issues of church-state separation in the United States are pretty much
limited to religious denominations, civil libertarians like the American Civil
Liberties Union (ACLU), and separatist zealots.[66] Among the foremost
single-issue advocates are Americans United for Separation of Church and
State and People for the American Way, the latter organized in reaction to the
evangelically based Moral Majority of the 1980s. Likewise with pornography,
the most visible single-issue group in the United States has been Citizens for
Decency Through Law. But the clash with constitutional guarantees involves
other groups "motivated by self-interest and principle ... [including] organizations of authors, presses, and distributors."[67] The reputable publishers,
librarians, and authors who rail against censorship are protesting censorship
on principled grounds of free expression—not from any profits they derive
from marketing obscene materials. Also right-to-die litigation during 1976-90
prompted medical organizations and single-issue groups, like Society for the
Right to Die and Concern for Dying, to author *amicus curiae* briefs favouring
passive euthanasia, while the opposition was limited to pro-lifers including
the Roman Catholic Church and advocates of the disabled who feared a slide
towards active euthanasia.[68]

Another single issue is gay rights. In the UK, gays formed the Homosexual
Law Reform Society (HLRS) to lobby for decriminalization. According
to Cowley, "[t]he campaign for the legalisation of male homosexuality ...
dated back to the establishment of the Wolfenden Committee (Committee
on Homosexual Offences and Prostitution) in 1954."[69] Homosexuals organize
to promote an identity politics that is self-interested, though not necessarily guided by economics (as a group, gays are relatively affluent). But what
groups are driven by their self-interest—economic or otherwise—to oppose
gay rights? The main opposition comes from conservative religious denominations for theological reasons. Margaret Ellis observes that "[t]he Christian
Right has been the major force behind efforts to enact antigay statewide referendums, notably Colorado's Amendment 2 in 1992 which was orchestrated
by Colorado for Family Values (CFV)."[70] A study of anti-gay campaigns in
American localities revealed that "the primary contestants against gay rights
were religious traditionalists," whereas "[b]usiness opposition was less general and more sporadic."[71]

Political conflict over language has surfaced in the United States with a
vengeance since the 1980s when most states enacted laws codifying English
as their official language (in 2002 Iowa became the twenty-seventh state to

do so). Yet backers of "English-Only" laws do not live amidst huge Hispanic communities, because most states with official language laws have many *fewer* Spanish-speakers than the American average. Although more than two-thirds of Americans favour these laws, this debate did not incite a large number of organized interests. Nativists have organized through the US English organization; the opposing coalition (once called EPIC, or English Plus Information Clearinghouse) includes the ACLU, and "Jewish organizations are aligned for ideological reasons, but the mainstay of EPIC's constituency are groups that represent non-English speakers ... educators who directly benefit from bilingual instructional programs ... and local single-issue groups."[72] The story of non-English-speakers illustrates how status anxiety has mobilized largely Hispanic groups to pursue identity politics in the United States. Surely material interests matter a lot to some groups, like salaried bilingual education teachers, but most supporters of English-Plus are not motivated by economic gain.[73]

Triggering Events

Often issues are boosted onto the policy agenda by unanticipated and dramatic human incidents, like a presidential assassination.[74] Similarly Kingdon conceptualizes the policy process as a "policy window" of opportunity that results from the confluence of three information "streams"—problem, policy, and political. The "problem stream" is his term for agenda-setting, and one factor drawing attention to a problem is a "crisis or prominent event," like a plane crash, or a major change in a widely reported social indicator, like a spike in the skin cancer rate.[75] Sometimes a powerful triggering event can ignite a full-blown social movement. During the take-off stage of mass mobilization, observes Claus Offe, one ingredient "from which a movement emerges is a widely publicized and highly visible event (or anticipation of an event) that triggers expressions of opinion and protest and helps to define the collectivity of those who are actually or potentially affected by it."[76] In these instances the triggering event does more than pinpoint one issue; it also "frames" an entire array of injustices that prompt political activists to demand a fundamental re-ordering of the social hierarchy. Most illustrative in North America are civil rights, gay rights, and animal rights.

TRIGGERING MOVEMENTS

Civil Rights
There is no more poignant example of the riveting impact of human injustice deeply personalized than the Rosa Parks experience in Montgomery, Alabama

in 1955. It launched the American civil rights movement and, perhaps even more important than mobilizing African-Americans, dramatized for white northern opinion the raw reality of racial separation. On December 1, 1955, Mrs. Parks boarded a bus after work and a few stops later was told to relinquish her seat to a white passenger. She refused, was arrested, and booked. Word quickly reached a local civil rights lawyer, who argued that Mrs. Parks did not technically violate the law and could be acquitted. But E.D. Nixon, ex-president of the Montgomery Chapter of the National Association for the Advancement of Colored People (NAACP), saw real potential in Parks's plight: "*This is the case.* We can boycott the bus line with this and at the same time go to the Supreme Court." A 382-day boycott of public transportation by the black community followed. Things got nasty, as city officials verbally blasted and the police intimidated civil rights activists, one being the Reverend Martin Luther King. As King recalled that pivotal moment in history, he said "a lady by the name of Rosa Parks decided that she wasn't going to take it any longer.... It was the beginning of a movement ... and the people of Montgomery asked me to serve them as a spokesman, and as the president of the new [civil rights] organization ... that came into being to lead the boycott. I couldn't say no." [77]

Gay Rights

As late as the early 1960s the number of gay and lesbian activists "remained small and their political influence limited," according to Button, Rienzo, and Wald, but "[b]y defining homosexuals as a sexual minority, similar to other ethnic and cultural minorities and entitled to the same rights and benefits granted other groups, these early activists aided the movement greatly." [78] As activist Urvashi Vaid explains, viewing gays as an aggrieved "sexual minority" like any ethnic or cultural minority "marked a profound definition of homosexuality" because that approach "moved homosexuality from the domain of illness and sociopathic deviance and into the public domain of civil rights." [79] It would not be long before gay rights burst upon the American political scene. In June and July 1969 the New York City police raided Stonewall, a Greenwich Village gay bar, and, by that assault, literally inaugurated the gay rights movement. "'Stonewall' has become an empowering symbol of global proportions," says Duberman,[80] adding that it was "*the* emblematic event in modern lesbian and gay history." Button, Rienzo, and Wald agree that it was "a crucial catalyst to the mass political mobilization of lesbians and gay men" across the United States. "Almost immediately following Stonewall, countless new lesbian and gay liberation organizations came into being. Mobilized by the women's movement, lesbians became a greater force in the new gay movement. More radical in tone and tactics than previous homosexual organizations, these new political groups not only challenged antigay policies but focused on sexual oppression more generally."[81]

While nothing comparable to Stonewall galvanized the Canadian gay rights movement, there were defining moments. Gay rights arrived in Canada in 1971, two years after Stonewall, when gay activists protested on Parliament Hill, published the first issue of *The Body Politic*, and established gay liberation organizations in Montreal and Vancouver. High profile "test" cases before provincial human rights commissions "were used in the gay and lesbian communities as levers for political action. They served as a rallying cry and as an assertion of the entitlement to equality." John Damien, a jockey and racing steward fired by the Ontario Racing Commission because he was homosexual, appealed to the Ontario Human Rights Commission. He lost, then filed a wrongful dismissal suit that was settled years later. Nonetheless Smith argues that "[t]he Damien case was the *cause célèbre* of the gay political community in the mid to late seventies and, from the beginning, gay liberation activists saw the potential of the case to mobilize its own constituency."[82]

Another episode during the late 1970s and early 1980s was police repression of homosexuals in Toronto. At that time "[b]y outing the issue of sexual orientation, early gay liberation groups had placed sexuality on the public and political agenda and had started to build urban communities, social movement networks, and political organizations," but these activities provoked a backlash. After a Toronto shoeshine boy was murdered in 1977, "the city was gripped by homophobia, stirred up by the mainstream media which depicted the murder as the result of homosexual depravity"; subsequently, the police raided the offices of *The Body Politic* for publishing immoral, indecent, and scurrilous material (two trials in 1979 and 1982 both ended in acquittals). Toronto police also stepped up their raids on bathhouses. After the bathhouse raids on February 6, 1981, "the largest gay rights demonstration that had ever occurred in Toronto was attended by 3,000 lesbians and gay men" and "[o]vernight, the RTPC [Right to Privacy Committee] was transformed, as 1,500 people came out to a community meeting to formulate the lesbian and gay community's response to the raids." Smith concluded that "[t]he very length of the [Damien] case, which facilitated the broader mobilization ... laid the groundwork for an ongoing gay and lesbian community that continued to assert rights claims at the provincial and federal levels in the seventies and beyond."[83]

Animal Rights

Equally explosive were the origins of the animal rights movement. *Animal Liberation* (1977) by Australian philosopher Peter Singer is considered to be the "bible" of the animal rights movement.[84] It had a formidable impact because "[f]or many people, this was their first exposure to the industries that produced the meat for their dinner or that subjected nonhumans to shocking, scalding, burning, and mutilation in the name of science." The late 1970s and early 1980s "marked the emergence of the *animal rights* movement," which claimed "that animals, like humans, have inherent value that must be respected. The rights view reflects a shift from the vague obligation to act 'humanely' to a theory of justice that rejects the status of animals as property and the corresponding hegemony of humans over nonhumans." [85] Rights are deemed the only appropriate remedy for injustice. "Many animal rights activists, seeing animals as yet another oppressed and invisible group, seized upon the language of rights to express their aims and agenda. They called upon the popular rhetoric of rights to empower their own [moral] crusade." [86]

The triggering event that specifically launched this grassroots movement was a highly publicized assault on a venerable institution in New York City by activist Henry Spira, who had been influenced by Singer. Since 1959 and with funding from the National Institutes of Health, the American Museum of Natural History in Manhattan had been conducting experiments on cats, which involved "removing parts of the brain, severing nerves in the penis, and destroying the sense of smell." For Spira, "bent on organizing a successful action, here was an ideal target. Located in New York City, a protest against the popular museum would attract broad public interest and media attention. Taxpayers were likely to be shocked to find that their tax dollars went to support the mutilation of cats in order to observe their sexual performance ... the exposé was likely to mobilize moral outrage." [87]

Spira penned a series of articles in a free weekly publication; organized a letter-writing campaign targeting the NIH, Congress, and the Museum; organized street demonstrations; and garnered newspaper space, including an editorial by Roger Simon on "Cutting up Cats to Study Sex—What Fun!" In the end he won, and the experiments were ended. The Museum "protest was one of the first visual expressions of the new 'animal rights' sentiments in action," and this victory "was indeed only the beginning. During the late 1970s and early 1980s, animal rights groups began appearing everywhere," including the quite militant People for the Ethical Treatment of Animals (PETA, one of whose founders also had been deeply influenced by Singer's book). [88]

TRIGGERING ISSUES

Although Swedish scientist Svante Oden as early as the 1960s had warned about the dangers of acid rain, what ultimately dramatized the issue for Americans was the 1978 Love Canal disaster in New York State. Daily reports on television, including an ABC News feature entitled "The Killing

Ground," led to congressional hearings about toxic waste, direct involvement by President Carter, and ultimately the enactment of the Comprehensive Environmental Response, Compensation, and Liability Act of 1980.[89] Given the social resistance to uprooting long-standing values, to justify a reordering of our moral values requires triggering events that galvanize public sympathies in highly *personal* terms, as Rosa Parks illustrated. Nothing can capture the public imagination like a human tragedy, so we believe that moral conflicts often are forced onto the systemic agenda by a *cause célèbre*. The issues of abortion, gun control, capital punishment, and physician-assisted suicide illustrate how agenda-setting can be shaped by triggering events that sensationalize human suffering.

Abortion

In 1962, Sherri Finkbine dramatized the need for abortion reform in the United States. Although illegal abortions had persisted since the nineteenth century, if not earlier, they were criminal acts and not publicized until a botched abortion resulted in death. Reformers early in the twentieth century directed their concerns to other professionals, not the general public, and abortion was considered a taboo subject, not suitable discussion in proper society. Moreover, a "gray" market existed whereby "[a]ffluent white women were granted practical immunities from pre-*Roe* abortion law" since physicians and hospitals bent the law to provide them with abortion services.[90] Poor and minority women could not take advantage of these "safe" abortions, and they also lacked the resources to mount a political challenge against state anti-abortion laws. The cause of abortion reform needed a white, married, middle-class, and professional woman of celebrity status to drive home its significance. That role was filled by Sherri Finkbine, a middle-class white woman who hosted a television program for children in Phoenix, Arizona. To calm her nerves during her pregnancy, she took thalidomide, just before reports from Europe indicated that the drug caused severe fetal abnormalities. Her request for an abortion at an Arizona hospital was approved, but was withdrawn when her story was publicized across America. Finkbine had to travel to Sweden for the procedure, which resulted in a grossly deformed fetus, and her travail galvanized the nation around the issue of "therapeutic" abortion reform.[91]

In France, feminists joined by Socialists and other Leftists were successful "in dramatizing the issue and expanding the conflict to the streets. Their symbol was Marie-Claire, the poor victim of the *faiseuse d'anges* [illegal abortionists]." Her plight in 1972 was viewed by lawyer Gisèle Halimi, who co-founded the pro-abortion feminist organization *Choisir*, as "the perfect case to illustrate the injustice of the 1920 [anti-abortion] law."[92] Seventeen-year-old Marie-Claire, her mother Michèle, and two other women were arrested for violating that

1920 law. Marie-Claire became pregnant from a rape, and, though it was easy to find a doctor willing to perform an abortion—for 4500 francs—Michèle, who was single and worked 10 hours a day in a Metro station to support three children, could only afford a *faiseuse d'anges*. Halimi and Marie-Claire's family collaborated to make their trial at Bobigny a political trial, as recounted by lawyer Halimi: "Because when the accused realize that they are fighting to defend a cause that goes beyond their own case, then the trial is political. And it is a political trial because the accused turn themselves into accusers, decide to use the court as a platform, and go over the heads of the judges to address themselves to the whole body of public opinion." The outcome, says Halimi, was "historic, for it enshrines the collapse of the [abortion] law of 1920."[93] According to Stetson, "[d]octors, biologists and prominent public figures ... put the law itself on trial, testifying for the need for change"; Marie-Claire was acquitted, and "[a]bortion was a taboo subject no longer."[94]

Gun Control

The United States has weaker gun laws than any other western democracy. What legislative success pro-control advocates have had usually followed a failed or successful assassination of a public official. New York State's Sullivan Law of 1911, the first modern state gun law, was prompted by the attempted murder of New York City Mayor William Gaynor, just as the first federal law, the National Firearms Act of 1934, was a response to the attempted assassination of President Franklin Roosevelt the year before. The assassination of President Kennedy in 1963 did not immediately result in new legislation; however, it did guarantee that gun control would remain on the agenda of government. Two years later, President Lyndon Johnson proposed sweeping new gun controls. What finally broke the legislative stalemate were two more high-profile assassinations. The "shooting deaths of Senator Robert F. Kennedy and the Reverend Martin Luther King, Jr, both in 1968, were more recent instances when public outrage over deaths from guns prompted a significant political reaction—passage of the federal Gun Control Act of 1968."[95]

From 1968 until 1988, however, no legislation to tighten gun controls reached the floor of Congress, but this quiescence abruptly ended. The "key event spurring control supporters was a senseless January 1989 schoolyard massacre in Stockton, California, when five children were killed and twenty-nine others were wounded in a shooting spree by a man using a Chinese AK-47 assault rifle"; within weeks 30 states considered bans on such weapons. One immediate result was that President George Bush reversed his opposition to assault weapons regulation and issued an executive order in March 1989 to temporarily, and later permanently, halt the importation of certain assault rifles. Two years later "the worst such massacre in American history" occurred in Killeen, Texas, when George J. Hennard killed 22 people and wounded 23 others in a cafeteria before killing himself.[96] Legislation curbing assault weapons had been introduced into Congress in 1989, but it was not until September 1994 when all the legislative hurdles were cleared and President Clinton signed the bill into law.

Although Canada has a history of stringent gun laws, added regulations in 1991 were a direct consequence of the massacre of 14 women at the University of Montreal by a man armed with a semi-automatic weapon. Within two years of those murders, a coalition of police, religious groups, public health, and victims groups joined forces as the Coalition for Gun Control to vigorously push their legislative agenda on Parliament Hill. That tragedy also caused 600,000 Canadians to sign petitions asking that military-style weapons be banned. All this impressed the ruling Progressive Conservatives to propose a 28-day waiting period for first-time firearm purchasers, enhanced screening of applicants for Firearms Acquisition Certificates, and the prohibition of converted automatic and military-style firearms (to limit their firepower) as 1991 amendments to the criminal code.[97]

Capital Punishment

Now consider capital punishment. Every abolitionist effort in the UK failed to stop judicial hanging until the British came to believe that there had been one hanging too many. The "renewal of the controversy in the middle 1950s can be attributed chiefly to the convergence of several forces at a particularly ripe moment in recent British history," namely, "the activities and the Report of the Royal Commission on Capital Punishment; a series of peculiar and much-publicized murder cases taking place in the early 1950s; and the formation and work of a new abolitionist organization, the National Campaign for the Abolition of Capital Punishment." Its report, however, had little impact on the authorities or opinion leaders and "would not have been sufficient to excite public or Parliamentary attention in such a way as to bring about changes in basic attitudes."[98] However, it helped lay the groundwork for a revival of the abolition crusade at a time when the public became gripped by the reality of injustice. James Christoph observes that "public concern was aroused by three sensational murder trials ... which ended in a hanging and raised the suspicion either that an innocent person had suffered an irrevocable punishment or that the rigidity of the law had required a penalty that was much too severe."[99]

The stories of those unfortunates—Timothy Evans in 1950, Derek Bentley in 1953, and Ruth Ellis (the last woman executed in Britain) in 1955—were highly publicized. In a few years "several books appeared to assert Evans' innocence and catalogue the misdeeds of the government officials.... None of them was a best seller, but each received extensive comment in the press and served to keep the facts and the allegations of the Evans-Christie saga before the public [John Reginald Halliday Christie eventually confessed to the Evans murders, and was hanged]. From 1953 onwards, no debate on capital punishment in either House of Parliament was complete without reference to the fate of Timothy John Evans." In its aftermath public support for capital punishment softened, with 34 per cent approving but 45 per cent disapproving a temporary suspension in hangings in 1956 (as compared to 13 per cent and 69 per cent, respectively, in 1948). Of all the factors that converged to bring about penal reform in the UK, Christoph argues that these miscarriages of justice were especially potent. "It is doubtful that abolitionist feeling in the nation would have been strong enough to force reconsideration of the issue by Parliament in the mid-fifties had not the Bentley, Evans-Christie and Ellis murders taken place and achieved their particular notoriety. The reformers were not influential enough to make their own opportunities; to a large extent they had to rely upon chance occurrences before a suitably large public could be created on the issue."[100] Ultimately on March 21, 1957 the first major bill in 90 years on capital punishment received Royal Assent. This Homicide Bill did not abolish capital punishment outright but made reforms in its application.

The abolition of capital punishment in France in 1981 was the result of even more of an insider strategy than what had happened in the UK. It was the culmination of a personal campaign by Robert Badinter, a lawyer long associated with Amnesty International, who was traumatized into action by witnessing the guillotining of a client in late 1972. A year later he wrote a highly acclaimed book on the French criminal justice system entitled *L'execution* ("The Executioner"). His window of opportunity came with the election campaign that ended the presidency of Valéry Giscard d'Estaing.

In November 1980 yet another attempt to end funding for the guillotine was rejected in the National Assembly, and afterwards President d'Estaing, seeking re-election, expressed his "distaste for the death penalty" but argued that supporting abolition "would go against the deepest sensibilities of the French people." His opponent, Socialist François Mitterrand declared on French television that "in my heart of hearts, I am opposed to the death penalty" and that he would not hide his views from the electorate.[101] That, recalls Badinter, was "a very important moment" in his campaign, despite a French public opinion poll that supported capital punishment.[102] In May 1981 Mitterrand, who was elected president of the French Republic with a big Socialist majority in the National Assembly, immediately commuted the death sentence of a cop-killer, and Badinter was named minister of justice. On August 26 the French cabinet proposed abolition legislation, which easily passed the National Assembly on a 369-116 margin before going to the French

Senate, which, despite control by the political opposition, voted 160-126 on September 30 to follow suit.

Physician-Assisted Suicide

What catapulted the issues of physician-assisted suicide (PAS) before the American public was the highly publicized court case of *Quinlan v. New Jersey* (1976). The name of Karen Ann Quinlan "became a household word" as her family's "travail was the nation's first public recognition that modern medicine's new power to prolong life had gone too far," and America needed "legal shelter" from medicine's grip.[103] The New Jersey Supreme Court ruled that Joe and Julia Quinlan could remove their 21-year-old comatose daughter, who had lingered in a vegetative state since mid-1975, from a respirator. However, Karen continued to survive in a comatose state for another 10 years, because her physician so gradually removed her from the respirator that she began to breathe on her own. Her ordeal "initiated an extensive public debate in the United States about end of life decisions. Quinlan broke the ice of secrecy and opened discussion of issues that were previously either taboo or occurred so infrequently that public discussion and debate were not required."[104] Adds Webb, "her case became the springboard for the growing body of end-of-life law ... for the wave of court cases after hers, and for the subsequent legislation ... such as living wills and health-care proxies" that were codified in state and federal law.[105]

MASS MEDIA AND PUBLIC OPINION

An assumption of the outside-initiative model of agenda-setting is "that the greater the size of the audience to which an issue may be appealed, the greater the likelihood that the issue will attain status on the systemic agenda and later move to the formal or institutional agenda."[106] Cobb and Elder specified three prerequisites for an issue to reach the systemic agenda: (1) "widespread attention" or awareness, (2) shared concern "of a sizeable portion of the public" that action is necessary, and (3) widespread perception that the matter is "an appropriate concern of some governmental unit" and falls under its authority.[107] Yet, how crying was the need for physician-assisted suicide or abortion in the United States? However compassionate we may feel towards women faced with an unwanted pregnancy or the desperately ill, in any given year those tragic victims do not number into the millions.

To gain access on the legislative agenda, logic suggests that morality policy would be most typified by the outside-initiative model. If so, then the most important political players are public opinion and the mass media, but how the cause and effect flows has been subject to scholarly disagreement. The relevant questions are whether the mass media leads or follows public opinion in defining the systemic agenda, and, afterwards, whether the mass media or public opinion have more impact on the institutional agenda.[108] It is not easy to empirically specify these relationships by looking at the time "lag" between media coverage and public opinion prior to an issue reaching the governmental agenda.

Abortion coverage in the American print media began in the 1950s and noticeably increased by 1973 when the Supreme Court constitutionalized first-trimester abortion. Heightened media coverage has continued, indicating that abortion remains on the systemic agenda despite that judicial ruling. A similar pattern can be observed in Canadian periodicals leading to the 1988 Supreme Court nullification of its 1969 criminal prohibitions on abortion.[109] A related issue is physician-assisted suicide (PAS), mentioned before, that leaped onto the popular agenda in the late 1980s. However, whereas public opinion followed medical opinion by coalescing around therapeutic abortion reforms, the issue of PAS gained a footing in lay publications before the professional medical journals were engaged. The PAS sequence of events is not typical in agenda-setting, Glick and Hutchinson explain, because usually "[e]xperts and professionals become aware of problems first, and their writings gradually are noted by reporters for the mass media" as had occurred with abortion and no-fault divorce reform in the United States.[110]

Because the defects of existing anti-abortion laws were already being discussed in the medical literature, the reform rationale gained much credibility when Sherri Finkbine's thalidomide-induced abortion made front-page headlines. For PAS, however, organized medicine was *not* beginning to discuss legalized euthanasia when the sensational acts of Dr. Jack Kevorkian burst upon the American scene. If anything, Kevorkian may have been a "negative" triggering event, helping to weaken public support for PAS legalization. Dr. Kevorkian had been assisting terminally ill patients to commit suicide, and he continued violating the law despite legal reprisals by the State of Michigan. Unlike the sympathetic reaction to Sherri Finkbine's case, Dr. Kevorkian was viewed less favourably, and one consequence may be the ambiguous feelings toward PAS by the American public. A bare majority of Americans were favourable in 1990, spiking to two-thirds by 1995, but then falling a year later to only 52 per cent (see opinion update in Chapter 8).[111]

Clearly, public opinion did not drive the environmental agenda during its early years. A leading expert observed that "[t]he fact that environmental issues were virtually ignored by public opinion pollsters in the early sixties indicates the low level of societal attention to such issues at that time," though the "situation rapidly changed in the latter half of the decade" as environmental activists inside and outside government began spearheading this cause. Yet, despite the "relatively strong consensus" for environmental protection and the "increased salience" of environmental problems by 1970, the environment was viewed "by only a minority of the public as one of the nation's most important problems."[112] Costain and Lester agree that American public opinion in the early 1970s was "'soft support,' meaning that it would dissolve in the face of concerns over economic development (or jobs over the environment)." It was not until the late 1980s that public opinion was "both strong and salient" on environmentalism.[113]

Saliency may not be enough to mobilize public opinion if intensity is lacking, which is why weakly held views by the majority are often overcome by "intense" minorities who feel more strongly about an issue. Though popular backing for passive euthanasia (withdrawal of treatment) jumped from 62 per cent in 1973 to 71 per cent in 1977 after the Karen Ann Quinlan case was publicized, public opinion "did not put the right to die on government agendas earlier or translate into public policy" for various reasons, including the fact that since "few polls reveal the depth of feeling, politicians are unlikely to feel secure about public opinion on this issue."[114] Similarly, if majority opinion favouring gun controls was all that mattered to Congress, the United States should have enacted strong legislation decades ago because most Americans have consistently held anti-gun views. Yet, there is evidence that gun control opponents were more likely to become politically activated, which helps explain why new federal gun laws typically depend upon a triggering event, namely a presidential assassination.[115]

Comparative research shows that Canadians are not necessarily more supportive of gun laws than Americans, even though police permits for handguns were required as early as 1913. More important in accounting for this policy divergence are regime differences, though another relevant consideration is the fact that "pro-firearms interest groups are much weaker in Canada" since "[t]here is no national-level lobby group representing Canadian firearms owners that has as much power and prestige as do those groups [National Rifle Association] in the United States." Rather "anti-firearms groups are somewhat stronger in Canada"; for example, they had cooperated directly with the justice minister to gain passage in 1991 of a 28-day waiting period and prohibitions on semiautomatic weapons.[116]

Looking Ahead: Strategy, Policy, and Institutions

Agenda-setting involves policy activists making strategic decisions about the most effective method of gaining access to political power and the odds of success. On the other hand, rank-and-file lawmakers (called backbenchers in parliamentary regimes) are likely to be more concerned with managing conflicts so that their political careers are not endangered. Although social activists and lawmakers may be motivated by different political interests, each must necessarily develop personal plans in which the means available, the ends sought, and the obstacles to be confronted are welded together in mental schemes. Mental schemes develop action in anticipation of the plans developed by others in our social world.

Since humans, unlike animals, are born into this world "instinctually deprived," they must create institutional arrangements to bring predictability to human affairs.[117] Experience leads us to search for *typicality* in daily events, meaning that we come to assume that those events and behaviours which we observed in the past will be repeated in the future.[118] Because almost all human action is *purposive*—oriented towards ends—and since our goals are often incompatible with those of others, our plans must often be revised under changing circumstances. According to Ludwig M. Lachmann, a plan is "the coherent design behind the observable action in which the various purposes as well as the means employed are bound together.... When men act they carry in their minds an image of what they want to achieve. All human action can be regarded as the carrying out of projects that are designed to give effect to imagined ends."[119]

If an individual plan is nothing more than a mental scheme by which one organizes the means, the ends, and the obstacles to be faced, a public policy "plan" is a generalization and coordination of individual plans for policy purposes.[120] In politics, the means—and obstacles— include voters, other political elites, money, ideology, and, most assuredly, governing *institutions*.

Since the 1960s behaviouralism has been the dominant paradigm in political science, as analyses of political behaviour replaced the age-old concern about political institutions, the law, and the formalities of governing. Recently there has emerged in political science a revival of institutionalism, a belated recognition that political behaviour occurs within institutional settings. We are relearning Lachmann's lesson: that institutions provide the means for realizing our ends or, alternatively, pose as obstacles to their realization. More specifically, political no less than other social institutions function, says Lachmann, as "signposts" for accomplishing our goals.[121] Political actors on both sides of the political equation—activists and legislators—learn to utilize some institutional signposts as opposed to others. They learn that particular rules and norms are more useful for the attainment of their ends than others. By helping the legislator, agency head, interest group, or individual citizen chart a policy course in a political environment full of uncertainties, political institutions not only determine the winners and losers but, as important, authoritatively allocate values throughout a society.[122]

THE SCOPE OF CONFLICT

In his classic study of political conflict, E.E. Schattschneider pointed out that politics is primarily a struggle between those who would keep politics "privatized" and those who would "socialize" conflict.[123] By following Schattschneider's lead, and combining his "socialization of conflict" idea with the concepts of a "policy plan" and "institutional signpost," we gain a better comprehension of the dynamics of policy process. We therefore hypothesize that two principal venues are available for legislators or political activists, although lawmaker and activist may use them for different purposes. In one arena socializers anticipate a favourable outcome; in the other privatizers expect to have the edge. Either strategy may be employed by social activists who, apart from their policy objectives, have no vested interest apart from the outcome. For the legislator, however, privatizing or socializing conflict implies a politics of *displacement* and avoidance of responsibility.

The first strategy—socialization of conflict—leads directly *downward* to the public referendum and the masses. As such, representatives avoid blame by wrapping themselves in the cloak of democracy. The issue, they maintain, is of such overriding importance that only a vote of the citizens can make the outcome truly legitimate. In this case, the ruling party and majority backbenchers seek to protect themselves from eroding parliamentary authority and avoiding a fall of the government and/or electoral retribution in the future. Still, other populist issues arise that do not lead to a referendum but are nonetheless so divisive, and cut across party lines so deeply, that individual legislators in parliamentary regimes will refuse to obey the party whip. At such times party unity is severely eroded, the discipline of the majority party is fractured, and normal patterns of decision-making are abandoned. Thus, constituency or conscience rather than the government whip dictates legislative behaviour, although the degree of ministerial intervention may vary.

The second strategy—privatization of conflict—leads *upward* to the centre of government, including its ministries, independent agencies and interdepartmental committees, nonpartisan government commissions, and the courts. Proponents of these strategies typically argue that legislatures are unequipped to deal with highly "complex" issues requiring the expertise of professionals in law, medicine, and science. This political manoeuvre, however, involves a deep paradox in democratic governance: executive and judicial elites, not the elected representatives of the people, are urged to resolve moral disputes.

For lawmakers, the overriding motivation to privatize or socialize conflict is the same: the avoidance of blame.[124] It has been said that the key motivation for a member of Congress, and presumably for members of parliamentary bodies as well, is political survival.[125] It seems logical that legislators would prefer to enact public policy that involves little rancour, and this risk-adverse mentality seemingly creates a bias against issues that fuel controversy in favour of those that inspire consensus. In the United States, for example, Theodore J. Lowi argues that distributive policies that spread government largesse to a huge number of congressional districts and states is a preferred policy, surely more preferred than morality conflicts (see Chapter 1).

If not carefully managed, highly contentious issues potentially are disruptive of established political expectations and political relationships. They must be controlled lest they get out of hand. Faced with a risky political environment because of a contentious controversy, the ordinary legislator is confronted with a limited range of unsatisfactory alternatives. First, one can vote according to one's conscience. In this scenario neither the party caucus nor leadership pressure can persuade the legislator to do otherwise. Or one can sacrifice one's principles and abide by the majority sentiment in the constituency. Either option may leave the representative with political scars, since a number of constituents—a sizeable minority if not the majority—would not be satisfied with the outcome. Most politically painful are those instances when constituency opinion is closely divided. Hence, there are compelling reasons why many parliamentarians may wish to *displace* controversial issues upon institutions *other* their own legislative body.

INSTITUTIONS MATTER

This understanding of the policy process, as one of policy plans oriented to institutional signposts, seems obvious if implicit in two contemporary scholarly literatures. In the first, one sees a growing awareness among American policy analysts that political activists make strategic choices on how the policy process is to be utilized. Thus, building upon Schattschneider's concept of the scope of conflict, Baumgartner and Jones identify "policy venues" as "the institutional locations where authoritative decisions are made concerning a given issue." An issue may be monopolized by one policy venue or shared among many. Related to the policy venue is "policy image," which means that policies "must be understood and discussed in some ways" rather than others.[126] In other words, political activists can engage in "venue-shifting" from one political institution to another in hopes of prevailing in the policy process, but the odds of their success will be influenced by policy image. This insight has special meaning for the United States because its system of federated and separated powers offers more opportunities for political activists to choose among national or sub-national decision-makers within the executive, legislative, or judicial branches.

The second literature includes the writings of social movement theorists, who postulate that one key variable affecting the mobilization of mass movements is what they call the "political opportunity structure."[127] According to Sidney Tarrow, it is the "consistent—but not necessarily formal, permanent, or national—dimensions of the political environment which either encourage or discourage people from using collective action." Most important are the changes that "result from the opening up of access to power, from shifts in ruling alignments, from the availability of influential allies and from cleavages within and among elites" within the political opportunity structure.[128] How open is the political system to new demands; what is the potential for coalition-building with allies; are political alignments in flux; are governing elites competitive or unified? In the jargon of political science, how "permeable" is the political system to outside pressures?

No other regime is as permeable as the political system of the United States. Since the UK and France are both parliamentary *and* unitary regimes, they have fewer access points than Canada or Germany which, though parliamentary governments, are also federal systems like the United States. Research on the anti-nuclear movement, which has obvious moralistic overtones, indicates that the varying political opportunity structures in four Western democracies made a difference in its degree of success. Kitschelt concludes that "[w]here political input structures were open and responsive to the mobilization of protest, as in Sweden and to a lesser extent in the United States, a search for new policies was triggered. Where they were closed, as in France and West Germany, governments insisted more intransigently on a predetermined policy course."[129] Similarly the pro-life movement faced differing institutional obstacles in different nations. Soper found that "British pro-life groups ultimately relied upon the support of key state elites and institutions, particularly political parties, to bring about political change," whereas in the United States pro-lifers "used the openness of America's federal political system, weak political party structures, and division of sovereignty among branches of the national government to become a much more vital force than British organizations."[130] This is also true in Canada, observe Meyer and Staggenborg, where "[n]one of the [Canadian] parties has any strong interest in nationalizing the abortion debate"; in contrast, in the United States "the Republican Party has been pushed to the right by the politics of abortion."[131]

The outside-initiative model of agenda-setting suggests that an issue will first appear on the systemic agenda by gaining media coverage and saliency in public opinion and then will jump onto the institutional agenda of government. Yet this two-step process is not the most extreme manifestation of the outside-initiative model. The ability to challenge political elites through popular plebiscites also serves to pry open the regime. Direct democracy means that citizens can define the public agenda and fashion their own policy resolution without interference from the political establishment. However, referendums are practically illegitimate in the UK, nor are they a viable policy option in Germany, France, or Canada. But in the United States morality policy is frequently the subject of popular plebiscite. This strategy intended to socialize moral conflict is discussed in Chapter 8.

One variety of inside-access agenda-setting is procedurally and substantively anti-democratic: resorting to judicial activism by means of a litigation strategy. In this scenario public opinion, the media, and representative government are sidetracked by organized interests and activist judges. While a long tradition of judicial activism has characterized the United States, the federal judiciary has become much more powerful in Canada since the 1982 Charter of Rights and Freedoms, and in France and Germany there are high courts with similar, if limited, powers of judicial review. Only the UK has not experienced judicial activism by an independent high court. However, recently the British have agreed to allow its citizenry to appeal directly to the European Court of Human Rights whenever statutory abuses of individual rights are alleged. This strategy to privatize conflict is discussed in Chapter 6.

The more conventional form of inside-access agenda-setting focuses on the legislative arena. The pivotal role of policy entrepreneurs effectively bypasses the systematic agenda, because decision-makers with the levers of power do not need to win over public opinion or the mass media. However group-based activists may be linked to those policy entrepreneurs, as illustrated by the private members' bills that promoted gay rights and abortion reform in the UK. But these policy entrepreneurs in parliamentary systems cannot succeed without the tacit approval of the government of the day. At the very least, morality policy orchestrated through the inside-access model cannot defy the parliamentary majority (though public opinion is another matter). The prospects for legislative success by using a strategy that is not thoroughly privatized nor entirely socialized is discussed in the next chapter.

Notes

1. Roger W. Cobb and Charles D. Elder, *Participation in American Politics: The Dynamics of Agenda-Building* (Baltimore, MD: Johns Hopkins University Press, 1972) 14.

2. See James E. Anderson, *Public Policymaking*, 4th ed. (Boston: Houghton Mifflin, 2000) 30-32; Barbara J. Nelson, *Making an Issue of Child Abuse* (Chicago: University of Chicago Press, 1984) 20-31.

3. Roger Cobb, Jennie-Keith Ross, and March Ross, "Agenda Building as a Comparative Political Process," *American Political Science Review* 70 (March, 1976): 126-38.

4. See literature review in Everett M. Rogers and James W. Dearing, "Agenda-Setting Research: Where Has It Been, Where Is It Going?," *Communication Yearbook* 11: 555-94.

5. J. Clarence Davies, "How does the agenda get set?," *The Governance of Common Property Resources*, ed. Edwin T. Haefele (Baltimore: Johns Hopkins University Press, 1974) 149-77.

6. Meier 247.

7. Theodore J. Lowi, "The Welfare State, The New Regulation and the Rule of Law," *Distributional Conflicts in Environmental-Resource Policy*, ed. Allan Schnaiberg, Nicholas Watts, and Klaus Zimmermann (New York: St. Martin's Press, 1986) 142.

8. Michael Howlett, "Issue-Attention and Punctuated Equilibria Models Reconsidered: An Empirical Examination of the Dynamics of Agenda-Setting in Canada," *Canadian Journal of Political Science* 30 (March 1997): 27.

9. Kathryn Harrison and George Hoberg, "Setting the Environmental Agenda in Canada and the United States: The Cases of Dioxin and Radon," *Canadian Journal of Political Science* 24 (March 1991): 26.

10. Mark J. Wattier and Raymond Tatalovich, "Issue Publics, Mass Publics, and Agenda-Setting: Environmentalism and Economics in Presidential Elections," *Government and Policy* 18 (2000) 121, 123.

11. Henry P. Caulfield, "The Conservation and Environmental Movements: An Historical Analysis," Lester, *Environmental Politics and Policy* 33, 39.

12. A.N. Costain, *Inviting Women's Rebellion: A Political Process Interpretation of the Women's Movement* (Baltimore: Johns Hopkins University Press, 1992) 42.

13. Stewart Hyson, "Governments on a Gamble in the Canadian Federation: The Case of New Brunswick's Video Gambling Policy," paper presented to the Annual Conference of the Atlantic Provinces Political Studies Association, 2000, Halifax, N.S.

14. Klaus Von Beyme, *The Legislator: German Parliament as a Centre of Political Decision-making* (Aldershot, UK: Ashgate, 1998) 20.

15. Beyme 33.

16. David P. Conradt, *The German Polity*, 6th ed. (White Plains, NY: Longman, 1996) 147.

17. F.L. Morton and Rainer Knopff, *The Charter Revolution and The Court Party* (Peterborough, ON: Broadview Press, 2000).

18. Elaine B. Sharp, "Agenda-Setting and Policy Results: Lessons from Three Drug Policy Episodes," *Policy Studies Journal* 20 (1992): 549.

19. Eric L. Jensen, Jurg Gerber and Ginna M. Babcock, "The New War on Drugs: Grass Roots Movement or Political Construction?," *Journal of Drug Issues* 21 (1991): 655, 662.

20. Elaine B. Sharp, "Paradoxes of National Antidrug Policymaking," *The Politics of Problem Definition: Shaping the Policy Agenda*, ed. D.A. Rochefort and R.W. Cobb (Lawrence, KS: University Press of Kansas, 1994) 112.

21. Wattier and Tatalovich 120.

22. Wattier and Tatalovich 124.

23. Some of this research is summarized in Tatalovich, *The Politics of Abortion in the United States and Canada* (Armonk, NY: M.E. Sharpe, 1997) 144-50 and 159-64. Also see Mark J. Wattier, Byron W. Daynes, and Raymond Tatalovich, "Abortion Attitudes, Gender, and Candidate Choice in Presidential Elections: 1972 to 1992," *Women and Politics* 17 (1997): 55-72; Elizabeth Adell Cook, Ted G. Jelen, and Clyde Wilcox, "Issue Voting in Gubernatorial Elections: Abortion and Post-Webster Politics," *Journal of Politics* 56 (February 1994): 187-99; and Elizabeth Adell Cook, Ted G. Jelen, and Clyde Wilcox, "Issue Voting in US Senate Elections: The Abortion Issue in 1990," *Congress and the Presidency* 21 (1994): 99-112.

24. Lipset and Rokkan 47.

25. Russell J. Dalton, *Citizen Politics: Public Opinion and Political Parties in Advanced Industrial Democracies* (Chatham, NJ: Chatham House, 1996) 108-09.

26. Claus Offe, "Reflections on the Institutional Self-transformation of Movement Politics: A Tentative Stage Model," *Challenging the Political Order: New Social and Political Movements in Western Democracies*, ed. Russell J. Dalton and Manfred Kuechler (New York: Oxford University Press, 1990) 232-50.

27. Dalton, *Citizen Politics* 152.

28. Ronald Inglehart and Paul R. Abramson, "Economic Security and Value Change," *American Political Science Review* 88 (June, 1994): 336-354; also see the rise of US postmaterialist values in comparative context in Nevitte, *The Decline of Deference*. On the weakening of class in American politics, see Robert Huckfeldt and Carol Weitzel Kohfeld, *Race and the Decline of Class in American Politics* (Urbana, IL: University of Illinois Press, 1989); Everett Carll Ladd, Jr. with Charles D. Hadley, *Transformations of the American Party System* (New York: Norton, 1975). On American politics and the materialist-postmaterialist divide, see Robert D. Brown and Edward G. Carmines, "Materialists, Postmaterialists, and the Criteria for Political Choice in US Presidential Elections," *Journal of Politics* 57 (May 1995): 483-94; Edward G. Carmines and Geoffrey C. Layman, "Value Priorities, Partisanship, and Electoral Choice: The Neglected Case of the United States," 19 *Political Behavior* (1997): 283-316.

29. Dalton, *Citizen Politics* 171, 190.

30. Geoffrey C. Layman and Edward G. Carmines, "Cultural Conflict in American Politics: Religious Traditionalism, Postmaterialism, and US Political Behavior," *Journal of Politics* 59 (August 1997): 752, 753, 768-69. The critics of Inglehart who they cite are Flanagan, "Value Change in Industrial Societies" 1289-1319, and Savage 431-51.

31. The racial thesis is developed by Edward G. Carmines and James A. Stimson, *Issue Evolution: Race and the Transformation of American Politics* (Princeton, NJ: Princeton University Press, 1987). Others who view race in the context of other issues include Alan I. Abramowitz, "Issue Evolution Reconsidered: Racial Attitudes and Partisanship in the US Electorate," *American Journal of Political Science* 38 (February, 1994): 1-24; Alan I. Abramowitz and Kyle L. Saunders, "Ideological Realignment in the US Electorate," *Journal of Politics* 60 (August 1998): 634-52. On abortion, see Geoffrey C. Layman and Thomas M. Carsey, "Why do Party Activists Convert? An Analysis of Individual-Level Change on the Abortion Issue," *Political Research Quarterly* 51 (September 1998): 723-49; Byron W. Daynes and Raymond Tatalovich, "Presidential Politics and Abortion, 1972-1988," *Presidential Studies Quarterly* 22 (Summer 1992): 545-61. On school prayer planks, see John A. Murley, "School Prayer: Free Exercise of Religion or Establishment of Religion?," Tatalovich and Daynes, *Social Regulatory Policy* 31-34. For gun control, see Robert J. Spitzer, *The Politics of Gun Control* (Chatham, NJ: Chatham House Publishers, 1995) 122-25. For the involvement of religion in political parties, see Geoffrey C. Layman, "Parties and Culture Wars: The Cultural Division of the Parties' Elites," paper presented at the annual meeting, American Political Science Association, 1994, New York City. Also see John C. Green and James L. Guth, "The Christian Right in the Republican Party: The Case of Pat Robertson's Supporters," *Journal of Politics* 50 (February, 1988): 150-65; John C. Green, James L. Guth, and Cleveland R. Fraser, "Apostles and Apostates? Religion and Politics Among Party Activists," Guth and Green, *The Bible and the Ballot Box* 113-36; James L. Guth and John C. Green, "Faith and Politics: Religion and Ideology Among Political Contributors," *American Politics Quarterly* 14 (July, 1986): 186-99; James L. Guth and John C. Green, "The Moralizing Minority: Christian Right Support Among Political Contributors," *Social Science Quarterly* 68 (September, 1987): 598-610; Byron E. Shafer, "The New Cultural Politics," *Political Science and Politics* 18 (Spring, 1985): 221-31; Byron E. Shafer and William J. Clagget, *The Two Majorities: The Issue Context of Modern American Politics* (Baltimore: Johns Hopkins University Press, 1995); Lyman A.

Kellstedt, Corwin E. Smidt, and Paul M. Kellstedt, "Religious Tradition, Denomination, and Commitment: White Protestants and the 1988 Election," Guth and Green, *The Bible and the Ballot Box* 139-58; Arthur H. Miller and Martin P. Wattenberg, "Politics from the Pulpit: Religiosity and the 1980 Elections," *Public Opinion Quarterly* 48 (Spring, 1984): 301-17.

32. Glen Sussman and Byron W. Daynes, "Party Promises and Presidential Performance: Social Policies of the Modern Presidents, FDR-Clinton," *Southeastern Political Review* 28 (March 2000): 125-26. Alan I. Abramowitz, "It's Abortion, Stupid: Policy Voting in the 1992 Presidential Election," *Journal of Politics* 57 (February, 1995): 176-86; Greg D. Adams, "Abortion: Evidence of Issue Evolution," *American Journal of Political Science* 41 (July, 1997): 718-37.

33. Hoover 201, 203. Also see Tom Flanagan, *Waiting for the Wave: The Reform Party and Preston Manning* (Toronto: Stoddart Publishing Company, 1995).

34. Dorothy M. Stetson, "Abortion Law Reform in France," *Journal of Comparative Family Studies* 17 (Autumn 1986): 279-80, 282, 284.

35. Joseph Szarka, "Green Politics in France: The Impasse of Non-Alignment," *Parliamentary Affairs* 47 (July 1994): 455.

36. David Butler and Donald Stokes, *Political Change in Britain: Forces Shaping Electoral Choice* (New York: St. Martin's Press, 1969) 354.

37. Donley T. Studlar and Ian McAllister, "A Changing Political Agenda? The Structure of Political Attitudes in Britain, 1974-87," *International Journal of Public Opinion Research* 4 (1992): 161, 163, 167.

38. Harold D. Clarke, Jane Jenson, Lawrence LeDuc, Jon Pammett, *Absent Mandate: Canadian Electoral Politics in an Era of Restructuring* (Toronto: Gage, 1996) 29.

39. Lorna Weir, "Social Movement Activism in the Formation of Ontario New Democratic Policy on Abortion, 1982-1984," *Labour/Le Travail* 35 (Spring 1995): 163-93; Gail Kellough, *Aborting Law: An Exploration of the Politics of Motherhood and Medicine* (Toronto: University of Toronto Press, 1996) 173-78.

40. Lisa Young, *Feminists and Party Politics* (Vancouver, Canada: University of British Columbia Press, 2000) 189-91, 197, 202.

41. Gary Mauser, "The Politics of Firearms Registration in Canada," *Journal on Firearms and Public Policy* 10 (Fall 1998): 1-26.

42. Rachel Carson, *Silent Spring* (Greenwich, CT: Fawcett Crest Books, 1962)—about its long-term impact, see H. Patricia Hynes, *The Recurring Silent Spring* (New York: Pergamon, 1989); Ralph Nader, *Unsafe at Any Speed* (New York: Grossman, 1965); Betty Friedan, *The Feminine Mystique* (New York: W.W. Norton, 1963); Millett.

43. Frances Fox Piven and Richard Cloward, *Regulating the Poor* (New York: Vintage Books, 1971) 62.

44. Hank Johnston, Enrique Laraña, and Joseph R. Gusfield, "Identities, Grievances, and New Social Movements," *New Social Movements: From Ideology to Identity*, ed. Enrique Laraña, Hank Johnston, and Joseph R. Gusfield (Philadelphia, PA: Temple University Press, 1994) 21, 23-24.

45. Joseph R. Gusfield, "The Reflexivity of Social Movements: Collective Behavior and Mass Society Theory Revisited," Laraña, Johnston, and Gusfield 70.

46. Mancur Olson, Jr., *The Logic of Collective Action: Public Goods and the Theory of Groups* (Cambridge, MA: Harvard University Press, 1965) 159-62.

47. Cobb and Elder 83.

48. Peter Clark and James Q. Wilson, "Incentive Systems: A Theory of Organizations," *Administrative Science Quarterly* 6 (1961): 129-66. See the essays by Jon Elster, Jane

Mansbridge, and Amartya Sen in Jane J. Mansbridge, ed., *Beyond Self-Interest* (Chicago: University of Chicago Press, 1990); Neera Kapur Badhwar, "Altruism versus Self-Interest: Sometimes a False Dichotomy," *Altruism*, ed. Ellen Frankel Paul, Fred Miller, Jr., and Jeffrey Paul (New York: Cambridge University Press, 1993); Kristin R. Monroe, "John Donne's People: Explaining Differences between Rational Actors and Altruists through Cognitive Frameworks," *Journal of Politics* 53 (May 1991): 394-433. Also see Carrie Menkel-Meadow, "The Causes of Cause Lawyering: Toward an Understanding of the Motivation and Commitment of Social Justice Lawyers," *Cause Lawyering: Political Commitments and Professional Responsibilities*, ed. Austin Sarat and Stuart Scheingold (New York: Oxford University Press, 1998) 31-68. On the question of altruism, see Eva Fogelman, *Conscience and Courage: Rescuers of the Jews during the Holocaust* (New York: Anchor Books, 1994); Kristen R. Monroe, Michael C. Barton, and Ute Klingemann, "Altruism and the Theory of Rational Action: Rescuers of Jews in Nazi Europe," *Ethics* 101 (October 1990), 103-22; Samuel P. Oliner and Pearl Oliner, *The Altruistic Personality: Rescuers of Jews in Nazi Europe* (New York: Free Press, 1988).

49. Carol J. C. Maxwell, "'Where's the Land of Happy?' Individual Meaning and Collective Antiabortion Activism," *Abortion Politics in the United States and Canada*, ed. Ted G. Jelen and Marthe A. Chandler (Westport, CT: Praeger, 1994) 90.

50. Paul Schumaker, "Moral Principles of Local Officials and the Resolution of Culture War Issues," Sharp, *Culture Wars and Local Politics* 196.

51. Hugh Miller, "Weber's Action Theory and Lowi's Policy Types in Formulation, Enactment, and Implementation," *Policy Studies Journal* 18 (Summer, 1990): 887-905, 888.

52. Miller 890, 891. In discussing value-rational action within the redistributive arena, Miller (896) makes these telling observations: "The location of an issue in the redistributive arena is not a matter of random selection but occurs when the debate takes on an ideological tenor regarding class privileges. As an argument about the rich and the poor, the bourgeoisie and the proletariat, the haves and the have-nots, the redistributive arena is, at its core, about values and contending world views." He mentions various Great Society programs enacted under President Johnson, for example the War on Poverty, as "examples of redistributive programs characterized by a high degree of ideological conflict during their formulation and legitimation" and, for that reason, "[t]he debate does not resemble interest group conflict so much as an ideological logjam."

53. Smith, *The Comparative Policy Process* 113.

54. Miller 894-95. Miller cites the Canadian flag debate on p. 899.

55. Theodore J. Lowi, "Foreword: New Dimensions in Policy and Politics," Tatalovich and Daynes, *Moral Controversies in American Politics* xiii-xxvii.

56. The careers of both these men are chronicled in F.L. Morton, *Morgentaler v. Borowski: Abortion, the Charter, and the Courts* (Toronto: McClelland and Stewart, 1992).

57. Tony Burkett, "The West German Deputy," *Representatives of the People?: Parliamentarians and Constituents in Western Democracies*, ed. Vernon Bogdanor (Aldershot, UK: Gower, 1985) 127-28.

58. Stetson 288, 278-79.

59. Christoph, *Capital Punishment and British Politics* 185.

60. David Marsh and Melvyn Read, *Private Members' Bills* (Cambridge: Cambridge University Press, 1988) 64.

61. Raymond Tatalovich and Byron W. Daynes, "The Lowi Paradigm, Moral Conflict, and Coalition Building: Pro-Choice Versus Pro-Life," *Women & Politics* 13 (1993): 39-66.

62. Tatalovich, *The Politics of Abortion in the United States and Canada* 131, 233. See also his Table 4.3 (122).

63. Tatalovich, *The Politics of Abortion in the United States and Canada* 126; Also see Ruth Ann Strickland, "Abortion: Prochoice versus Prolife," Tatalovich and Daynes, *Moral Controversies in American Politics* 16-22; Tatalovich and Daynes, "The Lowi Paradigm, " 39-66.

64. Tatalovich and Daynes, "The Lowi Paradigm," 49.

65. Leslie A. Pal, "Advocacy Organizations and Legislative Politics: The Effect of the Charter of Rights and Freedoms on Interest Lobbying of Federal Legislation, 1989-91," *Equity and Community: The Charter, Interest Advocacy and Representation*, ed. F. Leslie Seidle (Montreal: Institute for Research on Public Policy, 1994) 152-53.

66. Ted G. Jelen, "God or Country: Debating Religion in Public Life," Tatalovich and Daynes, *Moral Controversies in American Politics*, 144-46; also see Allen D. Hertzke, *Representing God in Washington* (Knoxville, TN: University of Tennessee Press, 1988); Clyde Wilcox, *Onward Christian Soldiers: The Religious Right in American Politics* (Boulder, CO: Westview Press, 1996); Robert Zwier, "Coalition Strategies of Religious Interest Groups," *Religion and Political Behavior in the United States*, ed. Ted G. Jelen (New York: Praeger, 1989) 171-86.

67. Byron W. Daynes, "Pornography: Freedom of Expression or Sexual Degradation?," in Tatalovich and Daynes, *Moral Controversies in American Politics* 242. The anti-pornography stance of this single-issue group has been tied to status anxiety. See Louis A. Zurcher, Jr. and R. George Kirkpatrick, *Citizens for Decency: Antipornography Crusades as Status Defense* (Austin TX: University of Texas Press, 1976).

68. Henry Glick, *The Right to Die: Policy Innovation and Its Consequences* (New York: Columbia University Press, 1994) 155-57. Groups representing medical, right-to-die, pro-life, and the disabled accounted for almost 91% of the total *amici* involved in such cases.

69. Philip Cowley, "Conclusion," *Conscience and Parliament*, ed. Philip Cowley (London: Frank Cass, 1998) 182; Melvyn D. Read and David Marsh, "Homosexuality," Cowley, *Conscience and Parliament* 26

70. Margaret Ellis, "Gay Rights: Lifestyle or Immorality?," Tatalovich and Daynes, *Moral Controversies in American Politics* 128. Herman argues that "[i]n the United States the opposition to gay rights is led, invigorated, and inspired by Christians, and the Christian faith." See Didi Herman, *The Antigay Agenda: Orthodox Vision and the Christian Right* (Chicago: University of Chicago Press, 1997) 11.

71. Button, Rienzo, and Wald 177.

72. Raymond Tatalovich, *Nativism Reborn?: The Official English Language Movement and the American States* (Lexington, KY: University Press of Kentucky, 1995) 17, 31, 83, 252.

73. Ronald Schmidt, Sr., *Language Policy and Identity Politics in the United States* (Philadelphia, PA: Temple University Press, 2000).

74. Cobb and Elder 84.

75. John W. Kingdon, *Agendas, Alternatives, and Public Policies*, 2nd ed. (New York: HarperCollins, 1995) 16.

76. Offe 236.

77. David J. Garrow, *Bearing the Cross: Martin Luther King, Jr., and the Southern Christian Leadership Conference* (New York: William Morrow and Company, 1986) 14. The King quote is from p. 57.

78. Button, Rienzo and Wald 25.

79. Urvashi Vaid, *Virtual Equality: The Mainstreaming of Gay and Lesbian Liberation* (New York: Doubleday, Anchor Books, 1995) 52.

80. Martin Duberman, *Stonewall* (New York: Dutton, 1993) xv.

81. Button, Rienzo and Wald 25.

82. Miriam Smith, *Lesbian and Gay Rights in Canada* (Toronto: University of Toronto Press, 1999) 3, 50, 52.

83. Smith, *Lesbian and Gay Rights in Canada* 67-68, 52.

84. Peter Singer, *Animal Liberation* (New York: Avon, 1977).

85. Francione 12, 1-2.

86. Jasper and Nelkin 22.

87. Jasper and Nelkin 27.

88. Jasper and Nelkin 29.

89. James P. Lester and Joseph Stewart, Jr., *Public Policy: An Evolutionary Approach*, 2nd ed. (Belmont, CA: Wadsworth Thompson Learning, 2000) 76-83.

90. Mark A. Graber, *Rethinking Abortion: Equal Choice, the Constitution, and Reproductive Politics* (Princeton, NJ: Princeton University Press, 1996) 6.

91. Tatalovich and Daynes, *The Politics of Abortion* 44-46.

92. Stetson 281, 286.

93. Gisele Halimi, *The Right to Choose*, trans. Rosemary Morgan (Brisbane: University of Queensland Press, 1977) 69-70.

94. Stetson 281.

95. Spitzer, *The Politics of Gun Control* 13.

96. Spitzer, *The Politics of Gun Control* 152.

97. Christopher D. Ram, "Living Next to the United States: Recent Developments in Canadian Gun Control Policy, Politics, and Law," *New York Law School Journal of International and Comparative Law* 15 (1995): 279-313.

98. Christoph, *Capital Punishment and British Politics* 76, 92.

99. Christoph, "Capital Punishment and British Party Responsibility," 26.

100. Christoph, *Capital Punishment and British Politics* 104, 117, 174-75. Books which chronicled the Evans tragedy were: R.T. Paget and Sydney Silverman, *Hanged—and Innocent?* (London: Victor Gollancz, 1953); Michael Eddowes, *The Man on Your Conscience: An Investigation of the Evans Murder Trial* (London: Cassell, 1955); Lord Altrincham and Ian Gilmour, *The Case of Timothy Evans: An Appeal to Reason* (London: The Spectator, 1956). This issue was kept alive during the 1960s with the publication of Ludovic Kennedy, *Ten Rillington Place* (London; Panther Books, 1961), which was popularized in a movie (1970) of the same name.

101. Michel Forst, "The Abolition of the Death Penalty in France," *The Death Penalty Abolition in Europe* (Germany: Council of Europe, May 1999) 112-13.

102. Edward Cody, "France Will Retire Its Guillotine and Abolish the Death Penalty," *The Washington Post* 18 September 1981: A16; James Lardner, "Fall of the Guillotine," *The Washington Post* 26 January 1983: B1.

103. Marilyn Webb, *The Good Death* (New York: Bantam, 1997) 127. Glick calls the 1976 Quinlan case a "galvanizing event which stimulated a rapidly rising chorus of concern" across the nation. See Glick 15.

104. Tim Newman, "Physician Assisted Suicide and Voluntary Euthanasia: the Links between Ethics and Policy," paper presented to the Annual Meeting, Midwest Political Science Association, April 1999, p. 11.

105. Webb 128.

106. Lester and Stewart 69.

107. Cobb and Elder 86.

108. Rogers and Dearing 569-73.

109. Tatalovich, *The Politics of Abortion in the United States and Canada* 24-25.

110. Henry R. Glick and Amy Hutchinson, "The Rising Agenda of Physician-Assisted Suicide: Explaining the Growth and Content of Morality Policy," Mooney, "Symposium" 754, 755. See Deborah L. Rhode and Martha Minow, "Reforming the Questions, Questioning the Reforms: Feminist Perspectives on Divorce Law," *Divorce Reform at the Crossroads*, ed. Stephen D. Sugarman and Herma Hill Kay (New Haven, CT: Yale University Press, 1990) 191-210. Initially the "leading proponents" of "no-fault reform were lawyers, judges, and law professors" (p. 195) and there is not a hint that public opinion played any role in this movement to liberalize the divorce laws.

111. Glick and Hutchinson 760.

112. R.E. Dunlap, "Public Opinion and Environmental Policy," Lester, *Environmental Politics and Policy* 95 and 101.

113. W. Douglas Costain and James P. Lester, "The Environmental Movement and Congress," *Social Movements and American Political Institutions*, ed. Anne. N. Costain and Andrew S. McFarland (Lanham, MD: Rowman and Littlefield, 1998) 197.

114. Glick 88.

115. Robert J. Spitzer, "Gun Control: Constitutional Mandate or Myth?," Tatalovich and Daynes, *Moral Controversies in American Politics* 172-74. Howard Schuman and Stanley Presser, "The Attitude-Action Connection and the Issue of Gun Control," *Gun Control*, ed. Philip J. Cook, *The Annals of the American Academy of Political and Social Science* 455 (May 1981): 40-47.

116. G.A. Mauser and M. Margolis, "The Politics of Gun Control: Comparing Canadian and American Patterns," *Government and Policy* 10 (1992): 208.

117. Peter Berger, "Foreword," Gehlen, *Man in the Age of Technology* vii-xii.

118. Alfred Schutz, "Tiresias, or Our Knowledge of Future Events," *Collected Papers: Studies in Social Theory*, ed. Arid Brodersen (The Hague, Netherlands: Martinus Nijhoff, 1971) 277-93.

119. Ludwig M. Lachmann, *Capital, Expectations, and the Market Process: Essays in the Theory of the Market Economy*, ed. Walter E. Grinder (Kansas City, MO: Sheed Andrews and McMeel, 1977) 68-69, 72, 101-02; Ludwig M. Lachmann, *Legacy of Max Weber* (Berkeley, CA: Glendessary Press, 1971) 20, 30.

120. For a discussion of these concepts—personal plan and public policy plan—see Smith, "A Phenomenology of the Policy Process" 1-5.

121. See Lachmann, *Legacy of Max Weber* 87-100.

122. The influential work of political scientist David Easton argued that the "authoritative allocation of values" for a society is the core function of a political system. See David Easton, *The Political System* (New York: Alfred A. Knopf, 1953) 129-31.

123. Schattschneider 7.

124. R. Kent Weaver, "The Politics of Blame Avoidance," *Journal of Public Policy* 6 (1986): 371-78. Also see the case studies in Leslie A. Pal and R. Kent Weaver, eds., *The Politics of Pain: Political Institutions and Loss Imposition in the United States and Canada* (Washington, DC: Georgetown University Press, forthcoming).

125. For the United States, the primary "constituency career" goal is re-election whereas having influence within Congress and making good public policy are both "Washington career" goals, according to Richard E. Fenno, Jr., *Home Style: House Members in Their Districts* (Boston: Little, Brown and Company, 1978) 215.

126. Frank R. Baumgartner and Byron D. Jones, *Agendas and Instability in American Politics* (Chicago: University of Chicago Press, 1993), especially 31-32.

127. Doug McAdam, John D. McCarthy, and Mayer N. Zald, "Introduction: Opportunities, Mobilizing Structures, and Framing Processes—Toward a Synthetic, Comparative Perspective

on Social Movements," *Comparative Perspectives on Social Movements: Political Opportunities, Mobilizing Structures, and Cultural Framing*, ed. Doug McAdams, John D. McCarthy, and Mayer N. Zald (Cambridge: Cambridge University Press, 1996) 1-20.

128. Sidney Tarrow, *Power in Movement: Social Movements, Collective Action and Politics* (Cambridge, UK: Cambridge University Press, 1994) 18.

129. Herbert P. Kitschelt, "Political Opportunity Structures and Political Protest: Anti-Nuclear Movements in four Democracies," *British Journal of Political Science* 16 (January, 1986): 84.

130. J. Christopher Soper, "Political Structures and Interest Group Activism: A Comparison of the British and American Pro-Life Movements," *Social Science Journal* 31 (1994): 325.

131. David S. Meyer and Suzanne Staggenborg, "Countermovement dynamics in federal systems: A comparison of abortion politics in Canada and the United States," *Research in Political Sociology* 8 (1998): 235-36. Also David S. Meyer and Suzanne Staggenborg, "Movements, Countermovements, and the Structure of Political Opportunity," *American Journal of Sociology* 101 (May 1996): 1628-60.

5

Politicians Strike Back: Legislative Restraints on Morality Policy

The twentieth century was unkind to those politicians and intellectuals who wished to slow the encroachments of powerful executives on legislative prerogatives. The liberal ideal of limited government during the nineteenth century gave way to the ascendancy of collectivist ideologies after World War I and the rise to power of social democracy in Westernized nations. The advent of a large welfare state required a robust state apparatus and policy experts to carry out the increasing responsibilities of government. Not only did communists and fascists of various shades reject parliamentary democracy as an outright sham, but even social democrats and many political conservatives regarded parliaments as inefficient and inadequate bodies for coping with the problems of modern industrial life.

It is within this historical context that the role of modern legislatures must be considered. The growing share of national income appropriated by the state, coupled with the emergence of the professional politician, has encouraged legislators to employ various political strategies for their electoral survival. But since the growth of big government has been accompanied by the rise of strong executive power, the effect of these forces means that legislators must cope with increasing demands from constituents while coping with executive encroachment. The vulnerability of rank-and-file legislators is especially great in parliamentary regimes that fuse executive and legislative power, though similar tendencies are observed in the United States Congress,[1] aptly called the most independent legislature on earth.

A Tale of Two French Regimes

There have been periods when ordinary MPs played a significant role in formulating contentious public policies, occasions when parliamentary procedures were weighed against governments and in favour of backbenchers.

Most striking is the comparison between the French Fourth Republic (1945-58) and today's French Fifth Republic. It is significant that MPs under the Fourth Republic were equipped with both the political and constitutional means to impose their will on the various governments of the day.

The Fourth Republic was characterized by a *multiparty* system. Governments typically lasted no more than a few months before a premier (prime minister) was compelled to dissolve his government, usually because a minister in the governing coalition was under pressure from his party to withdraw support. The existence of a Communist party on the Left with the support of roughly one-quarter of the electorate and an insurgent Gaullism and Poujadism on the Right, all eager to destroy the current party regime, allowed the moderate parties of the centre—primarily Socialists, Popular Republicans, Radicals, and Independents—little wiggle room to manoeuvre and maintain viable governing coalitions.

Also *collective responsibility* as a means to assure government *control* over the legislative process was ineffectual. Coherent party majorities were non-existent, so premiers called for a vote of confidence only at their peril. However, most governments were not toppled by votes of no confidence; a more likely occurrence was for any disgruntled member of the governing coalition to resign. Deputies did not have to fear government retribution, or new elections, because a vote against the government meant the dissolution of the National Assembly. The parliamentary manoeuvre by which successive governments were so often undermined in the National Assembly was the short debate ("interpellation") on any subject that the deputies wished to raise, followed by a vote of the National Assembly. Its purpose was to wear down ministers with a constant barrage of criticism in order to assure their subordination to Parliament. Thus, it was relatively easy to peal away part of a coalition by striking at its weak points.[2]

Parliamentary timetables in the National Assembly were decidedly open to a variety of influences. Some 19 legislative committees, whose membership reflected the parliamentary strength of each party, so thoroughly dominated the National Assembly that the original sponsors of legislation, whether cabinet ministers or individual deputies, lost control of the proposals once a standing committee agreed to consider them. Therefore, bills reaching the floor bore scant, if any, resemblance to their original versions.[3] According to one observer, the National Assembly "followed the recommendations of its own committees more readily than those of Cabinet ministers."[4]

The provisional legislative timetable for the National Assembly was developed by the President's Conference, a large body that included the chairs of all party groups with at least 14 members. Because its voting was weighted according to the numerical strength of each parliamentary party, that meant the governing coalition was represented within the President's Conference. Members of the Conference also were likely to become future ministers or even prime minister. When a government began losing control over the National Assembly, political tensions first would appear in the Conference. And finally, *private members' bills* played a much more important role in the legislative process; most of them were reported by the legislative committees and generally were unopposed on the floor.[5]

In all these respects, the Gaullist Fifth French Republic has broken with the pattern of its predecessor. First, either of two major political parties on the Right and Left coalesce with other minor parties to form a majority government. According to Frears, what makes the executive "so dominant in the Fifth Republic has been the unexpected emergence of a modernised party system and disciplined parliamentary majorities. Parliament has become more efficient at legislation and less of a destabilizer to effective government, but it has also ceased to be the central forum for political debate in France and has been singularly ineffective at checking abuses of executive power."[6] Thus, the balance of power between the government and Parliament has been transformed. Add constitutional reforms intended to strengthen the hand of the executive to a stable majority-party system and the result is that collective responsibility in France has become an effective weapon to be deployed against any backbench rebellion. The threat of government resignation if its legislative program fails enactment is almost always powerful enough to force government backbenchers into line. In addition, the parliamentary timetable is tightly controlled by the cabinet, and government bills hold priority, as ministers—not legislative committees—pilot them through Parliament. Since ministers now have disproportionate influence in the President's Conference, they usually decide how time is to be allocated, to whom, and for what purposes.[7] In the first two years of the new Republic, according to Goguel, 90 per cent of the parliamentary bills were government-sponsored.[8]

The status of private members' bills is a strong indication of the government's control over backbench opinion. In the first year of the Fifth Republic, private members' bills were cut to 200 from 800 in the last year of the Fourth Republic. The new constitution under the Fifth Republic gives private members the right to introduce bills, but it is the government that decides whether they will actually be placed on the agenda. Moreover, preference is given to members of the majority party(s) or sometimes to opposition members whose bills happen to be preferred by the government majority. As a consequence, the average annual number of private members' bills that became law fell from 225 in the earlier years and 175 in the later years of the Fourth Republic to 73 and 109 in the first two parliaments of the Fifth Republic, and their share of the legislative output dropped from about 30 per cent in the Fourth Republic to 7 per cent in the first Parliament and rose to 11 per cent in the second Parliament.[9]

While the rise of the welfare state has weakened the legislature relative to the executive, economic issues are fundamentally unlike issues of morality policy. One would think that, if the legislative branch of government is closest to the people, then its representatives would scrutinize closely and ultimately resolve morality issues. If legislative bodies have their collective ears closest to the ground, then these issues of importance to ordinary citizens ought to lead representatives to insist that moral and cultural issues get priority. What role do political institutions play in moral controversies? Do policies that compel the regulation of moral behaviour resist compromise and display substantially different political processes from "normal" issues? Do the political players in these dramas choose different strategies from those in other policy arenas? We believe that the answer is "yes" to all these questions. At base, parliaments (and the American Congress to a lesser degree) have become increasingly marginalized in dealing with morality policy.

Political Culture and Institutional Balance of Power

Particular cultural biases require particular kinds of political institutions that are supported by constitutional practices, legislative roles, and political norms. It is generally easier to resist the democratization of issues when hierarchical cultures are strong, as in the Netherlands, the UK, France, and, especially, Germany. Germany "does not have a strong civil libertarian tradition" and has defined "liberty largely in collectivist terms."[10] Where political hierarchies are strong, therefore, explosive issues will generally be diverted to elite levels, and our argument is that the parliamentary bodies of the UK, Canada, Germany, and France are more or less hierarchical, not egalitarian nor individualist, as manifested in the policy roles of ministers versus backbenchers.

Though we may fault them for causing much political instability during the Fourth French Republic, it was the backbenchers who gave expression to the major cultural conflicts that divided the French people. At that time the serious cultural battles that divided egalitarians from hierarchists were whether church schools should get public moneys, whether whole industries should be nationalized, whether France should retain her colonies, and whether the French should join the Germans in a single European army. All that has changed. Since morality policies usually are driven by activists opposed to the cultural status quo, unless there is an overlap between the interests of those cultural advocates and the governing elites, the government may be predisposed to exclude them from access to Parliament. In other words, to secure a place on government agendas in the Fifth French Republic, the UK, Germany, or Canada, morality policies must be congruent with the political interests of ministers and the party(s) in power.

For at least a generation cultural individualism and egalitarianism have posed a threat to hierarchical rule in Europe.[11] The rise of new social movements and citizen groups in Germany, for example, suggests to Conradt that "Germans are ready for a more direct democracy than that envisioned in the Basic Law," noting that in 1990 over 80 per cent endorsed the referendum for important issues of policy.[12] A climate of opinion has arisen where issues over status equalization and status creation have captured the imagination of many Europeans and Americans. Today individual rights and equality are often at the centre of the public debate. Hierarchical groups resist pressures for social and political democratization, since democratization is contrary to their predilection to have issues resolved by those whose leadership roles, reputations, and/or reputed skills command respect and deference. In politics, this predilection means that they are more likely to support their leadership rather than follow ordinary backbenchers and that they believe that, if possible, crucial issues ought to be removed from public scrutiny and parliamentary debate and should be resolved by the cabinet, cabinet committees, or ministers.[13]

In her study of abortion in the Netherlands, Joyce Outshoorn argues that three strategies have characterized how elites attempted to deal with the issue: "depolitization," "avoidance," and "postponement."[14] One may refer an issue to experts for resolution, or avoid taking a stand on the issue, or buy time by sending the issue to a study commission. The ostensible purpose of all three strategies is to reduce or eliminate the prospects of a direct and open confrontation between political groups, which could lead to a political crisis for the governing coalition. Abortion politics in the Netherlands, therefore, illustrates hierarchically driven cultural forces in a country where deferential attitudes are relatively strong.[15]

First, the depoliticization and referral strategies allow politicians to restrict political transactions to government officials, established interest groups, and recognized experts or professionals. Thus, participation by organized medicine in the Netherlands enabled governments to alter the terms on which the abortion issue was debated. Second, the use of government commissions and expertise, rather than laypersons, to resolve a moral issue suggests not only a powerful hierarchical bias favouring functional specialization but also the hierarchical propensity to shed blame in order to maintain the viability of the whole society. It would be a stretch to imagine that the deputies in the Fourth French Republic would acquiesce to elitist dominance of moral controversies.[16]

Compare Europe, where hierarchies are stronger, with the United States. In Europe the abortion issue has been dominated by government and judicial bodies other than Parliament, and in the United States an otherwise power-ful Congress also plays a subordinate role to the federal judiciary. While the policy process seems parallel—the issue is pushed upwards for resolution—the political motives have been different. In Europe, an entrenched hierarchy has been able to depoliticize the abortion issue, but in the United States pro-choice egalitarians, since they were unable to prevail through the elected branches, have turned to the courts to overcome the anti-abortion forces. To summa-rize, where hierarchies are relatively weak and a political climate of openness, publicity, and access by non-elites to elites is highly valued—meaning that individualism and egalitarianism are more powerful cultural forces—elite decision-making is more easily thwarted. Such cultural values have reinforced American constitutional and political practices to produce what Wildavksy and Lipset both term American "exceptionalism."[17]

We hypothesize that four institutional attributes of the legislative arena facilitate elite dominance of morality policy:

1. where parliamentary systems exist in which the ideal of government accountability before the legislature is closely, if not slavishly observed;

2. where the executive defines the legislative agenda and maintains control over the timetable for parliamentary debate;

3. where a party regime is characterized by a single party in charge, or a coalition government with one dominant party, or a "grand coalition" of two major parties; and

4. where higher courts exist to review the constitutionality of legislative bills or laws.

All four conditions of elite dominance are more indicative of an hierarchi-cal political culture than an egalitarian or individualistic political culture (see Chapter 3). This chapter discusses the first three conditions that involve parliamentary rule (the fourth is considered in Chapter 6).

The Norm of Collective Responsibility

Perhaps no constitutional practice is more sacrosanct to parliamentary democ-racies than the ideal of collective responsibility. Originally justified in England as essential to compelling the king's ministers to defend the Crown's request for additional revenue, today it is acclaimed as being fundamental to any parliamentary democracy. Its supporters term collective responsibility as the basic procedure by which governments are held accountable to the peoples' representatives and, ultimately, to the voters. In truth, however, the evolution of collective responsibility owes less to popular democracy than to the idea of keeping the executive accountable to Parliament, *not* to the people. In the UK, this position, argue Marsh and Read, is "underpinned by a conservative [read: hierarchical] view of responsibility which can be traced back to old Tory views, together with a limited liberal view of representation."[18]

Since British governments, for political reasons, "are unwilling to introduce bills which deal with contentious social and moral issues like abortion, animal experimentation, blood sports or obscenity," they are most likely raised through private members' bills, which rarely succeed. Marsh and Read urge parliamentary reform because "there seems to be little point in Parliament wasting time and money continually debating the same issues because parliamentary private members' procedure and practices do not allow them to be resolved."[19] So far, the prevailing cultural outlook is to resist democratizing the procedures governing private members' bills.

Collective responsibility functions as a means for governments to exercise domination over individual legislators. Read and Marsh point out that neither the Tories or Whigs in the eighteenth and nineteenth centuries nor the Liberals in the late nineteenth and early twentieth centuries interpreted "responsibility" to mean responsibility to voters.[20] Whatever disagreements those parties had pertained to how power was distributed between the monarchy, lords, and House of Commons. Nearly 50 years ago, as R.T. McKenzie noted in his classic study of British political parties, a Labour Party dedicated to political democracy was nevertheless compelled to displace its own democratic values in order to transform Labour into an effective governing instrument.[21] Labour's emphasis upon democracy as a means of intra-party organization was incompatible with the demands of governing in a system where collective responsibility prevailed. Because collective responsibility exists to maintain firm control over backbenchers, the representative function of Parliament accordingly receded into the background of debate, to be resurrected mainly during visits by MPs to their constituencies during election campaigns. Once it became necessary to organize the masses in elections, and after political parties were created to that end, backbench independence slowly gave way to control by the party's parliamentary whips. The need to form and maintain a government is alone sufficient inducement to compel obedience by parliamentary backbenchers. Others maintain that most parliamentarians assess party discipline in a more positive way, claiming that it provides political cover for MPs to escape the onus of blame for their votes in Parliament. The combination of disciplined political parties and collective responsibility, therefore, has severely reduced both the independence of Parliament as an institution and the influence of its parliamentarians who are accountable to their constituents.

Government ministers have become major political players involved in the definition of issues and the management of political conflicts.

In a word, parliamentary "sovereignty" has become an illusory ideal. Here the relevant question is the extent to which collective responsibility insulates ministers from the pressure of backbenchers who are concerned about morality policy and cultural demands. The use of "free votes" does not mean that morality policy is devoid of partisanship. In the UK, Cowley shows that "conscience issues *are* party issues" based on his study of 13 unwhipped votes from 1979 through 1997. Statistical analysis confirms that conscience issues "are more likely to cut *down* party lines than *across* them," meaning that morality policy in the British House of Commons "may split some of the parties some of the time, but they do not split all of the parties all of the time."[22] For example, there were splits among Conservatives on voluntary euthanasia, tightening divorce, lowering consenting homosexual acts to age 18, trying war criminals, and legalizing some embryo research; Labour was split on the same vote on euthanasia but also on obscenity regulation and limiting abortions. Labour has been especially consistent on capital punishment, as Cowley and Stuart take note that "not one Labour MP has voted for the death penalty in any of its manifestations."[23] Studies of parliamentary free votes on capital punishment and abortion in Canada similarly find that party is very important.[24]

CANADA

Among the five regimes we are studying, Canada appears to have the parliamentary system most unfriendly to backbenchers. Not only has the norm of collective responsibility been rigidly applied, but private members' bills are rarely successful, and free votes are few and far between. Like in the UK, many private members' bills "deal with moral or contentious issues which governments wish to avoid," but, of the hundreds submitted during 1944-74, says Thorne, only 14 were enacted.[25] Writing in 1979, Dianne Pothier observed that in "the past few decades there have been only two issues handled as free votes in the Canadian House of Commons," on capital punishment in 1966, 1967, 1973, and 1976 (when abolished) and the flag debate of 1964. Such conscience issues as abortion, homosexuality, and divorce were whipped votes in Canada, unlike the British use of free votes to resolve those morally charged policies. In 1966, not only was a free vote allowed but four backbenchers from three parliamentary parties were allowed to sponsor legislation to abolish the death penalty because Prime Minister Lester Pearson's cabinet was divided.[26] Once this precedent was established, future governments could not easily deny a free vote on three subsequent occasions when capital punishment was debated.

The Pearson government also had to confront the flag debate. Between July 17 and December 15, 1964, says Smith, "Canadians witnessed one of the most turbulent parliamentary sessions seen in many years," one that divided English and French Canadians. Previously "[v]arious governments had quietly shelved the issue out of an understandable fear that merely to raise it meant dividing the nation over a piece of cloth," but this time Liberal Prime Minister Lester Pearson, whose party was dominant in Quebec, decided to introduce to the Commons a new flag with three maple leaves. However, the opposition Progressive Conservatives under John Diefenbaker, who was known for his Anglophone sympathies, was not about to abandon the semi-official Red Ensign (which contained the British Union Jack and the Canadian coat-of-arms) as the symbol of Canada.

The debate lasted six months, involved some 308 speeches, pushed aside consideration of all other legislation, and violated procedural rules and norms of behaviour. Though most Liberal backbenchers supported the government, Pearson flip-flopped on a confidence vote, having "at first decided to make the issue a test of confidence in his government, although he conceded at the same time that the issue was fundamentally one for the individual MP to decide according to the dictates of his own conscience." Liberal backbenchers were unhappy about "being placed in a most ambivalent position," and, given mounting criticism, in August Pearson "did an about-face by designating the flag issue as a free vote after all." This kind of leadership was hardly typical of collective responsibility, concludes Smith: "Since he [Pearson] could not easily dominate events in the normal ways of parliamentary government, he tempered his intention to lead by withdrawing his prior decision to engage his government's responsibility."[27]

In the years since, free votes have not been so uncommon in the Canadian Parliament. In 1990, Prime Minister Brian Mulroney indicated that Progressive Conservative backbenchers would be allowed a free vote on abortion, but "Cabinet Ministers and those aspiring to Cabinet were sent a clear message to hold their noses and pass the bill." Bill C-43 was intended to partially recriminalize abortion following the *Morgentaler v. The Queen* (1988) ruling (see Chapter 6). According to Brodie and her associates, "passage of the bill seemed to be a foregone conclusion. The government had exerted strong pressure on its caucus to toe the party line and the debate itself was not well attended." The New Democratic Party (NDP), though formally pro-choice in its platform, released its MPs to vote their own consciences, and the Liberals, with a significant faction of pro-lifers, also declared Bill C-43 to be a free vote. All pro-life amendments were turned aside, but C-43 barely passed (and was later killed on a tie vote in the Senate).[28]

In 1996 the Liberal Chrétien government allowed a free vote on Bill C-33, designed to amend the Canadian Human Rights Act to include "sexual orientation" as meriting protection against non-discrimination. According to Rayside, the "Liberal caucus had always been divided over gay rights, and Prime Minister Chrétien's handling of the issue encouraged dissenters until very late in the debate." Symptomatic of his lacklustre support for gay equality, Chrétien's "decision to allow a free vote implied that gay/lesbian rights did not have the same standing as those for women, racial minorities, aboriginals, or the disabled." [29]

So determined have Canadian governments been to limit the possibility of backbench rebellion that, under Prime Minister Pierre Trudeau, the "question time" for ministers was actually removed from the House of Commons and turned over to parliamentary committees.[30] Any adverse majority vote against a bill carried the most serious consequence, the resignation of the government. Such rigid application of the accountability principle raises the costs of political resistance to unacceptable heights, and surely makes ministers less inclined to accommodate their backbenchers. Thus, Canadian cabinets have had more freedom to ignore their backbenchers on a greater number of issues, one consequence being that there is a long-standing tradition in Canada for the government of the day to sponsor morality policy.

The most celebrated example came in the late 1960s. Three private members' bills on abortion had been considered by the parliamentary Standing Committee on Health and Welfare in 1967, two authored by NDP MPs Grace MacInnis and H.W. Herridge plus a third from Liberal MP Ian Wahn. Without waiting for the Standing Committee to issue its interim report, the Liberal government proceeded to announce its omnibus reforms of the Criminal Code, which included abortion liberalization.[31] When Justice Minister Trudeau on December 21, 1967 tabled his 72-page, 104-clause omnibus reforms to the Criminal Code, he, says Morton, "disclosed the Machiavellian skill that would become his political trademark. By placing changes on abortion (and also homosexuality) in the midst of a bill touching such unrelated matters as drunken driving, firearms, lotteries, and harassing phone calls, the new Minister of Justice gained a tactical advantage." Moreover, this legislation was introduced days before the Christmas holidays, catching the opposition unprepared, and Trudeau "was able to hurry the bill through first reading the same day, only hours before Parliament adjourned for the holidays."[32]

Following their landslide victory in 1968, the Liberals under now Prime Minister Trudeau reintroduced the same omnibus reforms. In the House of Commons, the left-wing NDP strongly supported the legislation, and the Progressive Conservatives "suspended party discipline and allowed a free vote." Liberal backbenchers "were unusually quiet and somewhat uneasy during the abortion debate," and Trudeau "never approved a free vote, yet party leaders claimed that no Liberals were being forced to vote against their conscience." The only concession made by Trudeau was on May 9, "toward the end of the third reading, [when] he allowed a free vote on a motion to eliminate completely clause 18, the abortion provision."[33] It failed, and the entire legislative package was enacted.

Although in 1966 backbenchers had sponsored an unsuccessful measure to abolish the death penalty, the following year "the government took the initiative with a bill introduced by Solicitor General Larry Pennell," which banned executions for five years. In 1973 "Cabinet backing of Solicitor General Warren Allmand's bill [renewing the 1967 partial ban for five more years] was even more pronounced," as was the 1976 enactment that permanently abolished capital punishment, also authored by Allmand.[34]

In 1990, Bill C-43, the attempt to partially recriminalize abortion, was sponsored by Brian Mulroney's Progressive Conservative government . But Mulroney's legislative leadership on abortion policy was not the hallmark of executive dominance. It began on May 20, 1988 when a three-pronged motion (with pro-life, therapeutic, and pro-choice options) was placed before the Commons by the government to get the sense of Parliament. A free vote was planned, but, given the ferocious reaction from both pro-life and pro-choice sides, the proposal was withdrawn. A second attempt was made on July 26, but this time only the language of the therapeutic option was offered, though the government allowed both amendments from the floor and a free vote. Five amendments were voted on and rejected; then the Commons defeated the government's proposal by 76 to 147. Soon thereafter Mulroney dissolved Parliament, was re-elected in November 1988, and tried once again in late 1989 to resolve the political tangle over abortion. This time he formed a caucus of Progressive Conservatives, with both pro-life and pro-choice MPs, and charged them to forge compromise legislation, which became Bill C-43.

As the end of Mulroney's tenure approached, in December 1992 Justice Minister Kim Campbell introduced long-awaited amendments to the Canadian Human Rights Act, which included the addition of sexual orientation as prohibited grounds of discrimination but with other language stipulating that marital status was confined to heterosexual relationships. "Even this qualification failed to quell backbench dissent, and no attempt to put the measure before the House of Commons was made before the end of the parliamentary session."[35] On issues of gay rights, however, the incoming Liberals were hardly more decisive. Prime Minister Jean Chrétien assumed office in 1993, but it was not until June 1995 that his Liberal government sponsored Bill C-41 to amend the Criminal Code by adding "sexual orientation" to the mandate of stiffer sentences for hate crimes. And it was not until 1996 that the Chrétien government sponsored Bill c-33, which included "sexual orientation" on the list of prohibited forms of discrimination in the Canadian Human Rights Act.

THE UNITED KINGDOM

In the UK, the "golden age" of private members' bills was during the late 1960s.[36] According to an insider account, the Labour government elected in 1964 had campaigned on a platform of economic growth, but the parliaments of the mid-1960s "may well be remembered less for their economics and more for their reforms initiated by private members and approved by majorities acting independently of party.... [T]he Government gave some help, but the chief credit should go to their private sponsors and to the general 'liberal' composition of Parliament."[37]

The punitive British law against homosexual conduct began as an 1885 proviso to the Criminal Law Amendment Act that made all male homosexual acts illegal. The famous Wolfenden Committee of 1957 echoed that sentiment by drawing a distinction between homosexuality as a personal preference and illicit homosexual acts. Parliamentary ambivalence towards homosexuality persisted in the Sexual Offences Act of 1967. This reform of the law against homosexuality had to await the election of a Labour government in 1964, but, even then, the legislative vehicle was a private members' bill authored by MP Leo Abse, a Labour backbencher who was "a dominant force" in gaining its passage.[38]

However, the bill's provision decriminalizing the age of consent at 21 became an issue that Parliament was forced to address, since 16 was the consenting age for heterosexual relations. In the 1970s the government had been unresponsive to calls for a lowering of the age of consent, but a decade later there was increasing pressure from the gay rights lobby and its parliamentary allies to act. At the end of 1993 Stonewall, a gay activist group, "learned that a vote could come as early as January, and immediately started to piece together a three-party contingent of backbench MPs to propose the amendment," to be led by Conservative MP Edwina Currie.[39] Parliamentary debate came in 1994 when Currie introduced her amendment to the Criminal Justice and Public Order Bill to equalize the age of consent at 16. On this occasion "the government had agreed to allow the amendments and granted a free vote," but the gay rights lobby miscalculated its support among Labour. Not only did 14 Labour MPs abstain but 39 others voted no; "[m]any who had voted against [age] 16 came from the more traditional Labour strongholds or constituencies with large Catholic populations."[40] According to Rayside, "[a]lthough this was a free vote ... party whips were making their support or opposition to the Currie amendment visible. On the Labour side, the chief whip and two colleagues were standing prominently by the 'no' lobby, signaling that it was safe to oppose the amendment even if the party leader and most of the shadow cabinet were voting in favor of it."[41]

Parliamentary attitudes changed markedly four years later, when the House of Commons voted 336 to 129 to lower the age of consent to 16. This time the free vote came on legislation sponsored by Labour backbencher Ann Keen, whose son is gay, and with the backing of Labour Prime Minister Tony Blair, William Hague of the Conservative Opposition, and Paddy Ashdown, leader of the Liberal Democrats.[42]

Similarly, as Donley Studlar points out, the "maintenance of capital punishment as the ultimate punishment in British law was challenged by backbenchers, especially Labour and Liberal ones, through private members' bills from 1947 until its abolition as a form of punishment in the mid-1960s."[43] What ultimately led to its abolition was the determined efforts of one Labour backbencher, Sidney Silverman, whose personal campaign was abetted by growing disquiet over the hanging of Timothy Evans in 1950 (see Chapter 4). The first parliamentary step to reform abortion policy also was a private members' bill in 1965, from Labour MP Renee Short. It was introduced "under the ten minute rule"—a time when any MP can move consideration of any legislation; if the majority agrees to consider it, that bill can proceed through the legislative stages, although only during the time allocated to unopposed business; if any MP objects, then that bill is indefinitely postponed by being dropped to the bottom of the list of private members' bills. However, "[n]o parliamentary time was available for further discussion of this bill," although, at the same time, Lord Silkin offered a more ambitious measure that actually passed the House of Lords. "These preliminary measures effectively paved the way for the introduction of a private members' bill by Liberal MP David Steel," which "went on to form the basis of the Abortion Act of 1967."[44]

In recent decades there has been a marked change in how conscience issues are handled by British governments. Cowley notes that "the history of conscience issues since 1970 is littered with failed private member's bills." This is because "[s]ince 1970, and especially since 1979, governments have been extremely unwilling to grant time," with the consequence that even private members' bills "which have overwhelming support within the Commons have been obstructed to death by often quite small bands of dedicated opponents." This shift towards greater ministerial control likely explains why, even today, "[f]ree votes on conscience issues ... are the norm...[though] not the rule."[45] The recent trend for British governments to sponsor conscience legislation, therefore, resembles long-standing practice in Canada.

However, this strategy backfired badly when the Labour Party committed itself to abolishing the centuries-old practice of fox-hunting. In 1997, upon taking power from the Tories, Labour pledged a total ban on fox-hunting but "soon backed off from what seemed like an easy populist move when it realized that the sport was more than just an upper-class pastime for the horsy set in red jackets." Tens of thousands of rural jobs were at stake, such as blacksmiths, gamekeepers, feed merchants, and hunt assistants, who joined many other rural interests as the Countryside Alliance. Their political clout multiplied with the millions of affected pensioners, farm-workers, small-town professionals, and weekenders who enjoy fox-hunting as outdoors recreation. As a consequence, Prime Minister Tony Blair has refused to enforce party discipline on his huge parliamentary majority and, instead, postponed final votes in the House of Commons. Although the Labour government allowed a vote in March 2002, as it had in three previous years, it "always avoided a final showdown by denying the bill the legislative calendar time it needs to become law and by resisting resort to the Parliament Act, a coercive measure by which it can overrule the [House of] Lords."[46] Just as the Commons has signalled its willingness to abolish this blood sport, so has the Lords regularly affirmed its support. In this latest parliamentary skirmish, the Commons voted overwhelmingly to outlaw fox-hunting, the Lords shifted to support licensing the practice, but Blair proposed yet six more months of consultation towards finding a "common ground" on the issue.

Leading the fight against all blood sports were the various anti-cruelty-to-animals lobbies, which enjoy wide support. A July 1999 Market and Opinion Research International (MORI) poll showed that 63 per cent generally favoured banning hunting wild mammals (foxes and stags) with dogs, and in November 1999 59 per cent backed Prime Minister Blair's proposed ban over Prince Charles's support for the sport. In Scotland, an April 2000 MORI poll found that 70 per cent favoured the abolition of fox-hunting, as had been proposed by the regional Parliament of Scotland.[47] Blair also faced a major rebellion from his backbenchers. Labour MP Gordon Prentice tabled an amendment co-sponsored by 174 MPs aimed at forcing the ministers to propose legislation banning fox-hunting, rather than allowing them to fashion a compromise later in 2002. "There is no such thing as licensed cruelty," said Labour MP Tony Banks. "This is a moral issue, and as soon as you try and compromise on a moral issue you end up hacking everybody off."[48]

In sum, the morality policy processes in Canada and the UK are diverging and converging. A change in Canadian parliamentary procedure in 1986 was designed to facilitate the use of private members' bills, paradoxically at the same time that cabinet controls over backbench independence had been growing. Before 1986, debate and voting on private members' bills had to be accomplished in one hour, so 90 per cent of those measures were filibustered to death. The new reforms stipulate that no more than 20 private members' bills may be randomly selected for debate, and a special parliamentary committee designates which measures can be brought to a vote after a maximum of five hours deliberation.[49] Perhaps Canadian governments want to institutionalize the means for backbenchers to vent their grievances, given the quantum power shift towards the ministers since the days of Prime Minister Trudeau.

In the UK, government bills have displaced private members' bills as the primary vehicle for morality policy. British cabinets monopolize the introduction of legislation and assume direct control over the legislative agenda. In Canada, on the other hand, the formidable array of parliamentary weapons available to the government of the day make prime ministers even less inclined to allow a full-blown debate on controversial issues. Though there have been more free votes in the Canadian Parliament in recent decades than historically, there is no comparison with the British House of Commons where free voting remains commonplace on conscience issues. Indeed, generally speaking, any vote against the cabinet in the British House of Commons need not force its resignation, because the seriousness of a government measure is determined by the prime minister who signals in advance whether a given bill will be treated as a test of party loyalty. But even for unwhipped votes, as Cowley shows, the levels of party cohesion are high, suggesting that ideology and shared values unify parliamentary parties as much as threatened sanctions.

OTHER EUROPEAN COUNTRIES

In other European countries, where no formal apparatus exists for bringing a government to heel, it is not uncommon for minority governments to survive for some period of time without controlling the parliamentary majority. In Sweden (until 1967), Norway, and the Netherlands, no formal procedures exist to dismiss a sitting government, but, nonetheless, a government losing its majority on an important vote would undoubtedly feel strong pressure to offer its resignation, so, for all practical purposes, the political consequences are the same.

The institutional structure of Germany and France is very different from other parliamentary regimes. The balance of power between governments and parliaments results largely from the conviction by the founders of the French Fifth Republic and the architects of the Basic Law of the Federal Republic of Germany that the major source of political instability was the inability of their multi-party systems to surmount deep social and political divisions and their eagerness to bring down fragile coalition governments. To assure political stability, the French and German response was to arm the executive with the constitutional means to face down rambunctious political parties.

Let us first consider the German system. It was with the Weimar Republic in mind that the creators of the German Basic Law sought to strengthen the position of the chancellor (prime minister) at the expense of both Parliament and the president. First, it is the chancellor, not the cabinet, who today is accountable to the Bundestag, although members of the cabinet would surely resign if their leader failed to receive a majority of votes on a motion of no confidence. The chancellor could demand a vote of no confidence from the Bundestag and, if a majority voted against him, he or she could request the president to dissolve the Bundestag and call for a new election.

Second, or alternatively, the chancellor might simply refuse to resign. In order to avoid a repetition of the musical-chairs governments characteristic of the prewar Weimar Republic, the reformers gave the chancellor the so-called "constructive vote of no confidence." In this case, before a sitting chancellor can be overthrown by the legislature, it is necessary for an alternative chancellor to be selected by the Bundestag. Since it was assumed that the past could not be easily overcome, and that a resurrection of the traditional multiparty system would possibly rise again, one could not exclude the distinct possibility that anti-democratic parties of the extreme Right and Left might pose a threat to democracy. It was thought that the extremists could hardly agree upon a replacement, and a sitting chancellor could ride out the political storm.

But postwar Germany has been the picture of political stability. Contrary to the reformers' fears, usually either the Christian Democratic Union-Christian Social Union (CDU-CSU) or the Social Democratic Party (SPD) have formed governments in coalition with another, much smaller party, leading commentators to describe that regime as a two-and-a-half party system. An unintended consequence of Germany's oddly configured party regime has been to strengthen the political position of the chancellor. Either the CDU-CSU or the SPD have, on occasion, controlled or were only a few seats short of controlling an absolute majority in the Bundestag, so the likelihood that a chancellor would be turned out of office by a backbench revolt was unlikely. This is despite Article 38 of the Basic Law, which "guarantees deputies the right to regard themselves as only subject to the dictates of their own consciences [; thus,] party discipline and thus party 'cohesion' is as strong in the Bundestag as it is in Westminster."[50]

Relative to the executive, the Bundestag occupies a middle position between the United States Congress and the British House of Commons. Its influence results from the stronger role of standing committees, which make governments of the day more responsive to the demands of opposition MPs and the smaller parties. Opposition influence is based not only on the more extensive powers of the standing committees but also because committee membership *and* selection of committee chairs are decided according to the principle of proportional representation. David P. Conradt puts it well: "In the preparation of bills, even government bills, the Bundestag has more influence than the House of Commons. The German chancellor, in contrast to the British prime minister, also has less influence on the day-to-day schedule and agenda of the Parliament. The German executive must engage in more informal negotiations with the leadership of the parliamentary parties than in Great Britain. The Bundestag in committee can make major changes in a government bill without forcing the government to resign; numerous bills submitted by the government have in fact been extensively rewritten by the parliament with both government and opposition parties influencing the bills' final form."[51]

For this reason, the German Parliament is better positioned to resist proposals from ministers that ignore the wishes of a determined minority of backbenchers. In addition, backbenchers can appeal to the Federal Constitutional Court to challenge a parliamentary enactment constitutionally (see Chapter 6). In sum, governments are less likely to propose controversial legislation if they believe that a legal challenge by backbenchers may occur. The power of judicial review over legislation also is a major consideration in the political calculations of government, legislative, and party elites.

The hierarchical culture of German society is reflected in its brand of parliamentary government. Ideological debate and systematic criticism are somewhat muted in Germany. Committee work is stressed in which inclusion, not exclusion, of the opposition is the norm. Although the German Basic Law grants ministers the right to participate in parliamentary committee meetings, the independence of standing committees has been much less compromised than its constitutional authors would have supposed. The inclination to avoid extreme partisanship, the respect for expertise and specialization, the emphasis upon legislative rules and procedures, and the strong role of standing committees all connote a hierarchical political culture.

Turning to France, the political and institutional power of backbenchers is weaker than in Germany but relatively stronger than in the UK and especially Canada. In the long history of the guillotine, dating back to the French Revolution when 1,373 heads rolled, there had been periodic attempts in Parliament to abolish capital punishment. But the pace quickened between 1978 and 1981 when a cross-party group of backbenchers in the National Assembly organized a study group for the abolition of the death penalty. In 1978 this parliamentary group failed to halt expenditures for paying the executioner and maintaining the guillotine; the following year, several deputies close to the government tabled a private member's bill, thus forcing Justice

Minister Alain Payrefitte to openly debate the issue. No vote was taken, but momentum was building for 1981, when the newly elected Socialists abolished capital punishment.

In 1970 Dr. Claude Peyret, a Gaullist backbencher, introduced a private member's bill providing for therapeutic abortion reforms, but "the barriers to the passage of any reform were high," since President Pompidou and the Gaullists in the legislature were deeply divided over this issue. Minister of Health Jean Foyer declared his firm opposition to liberalized abortion, although the Peyret bill "brought the issue to public attention."[52] The pace of parliamentary agitation quickened in 1971 as the Communists started to file reform bills every year and increased in 1973 when Socialist deputies agreed to sponsor a bill authored by feminist pro-choice organization *Choisir* for abortion on demand. Following the 1973 elections, when the Gaullists lost ground to Centre and Left parties, President Pompidou and Prime Minister Pierre Messmer promised to review the abortion law. A signal of their intentions was the transfer of the Health Ministry portfolio from Foyer, a life-long pro-lifer, to Michel Poniatowski (an Independent Republican), who promised that the Messmer government would introduce legislation to reform the 1920 anti-abortion law.[53]

In June 1973 Justice Minister Jean Taittinger introduced a government bill to reform abortion along the lines of the 1970 Peyret bill. But neither side was satisfied, and a working group of the Cultural, Family, and Social Affairs Committee of the National Assembly heard testimony over four months from a multitude of interests. The end of the hearings found the committee majority opposed to the government bill, and "the committee threw out the bill and offered a substitute." The committee chairman drew from proposals authored by Dr. Peyret, the Socialist Party, the Communist Party, the Unified Socialist Party, and the Centrists to draft legislation allowing a woman endangered by pregnancy to obtain an abortion through the first 12 weeks with the consent of one physician. It barely passed the committee—31 to 30—but, despite that, the government decided to bring its own legislation before the National Assembly, although Justice Minister Taittinger agreed "not to force the Assembly to a decision or to try to discipline the government parties." Two days of intense debate led to a motion to refer the bill back to committee, but the Leftist parties wanted the debate to continue, and ultimately the "government acquiesced to the opponents of reform who killed the bill 255-212." A later effort to reform the abortion law cleared both the National Assembly and the French Senate in December of 1974, but this turbulent sequence of events led Stetson to conclude that "[o]nly on the issue of abortion do we see the *majorité des idées* that so frequently surfaced during the Fourth Republic."[54]

France's hydra-headed political system is a mixture of presidential and parliamentary government. Elected by a national majority independent of Parliament, the president is undoubtedly the dominant force in French politics. He appoints and dismisses the prime minister and ministers, presides over the government (the Council of Ministers), can dissolve the National Assembly and call for new elections, and may bypass Parliament by submitting proposals for approval by the people in national referendums. The president also can seek a reconsideration of parliamentary enactments within two weeks by requesting the Constitutional Council to rule on bills prior to their promulgation.

Despite these impressive powers, it is the government, according to the Constitution, which "shall determine and direct the policy of the nation" (article 20) and the prime minister who "direct[s] the operation of the Government" (article 21). Whereas the prime minister must seek the approval of the president when choosing cabinet members, at the same time the government is held collectively responsible to the National Assembly. Thus, the prime minister occupies an ambivalent position, caught between a president to whom he or she and other ministers owe their political existence and the parliamentary deputies to whom the government is constitutionally accountable.

Parliamentary Timetables and Agenda-Setting

The pressures from a multitude of demands from parties, interest groups, and citizens increases the value of time to political elites. Time spent on one policy cannot be spent on another. The scarcity of time, therefore, translates into a powerful resource for ministers to facilitate, or deny, access to the legislative floor. Cabinets tend to monopolize the power to determine the *order* in which bills will be considered, the *time allotted* to their consideration by the legislature, and the power to invoke *closure* of debate.

The President's Conference of the Fifth French Republic, which determines what oral questions will be allowed and how much time can be devoted to them, acts as a sounding board which enables the government to gauge legislative opinion and negotiate compromises with backbenchers. It also decides how any free time made available by the government will be utilized, though, even here, it is the government's prerogative to seize any available time for its purposes (thus effectively depriving the Conference of its power over the timetable).[55] Nor can the opposition offer much resistance, because the government's bills enjoy priority, not those from standing committees. Although the National Assembly debates the drafts of government legislation and standing committees may offer amendments, even bills unreported by a standing committee may be called up by the government. In Germany, membership on the Council of Elders, which sets the legislative agenda, is determined by proportional representation of the parliamentary membership. The fact that 40 per cent of the bills introduced by the deputies are passed implies that back-bench influence is greater in Germany. But that point ought not to be exaggerated, because it is estimated that 85 per cent of government bills are enacted.[56]

The crucial role of time in the British House of Commons is underscored by an insider account of the parliamentary debate on abortion reform. According to Hindell and Simms, "[e]ven before the [abortion] bill reached the report stage it was obvious that it could not possibly get through unless the Government allowed it extra time." Thus its sponsors made this appeal to the party leadership:

> In presenting the case they argued that the Commons must be allowed time in which to decide on the issue, one way or the other. If the private members' procedure could not bring this Bill to some definite conclusion, then the whole procedure and Parliament itself would fall into contempt.... Moreover ... Leo Abse's Sexual Offences Bill ... was also at a similar stage. It, too, had a strong bipartisan majority in the Commons, but its further progress could easily be stopped by a small minority unless it was granted extra time.

Time was allowed, as "[t]he Cabinet had already granted unlimited parliamentary time to Abse's Sexual Offenses Bill ... [so] [t]he Cabinet now decided that abortion should be completed." At that point "the opponents knew they were beaten in the Commons," and they "complained that the Government was not maintaining its professed neutrality, since the grant of extra time was tantamount to saving the Bill."[57] However, displeasure with the Abortion Reform Act of 1967, mainly from pro-lifers, led to 17 subsequent attempts to gain further changes, though none succeeded until the Conservatives in 1990 "promised time" to discuss a government-sponsored bill on human fertilization and embryology. On this occasion, "[t]here is some evidence that the government's decision to allow time for a discussion of abortion was taken in return for a promise from the parliamentary pro-life lobby that they would 'go away' for a while if they were allowed this opportunity." In the end the House of Commons agreed to amend the original legislation by imposing a 24-week limitation on abortions.[58]

The pivotal importance of time is vividly illustrated by how the Eden government controlled the political fate of backbench legislation to abolish capital punishment. Since the Tory leadership "remained adamant in its refusal to bring in an abolition bill of its own," abolitionist MPs tried to win the lottery for private member's bills that occurs at the start of each parliamentary

session, but they failed. Then Labour backbencher MP Sydney Silverman resorted to the ten minute rule. During the second reading of Silverman's bill,
several MPs did object, and it was dropped. In explaining this sequence of
events, Christoph speculated that "[t]hese Parliamentary dodges [by the gov-
ernment]...succeeded in keeping Conservative discontent below the surface
for the moment" but also "strengthened the abolitionists' belief that they had
considerable support on the Tory back bench" and that the Tory leadership
would have to accommodate that sentiment.[19] All this happened in late 1955.

Early in 1956 the Conservative government "was under considerable
pressure ... to permit a full-scale debate" on capital punishment, as Tory
backbenchers "were restive over the stalling tactics" being employed. The
government agreed to allow a debate, but was determined to win any free
vote, so a motion bearing the name of Prime Minister Eden was tabled that
would retain but reform the death penalty statute. Abolitionists countered
with an amendment calling upon the government to offer legislation to end or
temporarily suspend capital punishment and, when the time arrived to vote,
the abolitionist victory was "due to the desertion from the Government" of
48 backbenchers who joined "an almost solid Labour and Liberal phalanx on
this occasion." The government, having badly miscalculated, now had two
options—it could either sponsor its own abolitionist legislation or resurrect
the Silverman bill. After much argument within the cabinet, the government chose "an arrangement by which the Silverman bill was to be given
Government time for its further stages and free votes allowed throughout its
course. It was felt that this choice would permit the Government to stand by
its principles, avoid subsequent embarrassment, and still keep its word to the
House of Commons."[60] It was a fateful choice, because the Silverman bill was
able to successfully navigate the remaining legislative hurdles to gain passage
on third reading in June 1956.

The rigid application of collective responsibility combined with strict
limits on the time for debate and even "closure" of debate have undoubtedly
made the Canadian Parliament much more a bystander in the policy process
than its counterpart in the UK. Yet this was not always the case, as we saw
in the discussion above of the flag debate in 1964. Prior to the ascendancy
of the Trudeau government, prime ministers rarely resorted to closure of
debate; only eight times in the history of the Commons before 1964 had closure been invoked. However, "it became obvious early in the flag debate that
the Conservatives were deliberately resorting to filibustering tactics in order
to prevent a vote on the 'Pearson pennant' [a pejorative for the three maple
leaves design he sponsored]." After the Liberal government yielded, allowing
a multi-party select committee of Parliament to recommend any flag design
(it ultimately rejected both the Red Ensign and Pearson's tri-leaf in favour of

the present single-leafed design), the Conservatives continued their filibuster by delivering some 210 speeches "and refused almost totally to cooperate with the government on its legislative timetable," going so far as opposing a temporary delay in order to enact an interim supply bill.[61] The refusal of John Diefenbaker, the Conservative leader, to allow other legislation to proceed through the Commons caused many MPs to urge Liberal Prime Minister Pearson to resort to closure, something not done since a decade before. As one observer recalled: "Since the [natural gas] pipeline debate in 1956 an almost superstitious horror had grown up against using the ultimate weapon of closure to choke off debate. Both major parties, or large sections of them, really believed the Liberals had been turned out of office in punishment for using this sinful device, and to use it in so emotional issue as the flag seemed to be, was considered doubly dangerous." Nonetheless, Pearson did invoke a closure vote, which was approved by the parliamentary majority with a faction of Conservative backbenchers. On February 15, 1965 the red maple leaf centred on a white banner aligned with two red stripes became the official flag, and, observed Fraser, in its aftermath "[a]n issue which had terrified Canadian governments for forty years, and been a burr under Canada's saddle blanket for a century, had at last been disposed of forever."[62]

In June 1995 Prime Minister Jean Chrétien's Liberal government sponsored Bill C-41 to amend the Criminal Code by adding "sexual orientation" to the mandate of stiffer sentences for crimes "motivated by bias, prejudice, or hatred based on race, nationality, colour, religion, sex, age, mental or physical disability, or sexual orientation of the victim."[63] Though clearly a morality policy, the prime minister and his minister of justice refused to allow a free vote, which prompted Liberal backbenchers to table (introduce) several hostile amendments. However, because the government wanted C-41 enacted before the summer recess, 20 votes were scheduled at the report stage on June 14, and third reading occurred the very next day. It was passed.

Similarly, after the Chrétien government decided to sponsor legislation in 1996 to include "sexual orientation" under the non-discrimination provision of the Canadian Human Rights Act, its progress through the Commons was uneventful. Rayside explains, "Once the government was persuaded to proceed, the leadership was able to retain control of the legislative timetable and thereby contain dissent within the ranks.... The prime minister had conceded a free vote to Liberal opponents of the measure, but was still able to limit opportunities for his own caucus members to amend the legislation and to impose limits on debate with almost no dissent."[64]

Thus, the real political casualties of time scarcity in modern parliaments are not ministers and party leaders so much as backbenchers. Their ability to play a significant role is partly a function of their access to the legislative timetable. Caught in a temporal squeeze, backbenchers have less control than ever over their political destinies or their own constituency interests. Unlike the opposition which has little if anything to gain by supporting the government of the day, the backbenchers in the majority party are expected to ratify decisions made by their ministers.

Party Regimes and Policy Access

In an excellent analysis of one morality policy—abortion—Dutch political scientist Joyce Outshoorn observes that party elites in the Netherlands, like elsewhere in Western Europe, often are reluctant to place the abortion issue on the government agenda.[65] Apparently convinced that economic disputes are more easily resolved through the normal give-and-take of daily politics than issues of conscience, they seek to divert public attention from such issues as abortion to those revolving around socioeconomic cleavages salient to both parties and voters. In countries with multiparty coalitions, the need to maintain viable coalitions encourages party leaders to avoid issues which might make their parties unsuitable candidates for participation in future governments. Especially where Christian Democrats play an important role in the formation of governments—the Netherlands, Belgium, Luxembourg, Italy, and possibly Germany—there is concern that raising the abortion issue would probably end any prospects of them joining with secular parties in a coalition government.

In other nations—including France and the UK—the abortion issue has become incorporated into the traditional Left-Right ideological divide. There pro-abortion supporters are aligned with the political Left, and their anti-abortion foes tend to favour parties on the Right. While President Pompidou and Prime Minister Pierre Messmer governed through a majority coalition of Gaullist Union of Democrats for the Republic (181 deputies) and 55 Independent Republicans, many of their backbenchers were opposed to liberalized abortion, meaning that the government "needed the Left parties" and, hopefully, a few votes from the Centre and the Right. For their part, recounts Stetson, the Left wanted abortion on demand and, therefore, "needed either government sponsorship or at least silent acceptance for the committee bill to pass, and abortion on demand was unacceptable to the government." This deadlock was broken after Pompidou died, an election was held, and pro-abortion reform Valéry Giscard d'Estaing of the Independent Republicans emerged as the new President of France under a reconfigured Centre-Right parliamentary coalition. Because the government bill was very permissive, allowing unconditional abortions during the first 10 weeks and conditional abortions thereafter, most opposition came from Gaullist backbenchers, though it passed in the National Assembly (284 to 189) and the Senate (184 to 90). In the Senate "[a]s in the National Assembly, the government parties were divided and the Left unanimously supported the [Minister of Health] Veil bill."[66]

The French parliamentary debate over capital punishment was coloured also by the historic cleavage between Left and Right. Partisanship was the key, because abolition of capital punishment was a long-time priority for the French Socialist Party who finally redeemed their pledge in 1981, after winning the parliamentary majority and the presidency, despite a poll by *Sofres* for *Le Figaro* at that time showing that 62 per cent of French respondents favoured keeping the guillotine (see Chapter 8).[67]

In a multiparty government of three or more parties, the penalties for rebellion are unlikely to place as heavy a political burden upon backbenchers. On most occasions coalition governments do not usually fall because of a formal vote of no confidence. Rather, they usually fall apart when disgruntled party members within the coalition decide their own interests no longer coincide with those of the others in the coalition. As a result, the influence of backbenchers under multiparty conditions is greater than in systems in which a single party is dominant. Where a single party controls the government, as in the UK, or when a single party dominates a coalition government composed of much weaker allies, as in France today, the costs of rebellion by majority backbenchers may be quite high. When only a few backbenchers revolt and they cannot endanger the leadership, the parliamentary whip may be withdrawn. Thus, the nature of party systems shapes the relationship between the backbenchers and the frontbenchers who compose the government of the day.

A second consequence of party regimes is that they structure the political balance of power between the legislature and the executive. Once collective responsibility becomes an ingrained "rule of the game," all that is required to shift the centre of gravity decisively towards, or away from, the executive is a particular kind of party regime. In parliamentary systems, the number of parties contesting for political dominance will affect the distribution of political power between cabinets and legislatures. Other things being equal, influence flows to ministers when a single majority party or a dominant party within a coalition government controls the levers of power. In multiparty systems, on the other hand, the tendency is for political power to be more broadly distributed between government and Parliament, or, to be more precise, between ministers and the parliamentary standing committees. Under these conditions a window of opportunity is opened to rank-and-file legislators determined to influence public policy.

Consider France, where it makes all the difference whether the same parties do or do not control both heads of its dual-executive system. Suppose a president is elected who belongs to a different party or party majority than that of the National Assembly, hence the government. The consequence is an immediate shift in power from the presidency to the prime minister and the government. Conversely, when the same party or party coalition occupies both the Elysée Palace and the Hotel Matignon, power shifts perceptibly to the presidency. The first instance—the French call it "cohabitation"—means that constitutional and political power is shared, with the president maintaining some prerogatives in diplomatic and foreign policy. In the second instance, domestic policy is clearly dominated by the prime minister and his or her government.

Thus, in two-party systems the effects of collective responsibility are magnified, and the sources of influence independent of the ministry are significantly reduced. Legislative committees are much more likely to thrive under a multiparty system than under a strong two-party system. The only real policy option is appealing to an individual minister or a ministerial committee; otherwise, those backbenchers opposing ministerial control can look to judicial authorities for a review of parliamentary legislation, as in France and Germany (see Chapter 6).

Conclusion

Legislators who challenge the normative status quo in the major parliamentary democracies will confront a number of constitutional, procedural, and political obstacles along the way. Compared to other parliaments, British prime ministers in recent years have been somewhat more relaxed than their counterparts in Canada, Germany, or France. The British political system has relatively strong hierarchical tendencies, a strong commitment to the concept of collective responsibility before the House of Commons, and an adherence to single-party government. Also, much of the political class retains a fundamental belief in the ideal of parliamentary sovereignty. It is hardly surprising, therefore, that many current British citizens look with suspicion on the growth of institutional arrangements which might compete with Parliament in the formulation of law, as seen notably in the debate over the European Court of Human Rights (see Chapter 6).

Once the ministerial route to the House of Commons is foreclosed, there exists no readily available alternative venues to which aggrieved single-issue, moral-purpose groups and their parliamentary allies may turn. Unless morality policy can be integrated with the attitudes of party activists and party manifestos, political elites will be tempted to resist them outright or demand that these issues be put aside in the interests of party cohesion. In none of the other three parliaments are governments any less threatened by issues of conscience, but opponents of the moral status quo in Canada, and especially in the United States, may seek legal redress through high courts. The opposition and/or majority backbenchers in Britain have no equivalent of the French Constitutional Council or the German Federal Constitutional Court to petition for relief against the cabinet (see Chapter 6).

However, we cannot exaggerate these national differences. Today, in each of these parliamentary systems, either a single party or a dominant party has control of legislative policymaking. They effectively monopolize the parliamentary agendas and timetables, leaving their backbenchers with little means to alter policy, absent political division within the cabinet itself. Using a free vote in the British Parliament, for example, may be a guise for cabinets to give the appearance of indulging morality interests while simultaneously assuring that their ultimate effects will be minimal. Moreover, since they are so often offered as private members' bills, they may be easily killed when they are routed through the parliamentary process. Any real hope to utilize the private member's bill as a serious legislative vehicle for moral reform would require governments to relinquish their monopoly over agenda-setting and parliamentary time.

That seems unlikely, because morality policy is normally viewed by party leaders as politically divisive and inimical to party unity. Governments almost never make such issues the centrepiece of their election campaigns, since they may encourage intra-party divisions, carry unpredictable risks at the ballot box, and afterwards may hamper party elites in the effort to form a cabinet. Modern political parties and their leadership show no signs of sacrificing their monopoly control over their timetables and agendas for the sake of legislative democracy.

With respect to morality policy, therefore, collective responsibility in parliamentary regimes yields *political unaccountability* by the governing majority. It does not require a strident advocacy of elite theory to conclude that the linkage between the opinions of government and party elites, on the one hand, and mass opinion, on the other hand, is not one-to-one. Especially today in the UK, given the tendency for government-sponsored legislation to displace private members' bills on morality policy, Philip Cowley says that the one remaining criticism involves political accountability: "The frequent (if not inevitable) free votes that occur on such issues remain problematic by removing (falsely in most cases) an issue from party political battle: in a country where the electoral battle remains dominated by the concept of party, such a process in practice weakens the accountability of the elected."[68] Thus, Cowley wants conscience issues to be subjected to debate during election campaigns.

Notes

1. Morris P. Fiorina, *Congress: Keystone of the Washington Establishment* (New Haven, CT: Yale University Press, 1977).

2. Philip M. Williams, *Politics in Post-War France: Parties and the Constitution in the Fourth Republic* (New York: Longmans, Green, 1958) 157. Also Philip M. Williams, *The French Parliament: Politics in the Fifth Republic* (Westport, CT: Greenwood Press, 1977) 46-47.

3. Williams, *Politics in Post-War France* 234-39.

4. Herbert J. Spiro, *Government by Constitution: The Political Systems of Democracy* (New York: Random House, 1959) 315.

5. Williams, *Politics in Post-War France* 199-201, 203. Also Williams, *The French Parliament* 45.

6. John Frears, "The Role of the Député in France," Bogdanor, *Representatives of the People?* 112-13.

7. Williams, *The French Parliament* 45-46, 65.

8. Francois Goguel, "Parliament Under the Fifth Republic: Difficulties in Adapting to a New Role," *Modern Parliaments: Change or Decline?*, ed. Gerhard Loewenberg (Chicago: Aldine Atherton, 1971) 93.

9. Williams, *The French Parliament* 57,61; Goguel 93.

10. Conradt 93. Also see Leonard Krieger, *The German Idea of Freedom* (Chicago: University of Chicago Press, 1957).

11. Elias 1-43.

12. Conradt 92.

13. See Michael Thompson, Richard Ellis, and Aaron Wildavsky, *Cultural Theory* (Boulder, CO: Westview Press, 1990) 254-55.

14. Joyce Outshoorn surveys abortion policy across Europe in "The Stability of Compromise: Abortion Politics in Western Europe," Githens and Stetson 145-64.

15. Arend Lijphart, *The Politics of Accommodation: Pluralism and Democracy in the Netherlands* (Berkeley, CA: University of California Press, 1968).

16. Thompson, Ellis, and Wildavsky 59-60. On France, see Nathan Leites, *On the Game of Politics in France* (Stanford, CA: Stanford University Press, 1959).

17. Seymour Martin Lipset, *American Exceptionalism: A Double-Edged Sword* (New York: W.W. Norton, 1996); Wildavsky, *The Rise of Radical Egalitarianism* 39-47.

18. Marsh and Read 187.

19. Marsh and Read 189.

20. Marsh and Read 185-88.

21. Robert T. McKenzie, *British Political Parties* (New York: St. Martin's Press, 1955).

22. Philip Cowley, "Unbridled Passions? Free Votes, Issues of Conscience and the Accountability of British Members of Parliament," *Journal of Legislative Studies* 4 (Summer 1998): 81, 84. Also see John R. Hibbing and David Marsh, "Accounting for the Voting Patterns of British MPs on Free Votes," *Legislative Studies Quarterly* 12 (May 1987): 275-97.

23. Philip Cowley and Mark Stuart, "Sodomy, Slaughter, Sunday Shopping and Seatbelts: Free Votes in the House of Commons, 1979-1996," *Party Politics* 3 (1997): 125-26.

24. Diane Pothier, "Parties and Free Votes in the Canadian House of Commons," *Journal of Canadian Studies* 14 (Summer 1979): 80-96; L. Marvin Overby, Raymond Tatalovich, and Donley T. Studlar, "Party and Free Votes in Canada: Abortion in the House of Commons," *Party Politics* 4 (July 1998): 381-92.

25. Susan Thorne, "Private Member's Bill: Success Stories in Canada's Parliament," *The New Federation* (February/March, 1990): 21.

26. Pothier 80, 81. Peter Richards, *Parliament and Conscience* (London: George Allen & Unwin, 1970).

27. Smith, *The Comparative Policy Process* 113, 115, 118.

28. Janine Brodie, Shelley A.M. Gavigan, and Jane Jensen, *The Politics of Abortion* (Toronto: Oxford University Press, 1992) 99, 109-10.

29. Rayside 133, 135.

30. Robert J. Jackson and Michael M. Atkinson, *The Canadian Legislative System*, 2nd ed. (Toronto: Macmillan Canada, 1980) 38.

31. Brodie, Gavigan, and Jenson 32-33.

32. Morton, *Morgentaler v. Borowski* 22-23.

33. Morton, *Morgentaler v. Borowski* 24, 26.

34. Pothier 81.

35. Rayside 111.

36. Richards.

37. Keith Hindell and Madeleine Simms, *Abortion Law Reformed* (London: Peter Owen, 1971) 124-25.

38. Marsh and Read 67.

39. Rayside 49.

40. Melvyn D. Read and David Marsh, "Homosexuality," Cowley *Conscience and Parliament* 35. Also see 24-25 for background.

41. Rayside 51.

42. Warren Hoge, "Britain Lowers Gay Consent Age, Creating Single Standard," *New York Times* 23 June 1998: A11.

43. Donley T. Studlar, *Great Britain: Decline or Renewal?* (Boulder, CO: Westview Press, 1996) 193.

44. Susan Millns and Sally Sheldon, "Abortion," Cowley *Conscience and Parliament* 8.

45. Cowley, "Unbridled Passions?" 73, 75.

46. Warren Hoge, "Lawmakers in Britain Pursue Fox Hunters," *New York Times* 21 March 2002: A5.

47. "Fox Hunting Poll: Research Study Conducted for the Mail on Sunday," http://www.mori.com/polls/1999/ms990715.htm (15 July 1999); "Hunting Wild Mammals With Dogs," http://www.mori.com/polls/1999/hunting.htm (4 November 1999); "Massive Poll Boost for Anti-Hunt Bill," http://www.mori.com/polls/2000/ifawo300.htm (5 April 2000).

48. Kamal Ahmed, "Blair triggers hunt ban revolt," *The Observer* 17 March 2002). Also Warren Hoge, "Fox Hunters in England Win a Reprieve," *New York Times* 22 March 2002).

49. Thorne 21-23.

50. Tony Burkett, "The West German Deputy," Bogdanor 129.

51. Conradt 189, 190.

52. Stetson 280.

53. Stetson 282.

54. Stetson 283, 288,

55. Williams, *The French Parliament* 45-46.

56. Conradt 189.

57. Hindell and Simms 194-95, 199.

58. Millns and Sheldon 12, 14-15.

59. Christoph, *Capital Punishment and British Politics* 128.

60. Christoph, *Capital Punishment and British Politics* 129, 137, 139.

61. Smith, *The Comparative Policy Process* 120-21.

62. Blair Fraser, *The Search for Identity: Canada, 1945-1967* (Toronto: Doubleday Canada Ltd., 1967) 245, 247.

63. *Hansard* 22 September 1994: 6029.

64. Rayside 127-28.

65. Outshoorn 154-57.

66. Stetson 283, 285-86

67. Forst 113-14.

68. Cowley, "Unbridled Passions?" 85.

6

The Juridicization of the Morality Policy Process

The requirement of cabinet responsibility, ministerial control of parliamentary time and the policy agenda, and the emergence of majoritarian or dominant one-party coalition governments are not the only reasons for the political weakness of legislatures. There is also what Alex Stone terms the "juridicization" of the policy process as a result of intervention by high courts. Through judicial review, legislative enactments are increasingly crafted, directly or indirectly, by rulings from judges. Because parliamentary sovereignty is so deeply ingrained in continental legal scholarship and often divorced from the study of the policy process, many European academics have only recently begun to appreciate the extent to which high courts can encroach upon powers long said to belong to Parliament.[1]

Because British constitutional practice does not permit judicial review and parliamentary law is supreme, the British legislative process is the least juridicized. On the other hand, given the unique role of the French Constitutional Council, the French legislative system is probably the most thoroughly juridicized.[2] Unlike high courts in the other four regimes, the French Constitutional Council is unique because it may rule on the constitutionality of parliamentary bills *before* they are promulgated as laws. In this respect the German Constitutional Court operates slightly differently; it may be called upon by the legislature to rule on its own legislation, with this important difference: it may strike down parliamentary *statutes*, not parliamentary bills.[3]

In both Germany and France judicial review involves judges reading the legislative text and then determining whether the bill (France) or statute (Germany) conforms to the requirements of their respective constitutions. This format, termed "abstract review," does not require that judges decide *concrete* cases involving real disputes between opposing parties, as in the United States, the UK, and largely in Canada. The Canadian exception to the "cases and controversies" requirement of American jurisprudence are reference cases, instances when governments request an advisory opinion from the Supreme Court of Canada. Reference cases may only be initiated by the government of the day, not private parties, just as in France and Germany disputes about constitutional interpretation are initiated by the political authorities rather than private litigants. Hence, petitioners for redress before the German Constitutional Court are major political leaders: chancellor or cabinet, laender (state) governments, or one-third of the members of the Bundestag (lower House). In France only the president of the Republic, prime minister, presidents of the National Assembly and Senate, and 60 deputies or senators may petition the council to request a constitutional review.

Once judicial review becomes settled practice, the distinction between judicial and legislative policymaking is more unclear. Particularly in France, the threat to petition for judicial review can never be far from the minds of ministers, members of the majority party(s), or opposition backbenchers. At the same time, however, each of these groups often uses the courts to frustrate the plans of other legislative and ministerial players. The looming prospect of judicial intervention, therefore, makes cabinet ministers no less than backbenchers exceedingly mindful of the role played by judges in the legislative process. If the growth of judicial intervention has come at the expense of governments and parliaments, within the legislature the political shift has likely enhanced the leverage of majority backbenchers and the opposition parties. Unlike the UK, Canada, or the United States, the French (since 1974) and German constitutions permit backbenchers to directly challenge the constitutionality of legislation. To petition for judicial review offers backbench rebels, particularly in the majority, with a political strategy to avoid a direct confrontation with the government.

In France and Germany, therefore, judicial review arms backbenchers and cabinets with an additional means for avoiding responsibility when dealing with explosive political issues. Recall from our discussion of Schattschneider (Chapter 4) that legislators may push issues of conscience upwards for resolution or downwards to the public. Juridicization of the policymaking process essentially creates additional institutional signposts to which backbenchers may orient their policy plans, one purpose being to displace accountability upon non-parliamentary institutions and to avoid blame from constituents. According to Holland, "[b]ecause the losing side in Parliament frequently challenges, through abstract judicial review, a measure it initially opposed on political grounds, the [German] Constitutional Court effectively has become a participant in the legislative process."[4]

From the standpoint of those opposed to the policy status quo, "abstract review" may be a mixed blessing. It offers incentives for politicians to engage in displacement politics but, by substituting judge-made law for parliamentary law, it undermines the role of the legislator as the ultimate representative of the people. This debate over judicial review versus popular sovereignty, which raged for decades among American academics, was reignited in 1973 by the controversial ruling from the American Supreme Court that constitutionalized a right to abortion. While judicial review was established early in the United States (1803), relatively few federal statutes have been nullified by the high court. More controversial are the many rulings by its Supreme Court that have displaced legislative authority within the states.

As compared to Europe, and even Canada, the forces of cultural egalitarianism and cultural individualism are strongest in the United States. It is not simply that Congress is a very porous legislative system. Where majority support for morally charged issues is soft, if not hostile, those groups with a determined egalitarian agenda often try to shift policymaking from the national or state legislatures to the federal courts. This has been particularly true of such divisive issues as race (affirmative action, school busing, school vouchers), gender (abortion, gay marriage), and capital punishment. In Canada, similarly, demands from women, gays, the Inuit, First Nations, and linguistic minorities now routinely find their way to the federal courts. Direct appeal to British, French, and German high courts is not possible, but in the United States and Canada judicial review is a primary venue whereby activists for minority causes can avoid the political branches and seek redress from less democratic, and presumably more friendly, courts.

Exploiting litigation politics as a viable alternative to legislative lobbying depends not only on a tradition of judicial activism but also on a constitutionally "entrenched" bill of rights. Existence of the 1791 Bill of Rights in the United States, the 1982 Canadian Charter of Rights and Freedoms, or the supra-national European Convention for the Protection of Human Rights and Fundamental Freedoms (since 1950) is a necessary but not a sufficient condition for legal mobilization. A social movement or single-issue group must have the resources to take advantage of these attributes of the political opportunity structure.[5] Of course "rights" rhetoric can be exhorted as a tactic to mobilize political activists even before any judicial victory is secured. Based on her analysis of the Canadian gay rights movement, Miriam Smith hypothesizes "that changes in the political opportunity structure and, in particular, state structures themselves, may influence the mobilizing structures of movements and meaning frames."[6] Her point is that the Charter offered gays an entirely new policy venue to pursue a litigation—not legislative—strategy.

This point was also made by Stuart Scheingold with respect to the American civil rights movement. "It is possible to capitalize on the perceptions of entitlement associated with rights to initiate and to nurture political mobilization—a dual process of *activating* a quiescent citizenry and *organizing* groups into effective political units. Political mobilization can in this fashion build support for interests that have been excluded from existing allocations of values and thus promote a *realignment* of political forces." But there is a down-side to judicial activism, and Scheingold cautions the would-be activist that the "myth of rights" somehow implies that litigation can bring about social change when, to the contrary, a "sober assessment of the status of rights in American politics raises serious doubts about the capabilities of legal and constitutional processes for neutralizing power relationships. The authoritative declaration of a right is perhaps best viewed as the beginning of a political process in which power relationships loom large and immediate." Here Scheingold makes reference to the problems of "compliance" in the aftermath of controversial American Supreme Court rulings.[7]

One morality policy paradox is that the United States Congress—arguably the most powerful legislative body in the world—has played a role subordinate to the federal judiciary in addressing the most contentious disputes of the past 50 years. The emerging Canadian experience with litigation politics and judicial review in morality policy, therefore, invites comparison with its long-standing use in the United States.

United States

The so-called "Roosevelt Revolution" effectively ended judicial intervention in regulatory and redistributive policies (when Roosevelt was first elected, the high court nullified key New Deal laws but later capitulated). That halted Supreme Court activism in support of *laissez-faire* economics, so, according to Baum, "the Court's emphasis in the current era is on civil liberties. More precisely, the Court has focused primarily upon the interpretation of constitutional guarantees of protection for freedom of expression and freedom of religion, for the procedural rights of criminal defendants and other persons, and for equal treatment of racial minorities and other disadvantaged groups by the government."[8]

Scholars date the beginnings of contemporary "social" activism from the desegregation rulings in *Brown v. Board of Education* (1954). Koshner shows that "over the past 60 years the percentage of cases that meets the social impact criterion has increased from 8 per cent of the total docket [in the 1930s] to over 50 per cent through 1987" while "the percent of the docket that was taken up by economic cases has fallen dramatically."[9] *Brown* to this day inspires apologists of judicial activism, who argue that the courts are a necessary—indeed essential—forum for making policy to protect the rights of minorities and individuals, especially when legislative and executive authorities refuse to act. The loudest critics of judicial activism are political conservatives who argue that federal courts should not make public policy but should defer to the popularly elected branches of government.[10]

The debate over judicial activism versus judicial restraint was reignited after *Roe v. Wade* (1973) mandated a right to abortion without referencing any explicit constitutional language. Because it required 46 states and the District of Columbia to abandon their historic anti-abortion laws (typically banning abortions except to safeguard the mother's life or health), pro-life law professor John T. Noonan, Jr. declared that "*Roe v. Wade* and [its companion case] *Doe v. Bolton* may stand as the most radical decision ever issued by the Supreme Court."[11] John Hart Ely is another law professor who, though sympathetic to the outcome in *Roe*, nonetheless charged that "the Court claims no mandate to second-guess legislative balances [woman or fetus], at least not when the Constitution has designated neither of the values in conflict as entitled to special protection." Ely questions if the Court should assume this function on various moral conflicts:

> Laws prohibiting the use of "soft" drugs or ... homosexual acts ... can stunt "the preferred life styles" of those [groups]... It is clear such acts harm no one besides the participants...Yet such laws survive, on the theory that there exists a societal consensus that the behavior involved is revolting or at any rate immoral. Of course the consensus is not universal but it is sufficient, and this is what is counted crucial, to get the laws passed and keep them on the books.[12]

LITIGATING MORALITY POLICY

Pro-lifer John T. Noonan was correct in calling *Roe v. Wade* radical, because it embodied many features of an ideal litigation strategy.

1. By litigating in the federal courts that a Texas state law violated the Bill of Rights, the objective was not simply to invalidate the statute in that state but all such laws on the books of any state. This point requires some clarification. The Bill of Rights was adopted in 1791, and its "original intent" was to protect citizens and states *from* the newly created federal government. Indeed, the high court ruled in *Barron v. Baltimore* (1833) that a citizen could not invoke the Bill of Rights against a state. It was not until 1868, after the Civil War, that enough states ratified the Fourteenth Amendment to enforce national citizenship standards. Section 1 of the Fourteenth Amendment reads: "All persons born or naturalized in the United States, and subject to the jurisdiction thereof, are citizens of the United States and of the States wherein they reside. No State shall make or enforce any law which shall abridge the privileges and immuni-

ties of citizens of the United States; *nor shall any State deprive any person of life, liberty, or property, without due process of law*; nor deny to any person within its jurisdiction the equal protection of the laws" (italics added). This due process clause provides the constitutional basis for the Supreme Court to pursue "incorporation" jurisprudence, and scholars usually date its beginnings with *Gitlow v. New York* (1925). In *Gitlow*, New York State was warned that a state law regulating political sedition may violate the "free speech" guarantees of the First Amendment. So expansive has the reach of judicial review become vis-à-vis the incorporation doctrine, that this activist jurisprudence also has inspired a strong dissent among conservatives.[13]

2. *Roe v. Wade* was a "class action" lawsuit that plaintiff Roe filed on behalf of all women who faced an unwanted pregnancy and confronted other state anti-abortion laws.

3. Because of its pertinent facts, *Roe* was the perfect "test case" to challenge Texas's century-old anti-abortion law. The anonymous Jane Roe (later identified as Norma McCorvey) was approached by Linda Coffee and Sarah Weddington, two newly minted Texas lawyers with ties to feminist causes, whose motivation was "primarily ideological" since "[n]either woman had undergone an abortion nor had any firsthand experience with one." In a new legal twist, these lawyers believed that they needed a pregnant woman to challenge the 1859 Texas statute in order to launch a class-action broadside against all anti-abortion laws. However, since Coffee and Weddington could not easily bankroll their appeal to the Supreme Court, much needed financial help was provided by a Texas socialite, while legal research came from various sources, notably the Association for the Study of Abortion.[14]

4. This litigation was "sponsored" insofar as the plaintiff—unmarried and poor—could hardly afford this lawsuit without the legal resources, attorneys, and financial backing from feminist interests and civil libertarians. Major legal forays to the Supreme Court are costly propositions. Impoverished blacks could hardly have funded their own battle against racial segregation during the 1950s. Credit for developing that litigation strategy goes to the NAACP lawyers who spearheaded a series of lawsuits aimed at ending restrictive racial covenants, ultimately leading to their crowning achievement in the *Brown* case. Women's groups also have orchestrated lawsuits to promote their feminist agenda.[15] A recent innovation is "cause lawyering" where, explain Professors Sarat and Scheingold, the commitment is "to the kind of transformative politics that will redistribute political power and material benefits in a more egalitarian fashion" and whose "primary loyalty is not to clients, to

constitutional rights, nor to the legal process but to a vision of the good society and to political allies who share that vision."[16] Menkel-Meadow agrees that, because this kind of litigation "is less well compensated" and poses a variety of "risks" to those so engaged, what motivates cause lawyers is the desire to "*'do good'—to seek a more just world—to do 'lawyering for the good'*"(italics in original).[17]

5. In *Roe v. Wade*, 23 women's, health and medical, family planning, religious, and single-issue groups joined to file *amicus curiae* ("friend-of-the-court") briefs in order to supply legal arguments and factual data to bolster Jane Roe's case, a sharp contrast to the 11 pro-life groups who similarly lobbied the Supreme Court.[18] Ever since Professor Krislov alerted judicial scholars to court lobbying by interest groups, an academic cottage industry has arisen to study the agenda, strategy, and tactics used by these activists.[19] The number of *amici* in *Roe* was not exceptional; that record was set 15 years later in the famous "reverse discrimination" case (filed by a white man who successfully contested a medical school "quota" favouring minorities) of *Regents of the University of California v. Bakke* (1978).[20]

A decade later the volume of *amicus* litigation in *Bakke* was easily dwarfed by another abortion case, *Webster v. Reproductive Health Services* (1989), which threatened to reverse *Roe v. Wade*. For that reason *Webster* activated 316 pro-choice organizations and 65 pro-life groups as *amici*. More than the greatest outpouring of *amicus* activity by organized interests, *Webster* transformed the pro-choice coalition. The pro-choice briefs were orchestrated by the American Civil Liberties Union (ACLU) and Planned Parenthood Federation to "coordinate the arguments of numerous interest groups ... to minimize duplication and to ensure that each interest group made the arguments most appropriate to their constituency."[21]

Amicus filings can have a decisive impact on individual Supreme Court justices. In *Roe*, for example, Justice Blackmun's opinion for the majority referenced scholarship by Cyril Means on the feminist rationale for nineteenth-century anti-abortion laws (to safeguard the mother, not the fetus). Means had been an attorney active in the abortion reform movement, and his argument allegedly was published to influence the Court precisely on this point. *Amicus* briefs are not presumed to be even-handed, and empirical research verifies that they rally one-sided information to argue the strongest case possible.[22]

6. An effective litigation strategy depends on the justices and their ideological sympathies, and there were signs that the Supreme Court would be receptive to Jane Roe. The logic of *Roe*'s argument looked promising, given that the high court recently had incorporated the "right to privacy" in its *Griswold v.*

Connecticut (1964) ruling that overturned a Connecticut statute banning the distribution of birth control devices. Also the high court signaled its predisposition by its willingness to accept *Roe* on appeal rather than wait until other abortion cases had worked their way through the federal judicial system.[23]

JUDICIAL VENUES AND MORALITY POLICY

Richard Cortner was perhaps the first scholar to observe that litigation is utilized by "underdog" groups that "are temporarily, or even permanently, disadvantaged in terms of their abilities to attain successfully their goals in the electoral process, within the elected political institutions or in the bureaucracy."[24] During the 1960s civil libertarian and liberal groups engaged in litigation because "[t]he courts served as a forum in the broader political process in which groups denied access in other arenas got a hearing, and sometimes got their way."[25] Lee Epstein similarly referenced 10 studies affirming that a litigation strategy is "used when all else fails or as a technique to be employed when goals are clearly unattainable in other political forums."[26] In the decade following *Roe*, the Supreme Court was viewed as sympathetic to pro-choice claims, with the consequence that from 1973 to 1988 pro-choice groups were more likely to author *amicus* briefs to the Supreme Court, whereas pro-lifers more often lobbied the Congress.[27] The landmark *Roe* precedent obviously posed a barrier to pro-life litigation.

Obscenity Issues

Similar venue-shifting affected the obscenity issue. Analysis of several pornography cases during 1957 to 1984 determined that most *amici* opposed to censorship were literary groups, like the Association of American Publishers and Authors League of America, whereas more than three times as many groups that favoured government censorship directed their testimony to congressional committees.[28] Obscenity has never been considered a "protected" right under the Free Press Clause, but since the 1950s the Supreme Court seemed less able to define what obscenity was than what obscenity was not. After the Warren Court's permissive ruling in *Roth v. US* (1957), the term obscene all but disappeared. Later the high court in *Miller v. California* (1973) enumerated specific examples of obscenity and tried to shift policy back to states and localities. One significant victory for the opponents of pornography came when the Supreme Court in *New York v. Ferber* (1982) sided with states and Congress by upholding stricter standards whenever children were the objects of obscenity.

However the Supreme Court refused to accept feminist grounds for anti-pornography laws. The city of Indianapolis prohibited "all discriminatory practices of sexual subordination or inequality through pornography" (defined as "the graphic depiction of the sexually explicit subordination of women"), but a federal district court ruled it unconstitutionally vague and imposing prior restraint without adequate procedural safeguards. On appeal, the Supreme Court summarily affirmed that judgment in *American Booksellers Association v. Hudnut* (1986), and since then the high court has not entered this thicket of feminist jurisprudence.

The Christian Right and the Courts

Church-state separationists had virtually dominated the judicial battleground in their litigation advocacy, as Sorauf explains: "Those minorities, having failed to stop some public policy in the more usual political processes ... assert that the policies violate their constitutionally granted rights," and, therefore, in these "67 church-state cases it is chiefly the separationist interests that enjoy the plaintiff's position."[29] Because of the long line of Supreme Court precedents against public school prayer, the Christian Right in the 1980s chose to pursue its policy agenda in Congress, not the federal courts. Since these issues have special meaning for non-believers and non-Christians, usually the *amici* in church-state cases were the American Jewish Congress, Americans United for Separation of Church and State, and the American Civil Liberties Union. However membership turnover on the Supreme Court can fundamentally alter the political opportunity structure, and the late 1980s showed an upswing in high court litigation activity by Christian Right organizations.[30]

After President Nixon named Warren Burger to replace Earl Warren as Chief Justice, there was increased litigation by conservative groups who now believed that the justices would be more receptive to their arguments. Notable conservative *amici* were Citizens for Decency, involved in obscenity cases; Americans for Effective Law Enforcement; and the anti-abortion Americans United for Life.[31] Susan Olson argues that the 1960s "disadvantage theory" was time-bound, and she endorses the contemporary view that "[o]ften the same grievance can theoretically be remedied through favorable administrative action, state or federal legislation ... litigation, or even the popular ballot if initiative and referendum are available." Thus, says Olson, litigation is "just one among many political strategies groups may choose in their battles over public policies."[32]

The choice of a litigation strategy is influenced by many factors, including whether the Supreme Court is perceived to be a friend or foe. Adherence to the settled law is one canon of jurisprudence, but there is scholarly debate about whether the justices are constrained by legal norms and *stare decisis* (deciding legal points according to precedent). There is substantial evidence that the personal ideology of a justice matters a lot. Harold Spaeth concludes, "liberal Courts should overrule conservative precedents, and conservative Courts those that are liberal."[33] And they do. Since President Reagan elevated Associate Justice William Rehnquist to succeed Warren Burger as Chief Justice in 1986, the emergence of a 5-4 split on the Supreme Court favouring conservatives has caused some liberal activists to shift their litigation strategy towards state courts, using state constitutions.

Same-Sex Marriages

One highly publicized example of judicial venue-shifting involved same-sex marriages. It began with the decision of a lone judge in Hawaii that legislation disallowing homosexual unions violated the equal protection provision of the state constitution. The Hawaiian Supreme Court in *Baehr v. Lewin* (1993) upheld that ruling, thus paving the way for legal same-sex marriages in Hawaii but, at the same time, fueling a nationwide backlash. By mid-1998 all but two states had considered legislation banning the recognition of same-sex marriages, and thus far 35 states have adopted such policies, actions no doubt hastened by Congress's enactment of the Defense of Marriage Act of 1996, which not only stipulated that states are not required to recognize same-sex marriages but also prohibited homosexual couples from receiving any federal benefits related to marriage (like tax deductions). The Hawaiian judicial ruling, however, was ultimately rejected by the political branches and the electorate. A state constitutional amendment approved by the legislature and ratified by the voters caused the Hawaiian high court to reverse directions, ruling in December 1999 that the constitutional amendment had "validated" Hawaii's discriminatory marriage law by "taking the statute out of the ambit of the equal protection clause of the Hawaii Constitution."[34]

To date only one state authorizes same-sex unions, and again that morality policy was forced upon the state legislature by the judiciary. In December 1999 the Vermont Supreme Court unanimously ruled that the state must guarantee the same protections and benefits to gay and lesbian couples that are granted to heterosexual spouses. To extend equal rights to homosexual couples "who seek nothing more, nor less, than legal protection and security for their avowed commitment to an intimate and lasting relationship is simply, when all is said and done," declared the justices, "a recognition of our common humanity."[35] The court deferred to the legislature, giving lawmakers a "reasonable period of time" to consider reforms, and four months later a "civil unions" bill (legally parallel with marriage for heterosexuals) was signed into law.

It would require a fanciful imagination to believe that the United States Supreme Court under Chief Justice Rehnquist would uphold same-sex marriages as constitutionally permissible. One telling example of its ideological about-face, in fact, involves gay rights.

Gay Rights

Before 1961 all 50 states and the District of Columbia criminalized homosexual sodomy, and by 1969 only two states had repealed their anti-sodomy laws.[36] As late as 1979 American law "reveal[ed] systematic and pervasive discrimination against homosexual individuals in our courts and dispels the popular idea that, because homosexual individuals occupy every walk of life, there is no real discrimination against them. On the contrary, homosexual individuals are penalized in all aspects of their lives because of their sexual preference. They lose their jobs, their children, and numerous other previous rights as a result of many current judicial policies." At that time sodomy was criminalized by 29 states and the District of Columbia, whereas private, consensual, adult homosexual acts had been decriminalized in 21 other states.[37] The "right to privacy" precedent was established by the Supreme Court in *Griswold v. Connecticut* (1964), but the justices have not applied that precedent to consenting homosexual acts. The refusal of the high court to nullify the Georgia criminal anti-sodomy law in *Bowers v. Hardwick* (1986) caused one gay rights activist to view *Bowers* as completely "inconsistent with treating privacy as autonomy."[38] However, 12 years later the Georgia Supreme Court overruled that law, holding that such behaviour is protected under the privacy rights guaranteed in the state constitution. Georgia, thus, became the fifth state whose high court nullified anti-sodomy laws since *Bowers*.[39]

Nor was the ruling in *Bowers* an isolated case. In *Hurley v. Irish-American Gay, Lesbian and Bisexual Group of Boston* (1995) the Supreme Court upheld the South Boston Allied War Veterans Council's decision to exclude gay marchers from the St. Patrick's Day Parade. A lawsuit to bring homosexuals into American scouting also failed when the Supreme Court in *Boy Scouts v. Dale* (2000) reversed a decision by the New Jersey Supreme Court that had declared the expulsion of homosexual scoutmaster James Dale to have violated the state anti-discrimination law.

One exception to this poor track record on gay rights was *Romer v. Evans* (1996), when the Supreme Court overturned a voter initiated anti-gay rights amendment to the Colorado state constitution. The Christian Right in Colorado had orchestrated Amendment 2 to nullify anti-discrimination ordinances in Denver, Boulder, and Aspen that gave coverage to sexual orientation. But Amendment 2 violated the Equal Protection Clause, ruled the Supreme Court, because a state may not "deem a class of persons a stranger to its own laws." Some commentators viewed *Romer* as being as significant for homosexuals as the *Brown* desegregation ruling was for blacks,[40] but that assessment was premature in light of what soon happened in *Equality Foundation of Greater Cincinnati v. City of Cincinnati* (1998). Here the Supreme Court refused to hear a legal challenge to another voter initiated anti-gay amendment (Issue 3) to the city charter. In so doing, the Court let stand the reasoning of the federal Appellate Court for the Sixth Circuit, which ruled that Issue 3 barred only "special protection" for gays and lesbians and did not deprive them of general anti-discrimination protections.

Physician-Assisted Suicide and Medical Use of Marijuana

Advocates of physician-assisted suicide (PAS) also failed before the Rehnquist Court. They, too, based their legal arguments on the right to privacy to justify invalidating the criminal prohibitions on suicide that existed in every state but one. Forty-nine states draw a legal distinction between passive euthanasia (not providing life-sustaining drugs or devices) and active euthanasia (using drugs or devices to hasten death). Active euthanasia is illegal everywhere except Oregon, which legalized PAS. Two companion cases — *Vacco v. Quill* (1997) and *Washington v. Glucksberg* (1997) — appealed federal Appellate Court rulings that upheld anti-PAS statutes in New York State and Washington State, but the Supreme Court threw aside those privacy claims and ruled that the "right to die" is not constitutionally protected. States remain free to criminalize PAS.

The medical use of marijuana also was dealt a judicial blow in May, 2001 when the Supreme Court voted 8-0 that federal legislation criminalizing marijuana use included no exceptions for people seriously ill with such diseases as AIDS, cancer, and multiple sclerosis. By doing so, the Court in *United States v. Oakland Cannabis Buyers Cooperative* (2001) reversed a ruling from the Ninth Circuit Court of Appeals that "medical necessity" was a legal defence for skirting the federal ban. This issue surfaced after voters in Arizona, Alaska, Colorado, Maine, Nevada, Oregon, Washington State, and California as well as the District of Columbia approved ballot initiatives to legalize the medical use of marijuana (see Chapter 7). A ninth state, Hawaii, also legalized medical marijuana by statute.

Canada

As part of the Commonwealth of Nations for two centuries after the Americans declared their independence from England, Canada remained faithful to British legal customs by having no constitutionally entrenched bill of rights until 1982, when its Constitution was repatriated and a Charter of Rights and Freedoms was written. Two decades earlier (1960) the Canadian Parliament had enacted a statutory Bill of Rights that applied only to federal laws and, therefore, was not "fundamental" law. Nonetheless by 1975, as A. Paul Pross noted, one "striking feature of current writing on Canadian politics is the continual reiteration of concern at the lack of openness in the policy system," meaning that the policy process worked "principally through two relatively closed structures, the party and the bureaucracy, both of which achieve an apex in the cabinet." Even for trials seeking to politicize causes, Kenneth McNaught concluded that "our judges and lawyers, supported by the press and public opinion, reject any concept of the courts as positive instruments in the political process" because "political action outside the party-parliament structure tends automatically to be suspect—and not least because it smacks of Americanism."[41]

Less than a decade after the Charter's adoption (and four years after its equal rights provisions of Section 15 came into force), Michael Mandel characterized its impact as the "legalization of politics" in Canada and "admittedly a revolt against majoritarianism. But it does not substitute a new kind of democracy for it. In allowing individuals to short-circuit representative institutions and groups, and to advance claims which 'trump' more representative claims on the basis of consistency with abstract rights embedded in the status quo, it is a perversion of democracy."[42] Another Canadian judicial scholar, Peter Russell, believes that "the importance of judicial review in Canada at the present time equals if it does not exceed its importance in the United States."[43] And Morton and Knopff go even further, calling it a "Charter Revolution" because "parliamentary supremacy has been replaced by a regime of constitutional supremacy verging on judicial supremacy. On rights issues, judges have abandoned the deference and self-restraint that characterized their pre-Charter jurisprudence and become more active players in the political process."[44] The prospect of judicial activism has troubled the Right in Canada, as in the United States, but "until the Reform Party [now the New Alliance Party] came along, Canada's political parties ... had virtually ignored these growing concerns about judicial power."[45]

Indeed Alan Cairns anticipates far-reaching political consequences from a Charter that designates group entitlements for certain minorities. "The Charter is more than an instrument that hands out abstract rights equally to all Canadians and is indifferent to their various statuses defined by gender, ethnicity, official language status, and the presence or absence of disabilities. In fact it specifically mobilizes Canadians in terms of these categories. It encourages Canadians to think of themselves for constitutional purposes as women, as official-language minorities, as disabled, or as ethnocultural Canadians."[46] To this extent Les Pal agrees: "The advent of the Charter in 1982 therefore did not so much create new groups as new opportunities, though some organizations were spawned specifically to pursue new litigation strategies related to the Charter's equality provisions."[47]

It was not long before the Canadian Supreme Court broadcast its intentions in no uncertain terms. In *Law Society of Upper Canada v. Sapinker* (1984), it declared that its Charter jurisprudence would be "large and liberal" in scope, a welcome signal to advocacy groups who were organizing a litigation campaign. Unlike the United States, where interests groups rely on their own funding sources, the government of Canada made provision for advocacy groups wishing to sue the federal and provincial authorities in order to secure certain Charter rights. Best known is the Women's Legal Education and Action Fund (LEAF), founded the same year that Section 15 (equality rights) of the Charter was scheduled to take effect. During the decade 1985-95 LEAF submitted briefs (known as "factum" in Canadian law) in 23 cases and won 83 per cent of the time.[48] It goes without saying that this program was tailored to help victimized groups, but not every aggrieved minority. As Hoover and den Dulk point out, "Canada's conservative Christian organizations are *not* generally coming to the Court as beneficiaries of the Court Challenges Program. More often it is as *opponents* of these beneficiaries."[49]

That allegation is empirically confirmed by the most comprehensive study of interest group lobbying before the Canadian Supreme Court during the period 1988 to 1998. According to researcher Gregory Hein, Charter-designated minorities, aboriginal peoples, civil libertarians, and new-left activists—called "judicial democrats"—"believe that litigation has the potential to make our public institutions more accessible, transparent and responsive, if courts hear from a diverse range of interests, guard fundamental social values and protect disadvantaged minorities." With the exception of organized labour, such interests as groups of victims (from crime), social conservatives, and professionals rely much less on a litigation strategy. Moreover, to highlight the litigious role of corporate Canada is misleading, because "[h]alf of the actions initiated by corporations are civil claims against private parties" and "these cases rarely affect public policy," whereas what troubles the political right are the "Aboriginal peoples, Charter Canadians, civil libertarians and new left activists [who] bring 52% of the claims that attack Cabinet decisions and public policies. To win, these litigants have to persuade judges to accept a controversial role—to be full partners in the legislative process who use their skills to solve pressing problems and exercise their authority to improve society." Moreover, in terms of the number of groups they represent in Canadian society, the corporate sector is 55 times under-represented in court as compared to the judicial democrats. Thus, the bottom line is that "the interests that conservative critics blame for the expansion of judicial power are far more inclined to litigate than other groups."[50]

The grounds for legal "standing" to bring suit before the high court have been loosened considerably because, say Morton and Knopff, LEAF and the Canadian Civil Liberties Association (CCLA) "mounted a furious public relations campaign ... to persuade the Court to loosen the rules on intervention."[51] In *Borowski v. Minister of Justice et al.* (1982), the Supreme Court articulated a policy on standing that Morton calls "the broadest rule of standing in any common-law jurisdiction," given the increasing applicants for "intervener" status (analogous to *amicus curiae* in American law) and the rate of acceptance by the justices.[52] Thus Epp determined that, after 1980, a higher percentage of all cases on the Canadian Supreme Court docket attracted interest groups as interveners[53]

Abortion

Highly controversial decisions have been based on Charter provisions, and no ruling more than abortion shows the decisive impact of Charter litigation. In the 1970s pro-choice activist Dr. Henry Morgentaler asked the Supreme Court to nullify the 1969 abortion restrictions of the criminal code in *R. v. Morgentaler* (1975). The Court refused. That ruling, says Susan Mezey, illustrated that "the Canadian court's reluctance to intervene can be traced to the ambiguous nature of the 1960 Canadian Bill of Rights and its status as a 'simply statutory instrument' and not part of an established constitution." Morgentaler gambled that the Supreme Court would accept American legal precedents: "Morgentaler alleged that the Canadian Bill of Rights 1960, derived from the US Constitution, imported American common law decisions into Canadian law, and thus *Roe v. Wade* case law should be followed in Canada. He urged that women had a right to terminate a pregnancy, especially during the first trimester." But the Canadian Supreme Court unanimously rejected his constitutional arguments and, moreover, affirmed "that Parliament has in its judgment decreed that interference by another, or even by the pregnant woman herself, with the ordinary course of conception is socially undesirable conduct subject to punishment. That was a judgment open to Parliament in the exercise of its plenary criminal law power, and the fact that there may be safe ways of terminating a pregnancy, or that any woman or women claims a personal privilege to that end, becomes immaterial."[54]

Thirteen years later Morgentaler won. The difference between 1975 and 1988 was the Charter, specifically Section 7: "Everybody has the right to life, liberty and security of the person and the right not to be deprived thereof except in accordance with the principles of fundamental justice." In 1983 Morgentaler and two other physicians were charged with unlawfully performing abortions in his Toronto clinic. When appealed to the Supreme Court, the fundamental legal issue was whether the Criminal Code infringed on a woman's right to "life, liberty and security of the person" as guaranteed in Section 7. According to Dunsmuir, the ruling in *Morgantaler v. The Queen* (1988) meant "that the legislation interfered with the security of the person of a woman in limiting, by criminal law, her effective and timely access to medical services when her life or health was endangered. This criminalization was not in accordance with fundamental justice."[55] However, only one justice was receptive to following American precedent and establishing a constitutional right to abortion; furthermore, because the ruling was not grounded in privacy rights but rather hinged on the unworkable nature of the existing law, the majority opinion invited Parliament to rewrite the statute. Afterwards, the Progressive Conservative government tried to revise the abortion law, but failed, meaning that to this day Canada has arguably the most open-ended abortion policy of any western nation.

Less successful, however, was pro-life litigation. *Borowski v. Canada* (1989) was taken to the Supreme Court by Joe Borowski, formerly a minister in Manitoba's NDP government, who became Canada's foremost pro-life crusader. Borowski's final appeal to the Supreme Court argued that Section 7, granting "everyone" the "right to life, liberty and security" should be extended to the unborn. Borowski had lost twice in Saskatchewan, where courts held that the fetus is not a legal person, setting the stage for this high court review. Instead of ruling on the merits, however, the Supreme Court sidestepped the constitutional issue and countered that it was moot in light of the *Morgentaler* ruling. Although the Court again expressed some deference to Parliament, in fact, as Peter Russell observed, "Canadians prefer judges over legislatures as the final decision makers on questions pertaining to rights and freedoms."[56]

Physician-Assisted Suicide

Canadian advocates of physician-assisted suicide (PAS) had no more luck than their American counterparts. In *Rodriguez v. British Columbia* (1993), the appellant, Sue Rodriguez—who was suffering from the incurable disease, ALS, which affects the nervous system—argued that Section 241(b) of the *Criminal Code*, which prohibits assisted suicide, was unconstitutional based on three Charter provisions, mainly that it violated right to "security of the person" under Section 7. The Court of Appeal for British Columbia disallowed Sue Rodriguez's rights claim, and its ruling was upheld by the justices. The majority said that the long-standing historical roots of the ban on assisted suicide fulfilled the government's objective of protecting the vulnerable and human life (another right mentioned in Section 7), noting that "[n]o consensus can be found in favour of the decriminalization of assisted suicide," but rather "[t]o the extent that there is a consensus, it is that human life must be respected." Nine interest groups participated in this case as intervenors; Dying with

Dignity and the Right to Die Society of Canada were opposed by advocates representing the handicapped, pro-life groups, Catholics, and Evangelicals.

The Lord's Day Act

Americans may be especially perplexed by the ruling in *R. v. Big M Drug Mart* (1985), which struck down the Lord's Day Act banning Sunday sales as violating "freedom of conscience and religion" under Section 2(a) of the Charter. Three legal defences were raised by the attorney general of Alberta, namely, that a corporation cannot claim religious rights; that the Charter has no prohibition akin to the Establishment Clause in the First Amendment to the American Bill of Rights, which prohibits government from promoting religion; and that even the Supreme Court of the United States upheld Sunday observance laws. However, the Canadian Supreme Court held that a corporation could challenge the law's constitutionality, that its "purpose" was purely religious, and that American jurisprudence was irrelevant to understanding the Charter.

Equality Rights

What is very radical as compared to the equal protection clause of the American Constitution is Section 15 of the Canadian Charter. According to Peter Russell, "[p]ositive freedom is given precedence over negative freedom in the equality section of the Charter, which recognizes affirmative action to ameliorate the conditions of disadvantaged individuals or groups as legitimate grounds for modifying the right to equal benefit of the law."[57] Section 15 reads:

> (1) Every individual is equal before and under the law and has the right to the equal protection and equal benefit of the law without discrimination and, in particular, without discrimination based on race, national or ethnic origin, colour, religion, sex, age or mental or physical disability.

> (2) Subsection (1) does not preclude any law, program or activity that has as its object the amelioration of conditions of disadvantaged individuals or groups including those that are disadvantaged because of race, national or ethnic origin, colour, religion, sex, age or mental or physical disability.

Section 15 was employed by the Ontario Court of Appeal in *Haig and Birch v. Canada* (1992) to "read sexual preference into" the Canadian Human Rights Act, just as the Supreme Court later did with respect to the Alberta

Human Rights Act in *Vriend v. Alberta* (1998). The groundwork for this 1998 ruling was established in *Egan and Nesbitt v. Canada* (1995) when sexual orientation was added to Section 15 coverage. Morton and Knopff argue that *M v. H* (1999), which prohibited the state from defining spouse as "a member of the opposite sex, potentially affects more laws than all its previous Charter rulings combined—58 federal statutes and hundreds of provincial statutes."[58]

Unlike the American Bill of Rights, gender equity is given constitutional standing in Section 28: "Notwithstanding anything in this Charter, the rights and freedoms referred to in it are guaranteed equally to male and female persons." The Charter also explicitly identifies group rights. Sections 16 to 20 specify that only French and English are "official languages," meaning no other mother tongue enjoys equal constitutional status. Section 23 guarantees collective rights to English-speaking or French-speaking linguistic minorities, who are entitled to have their children educated in their own language in any province. Language policy illustrates judicial restraint "by design" in Canada and "by default" in the United States, argue MacMillan and Tatalovich, because the Canadian Supreme Court "has acted in league with the political establishment by legitimizing official bilingualism," while the American Supreme Court has refused three times to rule against Official-English laws.[59]

Language Rights

Of course language is the heart of Quebec identity, and its effort to codify a French-only language policy catapulted the Canadian Supreme Court into a political quagmire, though the legalities involved none of the languages clauses but rather "freedom of thought, belief, opinion and expression, including freedom of the press and other media of communication" in Section 2(b). The Charter of the French Language, known as Bill 101, had multiple purposes, including a requirement that all signs, posters, and commercial advertising in Quebec must be exclusively in French (religious and political messages were exempt). The Canadian Supreme Court overturned this prohibition on English sign usage (Section 58 of Bill 101) in the *Quebec Public Signs Case* (1988) as violating both the Charter—"freedom of expression"—and the Quebec Charter of Rights and Freedoms. Unlike the United States, a "notwithstanding clause" in Section 33 of the Charter allows the federal or a provincial legislature to *nullify* any judicial decision made pursuant to most sections of the Charter. This is precisely what Quebec did; it ignored the ruling though eventually its sign law was modified to accommodate the decision.[60]

Pornography and Hate Speech

Freedom of expression under Section 2(b) was also forced to yield to legislation banning pornography and "hate speech" by the Canadian Supreme Court in rulings that most likely would not have been rendered by the American Supreme Court. The Canadian Court accepted feminist arguments to ban pornography in *R. v. Butler* (1992). Under Section 163(8) of the Criminal Code "any publication a dominant characteristic of which is the undue exploitation of sex, or of sex and any one or more of the following subjects, namely, crime, horror, cruelty, and violence, shall be deemed to be obscene." Given that this act of Parliament seemingly violates Section 2(b) of the Charter, which includes freedom of the press, the Supreme Court had to determine if that infringement could be justified under Section 1 of the Charter, which "guarantees the rights and freedoms set out in it, subject only to such reasonable limits prescribed by law as can be demonstrably justified in a free and democratic society." The Court differentiated between obscenity that does not and obscenity that does "harm" women. The majority said that the harm to society "in terms of public morality" may not warrant "an infringement of the right of expression" but the "harm goes beyond public morality in this narrow sense." Rather "if true equality between male and female persons is to be achieved, we cannot ignore the threat to equality resulting from exposure to audiences of certain types of violent and degrading material. Materials portraying women as a class as objects for sexual exploitation and abuse have a negative impact on 'the individual's sense of self-worth and acceptance.'"

"This case is the first test of the obscenity laws under the charter's provision on freedom of expression," said LEAF lawyer Kathleen Mahoney. "But the charter also has a strong equality section. The court said that while the obscenity law does limit the charter's freedom of expression guarantee, it's justifiable because this type of expression harms women personally, harms their right to be equal, affects their security and changes attitudes toward them so they become more subject to violence."[61] Declared University of Michigan law professor Catharine A. MacKinnon, whose work influenced the feminist brief in *Butler*, "This makes Canada the first place in the world that says what is obscene is what harms women, not what offends our values."[62]

A free speech standard in American jurisprudence is not easily abridged unless harmful actions result, but the Canadian Supreme Court in *R. v. Keegstra* (1990) backed a parliamentary ban on "hate speech" unrelated to any behaviour. An Alberta high school teacher who made anti-Semitic comments was charged with violating Section 319(2) of the Criminal Code, which subjected anyone "who, by communicating statements, other than in private conversation, willfully promotes hatred against any identifiable group is guilty" to an indictable offence punishable by imprisonment not exceeding two years. By "identifiable group" the law specified those people "distinguished by colour, race, religion or ethnic origin." Again, the Supreme Court majority ruled that the law imposed a reasonable limit on freedom of expression. "Parliament's objective of preventing the harm caused by hate propaganda is of sufficient importance to warrant overriding a constitutional freedom. Parliament has recognized the substantial harm that can flow from hate propaganda and, in trying to prevent the pain suffered by target groups and to reduce racial, ethnic and religious tension and perhaps even violence in Canada, has decided to suppress the willful promotion of hatred against identifiable groups." In addition, "the international commitment to eradicate hate propaganda and Canada's commitment to the values of equality and multiculturalism in ss. 15 [equality rights] and 27 [multiculturalism] of the Charter strongly buttress the importance of this objective."

Europe

Before 1950, "the power of European courts to control the constitutionality of legislation was nearly unknown." Alec Stone points out, "From 1780 in Germanic states and from 1791 in France, judicial interpretation of statutes was explicitly prohibited by constitutions, and penalties were prescribed in the penal codes for any transgression."[63] Constitutional review by judicial authorities is largely a postwar development. Since World War II, observes Kenneth Holland, "the level of judicial influence in European governance has grown substantially" and such "[a]ctivism is not confined to constitutional tribunals," since "European courts are increasingly comfortable in striking down legislative enactments and administrative actions and are involved in a growing list of policy areas, from abortion to welfare reform."[64]

Principally through the expansion of international organizations—the European Union and the Council of Europe—"judicial review is becoming a democratic norm in Europe," though Holland feels it "unlikely that European judges will ever match the American judiciary's level of political influence."[65] The coming to the UK (also to France, Germany, and many more European countries) of a supranational rights document holds the potential for expansive human rights litigation. The European Convention for the Protection of Human Rights and Fundamental Freedoms was created in 1950 under the auspices of the Council of Europe (founded in 1949). The UK (which ratified it in 1953), France, and Germany are all signatories to that Convention, whose objective was to harmonize the national laws of its member states to assure human rights to all their citizens. Enforcement utilized a fact-finding European Commission of Human Rights, which sought conciliation from offending nations, and a European Court of Human Rights, whose decision must be enforced by the Committee of Ministers of the Council of Europe. But a growing backlog of cases led the Council of Europe in 1994 to adopt Protocol No. 11, replacing the Commission and the Court with a new Court of Human Rights. What is likely to revolutionize the international law on human rights is Protocol No. 9, which proposes to expand the Court's jurisdiction from inter-state complaints about human rights abuses to petitions from any person, non-government organization, or group of individuals who claim to be victims of human rights violations by a member state, a change which required ratification by all member states. Another change with far-reaching implications is the Framework Convention, also adopted in 1994 by the Committee of Ministers, which proposed the first legally binding instrument for protecting the cultural rights of minorities. To enter into force, the Framework requires ratification by 12 member states. These amendments will establish the European Convention on Human Rights as the most advanced and sophisticated supranational system for protecting human rights.

This regime of international human rights law undoubtedly will profoundly change the political opportunity structures that activists confront in all (41) member states. Consider Catholic Ireland. Though it joined the European Union in 1973 for purely economic reasons, the human rights agenda of the EU has forced changes in Irish morality policy. In the years since "the European Court of Justice and the European Court of Human Rights delivered judgments against domestic law, which were of a moral or cultural nature," one recent example being "the demand by the European Court of Human Rights that Irish laws discriminating against homosexuals be repealed."[66]

GERMANY

Arguably the most active national tribunal in Europe has been the German Constitutional Court, as more than 90 per cent of its caseload and 60 per cent of its rulings have involved individual challenges alleging violation of constitutional rights. Kenneth Holland notes that the 1949 German Basic Law, which incorporated constitutional review, "enshrines a detailed and lengthy bill of rights, including both positive and negative rights that obligate the government both to act and not to act in its relationship with individual citizens." He explains that the German Constitutional Court "has had a clear mission: instruct the political organs and the people in the principles of liberal democracy."[67] Similar to what Canadian surveys revealed about judicial activism following adoption of the Charter, polls in Germany "indicate that the German people have more confidence in the Federal Constitutional Court (FCC) than in any other public institution and that the level of public trust has continued to grow into the 1990s." After the German Parliament legalized divorce in 1970, for example, the German Constitutional Court upheld that action several times, thus setting the stage for its acceptance by the German electorate.[68]

So established is judicial review in Germany, says Holland, that "only one of its decisions has engendered high-level protest," namely, its 1975 ruling disallowing abortions.[69] An 1871 statute criminalized abortion unless performed to save the life or health of the mother, and several attempts to liberalize that law during the 1950s and 1960s failed, primarily because the Christian Democratic Union (CDU) was opposed and the ruling Social Democrat (SPD)/Free Democrat (FDP) coalition lacked the votes to force a change. After the 1972 elections increased the SPD/FDP's share of parliamentary seats, abortion reform was enacted in 1974, whereupon 193 members of the *Bundestag* (who had voted against reform) and six *Lander* (states) petitioned the German Constitutional Court to rule on its constitutionality. "The *Abortion Decision*, announced on February 25, 1975, struck down the newly passed reform statute for being in violation of the German Basic Law (the Constitution), particularly Article 2, Paragraph 2, Sentence 1, which declares, 'Everyone shall have a right to life.'"[70] The high court "reasoned that, since life began 14 days after conception, the State has an affirmative duty to protect unborn life from harm—even from the mother"; furthermore, because "[t]ermination of the pregnancy meant destruction of human life and penal sanctions were the only way in which the State could ensure the survival of the foetus ... women could be forced to bear an unwanted child unless contravening factors were present."[71] While party affiliation generally "does not seem to play a decisive role in the [Court's] decision-making process," on the abortion case it did, since "a majority of judges connected with the Conservative Christian-Democratic Party (CDU) invalidated the law over the protests of two dissenting members affiliated with the Socialist Party (SPD)."[72]

When polls showed that 50 per cent of West Germans opposed that ruling, compared to 32 per cent in favour, the "Revolutionary Women's Group" protested by bombing the Constitutional Court building in Karlsruhe. The vice-president of the Bundestag declared that women would not obey that edict, though the federal minister of justice retorted that the government would enforce the decision.[73] In response, the Bundestag passed another reform statute, criminalizing abortion except where the woman's life or health was endangered, where the fetus was substantially deformed, and where there is a serious danger of "distress" if the woman was forced to bear her pregnancy; in addition it stipulated a three-day waiting period and required counselling. Activists then challenged this law before the European Commission on Human Rights, but its legality was upheld.[74]

In 1993 an abortion law that reconciled East German and West German differences was struck down. During unification talks, polls showed that 77 per cent of East Germans wanted to retain its law, permitting abortion on demand during the first trimester, whereas the West German statute permitted abortions on narrow grounds if certified by a government-approved family planning service. In effect the West German Bundestag capitulated in 1992, approving a pro-choice measure that the Constitutional Court partially nullified on May 28, 1993. In 1995 yet another abortion law was enacted, now allowing abortions during the first trimester coupled with the requirement that the woman first visit a counselling centre. That same year the Constitutional Court was embroiled in a church-state controversy. It struck down a Bavarian school requirement that a crucifix be hung in every classroom, based on violations of religious freedom and government neutrality in Article 4 of the Basic Law. That decision was roundly criticized by Bavarian authorities, the Catholic Church, and even Chancellor Helmut Kohl.[75]

After the Social Democratic-Green coalition government legalized same-sex partnerships, despite opposition from the Christian Democrats, Bavaria and Saxony appealed to the Constitutional Court in Karlsruhe, but in mid-2001 the high court dismissed that appeal, which had argued that the law was an assault on family values enshrined in the Basic Law.[76]

Another recent judicial ruling, this time by the European Court of Justice, forced Germany to abandon its 50-year ban on women serving in the military (other than as medical personnel or musicians). Yet nearly one year elapsed before the first 244 female recruits were enrolled in boot camp. In the case of *Tanja Kreil v. Federal Republic of Germany* (2000), the European Court of Justice overturned the ban in Article 12a of the Basic Law that women "may on no account render service involving the use of arms." That prohibition effectively discriminated against women in the armed services, said the Court: "German legislation barring women outright from army jobs involving the use of arms is contrary to the [European] Community principle of equal treatment for men and women. However, derogations remain possible where sex constitutes a determining factor for access to certain special combat units." The case was brought by Tanja Kreil, a 23-year-old electrical engineer whose application for a position in the weapons electronics maintenance service of the Federal German army was rejected solely on the grounds that the law bars women from military positions involving the use of arms.[77]

FRANCE

There was no entrenched bill of rights in the 1958 French Constitution. Created by the Gaullists to curb parliamentary excess, the French Constitutional

Council remained subservient to the executive until 1971, when "the Council annulled its first piece of governmental legislation and in the process incorporated an expansive bill of rights into the constitution, which includes the 1789 Declaration of the Rights of Man, the preamble to the 1946 constitution, and the unnamed 'fundamental principles' recognized by the laws of the republic."[78] However, Holland says that this bold step gained political significance only after a 1974 constitutional amendment gave any 60 members of the National Assembly or the Senate the right to refer bills to the council. "By giving the opposition party the power to bring constitutional challenges, the law effectively guaranteed that every major controversial bill would be reviewed by the council before promulgation."[79]

Few morality policies have been referred to the Council, though issues of law-and-order have. When legislation authorizing unconditional legal abortions during the first 10 weeks of a pregnancy and conditional abortions thereafter passed both parliamentary chambers on December 19, 1974, it was soon referred to the French Constitutional Council, which in early 1975 declared it constitutional and not in violation of the European Declaration of Human Rights.[80] In 1977, after adoption of a government bill to give the police wider powers to stop and search automobiles, three petitions signed by 239 parliamentarians were referred to the Council. The Council "chose to discover and to enshrine a wholly new FPRLR [Fundamental Principles Recognized by the Laws of the Republic], which it named—without defining—that of 'individual liberty.'"[81] Overall, between 1959 and 1990 the opposition parties accounted for 93.4 per cent of all bills referred to the French Constitutional Council. Moreover, "[n]early every veto of a major bill ... has been on grounds of violation of individual rights guaranteed by the constitution."[82]

United Kingdom

Historically the UK has had no written constitution or entrenched bill of rights, and the judiciary (including the House of Lords, its highest court) did not possess the power of constitutional review. The UK had something akin to judicial oversight of administrative discretion but, even here, as Kenneth Holland underscores, "British administrative law is principally a series of doctrines that command courts to defer to bureaucratic lawmaking and to prefer the interests of government over that of individuals. Thus, the Parliament has systematically withdrawn from the jurisdiction of the courts all policy matters of vital interest to themselves."[83]

On October 1, 2000 the Human Rights Act of 1998, which the Labour government had included in its legislative program, for the first time incorporated into British law the protections embodied in the European Convention on Human Rights. British citizens now can sue in domestic courts to enforce the Convention rather than travel to Strasbourg, France, to plead their case. This development transforms "negative rights"—whereby Britons were allowed to do anything not prohibited by a specific law—into "positive rights" that overarch parliamentary or executive decrees. "We have always trusted the executive and judiciary to protect our rights, but it's been a matter of trust only," observes international human rights lawyer Julian Knowles. "This document sets out in clear terms what these rights are." Conservative critics are fearful that cases taken to the European Court of Human Rights may challenge the UK's strident laws concerning libel, freedom of the press, employment practices, immigration, criminal justice, and homosexuality. It also threatens parliamentary supremacy. "Our Parliament will be powerless to stop unelected and unsackable judges making the law because the Human Rights Act is so loosely and vaguely worded," wrote Norman Tebbit, former minister in the Thatcher government, in the *Daily Mail*. "They will give rights to some people—sex perverts, illegal immigrants, and criminals are top of the list—which will rob us of freedoms we have had for centuries."[84]

Although the UK had signed the Convention in 1953, and in 1966 finally agreed to allow its citizens to seek legal redress in Strasbourg, a lack of political will explains why it took so long to codify this "bill of rights" in domestic law. Signs are ripe that the ominous warnings from conservatives may be accurate. The British government has lost before the European Court of Human Rights over 50 times, "giving it one of the poorest records among European nations—and has had to rewrite various laws, however grudgingly, to take into account the rights guaranteed by the convention."[85] By one account "[c]ases under Article 5, the right to liberty and security of person, have involved complaints about the recall of prisoners released on license, the length of detention in police custody, and breach of the peace. Fairness under Article 6, the right to due process, applies to both pretrial process and trial procedures. Rights to privacy under Article 8 have been fiercely litigated in the fields of correspondence and sexual relations."[86] A very important decision on homosexuality was *Dudgeon v. United Kingdom* (1981), which ruled that criminalizing homosexuality infringed upon privacy rights, insofar as "a kind of 'domino effect' occurred in UK dependent territories"—and beyond. This means that "the Court and Commission's decisions in *Dudgeon, Norris* [*v. Ireland* (1988)], and *Modinos* [*v. Cyprus* (1993)] could ultimately result in a continent of Europe free of laws forbidding same-sex sexual activity" and, therefore, "suggests that the Convention has had an important impact in the area of sexual orientation discrimination."[87]

In 1998 the UK banned hitting schoolchildren with a cane, a routine punishment used for centuries, but the issue of corporal punishment did not end there. In *Case of A. v. The United Kingdom* (1998), the European Court of Human Rights unanimously agreed that a violation of Article 3 of the Convention had occurred when a nine-year-old boy had been beaten with a garden cane by his stepfather. Article 3 stipulates that "no one shall be subjected to torture or to inhuman or degrading treatment or punishment," and, although the stepfather was arrested under the Offences Against the Person Act of 1861, under English law the prosecution shoulders the burden of proof to convince a jury that an "assault" on a child was beyond "reasonable chastisement" in order to convict. In this case, a British jury acquitted the stepfather, but the European Court of Human Rights nonetheless ruled that British law "did not provide adequate protection to the applicant against treatment or punishment contrary to Article 3. Indeed, the Government have accepted that this law currently fails to provide adequate protection to children and should be amended."[88] Afterwards, however, the Labour government chose not to introduce new legislation but to defend the current law in light of a government survey that showed that 88 per cent of parents and guardians favoured corporal punishment as "reasonable chastisement" for children.[89]

In recent years two extremely controversial decisions by the European Court of Human Rights pertained to juvenile justice and gay rights. One involved the highly publicized 1993 murder of two-year-old James Bulger, who had been lured away from a suburban Liverpool shopping centre by Jon Venables and Robert Thompson. At age 11 when tried, they were the youngest murder defendants in a century, and the European Court of Human Rights ruled in late 1999 that the British Home Secretary erred by increasing their eight-year jail sentences to 15 years and, moreover, that judicial proceedings against minors must take into account "age, level of maturity and intellectual and emotional capacities." This decision, coupled with an adverse ruling from the House of Lords, forced the Labour government to ponder reforms in the juvenile justice system.[90]

The election of Tony Blair's Labour government in mid-1997 "gave hope" to gays that their policy agenda, including the equalization of the age of consent and lifting the ban on homosexuals in the armed forces, would be resolved. But, according to Read and Marsh, "Labour spokesmen quickly played down expectations, explaining that the government was not committed to changing the laws on homosexuality and arguing that it was a matter for private members' legislation." Therefore, the cause of gay rights in the UK owes much to international tribunals: "In almost every case where reform has occurred it has been an attempt to pre-empt a ruling from the European Court. And the retention of the ban on homosexuals and lesbians in the Armed Forces demonstrates just how willing any government, whether Conservative or Labour, is to resist change even though it accepts that change is inevitable due to the pressures of the European Court."[91]

In 1994 Euan Sutherland petitioned the European Commission on Human Rights in *Sutherland v. United Kingdom*, charging the Sexual Offences Act of 1967 and the Criminal Justice Act of 1994 violated the European Convention for the Protection of Human Rights and Fundamental Freedoms by mandating different ages of consent for homosexuals and heterosexuals. The Home Office announced that it would vigorously defend the existing law, but in May 1996 the European Commission on Human Rights disagreed and also requested a written report on another case being brought by a schoolboy, Chris Morris. With these signals that the UK would lose should a decision be rendered by the European Court of Human Rights, an out-of-court settlement was accepted that included "allowing a free vote on lowering the age of consent for homosexuals to 16, [but] government officials refused to concede an early vote," and they "would not take sides or promote the cause for changing the law." Thus, "although the issue was effectively resolved by the European Court's ruling that the law was discriminatory, the political and legal resolution would have to wait until the British government was ready."[92]

The Sexual Offences Acts of 1967 prohibited homosexual acts among armed forces personnel, a criminal offence until 1994, and the military reserved the right to discharge known homosexuals or lesbians. Four ex-personnel challenged that policy in court, but in June 1995 the Queen's Bench upheld the law, although commenting that the "tide of history" was against the Ministry of Defence. The military chiefs of staff strongly opposed lifting the ban, and their position prevailed in the Appeals Court, whereupon the plaintiffs sought relief in the House of Lords and, later, the European Court of Human Rights. The Conservative government was determined to oppose any change, and there was a split within the Labour Party as national elections approached.

Almost one year before the European Convention was domesticated into British law, Duncan Lustig-Prean, Graeme Grady, Jeanette Smith, and John Beckett—the four gays who were dismissed from the British military—won a landmark decision before the European Court of Human Rights. Its rulings in *Lustig-Prean v. United Kingdom* (1999) and (the companion case) *Smith and Grady v. United Kingdom* (1999) held that involuntary discharge from the armed forces violated the fundamental human right to privacy under Article 8 of the European Convention. Early the next year the newly elected Labour government announced a revision in the military code of conduct that ended the ban on openly gay men and women, thus bringing British policy in line with most other NATO countries, including Canada, France, and Germany. "The European Court of Human Rights ruling makes very clear that the existing policy in relation to homosexuality must change," said Defence Secretary Geoffrey Hoon to the House of Commons. "As all personal behaviour will be regulated by the code of conduct," he added, "there is no longer a reason to deny homosexuals the opportunity of a career in the armed forces."[93]

A much debated issue in the UK is whether the Human Rights Act "entrenched" fundamental rights against parliamentary repeal or amendment, as do the American Bill of Rights or the Canadian Charter of Rights and Freedoms. One analysis says that the Human Rights Act "has lower status than all other legislation," which explains how easily and quickly the Criminal Justice (Terrorism and Conspiracy) Act of 1998 was enacted after a bombing by the Real Irish Republican Army that killed 28 people and injured 220 more. Having been proposed on September 1 and quickly promulgated into law on September 4, this, argue Walker and Weaver, "does not bode well for the current levels of institutional entrenchment" of the European Convention.[94]

Not all lawsuits reach the European Court of Human Rights, but simply the presence of the European Convention has affected the pace of litigation in the UK, including a huge increase—76 per cent between 1995 and 2000—in sexual and racial discrimination lawsuits. What gives plaintiffs new legal leverage are provisos to the European Convention on Human Rights ratified by the 15-country European Union in mid-2000. For the first time, Article 13 of the Treaty of Amsterdam provides a uniform legal standard for combating discrimination based on race, sex, religion, age, or disability. Because of the Convention, "[t]he thinking of the courts will shift from 'How can we be a barrier to people achieving their rights?' to 'How can we be a springboard?'" declared Chris Myant, spokesman for the Commission for Racial Equality.[95] Article 13 shifted the burden of proof from plaintiffs to defendants and also allowed third parties like the British Equal Opportunity Commission to sue on behalf of individuals.

Morality Policy By Decree

In his inventory of 11 western democracies, Holland suggests that the level of judicial activism is highest in the United States followed by Canada, with Germany fourth-ranked, and France (eighth) and England (ninth) among those nations with the least active judiciaries.[96] Both the American and Canadian Supreme Courts are independent of the elected branches, whereas the German Constitutional Court and especially the French Constitutional Council are quasi-legislative partners in their parliamentary systems. Historically there has been nothing equivalent to judicial review in British jurisprudence, but today the UK is under assault by litigants who take their claims to the European Court of Human Rights.

Landfried argues that the German Federal Constitutional "Court with its far-reaching competence becomes inconsistent with democracy when the

Court exceeds its competence, as, for example, in the decision on abortion." Judicial review has manifested "an undue alliance of judges and Members of Parliament in strengthening the process of judicialization of politics" to the point where "judicial review contributes to an 'overexertion of the Constitution to the debit of the political process.'"[97] Pointing to France, Stone feels that the French Constitutional Court may be "in a much more vulnerable institutional position than are other European constitutional courts" because "politically initiated, abstract review is inherently more destabilizing than is concrete review, precisely because it poses 'countermajoritarian difficulty' unambiguously, from the moment it is initiated."[98] This is true from the standpoint of the parliamentary majority who enacted the law, but what about democratic accountability? The ability of a minority of backbenchers to overturn parliamentary enactments by judicial referral does look anti-majoritarian *within* the legislative assembly, but may be pro-majoritarian in terms of what the French or German people want. The relationship between morality policy and public opinion is considered elsewhere (Chapter 8), but, with respect to parliamentary rule, abstract judicial review in France and Germany obviously serves to empower backbenchers vis-à-vis the governing majority.

Odds are that many, if not most, decisions by a court empowered with judicial review is anti-majoritarian, which is precisely why individuals and minorities seek judicial redress. After reviewing abortion litigation Scheppele concludes that "[i]n the United States, Canada, Ireland, Germany, and perhaps soon Hungary as well, the high court has been dealing with the issue repeatedly as the losers from the previous round have come up with new constitutional arguments to bring back to the courts. Constitutional decisions don't usually settle the question when it has been framed as a choice among rights; these decisions simply provide a pause in the cycle of competing rights claims."[99]

Not every ruling by a high court goes against the parliamentary will or the popular majority, but those that do may be perceived as illegitimate and, therefore, not authoritative rulings. On parental use of corporal punishment, for example, even the Labour government of Prime Minister Tony Blair was not prepared to go against the popular sentiment of the British. The erosion of democratic politics and the failure of consensus-building are primary reasons why Mary Ann Glendon opposes abortion policy by judicial decree and why Martha Derthick is troubled when litigators seek to impose draconian tobacco controls on American producers and consumers.[100] In the United States, morality policy by judicial edict contradicts republicanism. In Europe it upends parliamentary supremacy.

Notes

1. Alex Stone, *The Birth of Judicial Politics in France: The Constitutional Court in Comparative Perspective* (New York: Oxford University Press, 1992) 9, 114. Stone acknowledges (253) that it was the eminent German jurist, Carl Schmitt, who opposed "constitutional review on the grounds that it would lead either to the 'judicialization of politics' or to a 'politicization of justice.'" Alex Stone, "Abstract Constitutional Review and Policy Making in Western Europe," *Comparative Judicial Review and Public Policy*, ed. Donald W. Jackson and C. Neal Tate (Westport, CT: Greenwood Press, 1992) 41.

2. Stone, *The Birth of Judicial Politics in France* 225-53.

3. Stone, "Abstract Constitutional Review and Policy Making in Western Europe" 45. Elsewhere Stone explains that "[p]olitical scientists, including myself, comparativists, and non-French legal specialists have consistently conceptualized the Council as something other than a court, and as fulfilling more a legislative than a judicial function." See Stone, *The Birth of Judicial Politics in France*, 234; see also Stone, *The Birth of Judicial Politics in France* 43-45.

4. Kenneth M. Holland, "The Courts in the Federal Republic of Germany," *The Political Role of Law Courts in Modern Democracies*, ed. Jerold L. Waltman and Kenneth M. Holland (New York: St. Martin's Press, 1988) 99.

5. Charles Epp, "Do Bills of Rights Matter? The Canadian Charter of Rights and Freedoms," *American Political Science Review* 90 (December 1996): 765-79.

6. Smith, *Lesbian and Gay Rights in Canada* 13.

7. Stuart A. Scheingold, *The Politics of Rights: Lawyers, Public Policy, and Political Change* (New Haven, CT: Yale University Press, 1974) 131, 84-85.

8. Lawrence Baum, *The Supreme Court*, 3rd ed. (Washington, DC: CQ Press, 1989) 22.

9. Andrew Jay Koshner, *Solving the Puzzle of Interest Group Litigation* (Westport, CT: Greenwood Press, 1998) 52. The "social impact" cases are those dealing with due process, substantive rights, and equality.

10. Advocates of judicial activism are Laurence Tribe, *American Constitutional Law* (Mineola, NY: Foundation Press, 1988); Jesse Choper, *Judicial Review and the National Political Process: A Functional Reconsideration of the Role of the Supreme Court* (Chicago: University of Chicago Press, 1980); Herbert Wechsler, "Toward Neutral Principles of Constitutional Law," *Harvard Law Review* 73 (November, 1959): 1-35. For critics of that view, see Robert H. Bork, *The Tempting of America: The Political Seduction of the Law* (New York: Simon and Schuster, 1990); Alexander M. Bickel, *The Least Dangerous Branch* (New Haven, CT: Yale University Press, 1986); John Agresto, *The Supreme Court and Constitutional Democracy* (Ithaca, NY: Cornell University Press, 1984).

11. John T. Noonan, Jr., "Raw Judicial Power," *National Review* (March 2, 1973): 261.

12. John Hart Ely, "The Wages of Crying Wolf: A Comment on *Roe v. Wade*," *Yale Law Journal* 82 (1973): 923.

13. Raoul Berger, *Government by Judiciary: The Transformation of the Fourteenth Amendment* (Cambridge, MA: Harvard University Press, 1977).

14. Marian Faux, *Roe v. Wade* (New York: New American Library, 1988) 11-12, 224.

15. Clement E. Vose, *Caucasians Only: The Supreme Court, The NAACP, and The Restrictive Covenant Cases* (Berkeley, CA: University of California Press, 1959); Mark Tushnet, *The NAACP's Legal Strategy Against Segregation, 1925-50* (Chapel Hill, NC: University of North Carolina Press, 1987); Richard Kluger, *Simple Justice: The History of Brown v. Board of Education and Black America's Struggle for Equality* (New York: Knopf, 1976); Karen O'Connor, *Women's Organizations' Use of the Courts* (Lexington, MA: Lexington Press, 1980).

16. Austin Sarat and Stuart Scheingold, "Cause Lawyering and the Reproduction of Professional Authority," *Cause Lawyering: Political Commitments and Professional Responsibilities*, ed. Austin Sarat and Stuart Scheingold (New York: Oxford University Press, 1998) 7.

17. Carrie Menkel-Meadow, "The Causes of Cause Lawyering: Toward an Understanding of the Motivation and Commitment of Social Justices Lawyers," Sarat and Scheingold, *Cause Lawyering* 37.

18. Tatalovich and Daynes, "The Lowi Paradigm" 58-59.

19. Samuel Krislov, "The Amicus Curiae Brief: From Friendship to Advocacy," *Yale Law Journal* 72 (1963): 694-721. A contrary view is expressed by Nathan Hakman, "Lobbying the Supreme Court: An Appraisal of Political Science 'Folklore,'" *Fordham Law Review* 35 (1966): 15-50. A review of behavioural literature on amicus activity is provided by Lee Epstein, "Courts and Interest Groups," *The American Courts: A Critical Assessment*, ed. John B. Gates and Charles A. Johnson (Washington, DC: CQ Press, 1991) 335-71.

20. See Timothy O'Neill, *Bakke and the Politics of Equality: Friends and Foes in the Classroom of Litigation* (Middletown, CT: Wesleyan University Press, 1985).

21. "The *Webster Amicus Curiae* Briefs: Perspectives on the Abortion Controversy and the Role of the Supreme Court," Symposium Issue, *American Journal of Law and Medicine* 15: 156. Tatalovich and Daynes, "The Lowi Paradigm" 56.

22. Cyril C. Means, Jr., "The Phoenix of Abortional Freedom: Is a Penumbral or Ninth Amendment Right About to Arise from the Nineteenth-Century Legislative Ashes of a Fourteenth Century Common Law Liberty?," *New York Law Forum* 17 (1971): 335-410. The allegation that Means's design was to influence the justices is made by Robert A. Destro, "Abortion and the Constitution: The Need for a Protective Amendment," *University of California Law Review* 63 (September 1975): 1268. Also, Jack E. Rossotti, Laura Natelson, and Raymond Tatalovich, "Nonlegal Advice: The *Amicus* Briefs in *Webster v. Reproductive Health Services*," *Judicature* 81 (November-December, 1997): 118-21.

23. William P. McLauchlan, "Supreme Court Abortion Policy: The Selection and Development of a Social Policy," paper Presented to the Annual Meeting of the Midwest Political Science Association, 1987, Chicago, IL.

24. Richard Cortner, "Strategies and Tactics of Litigants in Constitutional Cases," *Journal of Public Law* 36 (1968): 287-307. The increase in *amicus curiae* filings before the Supreme Court was greater for "underdogs" than "upperdogs" when Earl Warren was Chief Justice, according to Robert C. Bradley and Paul Gardner, "Underdogs, Upperdogs and the Use of the Micus Brief: Trends and Explanations," *The Justice System Journal* 10 (1985): 78-96.

25. Jonathan D. Casper, *Lawyers Before the Warren Court: Civil Liberties and Civil Rights, 1957-1966* (Urbana, IL: University of Illinois Press, 1972) 20.

26. Lee Epstein, *Conservatives in Court* (Knoxville, TN: University of Tennessee Press, 1985) 10. Among the studies cited by Epstein were: Jack Greenberg, *Judicial Process and Social Change: Constitutional Litigation* (St. Paul, MN: West, 1977); David Manwaring, *Render Unto Caesar: The Flag Salute Controversy* (Chicago: University of Chicago Press, 1962); O'Connor, *Women's Organizations' Use of the Courts*; Frank J. Sorauf, *The Wall of Separation: The Constitutional Politics of Church and State* (Princeton, NJ: Princeton University Press, 1976).

27. Tatalovich and Daynes, "The Lowi Paradigm" 60.

28. Byron W. Daynes, "Pornography: Freedom of Expression or Societal Degradation?," Tatalovich and Daynes, *Social Regulatory Policy* 62, 64.

29. Sorauf 30. The three groups that "dominated separationist activity in these [67] cases" (31)—the ACLU, American Jewish Congress, and Other Americans United for Separation of

Church and State—"enjoyed a markedly greater success in the United States Supreme Court than did other plaintiffs" (127).

30. Matthew C. Moen, *The Christian Right and Congress* (Tuscaloosa, AL: University of Alabama Press, 1989) 12; also see Mark Rozell and Clyde Wilcox, *Second Coming: The New Christian Right in Virginia Politics* (Baltimore, MD: Johns Hopkins University Press, 1996); Leo Pfeffer, "Amici in Church-State Litigation," 44 *Law and Contemporary Problems* (1981): 83-110; Gregg Ivers, "Please, God, Save This Honorable Court: The Emergence of the Conservative Religious Right," *The Interest Group Connection: Electioneering, Lobbying, and Policymaking in Washington*, ed. Paul Hernson, et al. (Chatham, NJ: Chatham House Publishers, 1998), 289-301; Dennis R. Hoover, "Conservative Religious Interest Groups and the Court: Comparing Canada," paper presented at Annual Meeting, Midwest Political Science Association, Chicago, IL, 1999; Stephen P. Brown, "The New Christian Right, Religious Liberty, and the Supreme Court," paper presented at Annual Meeting, Southern Political Science Association, Norfolk, VA, 1998; Keven R. den Dulk, "Representing Christ in Court," paper presented at the Crossroads Conference, Jackson, TN, 1998.

31. Epstein, *Conservatives in Court* 110; also Karen O'Connor and Lee Epstein, "The Rise of Conservative Interest Group Litigation," *Journal of Politics* 45 (May, 1983): 478-89.

32. Susan M. Olson, "Interest Group Litigation in Federal District Court: Beyond the Political Disadvantage Theory," *Journal of Politics* 52 (August, 1990): 856, 858.

33. Saul Brenner and Harold J. Spaeth, *Stare Indecisis: The Alteration of Precedent on the Supreme Court, 1946-1992* (New York: Cambridge University Press, 1995) 110-11; Jeffrey Segal and Harold J. Spaeth, *The Supreme Court and the Attitudinal Model* (Cambridge, UK: Cambridge University Press, 1993). An empirical study that found support for both the legal and behavioural models is Tracey E. George and Lee Epstein, "On the Nature of Supreme Court Decision Making," *American Political Science Review* 86 (June, 1992): 323-37.

34. "Hawaii's Ban on Gay Marriage," *New York Times* 20 December 1999: A38.

35. Carey Goldberg, "Vermont's High Court Extends Full Rights to Same-Sex Couples," *New York Times* 21 December 1999: 1, A23.

36. John F. Niblock, "Anti-Gay Initiatives: A Call for Heightened Judicial Scrutiny," *UCLA Law Review* 41 (1993): 159.

37. Rhonda R. Rivera, "Our Straight-Laced Judges: The Legal Position of Homosexual Persons In The United States," *The Hastings Law Journal* 30 (March 1979): 947, 949-51.

38. Vincent J. Samar, *The Right to Privacy: Gays, Lesbians, and the Constitution* (Philadelphia, PA: Temple University Press, 1991) 36.

39. Kevin Sack, "Georgia's High Court Voids Sodomy Law," *New York Times* 24 November 1998: A14.

40. "Gay Justice: Romer v. Evans," *The Nation* (June 10, 1996): 4.

41. A. Paul Pross, "Pressure Groups: Adaptive Instruments of Political Communication," *Pressure Group Behaviour in Canadian Politics*, ed. A. Paul Pross (Toronto: McGraw-Hill Ryerson, 1975) 18; Kenneth McNaught, "Political Trials and the Canadian Political Tradition," *Courts and Trials*, ed. Martin L. Friedland (Toronto: University of Toronto Press, 1975) 138.

42. Michael Mandel, *The Charter of Rights and the Legalisation of Politics in Canada* (Toronto: Wall and Thompson, 1989) 60. Mandell's counter-argument cautions social activists not to overestimate the power of Charter litigation because, though anti-democratic "both in form and in content," the effect of the Charter "has been to strengthen the already great inequalities in Canada" by having "weighed in on the side of power and ... undermined popular movements as varied as the anti-nuclear movement, the labour movement, the nationalist movement in Quebec, the aboriginal peoples' movement and the women's movement" (4).

43. Peter H. Russell, "The Growth of Canadian Judicial Review and the Commonwealth and American Experiences," Jackson and Tate 37.

44. Morton and Knopff 13.

45. Peter H. Russell, "Reform's Judicial Agenda," *Policy Options* 20 (April 1999): 12 ; Also see E. Preston Manning, "A 'B' for Prof. Russell," *Policy Options* 20 (April 1999): 15-16; and Peter H. Russell, "Prof. Russell Replies," *Policy Options* 20 (April 1999): 17-18.

46. Alan C. Cairns, "The Fragmentation of Canadian Citizenship," *Belonging: The Meaning and Future of Canadian Citizenship*, ed. William Kaplan (Montreal and Kingston: McGill-Queens University Press, 1993) 208.

47. Leslie A. Pal, "Advocacy Organizations and Legislative Politics" 148.

48. LEAF's success rate was calculated in Lori Hausegger, "The Impact of Interest Groups on Judicial Decision Making: A Comparison of Women's Groups in the US and Canada," paper presented to Annual Meeting, American Political Science Association, Boston, 1998. The 23 LEAF facta are catalogued in Women's Legal Education and Action Fund, *Equality and the Charter: Ten Years of Feminist Advocacy Before the Supreme Court of Canada* (Toronto: Edmund Montgomery Publications, 1996).

49. Hoover and den Dulk 16.

50. Gregory Hein, "Interest Group Litigation and Canadian Democracy," *Choices* 6 (March 2000) 19; frequencies of litigation in Figure 1, p. 9; see also 13-14, 16. To be precise, the ratio between 180,000 corporations and their 468 cases is 1:385 whereas the 1,600 groups comprising the judicial democrats litigated 234 cases, or a ratio of 1:7.

51. Morton and Knopff 55.

52. F.L. Morton, *Pro-Choice vs. Pro-Life: Abortion and the Courts in Canada* (Norman, OK: University of Oklahoma Press, 1992) 102. See Kenneth Swan, "Intervention and Amicus Curiae Status in Charter Litigation," *Charter Cases 1986-1987*, Colloquium of the Canadian Bar Association, ed. Gerald Beaudoin (Montreal: Les Editions Yvon Blais, 1987) ; Stephen Bindman, "Door Opens: Supreme Court Lets Groups Intervene," *Ottawa Citizen* 9 March 1987: B8. Both these sources are provided in Hoover, "Conservative Religious Interest Groups and the Courts: Comparing Canada."

53. Epp 765-79.

54. Susan Gluck Mezey, "Civil Law and Common Law Traditions: Judicial Review and Legislative Supremacy in West Germany and Canada," *International and Comparative Law Quarterly* 32 (1983): 700, 704, n. 103.

55. Mollie Dunsmuir, "Abortion: Constitutional and Legal Developments," Current Issue Review, 89-10E (Ottawa: Library of Parliament, Research Branch, Law and Government Division), rev. 3 September 1991: 11.

56. Russell, "The Growth of Canadian Judicial Review and the Commonwealth and American Experiences," 36. Polling showing popular support for the legitimacy of judicial review are discussed in P. Sniderman, J. Fletcher, P.H. Russell, and P. Tetlock, "Political Culture and The Problem of Double Standards: Mass and Elite Attitudes Toward Language Rights in the Canadian Charter of Rights," *Canadian Journal of Political Science* 22 (1989): 259-84. Also see Paul M. Sniderman, Joseph F. Fletcher, Peter H. Russell, and Philip E. Tetlock, *The Clash of Rights* (New Haven, CT: Yale University Press, 1996) 159-68. Canadians "prefer courts rather than parliaments to have the final say by a margin of two to one" (164).

57. Russell, "The Growth of Canadian Judicial Review and the Commonwealth and American Experiences" 35.

58. Morton and Knopff 72, 14. On 43-44 they explain that "the Trudeau government and the Parliamentary Committee on the Constitution rejected repeated requests by gay rights activists to insert protection for sexual orientation in the Charter.

59. C. Michael MacMillan and Raymond Tatalovich, "Judicial Activism vs. Restraint: The Role of the Highest Courts in Official Language Policy in Canada and the United States," *American Review of Canadian Studies* (forthcoming).

60. C. Michael MacMillan, *The Practice of Language Rights in Canada* (Toronto: University of Toronto Press, 1998) 108-17. Others forcefully argue that the Supreme Court actually aggravated federal-provincial relations by its ruling and harmed efforts to bring about a constitutional resolution of the long-standing issue of national unity. See Morton and Knopff 160-62.

61. Quoted in Tamar Lewin, "Canada Court Says Pornography Harms Women and Can Be Barred," *New York Times* 28 February 1992: 1, B9.

62. Quoted in Nadine Strossen, *Defending Pornography: Free Speech, Sex, and the Fight for Women's Rights* (New York: Scribner, 1995) 229.

63. Stone, "Abstract Constitutional Review and Policy Making in Western Europe," 41, 42.

64. Kenneth M. Holland, "Judicial Activism in Western Europe," *Handbook of Global Legal Policy*, ed. Stuart S. Nagel (New York: Marcel Dekker, 2000) 179.

65. Holland, "Judicial Activism in Western Europe" 203, 198.

66. Brian Girvin, "Ireland and the European Union: The Impact of Integration and Social Change on Abortion Policy," Githens and Stetson 167.

67. Holland, "Judicial Activism in Western Europe" 184, 196, 192.

68. Holland, "Judicial Activism in Western Europe" 185-86. On Canada, see Sniderman, Fletcher, Russell and Tetlock 159-68. Also Joseph F. Fletcher and Paul Howe, "Public Opinion and the Courts," *Choices* 6 (May 2000).

69. Holland 186.

70. Kim Lane Scheppele, "Constitutionalizing Abortion," Githens and Stetson 38.

71. Mezey 697-98.

72. Christine Landfried, "Constitutional Review and Legislation in the Federal Republic of Germany," *Constitutional Review and Legislation: An International Comparison*, ed. Christine Landfried (Baden-Baden: Nomos Verlagsgesellschaft, 1988) 148.

73. Holland, "The Courts in the Federal Republic of Germany" 100; Holland, "Judicial Activism in Western Europe" 186.

74. Scheppele 39.

75. Conradt 33, 246.

76. "Same-Sex Partners Win Legal Status in Germany," *New York Times* 2 August 2001: A3.

77. Press Release No 1/2000, Judgment of the Court of Justice in Case c-285/98, *Tanja Kreil v. Federal Republic of Germany* (January 11, 2000). Also see Roger Boyes, "German Army Rewrites Rules as Women Enlist for Combat," *The Times* 3 January 2001.

78. Stone, "Abstract Constitutional Review and Policy Making in Western Europe" 44.

79. Holland, "Judicial Activism in Western Europe" 185.

80. Stetson 286.

81. Stone, *The Birth of Judicial Politics in France* 77-78.

82. Holland, "Judicial Activism in Western Europe" 185, 184.

83. Holland, "Judicial Activism in Western Europe" 202.

84. Sarah Lyall, "209 Years Later, the English Get American-Styled Bill of Rights," *New York Times* 2 October 2000: A3.

85. Sarah Lyall, "Britain Quietly Says It's Time To Adopt a Bill of Rights," *New York Times* 3 October 1999: 6.

86. Clive Walker and Russell L. Weaver, "The United Kingdom Bill of Rights 1998: The Modernisation of Rights in the Old World," *University of Michigan Journal of Law Reform* 33 (Summer 2000): 506-08.

87. Robert Wintemute, *Sexual Orientation and Human Rights* (New York: Oxford University Press, 1995) 93-95.

88. *Case of A. v. The United Kingdom* (100/1997/884/1096), 23 September 1998. This case is discussed within the larger jurisprudence in Susan H. Bitensky, "Spare the Rod, Embrace our Humanity: Toward a New Legal Regime Prohibiting Corporal Punishment of Children," *University of Michigan Journal of Law Reform* 31 (Winter 1998): 353-474; Tania Schriwer, "Establishing an Affirmative Governmental Duty to Protect Children's Rights: The European Court of Human Rights as a Model for the United States Supreme Court," *University of San Francisco Law Review* 34 (Winter 2000): 379-408.

89. Jill Lawless, "Britain Keeps Law that Allows Spanking," *Chicago Tribune* 9 November 2001: 27.

90. Warren Hoge, "Europe Court Faults Trial of Boy Killers of Toddler," *New York Times* 17 December 1999: A6.

91. Read and Marsh, "Homosexuality" 37, 38-39.

92. Read and Marsh, "Homosexuality" 37.

93. Sarah Lyall, "British, Under European Ruling, End Ban on Openly Gay Soldiers," *New York Times* 13 January 2000: 1, A16.

94. Walker and Weaver 533-34.

95. Suzanne Kapner, "Britain's Legal Barriers Start to Fall," *New York Times* 4 October 2000: W1.

96. Kenneth M. Holland, "Introduction," *Judicial Activism in Comparative Perspective*, ed. Kenneth M. Holland (New York: St. Martin's Press, 1991) 2.

97. Landfried, "Constitutional Review and Legislation in the Federal Republic of Germany" 163-64.

98. Stone, "Abstract Constitutional Review and Policy Making in Western Europe" 55.

99. Scheppele 49-50.

100. See Mary Ann Glendon, *Abortion and Divorce in Western Law* (Cambridge, MA: Harvard University Press, 1987); Martha A. Derthick, *Up in Smoke: From Legislation to Litigation in Tobacco Politics* (Washington, DC: CQ Press, 2002).

7

Bypassing Elites:
Morality Policy by Plebiscite

Political elites occasionally will socialize conflict over morality policy by deferring hard choices to the electorate in popular plebiscites, but the more typical use of referendums is by single-issue activists who want to bypass the political establishment. One would expect that, with exceptions, parliamentarians would not encourage mechanisms of direct democracy designed to weaken representative government, although the governing party may seek to avoid policy responsibility or to engender political legitimacy on highly controversial issues. Gordon Smith says a favoured approach to classifying referendums is according to their scope and subject: decisions on the constitutional make-up of the regime, decisions on public policy, and "the resolution of 'moral' issues which have a social rather than a political salience."[1] Nearly a quarter-century ago Butler and Ranney concluded that—with the exception of Switzerland—European "referendums are held infrequently, usually only when government thinks they are likely to provide a useful ad hoc solution to a particular constitutional or political problem or to set the seal of legitimacy on a change of regime."[2]

More recently Bogdanor sees the increased use of referenda across Western Europe as a byproduct of party systems that are so grounded in class politics that they are unable to represent or resolve new postindustrial issues. Bogdanor recalls the seminal work on party systems by Lipset and Rokkan (see Chapter 4), whose "freezing hypothesis" claimed that the party systems of the 1960s reflected those social cleavages of the 1920s. Bogdanor observes that Western European referendums are largely used for constitutional and territorial issues or "issues of conscience ... [that] cut across the party system" and, "although they arouse deep feelings among many voters, they are not generally the most salient issues in general elections," with the consequence that they "have proved especially difficult for governing parties to resolve." One answer to this political dilemma is direct democracy.[3]

Actually the United States is one of only five Western democracies that has never held a national referendum,[4] but is unparalleled in its use of state and local referendums and popular initiatives. At the turn of the twentieth century the Progressives championed the referendum and popular initiative as methods of ending boss domination of parties, restoring popular democracy, and enacting programs to remedy social and economic ills. But times change, and what was envisioned as empowering Left-oriented causes has been expropriated by conservatives to challenge the liberal agenda of political elites and to reaffirm grass-roots sentiment in morality policy.

Direct Democracy in the United States

Mechanisms for direct democracy were embraced most quickly by western states during the Progressive Era.[5] Currently 22 states—17 of them west of the Mississippi River—allow the initiative and the *popular* referendum. The popular referendum allows the people through petition to require that a bill passed by the legislature be submitted to the voters for approval or rejection, whereas the *legislative* referendum is a proposition—for example, an amendment to the state constitution—submitted by a government agency like the state legislature to the voters. Mississippi and Florida permit the initiative only, whereas Kentucky, Maryland, and New Mexico authorize the popular referendum but not the initiative. An "initiative" permits activists to mount a petition drive in order to get the requisite number of signatures for putting an issue on the ballot, thus bypassing government elites. "There has been a resurgence of the use of the initiative since the mid-1970s," says David Magleby, as indicated by his statistics showing an annual average of 22 ballot propositions during 1970-99 as compared to 13 for 1900-69.[6]

Californians seem especially inclined to use popular plebiscites to enact morality policy. In the 1920s they prohibited Japanese from owning land and, in 1964, voted to repeal an open housing law for minorities enacted by the state legislature.[7] Seemingly, Californians have a political fetish to approve hard-nosed policies on crime. In 1978 they expanded the death penalty; in 1982 a winning initiative gave prosecutors access to pretrial evidence and curbed defendants' rights at preliminary hearings; in 1994 the infamous "three strikes" law was approved, subjecting felons convicted the third time to a mandatory minimum sentence of 25 years to life. This trend continued in 2000 when voters approved Proposition 18, extending capital punishment to arson and kidnapping cases, and Proposition 19, which increased penalties to life imprisonment for the second-degree murder of certain law enforcement personnel.

In recent memory, so it seems, not a year goes by without several states holding referendums on gun control, animal welfare and hunting, environmentalism, abortions, or some other variety of morality policy. In California, the state with more referendums than any other, patterns for 1912-76 show that issues of "public morality"—notably liquor, gambling, boxing, and racing—tied for second place (with revenue referendums) at 19 per cent, just under those initiatives on governmental and political process (21 per cent), whereas "environmental protection, land use" were only 3 per cent of the total 155 ballot propositions. An update for the 399 California ballot initiatives during 1978-92 found that propositions involving "public morality" were fourth-ranked (15 per cent), but now there were three times as many "environmental or land use" (9 per cent) initiatives. These trends for California are comparable to what Austin Ranney uncovered for 1,224 ballot initiatives across the United States from 1898 to 1976—initiatives over public morality totaled 171 or 14 per cent.[8]

David Magleby argues that no ideology monopolizes the use of initiatives: "Issues pushed by conservatives include tax reduction, opposition to expanding the rights of homosexuals, and school choice. Liberals have sponsored measures to protect the environment, to preserve abortion rights, and to limit the death penalty."[9] Note that three of Magleby's examples are pure morality policies, though he did not determine the win-loss record of liberal and conservative ballot initiatives. Austin Ranney made an admittedly impressionistic attempt to answer this question based on 43 referendums in six topic areas. By his scorecard, 12 right-to-work referendums (which unions oppose) showed an even split between conservative and liberal outcomes, as did six anti-nuclear power initiatives. Liberals dominated on tax referendums, but conservatives prevailed on all five aimed at prohibiting racial discrimination, on all four to restore capital punishment, and on three that tried to enact abortions on demand. These patterns, observed Ranney, were "consistent with the widely held view that American voters are predominantly liberal on economic questions and conservative on social issues."[10]

But what about today, a quarter-century after Ranney wrote? To assess the ideological impact of plebiscites in contemporary America, we categorized all referendums dealing with morality policy for the period 1980-2000. In total, 22 states held 166 referendums on 12 narrowly defined morality politics over those two decades (Table 7.1). Since a total of 635 referendums appeared on the ballot of these states, the 26 per cent represented by these referendums should be considered a conservative estimate since our statistics exclude other issues (race relations, criminal justice) that would quality. Surely one in four is much higher than what we would expect to find during the early years of the twentieth century. Overall, liberals were able to turn aside conservative challenges on 85 votes, but the conservatives prevailed on another 81.

TABLE 7.1

Outcome of State Referenda on Morality Policies
in the United States, 1980-2000

	Liberal Vote	Conservative Vote[a]
Abortion	13	3
Affirmative Action	0	2
Alcoholic Beverages	2	4
Animal Rights	17	12
Drugs	12	4
English Language	0	9
Gambling	24	29
Gun Control	3	4
Homosexuality	6	8
Obscenity	5	0
Physician-Assisted Suicide	1	4
Sunday "Blue" Laws	2	2
	85	81

[a] These statistics are not the percentages which approved or disapproved the referendums because, for example, a majority approving an anti-gay rights proposition would be coded as a "conservative" vote just as a majority disapproving an anti-gay rights proposition would be coded as a "liberal" vote. Thus, a "liberal" vote was one supporting abortion, affirmative action, alcoholic beverages, animal rights, decriminalization of illicit drugs, gambling, gun controls, homosexuality, and physician-assisted suicide, and one opposing obscenity regulations, Sunday "blue" laws, and English-only language laws.

Source: Tabulated from the historical archives of the Initiative and Referendum Institute, Washington, DC. These referendums are the universe of cases on 12 morality policies in the 22 states where they occurred.

However, there is tremendous variation in success rates depending upon the issue. Fifty-nine per cent of these referendums involved gambling, animal rights, and abortion. Liberals prevailed against efforts to tighten abortions or abortion funding 81 per cent of the time, safeguarded animal rights by regulating trapping and hunting (a 59 per cent victory margin), and loosened laws against illicit drugs or legalized marijuana for medical use (winning 75 per cent of the votes). They also prevailed on the few referendums on obscenity, holding state censorship at bay. Similarly, liberals evenly split the four votes on "blue" laws that regulate Sunday sales and employment and did reasonably well on gambling referendums (winning 45 per cent), which often authorized state-sponsored lotteries.

Apparently a referendum is the political modus operandi when a state lottery is contemplated. Like prohibition, gambling illustrates the evolution of morality policy from sinful behaviour, once outlawed by most states, to a recreational lifestyle with potential to enhance state treasuries. Clearly, the political establishment often chooses the risk-adverse strategy. Although the lottery dates back to the American colonies, public outcry over fraudulent gambling enterprises and agitation by church leaders led to a political backlash. "By January 1, 1894, the legal lottery in the United States was no more. In addition to the federal laws, thirty-five states had constitutional prohibitions and most of the remainder had strong statutes against such schemes. Thus, a device that once could claim country-wide acceptance was nationally denounced and its supporters muted by public opinion."[11] Six decades later, with renewed acceptance of legalized gambling, those constitutionally enacted prohibitions meant that most states seeking to restore lotteries could not resort to statutory law. Between 1964 and 1988 there were 30 referendums on establishing state lotteries—all but two won. As Clotfelter and Cook explain, not only did the "constitutional bars against lotteries in most states" necessitate the use of referendums or initiatives, but sometimes "legislatures were only too happy to pass the buck to the voters rather than take full responsibility for bringing a lottery into being."[12]

LEGALIZATION OF GAMBLING AND DRUGS

At first glance, gambling seems to be illustrate what Ken Meier calls a "one-sided" morality policy, certainly where public attitudes—if not elite opinion—is concerned. Except for 1938 when 51 per cent opposed state lotteries, national polls have shown that a plurality—and typically since 1964 a majority—supported government-sponsored lotteries. Yet, a "fundamental paradox" affects the politics of gambling, because "objections remain. Moral, mostly religious, opposition, where it exists, is uncompromising." Clotfelter and Cook add that "opposition to gambling continues to be part of the doctrine of mainstream Protestant churches in America," such as Methodists, Mormons, Baptists, and Lutherans for whom, "[a]lthough gambling is not explicitly forbidden in the Bible, religious opponents charge that gambling is based on selfishness, that it undermines the stewardship of resources, and that, by relying on chance, it denies providential control over human life." What we have with gambling is a classic example of an "intense minority" against a more apathetic majority, which explains the risk-adverse behaviour of political elites. In concluding their study, Clotfelter and Cook observe that "[i]n virtually every state it was the lottery's opponents, not its supporters, who were most outspoken in debate or who counted major political leaders as allies. With remarkable regularity state governors and legislators have opposed lotteries, only to yield in the end to majority opinion."[13]

By the end of the twentieth century, 37 states and the District of Columbia had established lotteries, yet, due to the reluctance of public officials to lead the charge, several were established by popular initiatives. Consider Louisiana, where three referendums were held during the 1990s: in 1990 its voters ended the constitutional prohibition on lotteries, and in 1996 there were two ballot measures, one to require voter approval for any expansion of gambling and the other to gain approval or disapproval for gambling within each parish (county).

The most widely publicized fights over lotteries in recent years involved South Carolina and Alabama, since both elected Democratic governors pledged to establish state lotteries and earmark those funds for educational reforms. After incumbent Republican Governor David Beasley of South Carolina was upset in 1998 by Democrat Jim Hodges, who had steadfastly campaigned for a lottery, many Republican legislators shifted from opposition to allowing the voters to decide the issue. South Carolinians agreed with Hodges by approving a state lottery in 2000, but the best-laid plans of Alabama's newly elected Democratic governor, Donald Siegelman, were upset by voters who cast 55 per cent of their ballots against the proposed state lottery. Alabama voter turnout was higher than normal, and the churches were unified. "Even the abortion issue—the sanctity of human life—has not come as close to bringing denominations together," said Reverend Joe Bob Mizzell of the Alabama Baptist Convention.[14]

More controversial than gambling today is the legalization of certain drugs. In defiance of federal and state authorities, by the end of 2001 voters in Alaska, Arizona, California, Colorado, Maine, Nevada, Oregon, and Washington, as well as the District of Columbia, had voted to legalize the medical use of marijuana. "In two states, Arizona and Oregon, people overthrew the politicians on drugs," said Sam Vagenas who led the movement in Arizona. "This is the biggest grass-roots movement since term limits."[15] Voters reversed laws enacted by the Arizona legislature the previous year that had gutted successful marijuana referendums in 1996. Oregon voters also nullified the action of their state legislature which, the year before, had imposed criminal penalties for marijuana possession, thus restoring marijuana's post-1973 legal status as a misdemeanour as well as legalizing its medical use. Groups called "Free Hemp in Alaska" and "Hemp 2000" were the leading advocates for Alaska's campaign, and "Californians for Compassionate Use" had authored Proposition 215, which California voters approved in 1996.

AFFIRMATIVE ACTION AND ENGLISH-ONLY PROGRAMS

On the other hand, conservatives won both votes rejecting state-sanctioned affirmative action programs (Table 7.1), and their victory in California (the other being Washington) sent a signal with powerful national political implications. The 58 per cent of Washington voters who said yes to Proposition 200 in 1998 were asked whether government should be "prohibited from discriminating or granting preferential treatment based on race, sex, color, ethnicity or national origin" in public employment, education, and contracting. Thus, Washington joined California in enacting into law a wide-ranging, anti-affirmative action policy. "It means that America is taking a great step forward to looking beyond race and minimizing its importance, rather than dwelling on it and magnifying its importance," argued John Carlson who headed the initiative drive. "It also, I think, will hasten the transition of affirmative action from a program based on race and ethnicity and occasionally gender to a program that is based on people's circumstances."[16]

Other votes with immense political significance were the referendums that either established English as the "official" languages of certain states or abolished bilingual education programs. The use of popular initiatives to codify "English-Only" language laws in Florida, California, Arizona, and Colorado—all with sizeable Latino populations—was a deliberate strategy in the face of resistance by the state legislatures. In other words, Latinos had the institutional means to block those enactments "only when [English-Only] policy advocates operated in a constrained political environment in which they could not circumvent legislative channels."[17] This relationship between direct democracy and morality policy has been empirically verified. In determining whether or not majority support for "official" English laws is translated into public policy, one vital factor "is the opportunity to bypass the state legislature and let the voters decide on the proposals for themselves. This opportunity matters more than other factors" such as the partisan composition of the state legislature, economic conditions, and the ideological bent of the state. And even though most states did not codify English by plebiscite, "the mere existence of the opportunity [for referendums] makes passage more likely, especially as the percentage of foreign-born residents increases."[18]

All these "English-Only" grass-roots movements by Anglos were labelled racist by the Latino opposition, but the tenor of this debate changed dramatically when Californians approved by 61 per cent a 1998 referendum—spearheaded by a wealthy Anglo but with backing from Hispanics—to end bilingual education and to mainstream Latinos in English immersion classes. A similar measure passed in Arizona in 2000; curiously, this referendum ending bilingual education was approved by 63 per cent whereas the hotly debated 1988 "official" English initiative barely passed with 51 per cent.

PHYSICIAN-ASSISTED SUICIDE

Conservative voters disallowed physician-assisted suicide (PAS) in 80 per cent of those referendums (only Oregon voted to legalize PAS) and emerged victorious by two to one on six referendums regulating alcoholic beverages, but did slightly worse defusing gun controls and defending the right to bear arms or in sidetracking gay rights and same-sex initiatives (both at 57 per cent). Since PAS and homosexuality reflect the latest wave of morality politics, both deserve further elaboration.

Advocates of physician-assisted suicide "have sought alternative institutions to achieve their goals, notably the popular initiative and the courts."[19] However, unlike other civil rights issues, such efforts to bypass the legislative branch also failed in courts of law (see Chapter 6) and public opinion. In 1988 the Hemlock Society and its allies tried, but lacked the necessary signatures, to put its Humane and Dignified Death Act on the California ballot, and later such initiatives were rejected by the voters of Washington (1991, by 54 per cent), Michigan (1998), and California (1998). Washington's Initiative 119 originated with activists who were frustrated when its "conservative legislature refused to respond to the health-care community's decade-long lobbying effort to amend the state's 1979 Natural Death Act with language that clarified the conditions under which physicians may withhold or withdraw medical treatment in the event of terminal illness."[20] Success finally came in Oregon when the Death With Dignity Act (Measure 6) barely passed in 1994 with a 51 per cent majority, only to be immediately enjoined by a state court. In 1997 Oregon voters reaffirmed their original decision by refusing to repeal Measure 6 by a whopping 60 per cent margin in a referendum ordered by the state legislature.

GAY RIGHTS

Attacking homosexuality at the ballot box is stock-in-trade of the Christian Right, because political elites are more likely to be persuaded by civil rights arguments, whereas citizen opinion is shaped more by lifestyle concerns. Analysis by Haider-Markel and Meier indicates that anti-gay initiatives exemplify morality politics because they are "partisan, seek nonincremental solutions, focus on deeply held values, and flourish in areas with competitive political parties."[21] Moreover, Donovan and Bowler do not anticipate "motivations based on self-interest to be a major factor structuring voting on anti-gay initiatives" except for gays and lesbians, that is, because for most vot-ers "changing laws dealing with the civil rights extended to gays and lesbians represent a policy that is unlikely to alter the status quo in a manner that is immediately perceptible to them." Consequently, "instrumental motivations ... are not likely to be analogous to vote motivations on other material issues" like spending and taxation.[22]

The decade of the 1990s witnessed "an upswing in the number of state-lev-el ballot issues addressing the rights of homosexuals," notably in the West.[23] In 1992 Colorado voters approved Amendment Two that overturned three local anti-discrimination ordinances that covered gays, a decision that was reversed by the American Supreme Court (see Chapter 6). However, in 1998 the anti-gay trend continued with Coloradans refusing to give homosexuals protection against discrimination. The "tools of direct democracy have been the OCA's [Oregon Citizen's Alliance] weapons of choice" in its state-wide culture war, beginning in 1986 when OCA's Measure 8 successfully repealed the executive order by Governor Neil Goldschmidt prohibiting discrimination in state em-ployment based on sexual orientation.[24] However, Oregonians subsequently rejected anti-gay initiatives in 1992 (Measure 9) and 1994 (Measure 13). Defeat also followed such attempts in Idaho in 1994 (Proposition One) and Maine in 1995 (Question One). Yet, Maine voters in 1998 did repeal a law that added sexual orientation to the state civil rights law, and Washington voters in 1997 defeated a statewide initiative to extend such protections to gays and lesbians. The victory of Amendment Two in Colorado was not much more lopsided (55.6 per cent) than the losing margins in Idaho (50.4 per cent), Maine (53.3 per cent), and Oregon in 1994 (51.6 per cent), to show that a sizeable anti-gay sentiment existed in all these states. Indeed, one year after the 44 to 56 per cent loss statewide by Measure 9 in Oregon, anti-gay activists put similar initiatives on the ballot in 18 Oregon cities, with all but one being approved.[25]

Nor is anti-gay agitation limited to the state governments. Between 1974 and 1993, the National Gay and Lesbian Task Force reported that anti-gay ini-tiatives were approved in nine of nine counties and in 35 of 45 cities where they occurred.[26] On November 3, 1992, the day Colorado approved Amendment 2, other referendums aimed at repealing city laws banning discrimination against homosexuals were approved in Tampa, Florida but rejected in Portland, Maine. Recent trends indicate that the use of initiatives to repeal local anti-discrimination ordinances that include sexual preference "in the 1990s has increased over 400 per cent over the 1980s."[27] In shifting the policy venue, Steven Shaw explains, anti-gay initiatives are especially appealing for "the New Christian Right to bypass the political elite, most of whom were seen as foes in the movement's culture war."[28]

In 1993 the electorate of Cincinnati, Ohio voted 62 per cent in favour of Issue Three, an amendment to the city charter which read: "No special class status may be granted based upon sexual orientation, conduct or relationships." Thereupon, gay and lesbian groups sued in federal court, charging that Issue Three was discriminatory, and the trial judge agreed that the amendment infringed upon the fundamental rights of homosexuals to engage in the political process. This judgment came in mid-1994; subsequently, a federal Appeals Court upheld the referendum (and the American Supreme Court refused to review it; see Chapter 6). Cincinnati was a window of opportunity for anti-gay activists, as the language of Issue Three was used by petitioners in Kalamazoo and Traverse City, both in Michigan, who sought city charter amendments to prohibit any policy on "protected status" based on sexual orientation. Also on the November, 2001 ballot in Huntington Woods, Michigan, was the question of whether to reject an anti-discrimination ordinance adopted by its city council. "Politicians will cave in to pressure from homosexual activists, but when the issue is put to a vote of the people, in most cases it is soundly rejected," said Gary Glenn, president of the American Family Association of Michigan who helped organize those grass-roots movements.[29] In addition, Miami Beach voters were asked to decide whether unmarried partners of city employees should get medical benefits, and a proposal to amend the Houston city charter would prohibit providing benefits to unmarried partners of city employees.

Same-sex marriages are the latest twist in the struggle over gay rights. In the wake of a lower court ruling favouring same-sex unions in Hawaii, the majority of states passed laws prohibiting their legalization. A few acted through referendums, as did Hawaii when its voters authorized the state legislature to *overturn* the state high court ruling that had legalized same-sex marriages. Alaskans in 1998 voted 68 per cent for a state constitutional amendment that defines marriage as a union between one man and one woman. Even Californians in 2000 approved by a 61 per cent margin Proposition 22 that "only marriage between a man and a woman is valid or recognized in California," thus outlawing same-sex unions. In doing so, California joined the ranks of 34 other states which passed similar enactments banning same-sex marriages.

A promising study of referendum usage determined that 11 per cent of all ballot propositions before the voters of California, Colorado, and South Dakota over the past 34 years involved morality issues, only ranking behind governance or revenue/taxation issues in frequency. Unlike any other category of ballot proposition, however, 71 per cent of them were put before the voters through citizen initiatives, not by legislative action, and, significantly, 73 per cent of these citizen-initiated morality issues were "exclusive" policies that did not benefit the entire community. While the language of citizen-initiated referendums does not equivocate about intentions, those referendums referred by legislatures to the electorate, and which presumably resulted from the give-and-take of the lawmaking process, were more appealing, since many fewer citizen-initiated referendums were approved by the voters of those three states.[30]

THE CONFEDERATE FLAG DEBATE

The Confederate battle emblem that represented the South during the American Civil War precipitated a statewide referendum in Mississippi to resolve what had become a nasty political fight. To whites, the flag symbolized Southern heritage, to blacks slavery and racism. African-American activists demanded that Mississippi redesign its state flag, as did Georgia, to remove the prominently displayed "stars and bars." Previously the NAACP resorted to a boycott to force the South Carolina state legislature to move the Confederate banner from atop the state capitol, where it accompanied the state flag, to a less visible site on the grounds.[31]

It would have been an uphill battle to get the Mississippi legislature to abandon the existing state flag. What began the debate was a May 2000 ruling by the Mississippi Supreme Court that, although the legislature had designated the state flag with its Confederate emblem in 1894, that action had been inadvertently excluded from a 1906 codification of all state laws. This ruling ended an on-again, off-again lawsuit by the state NAACP that challenged the flag as violating the equal protection clause of the state constitution, and, though the high court effectively had ruled against the plaintiffs, that legal glitch offered the opportunity to scrap the old flag. Democratic Attorney General Mike Moore welcomed the chance to redesign the flag, but newly elected Democratic Governor Ronnie Musgrove did not act expeditiously. A day after the high court ruling, Musgrove announced the appointment of a 17-member, bi-racial commission to "take positive action," though he voiced no opinion either way. "Symbols mean a lot," Musgrove said. "They mean a lot to all of us. We want a good, open, honest discussion."[32]

The process was moved along by an October 2000 decision by a Hinds County circuit court judge, who agreed with a lawsuit filed by a member of the Sons of Confederate Veterans that Mississippi voters should be allowed to decide this issue by year's end. The governor's commission proposed a new design, with the "stars and bars" replaced by a red box with 20 stars to represent Mississippi's admission to the Union as the twentieth state, and recommended that the issue be put before the voters. Thus, the referendum was approved by the state legislature despite the opposition of all 10 black senators, who pointed out that, even should the new flag be adopted, the 1894 version would be designated an "historic" banner permissible to be displayed at city halls or county buildings. The referendum ploy removed this contentious debate from the legislative agenda, given the popularity of the existing state flag with large numbers of white Mississippians. Apparently the Confederate emblem was not all that distasteful to a sizeable minority of black voters, as reflected in the April 17, 2001 referendum when 65 per cent of Mississippians voted to retain the old flag. Nonetheless, the "threat" posed by a growing number of African-Americans (at nearly 40 per cent of Mississippi's population) played a role, as Orey calculated that white support for the Confederate flag was significantly greater in areas with high black concentrations.[33]

Referendums in Canada, Australia, and New Zealand

REFERENDUMS IN CANADA

Since Confederation, only three national referendums have been authorized by the governing party in Canada. One at the turn of the twentieth century involved the consummate morality policy of that day: prohibition of alcoholic beverages was decided by plebiscite in 1898. The question of military conscription was the subject of referendums in Canada during World War II (1942), in postwar New Zealand (1949), and in Australia twice during World War I (1916 and 1917). The third Canadian referendum, in 1992, was a nation-building device, pursuant to the Charlottetown Accord on changes to the proposed repatriated constitution, but it failed, and Quebec was not granted the "special status" it wanted among the 10 provinces. Nationwide plebiscites are very rare in Canada because neither the British North America Act of 1867 nor the Constitution of 1982 provided for them.

During the flag debate of 1964, the Conservative opposition advocated a national plebiscite to resolve the issue, a prospect not only highly unusual but also painful because "many Canadians recall[ed] the plebiscite of 1942 on conscription for overseas service," which "severely split" the country between French-speaking Quebec and the rest of English-speaking Canada. Those memories led the Liberal government to refer the flag problem instead to an all-party parliamentary committee for resolution.[34] Something akin to the Canadian flag debate occurred in Australia, when voters were authorized in 1977 to select a national song from among four alternatives, as well as amending the constitution. Given that "Advance, Australia Fair" nearly won a majority of votes (43.3 per cent), "[t]he subsequent general acceptance of the song makes it likely that should a replacement for the present national flag be proposed, that choice too would be put to a referendum."[35]

More typically, referendums have been authorized by subnational author-ities in Canada to resolve controversial public policies, including morality is-sues. Since 1867 there have been only 54 provincial referendums, though many more have been held by Canadian municipalities. One inventory of 25 provin-cial referendums held from 1892 through 1971 shows the predominance of one morality policy—20 involved the prohibition or regulation of liquor—and three more focused on daylight savings time.[36] An admittedly nonscientific survey of 91 Canadian communities found that more than one-fourth of the 450 local referendums during 1955-65 involved fluoridation of public water supplies, with others devoted to such morality policies as Sunday "blue laws," liquor control, and daylight savings time.[37]

Though ostensibly a public health issue, fluoridation had moralistic overtones that aroused serious episodes of community conflict in the United States at roughly the same time. They prompted American sociologist James Coleman to differentiate among community conflicts based on economics, power, or authority, and "area of life" issues, the latter involving "*cultural values or beliefs*" as illustrated by disputes over school desegregation. These reflected "two deeply felt beliefs—ingrained attitudes toward Negroes and ingrained attitudes toward equality of opportunity," while anti-fluoridation drives "apparently touched on values of individualism and anti-scientism in provoking the resistance which has occurred." The defeats of fluoridation ref-erendums during the early 1950s were accompanied by large voter turnouts, indicating to Coleman that voting was done by "a larger component of per-sons uninvolved in and unattached to community affairs," just as the Canadian experience led Hahn to similarly conclude that fluoridation "seemed to offer a prime example of referendums that may provoke an outburst of immediate protest."[38] Other sociologists confirmed Coleman's hypothesis that negative voting was symptomatic of alienation by the mass public—presumably from lower socioeconomic groups. The finding that opponents "have greater feel-ings of helplessness" than proponents led Gamson to infer that "fluoridation somehow symbolized the buffeting one takes in a society where not even the water one drinks is sacrosanct."[39] From another perspective, however, Mueller suggested that "people who might be called 'non-economic liberals' tend *slightly* to vote for fluoridation."[40]

More recently there has been another wave of referendum politics in Canadian localities, this time orchestrated by the Christian Right against video lottery terminals (VLTs). In 1998, the former Conservative Premier of Alberta, Peter Lougheed, was one of thousands who signed a petition urging the Calgary city council to hold a referendum on VLTs, and similar petition drives took place in various communities, including Edmonton. Moreover, the city or town councils of Red Deer, Lethbridge, and Lacombe (all in Alberta) also authorized such referendums. This episode of a grass-roots, single-issue movement, according to Tom Flanagan, began with evangelicals in a rural area west of Red Deer, Alberta, but expanded to include Roman Catholics, liberal Protestants, Muslims, Sikhs, and the provincial Liberal, New Democratic, and Social Credit parties.[41] Previously held plebiscites had defeated VLTs in Rocky Mountain House, Sylvan Lake, and Fort McMurray, but this time the VLTs fared much better. Calgary defeated the bid to remove them by a sizeable 58 to 42 per cent margin, as did Edmonton barely (50.1 per cent favoured keeping VLTs). Overall the anti-VLT lobby lost in all 11 cities where referendums were held and were victorious in only eight of the 25 towns that held plebiscites.[42] Based on these outcomes, while gambling may be a salient concern for conservative Christians, it seems no more a "hot button" issue for most Canadians than it is for most Americans. Anti-VLT sentiment spread eastward to New Brunswick, where the Progressive Conservative government fulfilled a campaign pledge made during the 1999 provincial elections to enact Bill 19, the Video Lottery Scheme Referendum Act. It mandated a plebiscite in May 2001, which also resulted in a victory for the VLT lobby.

REFERENDUMS IN AUSTRALIA AND NEW ZEALAND

Australia and New Zealand—though both Commonwealth nations and culturally similar—have diverged with respect to direct democracy. Australia, ranked third behind Switzerland and Italy in the use of national plebiscites, incorporated the referendum in its constitutional system, whereas New Zealand has not. From 1944 to 1996 Australia conducted 25 nationwide referendums; one (1949) focused on off-track betting while 16 others involved drinking hours and alcohol policy.[43] Early in twentieth-century Australia, except for the purpose of amending its constitution, "the referendum was used mainly to settle those same WASP (White, Anglo-Saxon, Protestant) and rural-flavored moral issues: curbing the drink trade and promoting religious instruction in state schools (which was possible in the absence of an American-style First Amendment)." More recently, in Australia the referendum "cause is championed most vigorously by small political parties, usually labeled by some single-issue derivation of direct democracy—Citizens Electoral Councils, Citizens Initiated Referendum Alliance, and the like—even though they may promote a wider range of far Right causes. In New Zealand, the right-wing Social Credit movement has endorsed the initiative, and the Left-Libertarian Values party has increased use of the referendum."[44]

Of the 41 territorial or state referendums within Australia during the period 1903-93, the majority involved morality policy. In the first three decades of the twentieth century, issues of prohibition, liquor licences or regulated bar closings were subjected to 10 referendums, and five more took place through 1969. During the 1910s three referendums in Victoria and one in Queensland focused on questions of religious instruction in schools. In 1965 a South Australia referendum establishing a state lottery was approved, and three years later voters in Tasmania supported a casino at Wrest Point. Most reoccurring in recent years have been referendums on authorizing daylight savings time: 1976 in New South Wales, 1992 in Queensland, 1982 in South Australia, and three times (1975, 1984, 1992) in Western Australia. All were defeated, except the votes in New South Wales and South Australia. Explains Colin Hughes: "The general empathy for those experiencing the hardships of rural life undercuts the vote for commercial interests and relaxation in the largest cities. The outcome is likely to be a conservative vote for 'God's time,' which is what some rural people call standard time."[45]

European Referendums

One must go beyond France, Germany, and the UK to other nations, notably Switzerland, Italy, and Ireland, to illustrate the use of popular plebiscites in Western Europe. An inventory of all national referendums during 1944-96 in 17 European democracies (not including Switzerland) numbered 114, of which 13 qualify as morality policy narrowly defined—drugs (one), divorce (three), abortion (six), and hunting (three)—in addition to others on nuclear power (five), decertifying an official church (one), and environmentalism (three). These 22 represent 19 per cent of the total, with two nations—Italy and Ireland—accounting for 58 per cent of all national referendums and 86 per cent of those concerning moral conflicts.[46]

THE UNITED KINGDOM, GERMANY, AND FRANCE

Since the UK has no written constitution, there is no provision for any plebiscite, and, though Parliament could authorize its use, a referendum would strike at the heart of parliamentary supremacy, something the British hold dear. Therefore, a national referendum was conducted only once, when Conservative Prime Minister Edward Health in 1975 submitted the question of Britain's membership in the European Community to the voters.

Article 146 of the German Basic Law required its constitutional ratification by popular vote, and one provision provides for referendums to reorganize the boundaries of the states (*Land*). Since World War II through 1992, therefore, Germany has conducted no nationwide referendum.

In France, Article 3 of the Constitution of the Fourth French Republic had limited referendum use to "constitutional matters," declaring that "in all other matters, [the people] shall exercise it [their sovereignty] through their deputies in the National Assembly." But the contrasting Article 3 of the Fifth French Republic Constitution states: "National sovereignty belongs to the people, which shall exercise it through its representatives and by means of referendums."[47] Although President Charles de Gaulle utilized the referendum to promote his constitutional agenda, since his death the referendum has been used rarely. Between 1958 and 1992 only eight issues were put before the French people, and none involved morality policy.[48]

ITALY

The situation is very different in Italy. Because the French Constitution of 1958 was a response to the parliamentary chaos that existed under the Fourth Republic, it authorized the referendum to legitimate strong leadership. In contrast, the Italian Constitution of 1947 was a reaction to fascism and, as such, "was essentially an appeal by the people *against* Parliament."[49] No European country other than Switzerland has had more referendums, mainly because the Italian people are able to trigger their use. Article 75 of the Italian Constitution allows 500,000 voters or five regional councils to demand an abrogative referendum on any law except those dealing with finances, pardons, and treaty ratification. Such a popular veto can negate the entire law or only clauses and articles. However, Article 75 requires that voting turnout equal 50 per cent-plus-one of the total electorate in order to be binding.

Of the 47 referendums held in Italy during the period 1944-97, morality policy was the focus of at least 12: divorce (1974), abortion (two votes in 1981), hunting (two votes in 1990 and one in 1997), decriminalization of soft drugs (1993), anti-nuclear power (three in 1987), and environmentalism (1990 and 1993).[50] Probably the best known was the 1974 divorce referendum. Although Article 75 of the 1947 Constitution authorized the "abrogative" referendum—one to repeal an existing law—the necessary implementing legislation was never approved by the dominant Christian Democrats, who were disinclined to undercut their own control over the legislative process. What caused its implementation in 1970 was a division in the Centre-Left coalition government over the issue of divorce. The Christian Democratic Party assented to a law reforming divorce but only if legislation implementing the abrogative referendum was adopted. It was, and the first abrogative referendum was held in 1974. However, the law survived as only 41 per cent backed its repeal.[51]

The threat of the referendum "had persuaded the government to pass a law liberalizing abortion in 1978," but it also prompted opposition groups to support two abrogative referendums in 1981, one to repeal the law and another to further liberalize the statute by removing the 18-year age limit. Both were defeated. Says Bogdanor, "[t]he main effect of the divorce and abortion referendums was to reveal the Italian electorate as both more secular and more liberal than had been generally suspected." In sum, the referendum in Italy "offered the electorate a new weapon" that "did not lie in the hands of the political parties to determine how it would be used, nor how often it would be used." Between 1970 and 1987 the Radical party directly appealed to the electorage to reconfigure Italian society, having promoted 27 of 33 referendums on various subjects, including abortion.[52]

IRELAND

From 1944 through 1996 Ireland held 19 national referendums, with seven involving morality policies: de-constitutionalizing the status of the Roman Catholic Church (1972), abortion (1968 and three votes in 1992), and divorce (1986 and 1995). One consequence of the Irish referendum has been to ensure "that the conservative moral values of the Irish electorate rather than the liberal values of the legislature have been enshrined in the Constitution." Concludes Bogdanor, the most contentious referendums "in Ireland have been those on moral issues," though less combative was the 1972 vote that deleted provisions in Article 44 of the constitution that symbolically conferred special status to the Roman Catholic Church (it won 84 to 16 per cent).[53] Much more conflictual was the 1983 abortion referendum that was designed to shift the prohibition of abortion from statutory law to constitutional law. It was orchestrated by the Pro-Life Amendment Campaign which, luckily for them, began shortly before the 1982 national elections and caused both major party leaders to agree to support a constitutional amendment banning abortion. Despite legal ambiguities in its language, the referendum endorsing the constitutional prohibition was approved by 67 per cent of the electorate.

However, the confused legalities set the stage for another battle over abortion a decade later. The wording of the 1983 referendum was: "The State acknowledges the right to life of the unborn and, with due regard to the equal right to life of the mother, guarantees in its laws to respect, and, as far as practicable, by its laws to defend and vindicate that right." In 1992, the case of *Attorney General v. X* showed that the 1983 language did not entirely prohibit abortion. X was a 14-year-old girl, allegedly raped, who wanted to travel to Britain for an abortion and who threatened suicide were she not allowed to do so. The Irish Supreme Court ruled that a serious threat to the woman was justification for her going elsewhere for the abortion or even getting an abortion in Ireland. That ruling complicated the task of Prime Minister Albert Reynolds and the governing Fianna Fail Party, who had to devise a way to decouple the abortion issue from a scheduled plebiscite on ratifying Ireland's admission into the European Union. In November 1992, five months after the Maastricht Treaty was ratified, Irish voters confronted three abortion referendums: the first overturned the high court ruling in the "X" Case and eliminated the threat of suicide as a justification for abortion; the second ensured the right to information about abortion; and the third permitted the right to travel abroad for an abortion. This time the Irish electorate rejected the restrictively worded first referendum (66 per cent against) but proceeded to approve the second (by 64 per cent) and the third (by 67 per cent).[54]

Yet 1992 hardly ended the abortion saga in Ireland, as the Dail (Parliament) debated the Twenty-Fifth Amendment of the constitution (Protection of Human Life in Pregnancy), Bill 2001, which sanctioned yet another referendum on abortion for March 6, 2002. Faced with upcoming national elections for the summer of 2002, Prime Minister Bertie Ahern was under heavy pressure to redeem his earlier pledge to sponsor a plebiscite aimed at making abortion unconstitutional, not just illegal, except where the woman's life is endangered. Its purpose was to remove the threat of suicide—used by the woman in the "X" case to justify her travelling to Britain for an abortion—as a loophole in the law. As in 1983 and 1992, observed *The Irish Times*, the parliamentary debate was "engendering such divisions between, and within, parties as to make the brokering of a national consensus almost impossible."[55] The outcome was razor close, as the Irish electorate defeated the government's restrictive amendment by 10,556 votes of the 1.2 million cast.

Emboldened by its victory in the Irish abortion referendum of 1983, the Pro-Life Amendment campaign regrouped to oppose the 1986 referendum liberalizing divorce. Following his re-election in November 1982, Prime Minister Garret FitzGerald of the Fine Gael Party vowed to make the laws of the Republic of Ireland more palatable to Northern Ireland Protestants. Since the Roman Catholic Church did not formally oppose it and the parliamentary opposition Fianna Fail Party stayed neutral, the referendum was expected to pass, but it was defeated by 53 per cent of the voters.[56]

In Ireland "political parties naturally sought to distance themselves from the referendums on moral issues," which "perform the function of mirrors, reflecting as they do the deepest aspirations of a society." Which is why Bogdanor sees big differences between Ireland and Italy: "In Italy, voters in the divorce and abortion referendums proved *more* liberal than expected, while in Ireland they proved *less* liberal than expected."[57]

SWITZERLAND

Switzerland, observes Kris Kobach, "is the only nation in the world where political life truly revolves around the referendum." In the postwar era through

1993, its 414 nationwide referendums account for more than two-thirds of all popular plebiscites in the democratic world. In comparison, Australia only had 44.[58] The four types of Swiss plebiscites are (1) the constitutional referendum, submitted to popular vote by the government; (2) the constitutional initiative, which is requested by voter petition; (3) the facultative referendum, whereby 50,000 voters can challenge any law or decree passed by the Federal Assembly; and (4) an optional treaty referendum to safeguard Switzerland's long-standing tradition of neutrality. Most years Swiss voters must decide six to 12 referendums, including a few dealing explicitly with morality policy.

Although undoubtedly many more policy questions touched upon morality and value conflicts during the 1970-93 period—for example, votes regulating foreigners, taxing alcoholic beverages, or ending the use of nuclear energy—the more obvious cases of morality policy were those referendums to protect animals in 1973 and 1978 (both passed) or to ban vivisection in 1985 and animal experimentation in 1993 (both failed). Also a 1977 referendum supporting free abortions during the first 12 weeks of a pregnancy was defeated, as was another abortion plebiscite in 1978. An effort to ban liquor and tobacco advertising in 1979 was defeated, just as two referendums in 1993 devoted to those dual purposes were similarly rejected. A 1980 referendum to advance the cause of church-state separation lost. But in 1981 Swiss voters did approve equal rights for men and women, favoured a 1992 referendum decriminalizing sex between minors and homosexuality as well as defining rape-in-marriage, and voted in 1993 to legalize casino gambling.

There has been a decided change in the content of Swiss initiatives. One of "the most visible transformations in Swiss direct democracy," says Kobach, has been the growth of popular initiatives or parliamentary counter-proposals (made in response to initiated referendums). Five factors explain this development, including "a shift" in issue focus "from below, rather than from above" with respect to the "rise of postmaterialism" across Europe. Continues Kobach: "Initiatives on environmental protection, nuclear energy limitation, and road traffic restriction have figured prominently in the post-1969 initiative boom, particularly since 1974" as "[r]oughly a third of the initiatives" fell into this category. The "environmental banner was carried by 'outsider' interest groups and small parties, most notably the Green parties and the Independent party" who had been ignored by the Bern political establishment, but eventually their pressure from "using direct democracy bore fruit in Parliament" as a "coalition of Green parties won 2.8 per cent of the vote and five seats in the National Council in 1983." Their share of parliamentary seats rose to 6.1 per cent in 1991, so, like the Catholic Conservatives of the nineteenth century and the Social Democrats of the early twentieth century, "the Greens used initiatives to introduce themselves and their cause to the electorate."[59]

Majority Rule or Majority Tyranny?

By instituting direct democracy, do the initiative and referendum pose a threat to representative government? The effects of direct democracy on representation, in fact, are indirect as well as direct. Merely the existence of popularly initiated referendums increases the odds that laws will reflect the median voter preference, argues Gerber, because "legislators may want to anticipate the behaviour of the potential initiative proposers and draft laws to preempt their initiatives."[60] The use of mandatory referendums, more in Europe than in the United States, has a similar impact on parliamentary decision-making, says Bogdanor, since "knowledge that the electorate would have the right to pronounce upon a bill might encourage MPs to seek improvement in legislation so that it become more acceptable to the electorate."[61]

James Madison, considered the "father" of the American Constitution, designed republicanism to "refine and enlarge the public views by passing them through the medium of a chosen body of citizens, whose wisdom may best discern the true interest of their country and whose patriotism and love of justice will be least likely to sacrifice it to temporary or partial considerations."[62] Madison was not only troubled by the idea of a populace making decisions on the basis of their passions rather than reason, but also believed that representative government facilitates deliberation and the building of consensus through debate. Because morality policy is so amenable to emotionalism, symbolic appeals, and demagoguery (on both sides), even relatively dispassionate observers like David Magleby urge caution with respect to mechanisms of direct democracy.[63] Yet, their review of the consequences of direct democracy in the American states led Donovan and Bowler to conclude "that it is hard to support the argument that outcomes under direct democracy, while unique and potentially more responsive to public preferences, are vastly more responsible or irresponsible than those of elected legislatures."[64]

However, Magleby would argue that "direct legislation rarely reflects the most important political problems or issues on the minds of voters" and, moreover, the issues presented "tend to reflect the concerns of ideological or reform groups that have been unsuccessful in getting their way with the legislature, or who desire to elevate their issue as a result of the media attention that comes with getting a measure on the ballot." Thus, he notes that the economy, unemployment, and budget deficits were paramount concerns in 1992, yet those issues were rarely the subject of referendums. By those economic criteria, surely morality policies seem tangential; however, postmaterialists would allege that morality issues may grow increasingly important with the passing of time. Through the 1940s popular initiatives occasionally were used to promote socio-economic reforms, but that policy bias has declined markedly in recent decades.[65]

Thus, ultimately, Magleby joins the critics by noting that "referendum campaigns appeal to passions and prejudices, spotlight tensions, and may foster even greater conflict and disagreement."[66] Just as Derrick Bell once argued that the referendum was a democratic barrier to racial equality, today liberal critics view English-Only or anti-gay referendums as nothing less than the tyranny of the majority against unpopular minorities. Thus, Arington urges the courts to view English-Only laws "as symbolic statements" and not "as broad restraints on bilingual programs," given their "potential threat to language minority rights" and "concerns about the process by which many of these laws were enacted."[67] Similarly Niblock argues that "even if anti-gay initiatives do reflect the will of the majority of voters, courts should more closely scrutinize them than legislation that has passed through the representation filter."[68] From the same perspective, Gamble argues that civil rights referendums "separate us as a people," while Cain alleges that minorities would fare better from a legislature than from popular initiatives.[69] Therefore, the solution, many critics believe, is heightened scrutiny by the judiciary, who "not only balance competing rights and liberties but are the 'traffic cops' over the procedures and practices of direct legislation."[70] However, Eule believes the "electoral accountability of the state courts raises significant doubt about their desire to take a leading role in curbing voter lawmaking."[71]

In contrast to the insecure tenure of elected officials, all federal judges are appointed for life. The best-known examples of federal judicial intervention occurred in 1964, when Californians voted against open housing for minorities—although that referendum was nullified by the Supreme Court—and, in 1996 when the Supreme Court held that the denial of coverage to gays under local non-discrimination ordinances in Colorado was unconstitutional. Earlier, as Magleby recalls, between 1960 and 1980 only two successful California initiatives were *not* declared partly or wholly unconstitutional by state or federal courts. But even Magleby acknowledges the democratic dilemma of having anti-majoritarianism trump majoritarianism: "The need to rule on the constitutionality of initiatives places the courts, the least democratic branch of our government, in the position of overturning a majority vote, perhaps an extraordinary majority."[72]

Critics allege that judicial intervention is most defensible where direct democracy threatens fundamental political freedoms and civil rights. But inevitably that involves a slippery slope on where to draw the line, because the essence of morality policy is to balance individual liberties against public order. Our suspicion is that many morality policies involve legitimate disagreements and do not—and should not—implicate fundamental freedoms. Does underage drinking, or adult drug use, or access to pornography, or unregulated hunting engage rights equivalent to political freedom or human rights? Do we have an unfettered right to gambling, via casinos, or lotteries, or horse races? In sum, the vast majority of morality policies—even putting aside gay rights or race relations—ought not to enjoy the status of rights so fundamental that courts should regularly intervene, whether the enactment came about through direct democracy or representative government.

Strident critics of direct democracy seemingly operate on the assumption that minorities are never wrong but majorities are rarely right on morality policy. A proper response requires a case-by-case analysis of each policy impact, which is beyond our reach. Our immediate concerns are the policy process and what prompts citizens to bypass the political establishment. Obviously, the answer is that political elites are perceived as being unresponsive to public opinion and, furthermore, anti-majoritarian whenever they do legislate on morality policies. That much was inferred in Chapter 5 on parliamentary rule and made more explicit in Chapter 6 on judicial activism. Now in Chapter 8 we try to assess empirically the charge and, along the way, revisit the concept of morality policy as the redistribution of values.

Notes

1. Gordon Smith, "The Functional Properties of the Referendum," *European Journal of Political Research* 4 (1976): 5.

2. David Butler and Austin Ranney, *Referendums: A Comparative Study of Practice and Theory* (Washington, DC: American Enterprise Institute, 1978) 221.

3. Quoted in Vernon Bogdanor, "Western Europe," *Referendums around the World*, ed. David Butler and Austin Ranney (Washington DC: AEI Press, 1994) 90, 91. The Lipset and Rokkan source referenced was: Seymour Martin Lipset and Stein Rokkan, eds., *Party Systems and Voter Alignments: Cross-National Perspectives* (New York: Free Press, 1967) 50.

4. David B. Magleby, "Direct Legislation in the American States," Butler and Ranney, *Referendums Around the World* 218.

5. Charles M. Price, "The Initiative: A Comparative State Analysis and Reassessment of a Western Phenomenon," *Western Political Quarterly* 28 (June, 1975): 243-62.

6. Magleby, "Direct Legislation in the American States" 229, 232. The calculation is ours.

7. Raymond E. Wolfinger and Fred I. Greenstein, "The Repeal of Fair Housing in California: An Analysis of Referendum Voting," *American Political Science Review* 62 (September, 1968): 753-69; Howard D. Hamilton, "Direct Legislation: Some Implications of Open Housing Referenda," *American Political Science Review* 64 (March 1970): 124-37.

8. Eugene C. Lee, "California," Butler and Ranney, *Referendums: A Study in Practice and Theory* Table 5-4, 95. Magleby, "Direct Legislation in the American States" 238. Those on "[g]overnmental and political processes" were 26 per cent, 21 per cent involved "[r]evenue, taxation, bonds," and [r]egulation of business and labor" along with "[p]ublic morality" had 14 per cent each. See Austin Ranney, "United States of America," in Butler and Ranney, *Referendums: A Comparative Study of Practice and Theory* 78.

9. Magleby, "Direct Legislation in the American States" 237.

10. Ranney, "The United States of America," Butler and Ranney, *Referendums: A Comparative Study of Practice and Theory* 84.

11. John Samuel Ezell, *Fortune's Merry Wheel: The Lottery in America* (Cambridge, MA: Harvard University Press, 1960) 271.

12. Charles T. Clotfelter and Philip J. Cook, *Selling Hope: State Lotteries in America* (Cambridge, MA: Harvard University Press, 1989) 145-46.

13. Clotfelter and Cook 43, 46-47, 236. Also see their Table 3.1 on p. 44..

14. "Voters in Alabama Soundly Defeat State Lottery," *New York Times* 13 October 1999: A16; also see David Firestone, "Religious Leaders Prevail As Alabama Shuns Lottery," *New York Times* 14 October 1999: 1, A18.

15. James Brooke, "5 States Vote Medical Use of Marijuana," *New York Times* 5 November 1998: B10.

16. Sam Howe Verhovek, "From Same-Sex Marriages To Gambling, Voters Speak," *New York Times* 5 November 1998: B1, B10.

17. Wayne A. Santoro, "Conventional Politics Takes Center Stage: The Latino Struggle against English-Only Laws," *Social Forces* 77 (March 1999): 901.

18. Deborah J. Schildkraut, "Official-English and the States: Influences on Declaring English the Official Language in the United States," *Political Research Quarterly* 54 (June 2001): 454-55.

19. Glick and Hutchinson 62.

20. Sally B. Geis, "The Meaning of Death: Time to Talk," *Christianity and Crisis* (3 February 1992): 9-10; Also see Rob Carson, "Washington's I-119," *Hastings Center Report* (March-April, 1992): 7-9.

21. Donald P. Haider-Markel and Kenneth J. Meier, "The Politics of Gay and Lesbian Rights: Expanding the Scope of Conflict," *Journal of Politics* 58 (May 1996): 334.

22. Todd Donovan and Shaun Bowler, "Direct Democracy and Minority Rights: Opinions on Anti-Gay and Lesbian Ballot Initiatives," *Anti-Gay Rights: Assessing Voter Initiatives*, ed. Stephanie L. Witt and Suzanne McCorkle (Westport, CT: Praeger, 1997) 112.

23. Donovan and Bowler, "Direct Democracy and Minority Rights" 108.

24. Thomas L. Mason, *Governing Oregon* (Dubuque, IA: Kendall/Hunt, 1994) 37-38.

25. Reported in Donovan and Bowler, "Direct Democracy and Minority Rights" 125, n.24.

26. Donovan and Bowler "Direct Democracy and Minority Rights" 125, n.24.

27. Stephanie L. Witt, W. David Patton, and Jacque Amoureux, "Morality Politics: The Use of Local Initiatives in the Backlash Against Local Gay-Rights Ordinances," paper delivered to the Annual Meeting, Western Political Science Association, Seattle, WA, 1999: 17.

28. Steven Shaw, "No Longer a Sleeping Giant: The Re-Awakening of Religious Conservatives in American Politics," Witt and McCorkle 16.

29. "Voters in Five US Cities To Decide Gay Rights Issues," *The Washington Post* 4 November 2001: A02.

30. Richard Braunstein and Tricia Wempe, "The Best Custodians of Moral Principle: A Comparative Study of Legislative and Citizen Morality Policy Making," paper delivered to the Annual Meeting, Western Political Science Association, Las Vegas, NV, 2001.

31. Laura R. Woliver, Angela D. Ledford, and Chris J. Dolan, "The South Carolina Confederate Flag: The Politics of Race and Citizenship," *Politics and Policy* 29 (December 2001): 708-30.

32. David Firestone, "Mississippi Forms Commission To Design a New State Flag," *New York Times* 6 May 2000: A7.

33. Byron D'Andra Orey, "Racial Threat, Republicanism and the Rebel Flag," paper presented to the Annual Meeting, Midwest Political Science Association, Chicago, IL, 2002.

34. Smith, *The Comparative Policy Process* 118-19.

35. Hughes, "Australia and New Zealand," Butler and Ranney, *Referendums around the World* 169.

36. Ranney, "The United States of America," Butler and Ranney, *Referendums: A Comparative Study of Practice and Theory*, Table 4-3, p. 74.

37. Harlan Hahn, "Voting in Canadian Communities: A Taxonomy of Referendum Issues," *Canadian Journal of Political Science* I (December 1968): 462-69.

38. James S. Coleman, *Community Conflict* (New York: The Free Press, 1957) 6, 19. Also Hahn, "Voting in Canadian Communities" 467.

39. William A. Gamson, "The Fluoridation Dialogue: Is It an Ideological Conflict?," *Public Opinion Quarterly* XXV (Winter 1961): 536. Also see William A. Gamson and Peter H. Irons, "Community Characteristics and Fluoridation Outcome," *Journal of Social Issues* 17 (1961): 66-74; T.F.A. Plaut, "Analysis of Voting Behavior on a Fluoridation Referendum," *Public Opinion Quarterly* 23 (1959): 213-22; Maurice Pinard, "Structural Attachments and Political Support in Urban Politics: The Case of Fluoridation Referendums," *American Journal of Sociology* LXVIII (March 1963): 513-26; Arnold Simmel, "A Signpost for Research on Fluoridation Conflicts: The Concept of Relative Deprivation," *Journal of Social Issues* 17 (1961): 26-36.

40. John E. Mueller, "The Politics of Fluoridation in Seven California Cities," *Western Political Quarterly* 19 (March 1966): 57.

41. Tom Flanagan, "In Praise of Single-Issue Politics," *The Globe and Mail* 21 May 1998: A21.

42. These data were supplied by the Canada West Foundation, for which we are grateful.

43. Maija Setala, *Referendums and Democratic Government: Normative Theory and the Analysis of Institutions* (New York: St. Martin's Press, 1999) Appendix 2, 181-82, 187-88.

44. Hughes, "Australia and New Zealand" 158, 159.

45. Hughes, "Australia and New Zealand," Table 5-4, 167-68; 172.

46. Calculated from Setala Appendix 2, 181-88.

47. Bogdanor, "Western Europe" 49.

48. Butler and Ranney, *Referendums around the World*, "Appendix A: National Referendums, 1793-1993" 268.

49. Bogdanor, "Western Europe" 62.

50. Setala Appendix 2, 184-86.

51. Paul Furlong, *Modern Italy: Representation and Reform* (London: Routledge, 1994) 157-58.

52. Bogdanor, "Western Europe" 66, 68.

53. Bogdanor, "Western Europe" 80-81.

54. Bogdanor, "Western Europe" 82-84.

55. "Withdraw This Referendum," *The Irish Times* 3 December 2001; also see Sarah Lyall, "Increasingly, Irish Turn to Britain for Abortions," *New York Times* 24 December 2001: A3.

56. Bogdanor, "Western Europe" 85.

57. Bogdanor, "Western Europe" 85.

58. Kris W. Kobach, "Switzerland," Butler and Ranney, *Referendums around the World* 98.

59. Kobach, "Switzerland" 140, 143-44; a listing of referenda during 1970-93 is given in Table 4-1 on 120-29. Also see Kris W. Kobach, "Recent Developments in Swiss Direct Democracy," *Electoral Studies* 12 (1993): 342-65.

60. Elisabeth Gerber, "Legislative Response to the Threat of Popular Initiatives," *American Journal of Political Science* 40 (February 1996): 101.

61. Vernon Bogdanor, *The People and the Party System: the Referendum and Electoral Reform in British Politics* (Cambridge: Cambridge University Press, 1981) 14.

62. James Madison, Alexander Hamilton, and John Jay, *The Federalist Papers* (New York: The New American Library, Mentor Books, 1961) 82.

63. David B. Magleby, "Let The Voters Decide? An Assessment of the Initiative and the Referendum Process," *University of Colorado Law Review* 66 (1995): 13-46.

64. Todd Donovan and Shaun Bowler, "An Overview of Direct Democracy in the American States," in *Citizens as Legislators: Direct Democracy in the United States*, ed. Shaun Bowler, Todd Donovan, and Caroline J. Tolbert (Columbus, Ohio: Ohio State University Press, 1998) 20.

65. Magleby, "Let the Voters Decide?" 35, 16, fn 12.

66. Magleby, "Let the Voters Decide?" 44.

67. Michele Arington, "English-Only Laws and Direct Legislation: The Battle in the States over Language Minority Rights," *Journal of Law & Politics* 7 (1991): 328.

68. Niblock 197. See Derrick A. Bell, Jr., "The Referendum: Democracy's Barrier to Racial Equality," *Washington Law Review* 54 (1978-79): 1-29. Other critics of direct democracy are: Arington 325-52; Craig C. Burke, "Fencing Out Politically Unpopular Groups from the Normal Political Processes: The Equal Protection Concerns of Colorado Amendment Two," *Indiana Law Journal* 69 (1993-94): 275-98; Robert A. Wagner, "Evans v. Romer: Colorado Amendment 2 and the Search for a Fundamental Right for Groups to Participate Equally in the Political Process," *St. Louis University Law Journal* 38 (Winter, 1993-94): 523-51; James J. Seeley, "The Public Referendum and Minority Group Legislation: Postscript to *Reitman v. Mulkey*," *Cornell Law Review* 55 (1970): 881-910; Cynthia L. Fountaine, "Note: Lousy Lawmaking: Questioning the Desirability and Constitutionality of Legislating by Initiative," *Southern California Law Review* 61 (1988): 733-76; Marc Slonin and James H. Lowe, "Comment: Judicial Review of Laws Enacted by Popular Vote," *Washington Law Review* 55 (1979): 175-209.

69. Bruce E. Cain, "Voting Rights and Democratic Theory: Toward a Color-Blind Society," *Controversies in Minority Voting*, ed. Bernard Grofman and Chandler Davidson (Washington, DC: Brookings Institution, 1992) 270; Barbara S. Gamble, "Putting Civil Rights to a Popular Vote," *American Journal of Political Science* 41 (January 1997): 262.

70. Magleby, "Let the Voters Decide?" 46.

71. Julian Eule, "Crocodiles in the Bathtub: State Courts, Voter Initiatives and the Threat of Electoral Reprisal," *University of Colorado Law Review* 65 (1994): 736; Julian Eule, "Judicial Review of Direct Democracy," *Yale Law Journal* 99 (1990): 1503-90. Here Eule alleged that the federal courts "may well be the only line of defense against majoritarian tyranny" (1584).

72. Magleby, "Let the Voters Decide?" 40-41.

PART THREE

Uncompromising Ends of Morality Policy

8

Building Political Consensus and the Public Peace

Where Ronald Inglehart contemplated value consensus in the postmaterialist age, Scott Flanagan foresaw a "New Left" opposing a "New Right" on such issues as abortion, women's liberation, and gay rights. By again borrowing Kenneth Meier's distinction between "one-sided" and "two-sided" morality policy, we believe that both Inglehart and Flanagan are credible, depending upon issue and circumstance.[1] Some morality policies are really non-issues that exhibit widespread agreement in certain Western democracies, while others engender controversy. Those that exhibit a degree of consensus may still activate a minority of dissenters, but they do not pose risks to democratic politics and political stability. Politically more ominous are those issues that divide the national community, mobilize segments of the population, and delegitimize institutions of popular government.

This chapter focuses on consensus-building, specifically the role of mass opinion. We want to revisit the claim that two-sided morality policy is analogous to redistributive policy. We argue that two-sided morality policy cannot be analyzed solely on those terms, given how the concept of redistribution is commonly understood. Instead, we propose to integrate both redistributive and regulatory features into the morality policy process. In brief, the answer to this intellectual puzzle is to view the consequences—outcomes—of morality policy on society as a continuum of likely effects on the general public and target groups, rather than as one discrete policy impact.

Morality Policy Outcomes

Meier defines morality politics as meaning "one segment of society attempts by governmental fiat to impose their values on the rest of society" and "[a]s such they are a form of redistributive policy that is rarely viewed as redistributive because the policies redistribute values rather than income."[2] This statement reveals the underlying paradox of the "redistribution of values" concept, because there can be a vast divide between the formality of law and the acceptance of those new values by the general public, let alone the subgroups of the population who are targeted by the policy (gun controls on owners of firearms, for example). The reality of redistributing economic resources, conventionally understood, is that the winners—whether by force, votes, or rules—impose their will on losers in quite specific ways at particular moments in time. We do not mean to imply that people cannot change their perceptions and opinions, but *mental* goods—values—simply cannot be rearranged throughout society by government fiat. If anything, economic redistribution of wealth is probably easier to accomplish than (as we will demonstrate) bringing about value change. Indeed, to the degree that individuals are acting politically, based on value-rational and/or affective goals, they would be especially *resistant* to changing their values and world-view.

While there is no denying that the majesty of law *symbolizes* certain value preferences regarding abortion, or homosexuality, or capital punishment (or any moral issue), the adoption of *new* law does *not* necessarily represent a redistribution of social values leading to acceptance of abortion or homosexuality or the death penalty. There are legal scholars who view the law as an "expressive" instrument that should be utilized to move social norms in certain (progressive) directions.[3] Of course, in the United States there was no greater failure to impose a redirection of social norms by formal law than the Eighteenth Amendment to the Constitution, banning the provision of alcoholic beverages.

State *regulation* of social conduct also *symbolizes* a society's approval or approbation of various moral practices. To assert a redistribution of values overestimates what legal symbolism can achieve in the short run, though arguably some redistribution of values *may* take place in the long run. While public opinion can be changed by positive law given enough time, we are less sanguine about changing the views of those target groups whose lifestyle and values are directly assaulted by the new legal requirements.

In Figure 8.1 we schematize our continuum of outcomes from the point of legal enactment to show the hypothesized effect on the general public and the targeted groups.

We doubt that social values can be immediately realigned by the political process and government coercion. What *can* occur in the short term (depending upon whether authorities can comply unilaterally) is the regulation of public behaviours. Consider capital punishment. Despite what the public may believe, a moratorium on death sentences by the Supreme Court of the United States or abolitionist legislation by the French National Assembly would spare all prisoners on death row. There is no time lag, because the implementation

FIGURE 8.1

Hypothesized Outcomes of Morality Policy on Public and Groups

	Immediate	*Short Term*	*Long Term*
	symbolic reaction	regulation of public behaviour	redistribution of values
General Public	diffuse support	compliant	possible
Target Groups	focused hostility	resistant	improbable

process rests entirely with administrative elites. But often morality policy is more complex, requiring elaborate implementation strategies to reach all the affected public and private parties, meaning that the process of compliance could extend beyond the short term. For example, slow progress in the United States towards racial equality in employment, voting, and housing led Bullock and Lamb to conclude that "[a]ttempts to implement civil rights depend to a large degree on the response of various state and local officials and, sometimes, of private citizens.... It is not uncommon, therefore, for national policy objectives to depend on a number of people not directly answerable to the decision makers who propounded the policy."[4]

Even where more time is needed for implementation, the regulation of public behaviour can proceed regardless of whether the values and beliefs of those affected actually change. This reasoning was at the core of liberal arguments for civil rights legislation in the United States during the 1960s. A favourite cry by conservatives was that hearts are not changed by the law alone, while liberals countered that the law was not intended to convert the thinking of segregationists but rather to stop them from discriminating against blacks. Race relations is surely the American "dilemma," given the disconnect between attitudes and behaviour. On paper, say Smith and Sheatsley, "a massive and wide-range liberalization of racial attitudes has swept America over the last forty years" as "[w]hites have steadily abandoned beliefs in the desirability of segregation and the notion that blacks are and should be second-class citizens."[5] Yet Kinder and Sanders point to studies that "American cities are now more segregated by race than they were at the turn of the century" and that in big city schools "segregation prevails and may even be increasing." Thus, "white Americans express considerably more enthusiasm for the principle of racial equality than they do for policies that are designed to bring the principle to life," they conclude.[6]

Both traditionalists and empiricists should be able to agree that morality policies seek to regulate the overt behaviours of individuals whose personal values may or may not support the law. To regulate the behaviour of those groups steadfastly opposed to the new law is not an easy proposition, but to redistribute values among that target population is even more problematic. Nor can we presume that widespread value change is inevitable among the general public, though its prospects are likely better than what can be achieved among the target groups.

Targeted Groups and Compliance

Studies of self-reported compliance with criminal offences indicate that people were more likely to engage in "criminal" behaviours if they believe that those actions are not morally wrong.[7] Tyler explains that citizens voluntarily comply with the law either "because they view the legal authority ... as having a legitimate right to dictate their behavior" or due to "an internalized obligation to follow one's personal sense of what is morally right or wrong." Of the two, empirical analysis indicated that the "most important normative influence on compliance with the law is the person's assessment that following the law accords with his or her sense of right and wrong," Tyler concluded.[8] In sum, a mismatch between social norms and legal requirements gives rise to a problem of non-compliance.[9]

The activism of the American Supreme Court since the 1950s led to a flurry of compliance studies to determine the impact of its decisions on racial desegregation, school prayer, criminal procedures, and abortion implementation.[10] School prayer is one issue that will not go away despite the widespread acceptance of church and state separation in American constitutional jurisprudence. Notwithstanding the 1962 precedent that any state-sanctioned school prayer violates the establishment clause of the First Amendment, and probably because of it, there are instances to this day of non-compliance in the Bible Belt, huge majorities favour prayer in public schools, and upwards of three-fourths endorse a constitutional amendment to restore the practice.[11] Legalized abortion and gun control are two other high-profile issues in North America that also show resistance by the targeted groups.

ABORTION SERVICES: UNITED STATES AND CANADA

Legislation authorizing limited therapeutic abortions was enacted by the Canadian Parliament in 1969, the very law which the Supreme Court of Canada in 1988 deemed "unworkable" and thus null and void (today there is *no* abortion code whatsoever in Canada). In 1973 abortion was constitutionalized by the Supreme Court of the United States. But lawyers do not perform abortions; physicians do. As late as 1986, only 35 per cent of Canadian hospitals were complying with the 1969 law that mandated a Therapeutic Abortion Committee in order to perform abortions, literally a carbon copy of the American hospitals with obstetrics capacity that also offered abortion services (34.5 per cent). As would be expected, that percentage was much lower among Canadian (9.9 per cent) and American (6.3 per cent) hospitals with religious affiliations (indeed *no* Catholic hospital in the United States offered abortion services).[12]

Informed observers generally agree that the health care community has not acquiesced to deliver abortion services, just as pro-lifers have not capitulated to the rule of law in the quarter-century since *Roe*. The determined opposition of pro-lifers coupled with the apparent sentiment among physicians and other providers that stigmatizes an abortion practice has led to parallel developments in the United States and Canada: the number of hospital-based abortion providers has declined, and specialized clinics account for a larger share of abortions (93 per cent in the United States and 33 per cent in Canada).[13] Generally what motivates Canadian and American abortion opponents is their religiosity, and one study based on the 1991 World Values Survey showed that "subjective and behavioral religious indicators—importance of God and church attendance rates—clearly emerge as the most powerful predictors of positions on abortion." Thus, "[i]n light of the prominent role played by religious organizations in the pro-life camps, it comes as little surprise to learn that WVS data confirm previous American research that emphasizes the important role that religion plays in shaping public opinion on the abortion debate."[14]

GUN REGISTRATION: UNITED STATES AND CANADA

Gun registration is one contemporary issue with the potential to provoke non-compliance by some Canadian gun owners despite the fundamentally different gun-control regime that exists there compared to the United States. It was never such an issue in European societies, which lacked a frontier and where ownership of firearms was restricted to the upper classes. Both Canada and the United States had a frontier, though firearms played no special role in Canada since the western provinces were tamed by the Northwest Mounted Police prior to settlement, unlike the American style of frontier development. Not only has there been a long history of strong gun laws in Canada, but the 1982 Canadian Charter of Rights and Freedoms has no language analogous to the "right to bear arms" language of the Second Amendment in the American Bill of Rights. Also, gun controls are uniform across Canada because they are lodged in the federal Criminal Code, whereas great disparities exist among the 50 American states apart from whatever federal restrictions are imposed. Today there are nearly nine times as many firearms in the United States (263 million) as Canada (30 million), and 41 per cent of American but only 26 per cent of Canadian households report owning a gun.[15]

In Canada, a police permit to carry handguns under specific circumstances became a requirement in 1913, and registration of all handgun owners was required by 1934—something which no American state or the federal government requires, even today. On this, recent polls show that "Canadians have more restrictive attitudes toward handguns than Americans," since more than twice as many Americans (34 per cent) as Canadians (15 per cent) agree that "licensing handguns is just another step by government to interfere in people's lives and limit their freedom." Moreover, if the law required that all handguns be turned into the police, more than twice as many Americans (17 per cent) as Canadians (7 per cent) believe that nobody would obey such a law, whereas many more Canadians (42 per cent) than Americans (17 per cent) thought that half or most gun owners would comply.[16]

Perhaps "most surprisingly" to researchers Mauser and Margolis was their discovery that "a strong majority of Canadians believe that they, as Canadians, also have the 'right to own guns.'" In other words, despite the constitutional, developmental, and political differences between these two countries, "the Canadian public apparently shares much of the US culture, including some of the mythology about firearms."[17] There is clearly a gun culture in the United States that Spitzer believes "is a rural and southern phenomenon," given that the majority of both those groups owns guns.[18] Canadian political scientist Les Pal extends that logic to Canada, insofar as "gun use is higher among rural than urban residents and southern states and western/northern provinces and regions than the east."[19] Statistical analysis of public attitudes indicate that "belief in the effectiveness of gun-control legislation is the most important factor in determining support or opposition to additional firearms legislation in both countries," but also that "gender and gun ownership are strongly linked ... [because] men and gun owners tend to oppose such legislation." This comports with the view that attitudes toward gun control are not "the result of a purely rational decision." Like others who allege that "gun ownership is closely linked with a rural upbringing and is culturally determined," Margolis and Mauser "confirm this for the United States, but also show that gun ownership is important for determining attitudes toward firearms legislation independent of the respondent's upbringing."[20]

The underlying sentiment within the Canadian gun culture that there is a right to own firearms was provoked when the Liberal government forced through Parliament the Firearms Act of 1995, which, by requiring that all owners be licensed by January 2001 and all firearms registered by January 2003, "completely changed Canada's gun control regime, making it one of the toughest in the world."[21] One cannot say that most Canadians were opposed to this legislation, since 83 per cent expressed their support as early as November 1994. Since then, no fewer than 64 per cent have been supportive, and the most recent poll in October 2000 showed 70 per cent favouring "a law that would require all firearms in Canada to be registered with the federal government."[22] An Environics survey in October 1994 revealed that 90 per cent favoured registration of all firearms, 67 per cent would ban private ownership of handguns, and 75 per cent wanted ammunition sales controlled.[23] Although a survey taken by Mauser during the parliamentary debate over Bill c-68 confirmed that 84 per cent agree "that all firearms should be registered," Mauser believes that such views are not firmly held because they dissipate markedly when respondents are asked to consider the costs of enforcement and the prospect that police would be transferred from the street in order to deal with the paperwork.[24]

Almost immediately, however, a challenge was brought before the Supreme Court of Canada by Alberta, which was joined by the provinces of Saskatchewan, Manitoba, Ontario, New Brunswick, the Northwest Territories, and the Yukon. It was unsuccessful, as the Supreme Court unanimously upheld the gun law in June 2000, but the issue of non-compliance has surfaced since then. Only 150,000 (or 5 per cent) of the estimated 3 million owners of long-barreled firearms were licensed in the first 18 months of the new gun law. According to one report, "the majority of gun owners seem to be taking a very un-Canadian path: civil disobedience." A new group, Law-abiding Unregistered Firearms Association, boasted 15,000 members by May 2000. Six months later the Canadian Firearms Centre (CFC) estimated that 80 per cent of Canadian gun owners were in compliance with the new licence law, but with some bureaucratic assistance. Licence fees were slashed from $30 to $6.50; the application was reduced to one page from four; a massive advertising campaign was launched; and 400 outreach workers went into shopping malls and shooting clubs to sign up nearly 700,000 owners.[25] But Mauser has his doubts about those CFC claims because its survey estimates of the number of gun owners in Canada declined from 36 per cent to 17 per cent over the past decade, meaning that "estimates of firearm owners has dropped from about between 5.2M and 3.8M in the mid 1990s to 2.2M in 2001. In other words, between 1.6 and 3M gun owners must have divested themselves of their firearms. It is difficult to find strong evidence to support this magnitude of decline."[26]

Morality Policy and Value Change

Postmaterialists who follow Inglehart's lead anticipate an evolutionary process in which value change accompanies the transformation from industrialized to postmaterialist societies, and they—like us—proceed on the assumption that the status quo is conservative with respect to social values. Consistent with postmaterialist expectations, therefore, the long term in the United States has brought about changes in public opinion. Pointing to the liberalization of American social attitudes after 1946, Davis predicts that *"[c]ohort replacement will exert a broad and persistent liberalizing effect on American opinions for years to come"* (italics in original). Generally, attitudes shifted in a liberal direction on abortion, race relations, and sexual morality (though not on crime).[27] A cross-cultural analysis by Canadian political scientist Neal Nevitte also documents postmaterialist value changes for Europe, Canada, and the United States based on the World Values Survey (WVS).[28] Here we somewhat parallel his analysis by drawing upon the earlier 1981, 1990, and the updated 1995 WVS to reveal the degree of public acceptance of nine morality policies (Table 8.1). Shown is the percentage who believe that each moral practice can be "always" or "sometimes" or "never" justified.

At first glance, these findings comport with the prevailing interpretation that public opinion across our five Western democracies had liberalized over the 1980-91 decade—considering those respondents who "sometimes" approve homosexuality, prostitution, abortion, divorce, euthanasia, and suicide. But other morality policies showed retrenchment over this period. By 1991 upwards of two-thirds in every nation condemned the use of marijuana or hashish as being "never" justified;[29] smaller majorities of Canadians and Britons felt similarly about adultery (as did seven out of ten Americans); and sex with an underage person was deemed "never" acceptable by three-fourths of the British, nearly two-thirds of Americans, and a bare majority of Canadians and Germans. Clearly, the United States is an outlier given that the majority of Americans express a morally absolutist view of homosexuality, prostitution, and suicide, as well as drug use, adultery, and sex with a minor. There seems to be virtually a consensus in every country that divorce and abortion are "sometimes" justified. Consistent with the postmaterialist thesis, Nevitte was impressed with "the general trend" towards moral permissiveness in the World Values Survey, but, for us, another relevant fact is indicated in our summary statistics (see Table 8.1): values shifted at a glacial pace over 1980-91, and, in the five years since, some backlash has resulted.

The ideal scenario for validating the postmaterialist thesis would be evidence showing that those who "always" or "sometimes" justify moral practices have risen while the proportion of moral absolutists, who say such practices are "never" justified, declines. However, this ideal scenario does not apply to either time-frame. During 1980-91, those who can "never" justify these practices decreased, while those who can "sometimes" justify them increased three-fold; however, respondents who "always" justify them more often declined than increased over the period. On the other hand, although increases by those who "always" justified various moral practices outnumbered decreases by three to one, respondents who "sometimes" could justify them were ten times more likely to decrease since 1995; moreover, the moral absolutists who could "never" justify such behaviour were twice as likely to increase their numbers.

Law, Policy Change, and Public Opinion

Most important for evaluating the redistribution of values argument is the relationship between these trends in public opinion and the enactment of new legislation which reverses the normative status quo. To grapple with this research question, we focus on our case studies of public opinion towards capital punishment, abortion, and homosexuality in Canada, the United States, France, the UK, and Germany. Before doing so, however, we want to consider one especially poignant morality policy that has surfaced in recent years in Canada and the United States, namely, active euthanasia or physician-assisted suicide (PAS).

We have already reported that the Supreme Courts of Canada and the United States refused to constitutionalize a right to physician-assisted suicide (see Chapter 6), and Nevitte reminds us that "active euthanasia was a crime in every country," though "in nearly every country the issue was becoming increasingly controversial."[30] It is noteworthy that, despite the unified opposition of the political authorities, American public opinion is considerably in flux. Despite well-publicized referendum defeats for PAS in Washington, Michigan, and California during the 1990s, national polls indicate that public opinion is more supportive of PAS than not. One series during the early 1990s revealed majority support in all but one survey for "a law which would allow doctors to end a patient's life by some painless means if the patient and his family request it."[31] Yet Glick and Hutchinson believe that pro-PAS attitudes are soft insofar as "there is *much less public support* for PAS than the overwhelming nationwide support for the withdrawal or withholding of treatment from the terminally ill that existed when most of the states enacted living will laws in the 1980s."[32]

In Canada, this issue surfaced in 1997 when Robert Latimer was convicted of second-degree murder for the mercy killing of his severely disabled daughter. His efforts to overturn that conviction might have posed fewer difficulties

TABLE 8.1

Value Change on Selected Morality Policies in Five Western Democracies

	Always Justified			Sometimes Justified			Never Justified		
	1991	1990	1995	1981	1990	1995	1981	1990	1995
Using Drugs									
US	2	1	—	30	25	—	68	74	—
Canada	3	2	—	36	34	—	61	64	—
UK	2	*	—	22	23	—	76	77	—
France	2	1	—	22	17	—	76	82	—
W. Germany	*	1	—	18	17	—	82	82	—
Adultery									
US	2	1	—	34	29	—	64	70	—
Canada	2	2	—	40	45	—	58	58	—
UK	1	*	—	48	46	—	51	51	—
France	4	3	—	71	63	—	25	25	—
W. Germany	2	2	—	52	56	—	46	46	—
Sex with Minor									
US	2	1	—	35	35	—	63	64	—
Canada	2	3	—	41	46	—	57	51	—
UK	1	*	—	28	25	—	71	75	—
France	5	1	—	63	63	—	32	36	—
W. Germany	4	4	—	44	45	—	52	51	—
Homosexuality									
US	3	4	5	32	42	41	65	54	54
Canada	4	8	6	45	55	53	51	37	41
UK	7	5	8	50	53	57	43	42	35
France	6	7	—	47	53	—	47	40	40
W. Germany	10	14	19	48	54	52	42	32	29
Prostitution									
US	2	2	2	34	38	37	64	60	61
Canada	3	4	3	47	54	52	50	42	45
UK	3	2	3	51	54	59	46	44	38
France	3	4	—	52	50	—	45	46	—
W. Germany	6	7	9	55	61	60	39	32	31
Abortion									
US	4	5	5	53	61	57	43	34	38
Canada	4	9	7	58	71	65	38	20	28
UK	6	3	5	64	77	73	30	20	22
France	10	8	—	69	74	—	21	18	—
W. Germany	7	5	7	65	77	72	28	18	21

	Always Justified			Sometimes Justified			Never Justified		
	1991	1990	1995	1981	1990	1995	1981	1990	1995
Divorce									
US	6	6	7	72	76	75	22	18	18
Canada	6	9	8	75	78	76	19	13	16
UK	8	5	10	78	82	79	14	13	11
France	11	11	—	76	78	—	13	11	—
W. Germany	13	15	18	74	77	73	13	8	9
Euthanasia									
US	6	5	7	51	63	57	43	32	36
Canada	8	8	8	58	69	65	34	23	27
UK	8	7	7	64	70	68	28	23	25
France	10	9	—	64	69	—	26	22	—
W. Germany	10	8	9	63	62	62	27	30	29
Suicide									
US	1	1	1	27	38	34	72	61	65
Canada	1	2	2	34	46	41	65	52	57
UK	3	1	2	48	58	53	49	41	45
France	4	5	—	58	62	—	38	33	—
W. Germany	3	5	7	50	55	55	47	40	38

Summary Statistics	Always Justified		Sometimes Justified		Never Justified	
	N	Avg %	N	Avg %	N	Avg %
1981-1990						
Increase	16	1.7	32	6.7	11	4.0
Same	8	—	3	—	1	—
Decrease	21	1.6	10	3.4	33	6.8
	45		45		45	
1990-1995						
Increase	14	2.2	2	4.5	15	3.5
Same	6	—	2	—	2	—
Decrease	4	1.5	20	3.2	7	3.1
	24		24		24	

Source: 1981, 1990, and 1995 World Values Survey. The multi-pronged question was: "Please tell me for each of the following statements whether you think it can always be justified, never be justified, or something in between, using this card." For 1981 and 1990 the 24 items included these nine recorded above: "Taking the drug marijuana or hashish," "Married men/women having an affair," "Homosexuality," "Prostitution," "Abortion," "Divorce," "Euthanasia (terminating the life of the incurably sick)," and "Suicide." On the 10-point scale, all responses coded 2 through 9 are grouped as signifying "sometimes justified" in this table, since the question explicitly coded 1 as "never" and 10 as "always." Those items on drug use, adultery, and sex with a minor were not included in the 1995 WVS, and there were no data for France on the other items. The asterisk (*) indicates a value at .5 or below, whereas a value from .6 to .9 was rounded as 1.

if he had appealed to the high court of public opinion. A series of Gallup Polls showed that no fewer than 45 per cent (1968) but most often a majority ranging above seven in ten Canadians agreed to the statement: "When a person has an incurable disease that causes great suffering, do you, or do you not think that competent doctors should be allowed by law to end the patient's life through mercy killing, if the patient has made a formal request in writing?" More discerning questions asked in 1995, 1997, and 1998 determined that at least 75 per cent favoured mercy killing when a patient's incurable disease is "immediately life-threatening and causes that person to experience great suffering" though support fell to the mid-50 per cent range in cases where the disease "is not immediately life-threatening but causes that person to experience great suffering."[33] In this light, if Canada and the majority of American states were to legalize PAS, arguably they would be acting pursuant to public opinion, not against it.

Even more revealing are the attitudes by North Americans and Europeans toward capital punishment, abortion, and homosexuality. Capital punishment has been abolished by every nation in this study except the United States, so can we safely assume that only Americans today favour the death penalty? The most permissive abortion policies are found in Canada and the United States, followed by Germany and France, with the UK barely more restrictive. Do public attitudes toward abortion rank accordingly in these five nations? By now homosexuality has been decriminalized in most American states and nationally in Canada, the UK, France, and West Germany, so can we assume that Americans are any less tolerant of homosexual relations than the other nation-states? Since the time-frame of these legal innovations ranges from a few years to several decades, these case studies are especially useful in assessing the inter-relationship between public opinion and the formal law during the short term and the long term.

CAPITAL PUNISHMENT

Long-term public resistance to morality policy reversal is best illustrated by the debate over abolishing capital punishment. Indeed, one commentator (with abolitionist sympathies) took note that "[t]he Western liberal democracies, such as France, the UK, and Canada, have held steadfast to the view … that popular sentiment alone should not determine penal policy, that task being the responsibility of elected representatives exercising their own judgment. As is well known, abolition of the death penalty in these three countries took place even though a majority of popular opinion was opposed to it."[34] This philosophy, he goes on to say, is quite unlike the United States, where the issue of capital punishment has been decided by popular vote. We later deal with this defence of elitism in the morality policy process (Chapter 9); here we want to test the proposition whether new law (abolition) has transformed public opinion in France, Canada, and the UK in the years since capital punishment was ended (see Appendix A.1).

Capital Punishment: United Kingdom

In 1947 the British Gallup poll showed that 65 per cent favoured the death penalty, and the following year two-thirds expressed disapproval for a reform objective of "not hanging anyone for murder for five years." The Labour government in late 1948 appointed a Royal Commission on Capital Punishment, but no reforms were forthcoming, although reform agitation got a big boost in the early 1950s when the hangings of two men and one woman were clouded by suspicions of official wrongdoings. Nonetheless, "[p]ublic opinion polls taken during this period [1953 and 1955], for instance, showed continued majority support for the retention of capital punishment, despite perceptible movement away from *overwhelming* acceptance of it." In January 1956, one month before the House of Commons voted again on abolition, a survey by Mass-Observation for the *Daily Telegraph* showed 34 per cent favouring a suspension of the death penalty (45 per cent disapproved), which contrasted with the 13 per cent who had favoured a temporary halt to hangings in 1948. These opinion data led Christoph to conclude that "at no time were the abolitionists able to claim a majority for their position, but instead they had to base their case upon evidence that opinion was moving in that direction in a rather remarkable way."[35] While not abolished, the mangled attempt by a Conservative government to reform capital punishment eventually yielded the 1957 Homicide Act, but still no turnabout in public opinion seems to have resulted.

Indeed, abolition came in 1965, yet three decades later "[c]apital punishment surveys regularly show that some three-quarters of the electorate favour the return of capital punishment for murder."[36] Support for capital punishment among Britons is shown in a long line of polls dating back at least to 1938, when 55 per cent opposed its abolition.[37] A similar question was asked seven more times through 1970 (Appendix A.1). Usually upwards of two-thirds opposed abolition, and, what seems particularly odd since capital punishment was outlawed in 1965, the high-water mark of retentionist sentiment was reached in 1962 and 1964, when, respectively, 81 per cent and 79 per cent were opposed to banning it. An especially telling question was asked by Gallup in mid-1962, presumably to measure the miscarriage of justice in the Timothy Evans hanging (see Chapter 4): "If it were proved that an innocent man had been wrongly convicted of a murder and hanged, would this alter your views about the death penalty in any way?" Fifty-two per cent answered no; only

9 per cent favoured abolition. In the wake of abolition, Gallup changed the question to assess support for reintroducing the death penalty, and support exceeded 70 per cent for the murderers of army or police personnel, for terrorist murders, the murder of a woman after a sexual assault, and murder done "just for the fun of it." (Appendix A.1). Looking even longer term, by the end of the twentieth century, nearly seven in ten British respondents wanted a return to capital punishment. There is little doubt that Labour abolished capital punishment despite consistent and widespread feelings to the contrary among the British people.

Capital Punishment: United States and Canada

High levels of support for capital punishment have been the norm in Canada and the United States, except that public opinion had no impact on the decision by Canada to abolish the death penalty. However, popular attitudes have been decisive in causing 39 states not to abandon the ultimate penal sanction. In both countries the nadir of popular approval came during the permissive 1960s, but, during the past two decades, usually no less than three-fifths of Canadians and seven of ten Americans express their support. Since the 50 states and the federal government have authority over their own criminal codes, there cannot be a blanket abolition of capital punishment, as occurred in Canada where the Criminal Code is under federal jurisdiction. The closest approximation for a test to judge the impact of wholesale abolition on American public opinion would be the "moratorium" imposed on death sentences by the American Supreme Court.

By its ruling in *Furman v. Georgia* (1972), the Supreme Court held that the "relatively rare and arbitrary manner in which capital punishment was imposed" raised serious constitutional issues, thus causing 35 states including Georgia to reform their death statutes to remedy the injustices. Since that ruling effectively set aside the sentences of over 1,000 inmates on death rows and because some justices in the majority believed that capital punishment was inherently a "cruel and unusual" violation under the Eighth Amendment, the perception of the illegitimacy of capital punishment could have had some short-term impact on American public opinion. It was not long, however, before the Supreme Court reconsidered this issue in *Gregg v. Georgia* (1976), which upheld the revised Georgia death statute and gave the green light to a resumption of executions nationwide. Did this episode have any impact on the attitudes of Americans? The plurality of 49 per cent that supported capital punishment in 1971 rose by eight percentage points by 1972 and then jumped to two-thirds in 1976, the year *Gregg* was announced. Indeed, taking note that 35 states reaffirmed capital punishment after *Furman*, the *Gregg* majority signaled that the Supreme Court was *following* public opinion.

Prior to 1961, anybody convicted of murder in Canada was automatically sentenced to death, unless the sentence was commuted by the governor general. In late 1967 the Canadian Parliament limited the death statute to the murderers of police officers and prison guards for an experimental five-year period. After that suspension expired, in January 1973, the solicitor general introduced legislation to Parliament—which passed it—to extend that partial ban on capital punishment. In 1976 Parliament made its abolition permanent. During the period from 1966-67 to 1976 the issue of capital punishment was debated not only in Parliament but on the editorial pages and in public opinion, and the Liberal government even commissioned an independent study to evaluate its deterrent effects. Nonetheless, Canadian public opinion seems not to have been much influenced by those events, according to one scholarly analysis: "The best estimate of the trend in public opinion over the past decade is that, in the mid-1960s, there was stable approval of the death penalty at between 50 and 58 per cent of Canadians and stable disapproval of it, between 33 and 40 per cent. A period of instability in the late 60s seemed to generate an increase in support of the death penalty to between 60 and 66 per cent of Canadians and a lessening of abolitionist opinion to 27-33 per cent." That is, support for capital punishment increased just as Parliament voted the partial ban, and this best estimate was probably no statistical anomaly given future opinion trends. The question asked in 1970—whether the death penalty should be reinstated for the kidnappers of public figures—"generated the strongest retentionist sentiment in twenty years" and was attributed to "a widely publicized kidnapping and murder of a politician in Quebec" by separatists turned political terrorists.[38]

But that spike in popular approval of capital punishment has not abated since, because Canadians have expressed high levels of support for the death penalty despite its abolition. The ultimate sanction was abolished for ordinary crimes in 1976, yet two years later polls showed that 68 per cent supported capital punishment (Appendix A.1). Analysis of CIPO surveys in 1965, 1975, and 1982 led Richard Johnston to conclude that "opinion was one-sidedly pro-capital punishment in each year," and the "restorationist sentiment of the 1980s was not a reaction after the fact of abolition" but rather "the abolition of the death penalty itself came in defiance of public opinion."[39] Polling trends from 1978 through 1998 show that support for the death penalty hit its recent nadir in 1996 (55 per cent) but has since risen slightly to 61 per cent in 1998—the year that Canada fully abolished capital punishment for all crimes.

Capital Punishment: France

The French experience is more suggestive that some shifting public opinion did materialize after capital punishment was ended. One informed account, which supports abolition, argues that the ebb and flow of French opinion is heavily influenced by grisly murders that are highly publicized. In mid-1969 President Georges Pompidou reprieved six prisoners sentenced to death, and polls showed the minority of French who favoured capital punishment dropping from the 39 per cent level (50 per cent were opposed) in May to 33 per cent by October (with 58 per cent now opposed).

But in September of 1971 two prison inmates took a nurse and guard hostage, and, after the building was stormed, both hostages were found dead with their throats cut. The press and public outrage that ensued shifted popular sentiment towards capital punishment by a 53 per cent to 39 per cent margin. Both prisoners were executed, and it was not until 1977 that a French jury convicted but refused to condemn a child-killer (who was defended by abolitionist crusader Robert Badinter; see Chapter 5). Five years later, during the precise month—September 1981—when the Socialists under President François Mitterrand enacted a statutory ban on capital punishment, a poll by *Sofres* for *Le Figaro* revealed that 62 per cent of the French public would keep the guillotine. Yet three years after its abolition, a poll by IFRES showed that public opinion shifted again, with 49 per cent now favouring abolition and 46 per cent opposed.

The French National Election Surveys probed whether "the death penalty should be reestablished" and found that the percentages of affirmative responses declined from 1988 (64 per cent said yes) to 1995 (56 per cent) and 1997 (50 per cent). This trend led the researcher to conclude "after a long period of declining law and order in the 1970s and 1980s, public opinion in support of the death penalty perhaps is beginning to decline, having succumbed to the rising power of the discourse of the cultivated elite, whose voice is one with that of a growing highly educated population."[40] A less optimistic prognosis is offered by one abolitionist who, after concluding that after "more than twenty years without an execution [that being in 1977], the majority of the French public are still not convinced [about abolition]" and cites two surveys taken the same month (in the late 1990s). Abolitionists were at 54 per cent when an IFOB poll asked "[a]re you in favour of restoring the death penalty?," but in the minority (46 per cent versus 50 per cent) when asked by a BVA poll "[a]re you in favour of the death penalty?"[41]

In sum, France is a mixed case, showing greater volatility in public opinion than the United States, Canada, or the UK, where retentionists always represented the prevailing viewpoint. In the short term (meaning at least one decade) following its 1981 abolition of capital punishment, polls showed that the majority of French were retentionists, and the activists most engaged in this historic campaign to rid Europe of the death penalty were not entirely convinced that they had won the intellectual battle for public opinion in

France. Yet if the minority retentionist view recorded in two polls of the late 1990s is a harbinger of the future, then this trend may signal that a long-term redistribution of values has occurred top-to-bottom in French society.

Capital Punishment: Germany

Article 102 of the Basic Law of the Federal Republic of Germany, dated May 23, 1949, declares "Capital punishment shall be abolished." Indeed, the movement to abolish capital punishment following the 1848 revolution was nearly successful, after which reformers were able both to reduce the number of crimes punishable by death and to slow down the pace of executions. This trend towards leniency ended under the Nazi regime, when over 16,000 death sentences were levied by civilian criminal courts. According to one official in the Federal Ministry of Justice, "[i]t was above all the impression of the abuse of capital punishment during the Nazi regime that, in 1949, the Parliamentary Council resolved to abolish capital punishment in the constitution of the Federal Republic of Germany." This backlash among elites yielded "a firm rejection of the death penalty" insofar as "[t]he vast majority of learned writers ... deny that it has a right to exist," although "[n]ot quite the same clear certainty exists ... when we come to the attitude of the general population in the Federal Republic of Germany."[42]

This observation is confirmed by opinion trends (Appendix A.1). One year prior to 1949 virtually three-fourths of Germans backed capital punishment despite the Nazi experience; one year later 55 per cent had not changed their minds. Majority support among Germans for capital punishment continued through the 1950s and 1960s, according to the Allensbach Institut, but dropped to a plurality in 1971. Afterwards, abolition was favoured by a plurality but not the majority (except for 1972 and 1979) until the 1983-95 period, when German opinion favouring capital punishment was a decidedly minority viewpoint. Yet an EMNID poll in 1958 indicated that eight out of ten Germans supported capital punishment for murder, with that percentage also falling to a bare majority in 1973, although support for capital punishment in murder cases rebounded to 60 per cent in 1977. The long-term trend clearly shows a stronger abolitionist constituency, although the upward spikes in public opinion favouring capital punishment in 1977 and again in August of 1986 were attributed to terrorist slayings and showed "the volatility of certain sectors of the population under the influence of recent events. Certain indicators suggest that a large number of persons who claimed not to have made up their minds may include a substantial number of supporters of capital punishment."[43] Surely, anti-abolitionist sentiments remain as tenacious as they are volatile, because a 1997 EMNID Institut survey found that 55 per cent of Germans favoured the reintroduction of capital punishment for the "most severe" crimes, like sexual murder or the murder of children. In sum, it is beyond doubt that Germany abolished capital punishment at a time when public opinion firmly supported it, that majority support persisted two decades after its abolishment, and that even 50 years later we cannot say with assurance that public opinion in Germany conforms with elite opinion, or the 1949 law, because a 1996 Allensbach Institut survey reported a drop in abolitionist sentiment to 45 per cent.

ABORTION POLICIES

Our second group of cases involve abortion policy, arguably a more contentious morality policy in these five Western democracies than capital punishment. Unlike the death penalty, where abolition was accomplished by an act of Parliament, abortion has been the subject of judicial intervention in the United States, Canada, and Germany; in examining these situations closely, we begin to appreciate whether or not public opinion is affected more or less by judge-made law as opposed to legislative enactment (Appendix A.2).

Abortion: United States and Canada
We first consider Canada and the United States together since a detailed case study by Tatalovich found striking parallels between these two countries in how abortion policy evolved.[44] In both, there were two junctures at which the intersection of law and opinion can be evaluated, the first being the 1960s when 14 states liberalized their nineteenth-century anti-abortion laws (four others repealed them entirely) and when the Canadian Parliament (1969) approved a new abortion law that provided for restricted therapeutic abortions. A poll taken in June 1965 by the Canadian Institute of Public Opinion (Gallup) showed that 72 per cent of Canadians supported therapeutic abortion "to preserve a mother's physical or mental health." Following the enactment of those provisions, a poll in January 1970 showed the public narrowly opposed to abortion (43 per cent to 48 per cent) "at any time during the first three months" and was even more divided in November when 45 per cent opposed (but 44 per cent favoured) revising the law "to permit an abortion for all who wish to have one." In sum, a few Canadian surveys but substantial polling in the United States indicate public support for therapeutic abortions on medical grounds even *before* these reformed laws were enacted.[45] Thus, we can safely conclude that the new abortion laws were brought into conformity with medical practice and public opinion during the 1960s, a time when many North American and European countries were reassessing their historic prohibitions on abortion (except for endangerment to the mother).[46]

The second policy change is more important for contemporary morality politics, namely, the interventions by the Supreme Court of the United States in *Roe v. Wade* (1973) and the Canadian Supreme Court in *Morgentaler v. The Queen* (1988). What was the trajectory of public opinion leading up to those rulings and in their aftermath? While Americans and Canadians are opposed to recriminalizing abortion, surveys indicate that the "contours of public opinion on abortion are fundamentally the same in Canada and the United States, though Canadians may be somewhat more liberal. Most people in both countries favor abortion under certain conditions, namely therapeutic ones, rather than elective abortion."[47] Almost a decade after the 1969 Canadian therapeutic abortion law was enacted, a study in Edmonton concluded that it remained "generally congruent with public opinion" and may be characterized as "custom reinstitutionalized," such that the law "is unlikely to change in the immediate future," though discontent would be directed "at the regulatory and judicial level."[48]

With respect to value change, the evidence shows that Americans exhibited greater support for therapeutic abortion *before* 1973 and that *Roe* had decidedly less impact on liberalizing public opinion. Indeed, *Roe* actually had a polarizing impact on American public opinion with respect to "discretionary" abortions, which "raises questions about the role of the Court as a legitimizing agent for policy positions."[49] But the most telling observation is that the American public has not rallied around elective abortion in the quarter-century since *Roe*, nor have Canadians in the decade following *Morgentaler* (see Appendix A.2). Recent polls show virtually a tie, with three in ten Americans and Canadians approving abortion under "any" circumstance. Maybe that picture is optimistic, given the results of the 1981 and 1990 World Values Survey that asked Americans and Canadians "whether you think it (abortion) can always be justified, never justified or something in between?" While Nevitte, Brandon, and Davis were impressed that those choosing "never" dropped from 42 per cent to 33 per cent in the United States and from 38 per cent to 21 per cent in Canada—suggesting to them the rising strength of the moderates in both countries—more relevant for us is the fact that by 1990 only a small fraction of Americans (5.3 per cent) and Canadians (8.5 per cent) endorsed abortion as "always" being justified.[50]

Abortion: United Kingdom

Any legal development in the UK has special meaning for Canada, though word of its abortion reforms also spread to the United States. Throughout the 1950s and 1960s none of the private members' bills on abortion were successful. What rekindled the reform movement was public concern over the thalidomide tragedy of 1961 (see Chapter 4). The Abortion Act of 1967 was quite liberal for its time, authorizing abortions where continuation of the pregnancy (1) involved a risk to the life or physical or mental health of the woman or "any existing children," and (2) where "a substantial risk" existed that the child would be born with "such physical or mental abnormalities as to be seriously handicapped," with a social caveat to (1) which stipulated that, in determining "such risk of injury to health" that "account may be taken of the pregnant woman's actual or reasonably foreseeable environment." Although the provision on fetal deformity was the important addition to existing British legal precedents, it was this social cause that provoked much of the outcry during the parliamentary debate.

It is solely for this reason that one cannot conclude that the 1967 reformed abortion law was not a perfect match with public sentiments, although undoubted purely therapeutic grounds for abortions were widely accepted. Indeed, what inspired the activists to redouble their efforts were early polls showing that their worries about an unsympathetic British public were ill-founded. A National Opinion Poll in July 1962 found that 72 per cent approved the termination of pregnancy "where there is a good reason to believe that the baby would be born badly deformed," and another in March 1965 showed that two-thirds believed that abortion should be legalized in some cases, as opposed to one-fourth wanting abortion illegal in all cases. Two National Opinion Polls commissioned by the Abortion Law Reform Association, the leading advocacy group, reported that 65 per cent of voters agreed in mid-February 1967 that abortions should be allowed on social grounds, and later, in September, large majorities supported abortion where the mother could not cope with more children, in cases of risk of fetal deformity, and where pregnancy resulted from a sexual crime.[51] Clearly, these polls were strategically employed to influence voting in the House of Lords, though they are not totally dissimilar from Gallup.

Gallup polling since 1966 (Appendix A.2) shows no fewer than seven in ten Britons approved abortions to safeguard the mother's health and in cases where the child would be born deformed, whereas lack of family income elicited 33 per cent approval in 1966 and 45 per cent in 1998. No more than about one-fourth of the British public supported on-demand abortion, however, which was technically not permitted under the 1967 law. Compared to the mismatch between the law and public opinion in the United States and Canada following judicial intervention, there seems a closer overlap between British opinion and British law on abortion.

Abortion: France

Compared to many European countries, "France appears to have legalized abortion late, rather slowly, and in a fairly restrictive way."[52] Before the 1975 reforms, legislation first enacted in 1920 and strengthened in 1923 made criminal abortion punishable by a large fine and imprisonment, with endangerment to the mother's life being the only therapeutic exception. However, there is scholarly debate about how restrictive the French law was in practice. Although the 1975 statute explicitly permitted abortion to protect the life of the mother as well as her physical and mental health, in addition to fetal abnormality, another provision stated that any adult woman suffering a "state of distress" could terminate her pregnancy up to the tenth week of pregnancy. It was this short eligibility period that led some commentators to view the French law as overly restrictive, though Dorothy Stetson argues that the determination of "distress" actually empowered women by removing that decision from the control of physicians.[53] The abortion reforms that were provisional under the 1975 law were made permanent in 1979, and by 1982 abortion services were covered under the health service. Thus, "nearly ten years elapsed between the first debate in the National Assembly and the enactment of the legislation in force today."[54]

So what was the state of public opinion during this period of institutionalization of abortion policy (see Appendix A.2)? In 1969 a slightly larger plurality opposed (47 per cent) rather than favoured (43 per cent) "a law allowing a pregnant woman of less than three months to terminate her pregnancy with the approval of her doctor." More important was the battery of questions in 1973, the year when the first (unsuccessful) bill to reform the abortion law was considered. One survey determined that a large majority of French supported some kind of reform, since only 13 per cent backed "maintaining the law as it stands," with more accepting the need for abortions "in the event of abnormal births" (41 per cent) than for "psychological trauma" as well as abnormal births (21 per cent). Only 22 per cent endorsed "total freedom of choice."

When asked about specific indications for abortions, the French in 1973 seemed decidedly more permissive than the British, Canadians, or Americans although not supportive of on-demand abortions. To the question "what is the best legal solution to the abortion question?," only 22 per cent would "sanction abortion in general," whereas 65 per cent would "sanction abortion in accordance with new and more liberal laws." A similar question forced respondents to choose "the most preferable for the present era" from three alternatives: sanctioning abortion "in cases in which the woman feels that either her material or moral circumstances are prohibitive to her having a child" (48 per cent), or "in limited and circumscribed situations only" (25 per cent), or "only in the event of possible danger to the mother's health" (24 per cent).[55]

A final question indicated that the acceptable circumstance for a legal abortion were far-reaching for large numbers of French people. In 1973 there was consensus regarding the mother's "physical or mental condition" (90 per cent) and where the "child may be abnormal" (88 per cent); beyond those, growing majorities endorsed abortions for a mother under age 18 (55 per cent), for a mother who "lives alone, without sufficient economic means" (69 per cent), where the "household already contains as many children as economic circumstances permit" (76 per cent), and where the "father or mother would be either physically or mentally incapable of raising the child" (82 per cent). Going further, the French split nearly evenly with a plurality favouring abortions for an unmarried mother or where the "happiness of the future mother or of the couple will be adversely affected by the birth of another child" (both at 44 per cent). In sum, these multiple results suggest that the 1975 reforms likely did not range widely from what French opinion was willing to accept.

Abortion: Germany
The story of abortion reform in Germany is complicated by the intervention, on two occasions, of the German Constitutional Court and by the reunification of East Germany and West Germany. The West German law of 1871 criminalized abortions except those performed to save the life or health of the mother. In 1974 the Bundestag enacted a permissive bill that allowed elective abortion during the first 12 weeks and, thereafter, extended abortions to 22 weeks to save the life or health of the woman, and where the fetus suffered from an incurable injury to its health. After enactment, however, 193 opposition legislators along with the governments of six German *Lander* (states) filed suit in the German Constitutional Court. In 1975 the Court struck down the abortion reforms as violating the "right to life" in the German Basic Law (see Chapter 6).[56]

The legal status quo in 1976, says Outshoorn, "was more conservative than German opinion, leading to a constant level of mobilization of both sides of the issues and to women 'voting with their feet,' going abroad or to the North for an abortion."[57] Based on one 1973 poll by Allensbach Institut, the parliamentary enactment of 1974 represented left-wing anti-majoritarianism and the 1975 ruling by the German Constitutional Court illustrated right-wing anti-majoritarianism. Of the two, the judicial intervention was more egregious because 38 per cent of West Germans favoured elective abortion during the first trimester and another 41 per cent would accept abortions for therapeutic or socio-economic reasons. The German Constitutional Court was much further to the right of public opinion than the Bundestag was to the left.

After the court nullification, the Bundestag enacted another reform statute that criminalized abortions unless the woman's life or health was endangered, the fetus was substantially deformed, or to "avert the danger of a distress which is so serious that the pregnant woman cannot be required to continue the pregnancy and cannot be averted in any other way she can reasonably be expected to bear." It was this more restrictive law that came under challenge with reunification talks in 1990, because the formerly Communist East Germany in 1972 had enacted a law permitting abortions during the first trimester and in cases of threats to the woman's life, her physical and mental health, the health of the fetus, and also socio-economic circumstances.[58] Since negotiators from the East and West were unable to resolve their differences on abortion, they agreed to allow each territory to retain its own jurisdiction pending a two-year deadline for a final solution.

In June 1992 the Bundestag again passed a law permitting abortion without restrictions during the first trimester so long as the woman underwent counselling and followed the three-day waiting period. Undeterred, yet again 249 legislators from the Christian-based political parties appealed to the Constitutional Court, but this time it equivocated by saying "abortion remain[ed] a criminal offense under German law for those cases that still fell outside the Court's 1975 list of acceptable circumstances, but normative counseling that was designed to persuade the woman to have the child could be used instead of criminal sanctions to reduce the number of actual abortions that German women would have."[59] The result of a 1995 revision authorizes first-trimester abortions so long as the woman visits a counselling centre, which means that the abortion law of unified Germany is much more liberal than the old criminal code of West Germany. Does this latest abortion revision comport with German public opinion? Our guarded answer based on several polls (see Appendix A.2) is probably not.

Four surveys taken in West Germany across the 1980s show that support for elective first-trimester abortion declined from 35 per cent in 1980 to 22 per cent in 1988, with the majority accepting abortions in special cases rising from 47 per cent in 1980 to 61 per cent in 1988, on the eve of reunification talks. Beginning in 1990, yearly polls showed that East Germans were much more willing to endorse first-trimester abortions. The differential between West and East Germans ranged from 20 per cent (1990) to 29 per cent (1992), leading us to suspect that overall the majority of all Germans would *not* have favoured the unified abortion policy. In 1995, for example, the 31 percentage point differential between East and West Germans yielded a 50 per cent margin favouring first-trimester abortions in the unified sample. Therefore, assuming that comparable samples were drawn from 1990 to 1993 (in 1994 majorities of East and West Germans supported first-trimester abortions), the fact that the differentials for 1990, 1991, 1992, and 1993 were smaller as compared to 1995 would imply that the majority in those unified samples were opposed to abortions during the first three months. When Allensbach Institut added a fourth option—abortion with counselling—to its standard three-pronged question, in 1992 and 1995 support for elective first-trimester abortions dropped in West

and East Germany. The odds seem high that since 1990 the majority of unified Germans have not approved of the permissive abortion policy adopted by
Bonn. Thus, the 1992 parliamentary act is another example of left-wing anti-
majoritarianism.

HOMOSEXUALITY

Although the issue of homosexuality had surfaced during the late 1960s in
Canada and the United Kingdom, we cannot say that the status of homosexuality has been resolved in those countries any more than in the United States
or Europe. While consenting homosexual relations between adults have been
decriminalized for the most part, the latest wrinkle in this morality policy has
been the issue of same-sex marriages. Thus, homosexuality allows us to judge
the relationship between public opinion and the older question of legalizing
consenting sexual relationships as opposed to the new debate over formally
institutionalizing same-sex arrangements (Appendix A.3).

Homosexuality: United States
The story of gay rights is more complicated in the United States because there
is no uniform national policy but 50 state policies, although clearly the once
unified front against sodomy by the states has given way to more tolerance.
On the question of consenting homosexual relations, public acceptance of
homosexuality has lagged behind decriminalization. As late as the early 1960s
every state had some form of anti-sodomy legislation (prohibiting heterosexual and/or homosexual acts), but the number of states still with criminal
penalties fell to 29 in 1979 and dropped well below the majority (19) by 1998.

On the question of legalized homosexual relations, the American public
has been closely divided since the first Gallup Poll of 1977 showed a 43 per
cent/43 per cent split. Since then, at times a plurality has favoured decriminalization, but it was rejected by a majority in the 1980s. Support for legalization
reached 50 per cent in 1999 and won over the majority in 2001, a major shift in
American attitudes if this trend holds true. However, the degree of legal acceptance has never translated into moral approval, as many more Americans
disapprove of homosexuality. A series of almost yearly NORC polls show that
73 per cent believed that same-sex relations were "always wrong" and that
roughly three-fourths of Americans continued to hold that viewpoint from
1980 through 1991, whereupon there was a marginal shift in public opinion.
By the end of the century, that rigid position was held by 59 per cent, whereas
28 per cent now believed that homosexual relations were "not wrong at all"
(Appendix A.3).

On the other hand, the consensus today among Americans is that gays should have "equal rights in terms of job opportunities," as the 56 per cent who agreed with that viewpoint in 1977 grew to 85 per cent in 2001. When asked about specific jobs, in 1977 a minority would accept them as elementary school teachers (27 per cent), clergy (36 per cent), and doctors (44 per cent), while a bare majority (51 per cent) would allow homosexuals in the armed forces; for 68 per cent, being a salesperson was acceptable. A more extensive inventory in 2001 found majority support for employing homosexuals as clergy (54 per cent), elementary (56 per cent) and high school (63 per cent) teachers, while upwards of three-fourths would accept gays in the armed forces (72 per cent), in the presidential cabinet (75 per cent), or employed as a doctor (78 per cent) or salesperson (91 per cent).[60] These data are consistent with the conclusion by two observers that "the mass public appears to have a firm (and somewhat increasing) commitment to broad concepts of civil rights for homosexuals and a corresponding disdain for gays and lesbians as a group (although there are signs of greater acceptance)."[61] Similar sentiments were registered on the attitudinal "feeling thermometer" questions on the 1992 American National Election Study that asked respondents to rate various social groups. Gays and lesbians were viewed more negatively than any other group except illegal immigrants. Also, research shows that "[a]mong the poorly educated, homophobia plays a significant role in policy reasoning" with respect to AIDS policy and civil liberties for homosexuals.[62]

Recent surveys affirm that American public opinion buttresses the legal code in opposing same-sex marriages. When the Hawaii Supreme Court declared that banning same-sex marriages was constitutionally suspect under the state equal protection doctrine, there was a widespread legislative backlash culminating in the federal Defense of Marriage Act of 1996. At the time of the Hawaii ruling, only seven other states explicitly prohibited same-sex marriages, although 30 more legally defined marriage as a civil union between a man and a woman. By early 1998, however, all but two states had considered legislation banning the legal recognition of same-sex marriages, and by 2000, 34 states had enacted such bans. Polls taken during the 1990s consistently show that more than six in ten Americans were opposed to legalizing same-sex unions, but by 2000 the opposition had fallen to a small majority (Appendix A.3). In sum, both public opinion and the legal code defend the marriage status quo.

Homosexuality: Canada

It was 1967 when Justice Minister Pierre Elliott Trudeau famously declared: "The state had no business in the bedrooms of the nation."[63] He introduced a package of reforms (divorce, abortion, birth control) that included decriminalization of homosexual relations, all of which were eventually passed with little fanfare. One cannot say that Trudeau's determination matched Canadian public opinion based on the results of a September 1968 Gallup Poll, which asked: "Do you think that homosexual behaviour, if it is conducted in private between men aged 21 and over, should or should not be a criminal act?" Forty-one per cent said it should; 42 per cent said it should not. Like their British counterparts, a bare plurality of Canadians anticipated what the government would do a year later.

Looking at opinion polls retrospectively, Rayside and Bowler say that "[o]ver the course of a generation, a major shift towards a more liberal position on the principle of equality rights for lesbians and gay men has been evident," yet "[s]trong moral disapproval of homosexuality persists ... as do fears rooted in traditional stereotypes which characterize homosexuals as deviant or sick, and threatening to children." These researchers, pointing to the 1968 Gallup poll, make the argument that mass opinions "show a dramatic shift at the time of the 1969 Criminal Code amendment on the subject, and those opinions were no doubt influenced by the change in law," insofar as "[n]ine years later, the numbers favouring decriminalization had increased from 42 to 70 per cent." In essence, argue Rayside and Bowler, attitudes towards homosexuality are soft and volatile. The "liberalized public opinion towards gay equality rights co-exists with strong heterosexist assumptions about what is normal and abnormal, healthy and sick, right and wrong."[64] As Rayside and Bowler predicted, more than two decades later less than one-fourth of Canadians believe that homosexuality can "always be justified."

The Liberals in Ottawa seem poised to formally extend legal benefits and obligations of married couples to common law couples regardless of sexual orientation, notwithstanding Canadian public opinion. Perhaps anticipating legal change, public opinion towards same-sex marriages began to soften as reported in a Gallup poll in February 2000 when 48 per cent were opposed and 43 per cent favoured "marriages between people of the same sex." When Gallup first polled Canadians in mid-1992, 61 per cent were opposed, but that proportion dropped to 52 per cent in April 1998, and then rebounded to 56 per cent one year later, before falling below the majority threshold in 2000.[65]

In sum, huge majorities of Canadians—bordering on consensus in some cases—believe that homosexuals should have "equal rights" in job opportunities, and they would not bar gays from being a junior school teacher, clergy, MP, doctor, salesperson, member of the armed forces, or prison officer. Americans also are willing to extend civil liberties to homosexuals and protection against discrimination (though the issue of gays in the American military is more contentious). On the other hand, Canadians—unlike Americans—are more accepting of homosexual relations, although—like Americans—they do not approve of same-sex marriages or homosexual adoption of children. Yet six in ten Canadians agree "that homosexual couples, who are living as married, should receive the same tax and employment benefits as heterosexual married couples."[66]

On the status of homosexuality, therefore, Canadians express more liberal views than Americans, so arguably it may not be too long before the Canadian public registers its support for codifying same-sex marriages. At this point in time, however, public opposition is represented in Canadian law. Should it be revised by the Liberals anytime soon, that action would signal the kind of political trauma that confronted Ontario in 1994, after the New Democratic Party won election to give Ontario its first NDP government. NDP Premier Bob Rae proceeded to fulfill a campaign pledge to guarantee equal protection for homosexuals by drafting Bill 167 (Equality Rights Statute Law Amendment Act), which included homosexual unions, adoption rights, and access by same-sex partners to employment benefits. After much controversy, the bill failed on a free party vote, though polling of Ontario citizens showed majority support for same-sex benefits and adoption rights (the question of same-sex marriage was not specifically asked).[67]

Homosexuality: United Kingdom

In 1553 Henry VIII removed sexual offences from church jurisdiction but retained the penalty of death in the criminal code. Homosexuality was not a crime but homosexual behaviour was. This legal regime ended with the decriminalization of consenting, adult homosexual relations in the Sexual Offences Act of 1967, although the gay community was not pleased with its overly restrictive provisions (it applied only to England and Wales, but not to the merchant navy or armed forces, for example, and the age of consent was set at 21). Nonetheless, a legal hurdle had been overcome, despite lukewarm support from the British public. In 1966, only 39 per cent favoured decriminalization, whereas 44 per cent were opposed; apparently, however, that sentiment has changed markedly. From 1979 through 1985, six in ten British respondents supported legalization, with a dip (to 55 per cent) coming in 1986, after which the level of support hovered around two-thirds into 1993 (Appendix A.3). The slight reversal during the mid-1980s, also indicated by the plurality opposed to homosexuality as an "accepted" lifestyle, may have reflected the conservative views of Prime Minister Thatcher. Because no polls are reported for the ten years after 1967, our tentative conclusion that the new law facilitated a shifting of values about homosexuality is based on the high level of public support for legalized homosexuality recorded in 1979 and afterwards. It would seem more likely that a majority of Britons would have been inclined to support decriminalization by 1977, if not earlier, rather than for us to assume the contrary.

Homosexuality: France and Germany

In the eighteenth century France (1791) along with Belgium and Luxemburg (1792) decriminalized homosexual relations, though no age of consent was imposed before 1832, when it was set first at 11 (until 1863) and then 13 until 1942, at which time it was increased to 21 under the pro-Nazi Vichy regime. There it stayed until 1978, when the age of consent lowered to 18, and finally to age 15 for both homosexuals and heterosexuals in 1982.[68] Given the centuries-old experience of France, this case is excluded from our summary analysis (see Figure 8.2).

An 1871 law outlawed homosexual relations in Germany, and gays were a persecuted minority during the Third Reich. Following World War II, homosexuality was not decriminalized until 1969 in West Germany, when the age of consent for gay men was codified at 21, being reduced to 18 in 1973. In East Germany, homosexual acts were criminalized until 1968, when they were legalized and the age of consent was established at 18; a common age of consent of 14 was specified for homosexuals and heterosexuals in 1989.[69] Decriminalization occurred despite the views of most West Germans. In 1963, large majorities of men and women wanted homosexuality punished, especially male homosexual acts, but that sentiment eased considerably by 1968, when the Allensbach Institut polled Germans specifically on Bonn's proposal to legalize homosexual relations. To that, 38 per cent supported the official position, but 45 per cent disagreed. Nearly 20 years later one survey indicated that many fewer Germans (11 per cent) would still punish adult homosexuality as compared to homosexual acts involving under-aged youth (42 per cent). The absence of polling in the aftermath of the 1968 law that decriminalized gay relations makes our conclusion very tentative. Clearly, there was a marked shift in public opinion between 1963 and 1968, and, furthermore, there was an accompanying change in how Germans perceived homosexuality. When asked how they "feel about homosexuality," the most common views among German men in 1949 was that it was a vice (53 per cent) or a disease (39 per cent), and those percentages fell slightly in 1963 (to 47 per cent and 38 per cent respectively). By 1976 only 25 per cent viewed homosexuality as a vice, more men judged it to be a disease (49 per cent), but still only 13 per cent of German men (and 20 per cent of German women) accepted homosexuality as natural.[70] The historical trend, while favourable to legalization, did not show majority support at the time of enactment, and, to this extent, this case illustrates left-wing anti-majoritarianism. If public acceptance of legalized homosexuality had occurred one decade earlier than 1987, when only 11 per cent would still punish it, then this espisode could have been coded as a redistribution of values. However, because so few Germans viewed homosexuality as "natural" in 1976, obviously the new legislation did not profoundly enlighten German public opinion.[71]

A breakthrough for gay rights in Germany came in 1994 when Parliament repealed a 1949 law that prohibited homosexual or heterosexual acts between an adult and a minor aged 16 to 18. In 1995 the Green Party launched a campaign to legalize gay unions, but same-sex marriages were not legalized for another five years. In mid-2000 another gay marriage bill was debated in Parliament, this time backed by Chancellor Gerhard Schroeder's Social Democrats (SPD) and their coalition partner, the Greens. It was anticipated that the bill would pass the Bundestag (lower house) but might be blocked in the Bundesrat (upper house), which was dominated by the Christian Democratic alliance, despite a Forsa Institut poll conducted for N24 television that found 56 per cent favouring the legislation.[72] In fact, the bill was approved and in August of 2001, amid "wide public support for the partnership registration," the first exchange of vows between a same-sex couple took place in Berlin.[73]

Given this latest poll, German opinion apparently has shifted since 1998, when a narrow 53 per cent were opposed to same-sex marriages according to Demoskopie Allensbach (Appendix A.3). How can we characterize the relationship between German public opinion and this same-sex enactment? Redistribution of values means that new law precedes attitude change; post-materialist shift means that changing attitudes preceded new law. Clearly this is a close call, but, assuming that the most recent poll accurately reflects popular feelings, then shifting attitudes likely accompanied the parliamentary debate—though they preceded the actual day of enactment. Thus we cautiously code this episode as a postmaterialist shift (see Figure 8.2).

Same-sex unions yielded a contrary political scenario in France. It took roughly 18 months before the Socialist government gained approval for its Civil Solidarity Pacts (PACS), which extends new legal rights to unmarried homosexual and heterosexual couples. It permits cohabiting couples to register their union and thereby gain inheritance, housing, and social welfare rights in addition to the ability to file joint income tax returns. The issue originated with a promise by Socialist Prime Minister Lionel Jospin to recognize gay relationships, but parliamentarians expanded the language to cover virtually any two people sharing a home. Despite assurances from the government that PACS is not same-sex marriage, the parliamentary "[d]ebates over the bill were among the stormiest the country has seen as impassioned legislators railed at each other."[74]

Moreover, the debate flowed onto the streets, with the outcry that France would become the first Catholic country to recognize homosexual unions. Earlier in the year, 200,000 protesters marched in Paris, activists called "Future of the Culture" mailed Jospin 60,000 postcards saying that the bill would "destroy the remains of civilization still separating us from barbarism," and roughly half of France's 36,000 mayors said that they would not officiate at such unions.[75] Undeterred by several parliamentary delays from conservative lawmakers as well as noisy demonstrations outside the National Assembly building, the Socialists prevailed by a vote of 315 to 249. Since it was reported that opinion surveys indicated that under one-half of the French people favoured PACS for homosexuals, though more favoured PACS for other cohabiting relationships, at first glance this episode represents more anti-majoritarianism. However, although public attitudes toward same-sex marriages were ignored in both Germany and France, the politics represented a right-wing elitism in Germany and left-wing elitism in France. Final enactment was scheduled for mid-1999, but the parliamentary losers already were planning an appeal to the French Constitutional Council (see Chapter 7).

A Schematic Summary

The relationship between public opinion and law and changes in either or both involves more than one scenario. Thirty-two cases are summarized in Figure 8.2. Twenty-three address our case histories of capital punishment, abortion, and homosexuality, and nine more are included on school prayer (United States), gun control and physician-assisted suicide (in both the United States and Canada), state lotteries (United States), English-Only laws (United States), and fox-hunting (the UK) where sufficient information has been provided to make an informed judgment.

Logically there are eight different possibilities, of which only one indicates a redistribution of values. That occurs whenever traditional public attitudes, after the enactment of a new law, are transformed in consistency with that legislation. The most likely episodes were the acceptance by Canadians of consenting homosexual relations and their embrace of a new Canadian flag. Adoption of the maple leaf in 1964 ended that political controversy and rallied the nation around the new flag. Since the 1940s more Canadians believed that the nation should have a national flag "of its own" rather than use the Union Jack or the Red Ensign, a sentiment voiced by 45 per cent to 46 per cent in the early 1960s.[76] Another probable case of value redistribution was decriminalization of homosexuality in the United Kingdom, which occurred in 1967. No polling was reported for the decade that followed but, beginning in 1979, a series of surveys reported that over three-fifths of the British supported the new policy.

For those seeking an end to the old normative order, a better strategy may be to educate public opinion in advance of changing the law, which is consistent with the *postmaterialist* thesis. Parliamentary decisions to reform

FIGURE 8.2

Schema of Linkages Between Opinion Change and Legal Change

Type	Time 1	Time 2	Time 3	Morality Policy Cases
Left Anti-Majoritarian	old opinion	changed law	old opinion	same-sex marriage: F capital punishment: C, GB, F, G abortion rights: US (1973), C (1988) abortion reform: G (1974), (1990) homosexual relations: US, G *school prayer: US*
Redistribution of Values	old opinion	changed law	new opinion	homosexual relations: UK, C *national flag: C*
Popular Backlash	new opinion	changed law	old opinion	
Postmaterialist Shift	new opinion	changed law	new opinion	abortion reform: C (1969), UK, F same-sex marriage: G *gun control: C* *state lotteries: US*
Status Quo	old opinion	unchanged law	old opinion	same-sex marriage: US, C, UK capital punishment: US *English-Only language laws: US*
Futuristic Shift	old opinion	unchanged law	new opinion	
Political Fad	new opinion	unchanged law	old opinion	
Right Anti-Majoritarian	new opinion	unchanged law	new opinion	abortion reform: US (1960s), G (1975) *gun control: US* *assisted suicide: US, C* *fox hunting: UK*

Note: capital punishment, abortion, and homosexuality cases in regular type; others in italics.

abortion law in the UK in 1967 followed by Canada in 1969 and France in 1975 occurred in the wake of changed attitudes favouring abortions for therapeutic and socio-economic reasons. Similarly, Canada's stringent gun control regime of 1995 generally reflected the long-standing support for strong gun laws by the majority of Canadians. Our tentative judgment was that enacting same-sex unions in Germany occurred in the wake of a marginal shift in the polls, whereby a narrow majority of Germans supported in 2000 what they had opposed two years earlier. Finally, recall the chronicle of state lotteries in the United States. At the turn of the nineteenth century constitutional bans on state-sponsored gambling were widespread, but in recent decades the rush by states to enact lotteries followed in the wake of a supportive public opinion.

And the vast majority of lotteries that required popular referendum were approved by the voters.

The normative *status quo* pertains whenever past and present public opinion remains unchanged and is reflected in formal law. Legal proscriptions against same-sex marriages in the United States, Canada, and the UK affirm the majoritarian viewpoint that marriage is a union between heterosexual couples. Capital punishment in the United States is widely accepted both in public opinion and in the laws of 39 states and the federal government. Codifying English-Only is odd only because 27 states chose to legally embody the linguistic value that huge majorities have always—and still—believe is the trademark of being an American.

There are several cases of anti-majoritarianism where a morality policy was changed by political elites on the Right or (more commonly) on the Left despite public opinion. Figure 8.2 identifies six cases of right-wing anti-majoritarianism. Notwithstanding widespread and consistent support for stronger gun controls, the lacklustre collection of state and federal laws provide the United States with arguably the weakest gun control regime of any western nation. Recent polls show that large majorities of Canadians and Americans favour physician-assisted suicide, yet the law, buttressed by high court rulings, disallow the practice. The early agitation for abortion reform in the United States also reflected a right-wing anti-majoritarianism only because public consensus behind therapeutic abortions was developing more rapidly than the pace of state legislative changes. In Germany, the 1975 mismatch between a more liberal public opinion and the restrictive legal code was the result of a ruling by the German Constitutional Court that nullified a reformed abortion law enacted by the Bundestag. And fox-hunting, a politically explosive conflict in the UK, finds Prime Minister Tony Blair fearful of asking a willing House of Commons to follow public opinion and abolish this blood sport because of monumental opposition from the House of Lords and rural interests. On this occasion Blair's "New Labour" philosophy is being manifested as right-wing anti-majoritarianism.

Of the 12 cases of left-wing anti-majoritarianism (Figure 8.2), three can be attributed to rulings by judicial elites. The 1962 ban on school prayer and the 1973 decision constitutionalizing a right to abortion during the first trimester were actions of the United States Supreme Court that leapfrogged ahead of public opinion—even today there is no consensus among Americans on either issue. Nor has Canadian public opinion rallied behind the ruling of its Supreme Court that nullified the 1969 law and left Canada with no abortion law whatsoever. The other 9 cases resulted from legislative elites enacting morality policies at odds with popular attitudes.

Our reading of the British reforms of abortion and homosexuality during the 1960s is not entirely consistent with Pym's observation that "[c]ampaigns like that mounted by the HLRS [Homosexual Law Reform Society] between 1958 and 1966 or that of ALRA [Abortion Law Reform Association] from 1963 onwards made people rethink their attitudes towards homosexuality and abortion. These groups' activities stimulated wider and more liberal coverage of the issues in the mass media, and ... these vigorous [abortion] campaigners cultivated a public climate in which reform was possible."[77] As noted, liberalized abortion was supported by most Britons, but polling in 1966, one year before decriminalization of homosexual relations occurred, showed that the majority did not support legalized homosexuality.

Nor did most Germans approve legalizing homosexuality in 1968, one year before the Bundestag did so. And those enactments by a minority of American state governments to decriminalize consenting homosexual relations occurred at a time when national polls showed that the majority of Americans disapproved. To correctly assess the overlap between public policy and public opinion on this issue, within-state polling is required to judge whether each enactment was or was not representative. Still, even if we acknowledge that a long-term shift towards American acceptance of legalized homosexuality came after the majority of states adopted decriminalization, thus implying a redistribution of values (which cannot be proved since other factors may have "caused" the rising tolerance for the gay lifestyle), we can argue more persuasively that those state legal reforms of the 1970s did not have much short-term impact on public opinion nationwide.

In 1999 the French Socialists prevailed in the National Assembly on a bill to legalize same-sex unions, despite much public outcry and a tepid response from the majority of French citizens. One issue on which all these four countries—and likely many others across Europe—are left-wing anti-majoritarian is capital punishment. The abolition of the death penalty in the UK, Canada, Germany, and even France occurred at a time when public opinion was not supportive. Today polls continue to find lopsided majorities favouring the restoration of capital punishment in all those countries, except France.

Two attempts to reform the German abortion law were left-wing anti-majoritarian. The first came in 1974 when the Bundestag authorized elective first-trimester abortion despite the fact that a minority of West Germans held that position, the second after the 1990 reunification of East and West Germany that yielded a parliamentary enactment more closely mirroring the permissive first-trimester law of East Germany than the criminal code of West Germany. Our best estimation is that most people in a unified Germany would not favour elective abortion during the first three months of a pregnancy.

In the next—and final—chapter we will make explicit what has been implied throughout this discussion—morality policy is not democratic. And because the *content* of morality policy is non-representative of public opinion, that finding also casts doubt on the morality policy *process*. Thus, morality policy is fundamentally unlike distributive, regulatory, or redistributive policy. Recall that Theodore J. Lowi (Chapter 1) argued that distributive policies are privatized as negotiated settlements, whereas regulatory policies illustrate vintage pluralism, engaging rival interest groups, and redistributive policy provokes class-based struggles. In contrast, morality policy and politics at the national level is *elitist* (even direct democracy in the Unite States is limited to states and localities). This will be the normative lesson of Chapter 9.

Notes

1. Inglehart; Flanagan; Meier 246-47.

2. Meier 4.

3. R. Cooter, "Expressive Law and Economics," *Journal of Legal Studies* 27 (1998): 585-607; C.R. Sunstein, "Social Norms and Social Roles," *Columbia Law Review* 96 (1997): 903-68.

4. Charles S. Bullock, III, and Charles M. Lamb, *Implementation of Civil Rights Policy* (Monterey, CA: Brooks/Cole Publishing, 1984) 3.

5. Tom W. Smith and Paul B. Sheatsley, "American Attitudes toward Race Relations," *Public Opinion* 14-15 (October/November, 1984): 50.

6. Kinder and Sanders 4, 6-7. Also see Paul Sniderman and Thomas Piazza, *The Scar of Race* (Cambridge, MA: Harvard University Press, 1993).

7. M. Silverman, "Toward a Theory of Criminal Deterrence," *American Sociological Review* 41 (June, 1976): 442-61; H.G. Grasmick and D.E. Green, "Legal Punishment, Social Disapproval and Internalization as Inhibitors of Illegal Behavior," *Journal of Criminal Law and Criminology* 71 (Fall, 1980): 325-35.

8. Tom R. Tyler, *Why People Obey the Law* (New Haven, CT: Yale University Press, 1990) 25, 64. The "person's feeling of obligation to obey the law and allegiance to legal authorities" was the second strongest factor among the various demographic variables tested.

9. P.H. Robinson and J.M. Darley, *Justice, Liability, and Blame* (Boulder, CO: Westview Press, 1997); P.H. Robinson and J.M. Darley, "The Utility of Desert," *Northwestern University Law Review* 91 (1997): 453-99.

10. Two inventories of the early research were Theodore Becker, *The Impact of Supreme Court Decisions: Empirical Studies* (New York: Oxford University Press, 1969) and Stephen L. Wasby, *The Impact of the United States Supreme Court: Some Perspectives* (Homewood, IL: The Dorsey Press, 1970). On specific issues, see Murley 36-39 and Tatalovich, *The Politics of Abortion in the United States and Canada* 199-202.

11. Murley 23-25.

12. Tatalovich, *The Politics of Abortion in the United States and Canada*, Table 7.5, 211; footnote on 212.

13. Tatalovich, *The Politics of Abortion in the United States and Canada* 202-13; see update in Raymond Tatalovich and Melissa A. Haussman, "Provincial Policies on Abortion Since

Morgentaler," paper Delivered to the Annual Meeting, Canadian Political Science Association, Quebec City, 2000.

14. Nevitte, Brandon, and Davis 24, 25.

15. Leslie A. Pal, "Gun Control: US and Canada," Pal and Weaver.

16. Mauser and Margolis 196-97.

17. Mauser and Margolis 207.

18. Spitzer, "Gun Control: Constitutional Mandate or Myth?" 124.

19. Pal, "Gun Control: US and Canada."

20. Mauser and Margolis 205-06.

21. Pal, "Gun Control: US and Canada."

22. These Gallup polls were publicized by the Coalition for Gun Control, Press Release (23 November 2000) http://www.guncontrol.ca/Content/Poll.htm.

23. Christopher D. Ram, "Living Next to the United States: Recent Developments in Canadian Gun Control Policy, Politics, and Law," *New York Law School Journal of International and Comparative Law* 15 (1995): 279-313. Polling results in footnote 95, 302-03.

24. See Mauser, "The Politics of Firearms Registration in Canada" 1-26.

25. James Brooke, "Canada fighting internal battle over gun registration," *New York Times* 8 May 2000; James Brooke, "Canadians Said to Obey Gun Law, After All," *New York Times* 26 December 2000: A11.

26. Gary A. Mauser, "The Case of the Missing Canadian Gun Owners," paper delivered at the Annual Meeting, American Society of Criminology, Atlanta, GA, November 2001.

27. James A. Davis, "Changeable Weather in a Cooling Climate Atop the Liberal Plateau," *Public Opinion Quarterly* 56 (1992): 294. Also see Tom W. Smith, "Liberal and Conservative Trends in the United States since World War II," *Public Opinion Quarterly* 54 (1990): 479-507; and Tom W. Smith, "Atop a Liberal Plateau? A Summary of Trends since World War II," *Research in Urban Policy: Coping with Urban Austerity*, Vol. 1, ed. Terry Nichols Clark (Greenwich, CT: JAI Press, 1985) 245-57.

28. Nevitte 218.

29. This result is consistent with Gallup polls in the United States showing that opposition to legalizing marijuana ranged from a low of 66 per cent in 1977 to a high of 84 per cent in 1969, with the mid-1990s showing almost three-fourths of Americans opposed. *The Gallup Poll Monthly* 368 (May 1996): 3.

30. Nevitte 217, 219.

31. *The Gallup Poll Monthly* 368 (May 1996): 4. The percentages approving were 65 per cent in 1990, 75 per cent in early April, and 68 per cent in late April 1996. This revised question elicited lower levels of support in January (58 per cent) and June (57 per cent) 1997, in June 1998 (59 per cent), and in March 1999 (61 per cent): "When a person has a disease that cannot be cured and is living in severe pain, do you think doctors should be allowed by law to assist the patient to commit suicide if the patient requests it, or not?" George Gallup, Jr., *The Gallup Poll 1999* (Wilmington, DE: Scholarly Resources, Inc., 2000) 161.

32. Glick and Hutchinson 66.

33. Gary Edwards and Josephine Mazzuca, "Three Quarters of Canadians Support Doctor-Assisted Suicide," *Poll Releases* (Princeton, NJ: The Gallup Organization, 24 March 1999), http://www.gallup.com/poll/releases/pr990323.asp.

34. Roger Hood, *The Death Penalty: A World-Wide Perspective* (New York: Clarendon Press, 1996) 213-14.

35. Christoph, *Capital Punishment and British Politics* 109; earlier surveys referenced are found on 43, 53-54; see also 116; survey data on 117.

36. Bill Jones, "Crime and Punishment," *Political Issues in Britain Today*, ed. Bill Jones (New York: Manchester University Press, 1994) 369.

37. Gallup, *The Gallup International Public Opinion Polls: Great Britain 1937-1975*, Vol. 1 (New York: Random House, 1976) 11. To the question "Should the death penalty be abolished?," 45 per cent said yes and 11 per cent had no opinion.

38. David B. Chandler, *Capital Punishment in Canada* (Toronto: McClelland and Stewart, 1976) 52-53, 51.

39. Richard Johnston, *Public Opinion and Public Policy in Canada: Questions of Confidence* (Toronto: University of Toronto Press, 1986) 79, 81.

40. Etienne Schweisguth, "The Myth of Neoconservatism," *How France Votes*, ed. Michael S. Lewis-Beck (New York: Chatham House Publishers, 2000) 183; see survey results on 179 and the question on 175.

41. Forst 115-16.

42. M. Mohrenschlager, "The Abolition of Capital Punishment in the Federal Republic of Germany: German Experiences," *Revue Internationale de Droit Penal* 58: 512-13.

43. Mohrenschlager 513-14.

44. Tatalovich, *The Politics of Abortion in the United States and Canada*.

45. Monica Boyd and Deirdre Gillieson, "Canadian Attitudes on Abortion: Results of the Gallup Polls," *Canadian Studies in Population* 2 (1975): 53-64. Several American polls are surveyed in Tatalovich and Daynes, *The Politics of Abortion* 116-20.

46. See Rebecca J. Cook and Bernard M. Dickens, "A Decade of International Change in Abortion Law: 1967-1977," *American Journal of Public Health* 68 (July 1978): 637-44.

47. Tatalovich, *The Politics of Abortion in the United States and Canada* 142; see also polling trends on 111-13.

48. Timothy F. Hartnagel, James J. Creechan, and Robert A. Silverman, "Public Opinion and the Legalization of Abortion," *Canadian Review of Sociology and Anthropology* 22 (1985): 424-25.

49. Charles Franklin and Liane C. Kosaki, "Republican Schoolmaster: The US Supreme Court, Public Opinion, and Abortion," *American Political Science Review* 83 (September 1989): 762.

50. Neil Nevitte, William P. Brandon, and Lori Davis, "The American Abortion Controversy: Lessons from Cross-National Evidence," *Politics and the Life Sciences* (February 1993): 26.

51. Cited in Hindell and Simms 122-23, 184, 210-11.

52. Janine Mossuz-Lavau, "Abortion Policy in France under Governments of the Right and Left (1973-84)," Lovenduski and Ooutshoorn 86.

53. Dorothy McBride Stetson, "Abortion Policy Triads and Women's Rights in Russia, the United States, and France," Githens and Stetson 109.

54. Mossuz-Lavau 86.

55. Gallup, *Gallup International Public Opinion Polls: France 1939, 1944-1975*, Vol. 2: 1065.

56. Scheppele 38.

57. Outshoorn, "The Stability of Compromise" 161-62.

58. Cook and Dickens 643.

59. Scheppele 40.

60. *The Gallup Poll Monthly* 375 (December 1996): 13 and 429 (June 2001): 6-7.

61. Donovan and Bowler, "Direct Democracy and Minority Rights" 111-12.

62. American National Election Study, Survey Research Center, University of Michigan, 1992. On the impact of homophobia, see Paul M. Sniderman, Richard A. Brody, and Philip E. Tetlock, *Reasoning and Choice* (Cambridge, UK: Cambridge University Press, 1991) 47.

63. George Radwanski, *Trudeau* (Toronto: Macmillan, 1978) 90.

64. David Rayside and Scott Bowler, "Research Note: Public Opinion and Gay Rights," *The Canadian Review of Sociology and Anthropology* 25 (November 1988) 649, 650-51, 656.

65. Gary Edwards and Josephine Mazzuca, "About Four-in-Ten Canadians Accepting of Same Sex Marriages, Adoption," *Poll Releases* (Princeton, NJ: The Gallup Organization, 7 March 2000), http://www.gallup.com/poll/releases/pr000307b.asp.

66. Edwards and Mazzuca, "About Four-in-Ten Canadians Accepting of Same Sex Marriages, Adoption."

67. Rayside 152.

68. Peter Tatchell, *Out in Europe: A Guide to Lesbian and Gay Rights in 30 European Countries* (London: Channel 4 Television Publications, 1990) 3, 16.

69. Tatchell 17, 27.

70. Elisabeth Noelle-Neumann, ed., *The Germans: Public Opinion Polls, 1967-1980* (Westport, CT: Greenwood Press, 1981) 251.

71. When asked about homosexuality between men in 1987, we only reported (Table A.3) that 11 per cent would punish adult homosexual acts and 42 per cent would punish homosexual acts with under-aged youth. But the multi-pronged question allowed respondents to choose more than one answer. In addition, seven other responses had varying negative connotations: (1) disgusts/sickens me—40 per cent; (2) I can't understand it—40 per cent; (3) is a topic which makes me uneasy—27 per cent; (4) is a sickness—22 per cent; (5) damages your health—17 per cent; (6) is something I don't want to talk about—14 per cent; (7) one should resolutely combat it—12 per cent. In contrast, four benign or favourable assessments elicited fewer responses: (1) people shouldn't make such a big deal of it—29 per cent; (2) doesn't bother me—29 per cent; (3) one shouldn't make fun of it—25 per cent; (4) is a very natural thing—12 per cent. See question in footnote (f) in Table A.3.

72. "Gay Marriage Bill Set to be Rejected by German Parliament," *Deutsche Presse-Agentur* July 7, 2000.

73. "Same-Sex Partners Win Legal Status in Germany," *New York Times* 2 August 2001: A3.

74. Suzanne Daley, "France Gives Legal Status to Unmarried Couples," *New York Times* 14 October 1999: A3.

75. Daley.

76. See poll trends in Mildred A. Schwartz, *Public Opinion and Canadian Identity* (Berkeley, CA: University of California Press, 1967) 107.

77. Bridget Pym, *Pressure Groups and the Permissive Society* (Newton Abbot, G.B.: David and Charles, 1974) 117-18.

9

Conclusion:
Morality Policy and
Democratic Governance

This book has investigated morality policy in five democracies. In his inventory of such disputes in 22 westernized nations, Donley Studlar lists these: abortion, gambling, alcohol/drugs, religious education/Sunday observance, animal rights, homosexuality, capital punishment, pornography, divorce, euthanasia, women's rights, ethnic/racial minorities, and gun control. However, their frequencies vary widely, because some are so old that they are no longer contentious, whereas others are too new to hit the political radar screen. First ranked is abortion, having been debated in every country; third-ranked homosexuality was politicized in nine nations; but capital punishment was subjected to political debate only in four (United States, Canada, France, and the UK). The contagion of morality politics among this group of nations shows, not surprisingly, that "the United States has the most morality disputes" (with 13), followed by the UK and Canada (both with 11), as well as France (7) in the top quarter, but Germany (3) far down the list. These patterns, concludes Studlar, are "prima facie confirmation of Anglo-American moralism and a distinction between continental countries and the English-speaking ones on the amount of moral controversy in their politics."[1]

No scholar would have any qualms with Studlar's list of morality policies, or those defined as conscience issues by Philip Cowley,[2] but policy analysis needs more than a periodic updating of lists. We need a conceptualization of morality politics that stands the test of time, that can look back to the issue of slavery in the nineteenth century, to Prohibition in the early twentieth century, and to animal rights in the twenty-first century. Policy analysts also would agree with Studlar's attributes of morality policy:

> Its debate is framed in terms of fundamental rights and values, often stemming from religious imperatives, by competing promotional groups whose members have little or no direct economic interest in

the outcome. Advocates invest considerable emotional capital in the values that they want their society and government to promote or protect. These issues are nontechnical in the sense that they do not require specialized expertise to hold an "informed" opinion. For these reasons, most morality policy issues also have relatively high public visibility.

Finally, adds Studlar, "[c]onflict of basic identities ... including nationality, race, religion, language, ethnicity, gender, and sexual identity, are likely to lead to morality politics," whereas disputes over social class and the economic sector "are less likely to lead to such disputes, at least without the added impetus of one or more of the basic identities."[3]

Fundamentalist religious beliefs are strongly related to hostility to gay rights, but what about animal rights? Does it immediately come to mind what "basic identities" provoked political brawls over daylight savings time in Australia or New Zealand and over fluoridation of water supplies in the United States and Canada? Does the perennial issue of gun control in the United States mean that the Western "gun culture" is a basic identity like race and gender? The environment did not make Studlar's list, nor Cowley's (though the Greens are politically active all over Europe), so presumably environmental activists are *not* driven by values or "first principles"—like Nature.[4] In other words, everything that Studlar says is true, and we heartily agree that identity lies at the core of moral conflict, but no list can include all possible examples, nor can a summary of their policy attributes provide enough theoretical power to explain the emergence of morality politics or to account for their future manifestations.

We have tried to fill this theoretical vacuum with culture theory. Culture theory does not depend upon "basic identities" like race, gender, or language. Religion *is* important, but culture theory does not need religion to explain moral conflict in the highly secular nations of Europe. All observers of morality politics, whether case analysts or quantitative empiricists, agree that economic class—conventionally understood—plays little or no role in these disputes. The logic of culture theory is that moral conflicts are struggles between the forces of *status-differentiation* and the forces of *status-egalitarianism*. The first reflects the hierarchical bias that looks fondly upon traditional societies in which individuals and groups know their place. The latter includes other elites of many stripes on the Left who believe in universal principles of human dignity and human rights.

And what about the masses? Morality policies can differentiate elites from masses—with political elites going one way and the masses another. The forces of status-differentiation, therefore, are sometimes aided by so-called "working-class authoritarianism," a phrase coined by sociologist Seymour Martin Lipset decades before postmaterialism was in vogue. Lipset said that "intolerant movements in modern society are more likely to be based on the lower classes than on the middle and upper classes [and this] has posed a tragic dilemma for those intellectuals of the democratic left who once believed the proletariat necessarily to be a force for liberty, racial equality, and social progress."[5] His observation was not limited to the American working-class, though early in the abortion debate in the United States Peter Skerry also noticed that abortion represented more than single-issue politics: it revealed "the upper-middle-class bias of the women's movement from which it emerged. Some [abortion] reformers explicitly link their efforts to a critique of the nuclear family and traditional sexual morality."[6] Attitudinal research by Granberg found that anti-abortion views among Americans did not relate to any coherent pro-life ideology nor to political conservatism but rather to "a traditional or conservative approach to matters of personal morality."[7] The clustering of attitudes shows opposition to abortion as well as to sex education, access to birth control information, premarital sex, easy divorce, homosexuality, and pornography.

Anti-Majoritarianism

From this comparative analysis of morality policies we find two conclusions to be especially compelling. The first is *anti-majoritarianism*; the second is *political unaccountability*. Perhaps the finding of anti-majoritarianism should not have surprised us, given that several studies of representation in Western democracies show "little evidence of policy agreement between constituents and their legislators."[8] Both right-wing and left-wing elites are responsible for this state of affairs, though clearly a larger share of the blame can be apportioned on the Left, given its advocacy of identity politics. This book was organized around three issues—capital punishment, abortion, and homosexuality—though other issues were added where especially apt. The relationship between public opinion and formal law summarized in Figure 8.2 revealed 21 anti-majoritarian policies of the 32 discussed, meaning that polls showed that the *majority* was not supportive of legal change at the time those parliamentary or judicial decisions were made (although a plurality may have been). Twelve involved left-wing anti-majoritarianism; six reflected right-wing anti-majoritarianism; and three represented a "redistribution of values." By its nature, any attempt to redistribute values is anti-majoritarian, notwithstanding the presumption that changes in the law will force changes in attitudes. Of these redistributive cases, only with respect to the maple leaf flag debate in Canada in 1964 did polls show that a plurality of Canadians had signaled their willingness to replace the historic English banner, and afterwards most Canadians relatively quickly accepted the "new" design. Similarly, homosexuality was legalized in Canada at a time when a bare plurality favoured decriminalization, but within a few years polls registered approval by most Canadians. Based on available survey data, our best guess is that public opinion in the United Kingdom also shifted in the wake of the 1967 act that decriminalized homosexuality.

In distinguishing between a redistribution of values and a postmaterial-ist shift, therefore, the meaning of short term and long term comes into play. To err on the liberal side, our feeling is that majority opinion would have to be transformed within 10 years of a legal enactment in order to conclude that a redistribution of values has occurred. Thus, gradual long-term changes in public opinion likely result from other factors, not simply legal change, and signal a postmaterialist shifting in the majority point of view. Majority acceptance of legalized homosexuality in the United States, based on polls taken around 2000, lagged well behind state laws decriminalizing those relationships, just as the rise of abolitionist sentiment in France required a nearly two-decade long adjustment in public opinion. In sum, these cases affirm what Morton and Knopff say about Canada, that anti-majoritarianism in morality politics is more often a curse of the Left.[9] And in the UK, as Read, Marsh, and Richards observe based upon their analysis of conscience votes in the House of Commons, "Once again, these results show that on homosexuality law reform, as on capital punishment, Parliament is more liberal, on occasions considerably more liberal, than the general public."[10]

An integral feature of our analysis has been Kenneth Meier's distinction between one-sided and two-sided morality policies, since democratic respon-siveness has different implications for each type. Meier strongly implies that one-sided morality policy smacks too much of majoritarianism. The "status quo" (Figure 8.2), when the law reinforces traditional values, represents Meier's politics of sin: capital punishment and English-Only language laws in the United States and bans on same-sex marriages in the United States, Canada, and the UK. Since a two-sided policy conflict forecasts a divided public, organized interests mobilized on both sides, and disunity within the political establishment, to transform this kind of ideological polarization into a zero-sum policy outcome does more than show contempt for majority rule. It plays fast and loose with the political rules of the game.

The worst-case scenario of anti-majoritarianism was the abolition of capital punishment in the UK and Germany, likely in France, and especially in Canada. Ottawa ended the death penalty despite long-standing support for it from Canadians that has been only marginally below the levels registered in the United States. Polls show that most Americans justify the death penalty in terms of revenge or its deterrent value.[11] One study found that "as support for the death penalty has increased so has willingness to endorse retribution as a motive," and, furthermore, while "a large proportion of the American public ... believe the death penalty is unfair, [they] support it nonetheless."[12] Scholarship also finds that support for capital punishment in the United States and Canada has an emotional and symbolic function unrelated to the risk of being victimized. Research that compared the "symbolic" against the "instrumental" explanations for public opinion found that "[c]itizens' policy preferences concerning the use of the death penalty are a reflection of their basic [political-social] values, not a result of their specific concerns about crime."[13]

These findings provide intellectual ammunition for abolitionists who argue that political elites are justified in ignoring public sentiments on the death penalty. The 1973 parliamentary debate in Canada, for example, found retentionist MPs bolstering their argument with polling statistics, whereas "many abolitionists countered with the position that a Member of Parliament is much more than a mere representative of his riding [district], much more than a rubber stamp of his constituency's wishes" who, in the face of majority support for retention, "were reduced to disdaining the 'mere' representative role of an elected official in the United States House of Representatives."[14] Director Michel Forst of Amnesty International, France, asks—in the face of polls showing majority retentionist support 20 years after the last execution—"[y]et is this a well-informed opinion, is there a thorough understanding of the facts and the risks involved in the death penalty ... what value and significance should be given to opinion polls?" His answer is not much: "Amnesty International believes that respect for life and the human rights that protect it must never depend on public opinion, but that those responsible for policy in this area have a duty to ensure that the public is well-informed."[15] A similar rationale was heard in Germany where, despite polls to the contrary, M. Mohrenschlager of the German Federal Ministry of Justice articulated this abolitionist argument: "The vast majority of learned writers dealing with the problems of capital punishment also deny that it has a right to exist," in addition to its "firm rejection" by the political class. To those victims and survivors who demand atonement, retaliation, and revenge, he says that such sentiments have no place in criminal law, because "[a]s a matter of principle, all members of the community, even criminal offenders, are entitled to the right of life which is embodied in the constitutions of many States and in the international covenants of human rights."[16] Dignity means equality; equality means rights; rights means *status*—even for the worst among us.

Elite arrogance underlies the willingness of parliamentarians to act contrary to public opinion. There is surely a cultural divide between how political elites and the masses assess capital punishment. The average citizen has no difficulty drawing a line between their "status" as law-abiding citizens and murderers who deserve final retribution. Yet, political elites abetted by scholars believe that "deterrence" is the only legitimate standard by which capital punishment can be judged. Nor is any huge leap of faith required for them to believe that ordinary citizens would endorse abolition if only they were educable and had enough information.

Discounting Democracy

If elites can justify parliamentary aloofness from public opinion, the critics of direct democracy can rally similar arguments to delegitimize the popular will. One common line of attack is that the public is ill-informed. Worse yet, the volatility of public opinion, which shows that events have great influence on public attitudes—as in France regarding capital punishment—is taken as *prima facie* evidence that the attitudes of ordinary citizens are not grounded in reason. If that is the case, then how can the relative stability of American and Canadian attitudes favouring capital punishment be explained? On the other hand, liberals in the United States point to sustained public support for stronger gun laws as evidence that intense minorities are denying the majority will. If stable opinions on gun control are compelling evidence in favour of majoritarianism, why are similar trends in attitudes toward capital punishment not accepted with equal validity? We already noted that an assassination of a political figure so influences the climate of American opinion that new gun control legislation is often forthcoming. Maybe there is a simple answer to this contradiction, namely, that liberals favour gun control but oppose the death penalty.

A second line of attack is that the wording of polling questions or popular plebiscites elicits different responses. On the death penalty, for example, the degree of support for capital punishment goes down when life imprisonment without parole is juxtaposed as the alternative. True enough, but this methodological bias affects any poll on every issue. Abortion polling, according to pro-choice advocates, shows that Americans and Canadians favour a woman's right to choose. But we know that any abstract question, particularly those with libertarian connotations, will elicit high levels of approval, as, for example, when abortion is framed as a decision between the woman and her physician and when it is mentioned that abortion is legal or has the sanction of judicial authorities. Nonetheless, polling over decades also shows that the majority of Canadians and Americans support abortions for various therapeutic reasons, but not as an elective procedure. And although Canadians are more inclined than Americans to favour gun registration and licencing owners, Mauser shows that those attitudes soften considerably when respondents are asked to consider policy trade-offs, like the costs involved or the reassignment of police personnel from law enforcement to administration. Thus, the nature of public attitudes is likely too complex to be revealed in any one survey question. As a result, such criticisms of direct democracy are ploys to circumvent popular sovereignty and are used selectively by elites to disparage majoritarianism. The political reality is that public opinion is no less informed on morality policies than on foreign affairs or economic policies. It is the nature of democracy, the price we pay for popular sovereignty.

Political Unaccountability

Social scientists know that political elites are more issue-oriented and ideologically driven than ordinary voters. This explains why, as Cowley pointed out, parliamentarians vote ideologically on morality policies even when the party whips are withdrawn. But why is ideology among elites no less a constraint on reason than weakly held opinions or ignorance on the part of the masses? So long as ideology is aligned on a Left-Right axis in terms of class conflict and economic interests, it works to obstruct rather than facilitate political representation. Representative governments are supposed to keep their political leadership accountable to the citizenry. Why has the representational relationship broken down despite the fact, as every observer agrees, that morality policies are highly salient and emotional disputes, which cut to core social values?

The answer is that the political processes and party systems in parliamentary regimes operate to isolate the elected from the electors. Not only do the hierarchical attributes of collective responsibility and disciplined parties in parliamentary regimes obstruct public opinion, but an ideological bias discounts popular sovereignty (except as expressed through elections). One can react to this democratic dilemma with a yawn, make a value-free reference to Harold Laswell's politics as "who gets what, when, and how," and entirely dismiss the policy outcome. That might work if morality policies were routine or pedestrian, but they are not. As British political scientist Cowley says, the law on capital punishment, abortion, homosexual relations, hunting, "and a whole host of similar questions, are far from peripheral or unimportant."[17]

Perhaps the fact that most citizens are not directly affected by morality policy offers a rationale for some loosening of democratic tenets. We have argued that the "target" group for each of these morality policies is not large, based upon an objective assessment of (not necessarily economic) self-interest. Those convicted murderers who could face the death penalty, those desiring to terminate a pregnancy, and those who are homosexual are a minority, if not a fraction, of the British, French, German, Canadian, or American societies. For those directly affected, such policies have paramount significance that they do not have for the public at large, though citizens may become active when their personal values are offended. In other words, a widely distributed tax benefit, new social entitlements, or even a nation at war has an immediacy for most citizens that is lacking with morality policies.

Saying that morality policies may not hold high priority for voters or that citizens may lack information about them is no defence for a lack of parliamentary accountability. Cowley discounts the argument that, because elections provide voters with the opportunity to hold MPs accountable for their actions, their failure to do so implies that these morality issues do not matter to the electorate. While he agrees that the citizenry does not rank conscience issues as serious matters for public concern, the paradox is that the party whips are "regularly applied" to other votes "about which the public know[s] little and care[s] less. If we were only to have whipped votes on those issues about which the public were very interested, free votes would be the norm not the exception." From this perspective, morality policies represent "a small but important group of issues which are treated differently—and in a system largely dominated by party such treatment causes clear problems of democratic accountability."[18]

Cowley could have pointed to another political fact about free votes: they are accompanied by a not insignificant number of abstentions. The research we reported on free votes in Canada on abortion and capital punishment and in the UK on a variety of conscience issues, including homosexuality, showed many abstentions. Are not the odds higher that parliamentary abstainers would have been "no" votes, absent the party whips? Probably, because abstentions identify those MPs who, for reasons of personal morality or constituency opinion, are risk-adverse to following the subtle signals from the government to vote yes (to even reach the floor there must be some degree of government acquiescence). Thus, the likely impact of parliamentary abstentions is to facilitate the passage of measures, because in non-parliamentary systems like the United States such legislators, who are placed in a conflicted position vis-à-vis their party and constituency opinion, tend to vote their constituencies.

Morality policy by plebiscite is often criticized on the grounds that voter turnout affects the policy outcome, as noted in fluoridation referendums, the implication being that a small number of voters skew the outcome. Thus, the inclination among informed opinion is to tolerate, if not praise, parliamentarians despite their cowardice but to condemn voters because of their passivity. In other words, non-voting hurts, but parliamentary abstentions help. In our opinion, to explain away the refusal of MPs to take a stand on these controversial issues as "pain avoidance" is too benign, for it covers up the obfuscation of political accountability. In fact, non-voting by parliamentarians is less defensible than voter non-participation because MPs are politically entrusted to "represent" their constituents, whereas voters are themselves sovereign in such matters.

But the political obstacles to accountability run deeper than unwhipped votes and abstentions. Most fundamental is the tendency for political parties in Canada and Europe to run away from these issues during election campaigns. As was shown (Chapter 4), party leaders emphasize their tried-and-true economic agendas that mobilize class-based constituencies. There was no "mandate" in 1968 for the Canadian Liberals to sponsor omnibus reforms of abortion, legalized homosexuality, gambling, and divorce any more than what catapulted British Labour to power in the 1960s, after which capital punishment was abolished and homosexuality decriminalized. Since then, four British elections over the 1970s and 1980s continued to focus on economics, and the Tories no less than Labour chose to ignore the contentious issues of race and abortion. The instances when party leaders make explicit their morality policy agenda—as when Mitterrand promised to abolish capital punishment in France—are few and far between.

We did not begin this project with any presumption that morality policy is anti-majoritarian and politically unaccountable. Being too well-versed in American politics is a partial explanation, or apology, as we may have presumed too much about the responsiveness of parliamentary regimes. As Russell Dalton explains: "While the representation process may be based on individual legislators in the United States, political representation in Western Europe largely follows the party government model."[19] The fact that the United States has the most open political opportunity structure of any nation, one inhabited by policy entrepreneurs unhampered by strong parties or disciplined whips, plus arguably the largest array of unsettled moral conflicts coupled with the most ideologically conservative and religious body politic in the democratic world, says volumes about risk-adverse American legislators trying to grapple with social activists in the context of a cautious American electorate that casts ballots very often as compared to voters in Canada, the UK, or Europe.

The charge by Morton and Knopff that Canadian judicial elites are biased towards postmaterialist values extends to parliamentary elites within the Canadian Liberal, British Labour, and French Socialist Parties. Inglehart determined that there were nearly three times as many postmaterialists among the candidates for the multi-national European Parliament as compared to the general public.[20] Morality policy-making in Canada and Europe is more *un*accountable to the body politic than what transpires in the United States. A partisan alignment with moral issues is transparent in America. Elsewhere, it is obscured, although party elites are the driving force behind morality policy, which seemingly contradicts the Inglehart and Flanagan thesis that postmaterialism causes a realignment in western party systems. Yet, the contraction is more apparent than real. Inglehart and Flanagan were debating partisan dynamics in the electorate, to assess strains within the proletariat and bourgeoisie that would cause a shifting of partisan loyalties towards a reconfigured New Left versus New Right. Our concern is with party-in-government: elites.

This sampling of morality policies illustrates how often existing party leaders—and governments—have adopted postmaterialist goals as their own, especially Leftist parties. Looking at the alignment of 14 political parties in the UK, Germany, and France, Dalton found that party elites and their voters among the Socialists and Communists held liberal views on abortion, whereas the voters and leaders of Rightist parties were more conservative.[21] Joyce Outshoorn's observation about a traditional Left-Right division over abortion in France and the UK applies with equal force to capital punishment and gay rights in France, both orchestrated by the Socialists, as well as the Canadian Liberals' embrace of a host of morality policy reforms from Trudeau through Chrétien: abortion reform, legalized homosexuality, divorce liberalization, birth control, abolition of capital punishment, hate crime legislation, gun controls, and gay rights. In the UK, the guise of free voting does not disguise the fact that legislation to legalize consenting homosexual relations and abolish capital punishment would never have passed without overwhelming support from Labour backbenchers.

Can we point, therefore, to any example of morality policy where politics better accommodates policy? Yes, and it offers a normative baseline for judging the morality policy process in any democratic system. By our lights the most benign scenario from the perspective of representative government, democratic politics, and consensus-building is the "postmaterialist shift" (Figure 8.2). This is how abortion policy was reformed across many western democracies during the 1960s, as illustrated by Canada and the UK, and later in France. Allowing therapeutic abortions paved the way towards eventual legalization. The agenda-setting process catapulted this issue onto the political agenda and, along the way, cultivated popular support for abortion reforms as urged by organized medicine. Canadian Prime Minister Trudeau did not disrupt the emerging policy consensus favouring abortion reform as much as codify it.

One More Case: Euthanasia in the Netherlands

On legalized physician-assisted suicide the Netherlands is the world's maverick, as liberal in its social mores as the United States is conservative.[22] Yet, the Dutch experience is exemplary as to how the morality policy process *ought* to proceed in order to achieve policy consensus and assure political civility. The political gestation period took at least a decade before the Dutch Parliament acted, and its legislation was shaped by prevailing medical practices. Essentially the law followed in the wake of non-compliance by the "target" group—physicians—with an outdated penal code.

Legalized euthanasia in the Netherlands is another example of a postmaterialist shift (see Figure 8.2), because public opinion was supportive prior to legal enactment and, afterwards, has not diminished. Of the 12 countries included in the World Values Survey, only citizens of Denmark and the Netherlands exhibited majority support for active euthanasia, or physician-assisted suicide. However, between 1981 and 1990 support among the Danes fell (64 per cent to 54 per cent) but increased among the Dutch (53 per cent to 60 per cent).[23]

"One of the most striking features" of Dutch euthanasia, says Griffiths, was "the key role that self-regulation has played in the process of legal development. The rules and procedures that govern euthanasia were largely worked out within the medical profession before being adopted in the case law and in (proposed) legislation." Perhaps it is not excessive to characterize the prelegislative history of modern Dutch history of euthanasia as professional non-compliance with an outdated criminal ban. By self-regulation Griffiths means "a process of legal change in which the group whose behaviour is the object of regulation takes the initiative in developing rules and procedures that come ... to be considered 'legal.'" Section 293 of the Criminal Code "flatly prohibited" anyone from "[c]ausing a person's death at the person's request," but that posed no practical barrier since "in the early 1970s it began to become apparent that an absolute prohibition of euthanasia was not consistent with the demands of medical practice as seen by doctors" whose voice was pivotal in the debate. Griffiths continues, "Although there were developments in public opinion, in legal opinion, and in political opinion in the same period, the new attitude of doctors was increasingly expressed not only in the form of contributions to the public debate but in the form of self-made regulations applicable to precisely the behavior apparently forbidden altogether by section 293."[24]

During the 1970s and 1980s some physicians were brought to trial for violating Section 293; in the process, courts in the *Postma* (1973) and *Wertheim* (1981) cases laid out guidelines for euthanasia that would pass legal scrutiny. In 1984 the Royal Dutch Medical Association's Executive Board issued new policy guidelines for euthanasia; apparently, its change of heart influenced the Dutch Supreme Court to rule in *Schoonheim* (1984) that a violation of Section 293 can be justified "according to responsible medical opinion, subject to the applicable norms of medical ethics" for the doctor who performs euthanasia. The doctor involved in this case was ultimately acquitted, showing that the Dutch high court acted to legitimize the emerging policy consensus. In 1985 the State Commission on Euthanasia issued its recommendations that PAS be legalized, and by 1994 77 per cent of hospitals and 57 per cent of nursing homes had adopted written policies permitting euthanasia under specific conditions. All this preceded new legislation. The policy process, says Griffiths, was largely "self-regulation followed by legal assimilation, and in fact this is precisely what the courts (and probably, in its secret heart, the legislator) wanted."[25]

Thus, when the Dutch Parliament finally acted, the reported 2,216 physician-assisted suicides in 1999 grossly under-represented the actual number (estimated to be closer to 5,000), and polls indicated that only 10 per cent of the Dutch citizenry and 10 per cent of Dutch physicians were adamantly opposed to the new law. The final parliamentary vote reflected more consensus than conflict, since the division in the lower parliamentary chamber was not even close (104 to 40). "Doctors and healers everywhere have helped people put an end to their suffering and helped them die," said Rob Jonquière, director of the Netherlands Association for Voluntary Euthanasia. "This will end a gray area. We don't want something of this importance to go on underground."[26]

The legislative success of legalized euthanasia in the Netherlands invites comparisons with the failed enactment of physician-assisted suicide (PAS) in the United States and Canada (see Chapter 8). It also calls to mind the rupture in the development of abortion policy in the United States and, to a lesser degree, in Canada. Put bluntly, all four of these cases involved judicial activism but, unlike the Dutch Supreme Court, the American and Canadian high courts acted contrary to the preferences of public opinion. *Roe v. Wade* constitutionalized the pro-choice agenda despite opposition from the political branches, ardent pro-lifers, and an American public not inclined to accept abortion on demand. The same can be said for the Canadian Supreme Court's *Morgentaler* (1988) ruling decriminalizing abortions except, to its credit, the high court invited Parliament to revisit abortion policy.

Liberals, feminists, and civil libertarians applauded these abortion rulings as being "principled" policymaking notwithstanding the majority will. Now fast forward to 1993, when the Canadian Supreme Court refused to extend the Charter's "security of the person" guarantees to allow Sue Rodriguez to end her own tragic life with dignity, and to 1997 when the American Supreme Court upheld 49 state laws banning PAS. Both high courts acted despite polls showing that a majority of Americans, and an even larger majority of Canadians, supported the practice. It was a shaky majority in the United States, but more a majority than what existed when abortion was legalized in 1973.

Conclusion

Morality politics under conditions of political unaccountability and anti-majoritarianism is, at best, problematic if not illegitimate. Recall that when the French Socialists faced a two-sided morality dispute over same-sex unions, what began as a campaign pledge to gays was reworked by the National Assembly to include any cohabiting relationships, in an attempt to win over conservative deputies. Such efforts at building coalitions bespeak representative government and the larger cause of consensus-building. Thus, if forced to choose, we join the critics of judicial activism who prefer a legislative resolution to any morality policy.

Notes

1. Donley T. Studlar, "What Constitutes Morality Policy? A Cross-National Analysis," Mooney, *The Public Clash of Private Values* 45-47.

2. Cowley, "Unbridled Passions?" 70. Cowley's list includes corporal and capital punishment, abortion and embryo research, hunting, contraception, the punishment of war criminals, Sunday entertainment and trading, homosexuality, prostitution, euthanasia, censorship, divorce, and (less definitely) disability rights and the wearing of seatbelts.

3. Studlar, "What Constitutes Morality Policy?" 39.

4. Christopher Mooney argues that morality "policy and its politics are characterized, first and foremost, by debate over first principles." As he explains: "At least a significant minority of citizens has a fundamental, first-principled conflict with the values embodied in any morality policy." See Mooney, "The Public Clash of Private Values" 3, 4.

5. Lipset, *Political Man* 87.

6. Peter Skerry, "The Class Conflict over Abortion," *Public Interest* 52 (Summer 1978): 70.

7. Donald Granberg, "Pro-Life or Reflection of Conservative Ideology? An Analysis of Opposition to Legalized Abortion," *Sociology and Social Research* No. 62 (1978): 423. Also see Donald Granberg and Beth Wellman Granberg, "Social Bases of Support and Opposition to Legalized Abortion," *Perspectives on Abortion*, ed. Paul Sachdev (Metuchen, NJ: The Scarecrow Press, 1985) 201-02; Donald Granberg, "The Abortion Activists," *Family Planning Perspectives* 13 (July/August 1981): 157-63; Donald Granberg and Donald Denney, "The Coathanger and the Rose," *Society* Magazine 19 (May/June 1982): 39-46.

8. Dalton, *Citizen Politics* 246. Those studies are referenced here.

9. See Morton and Knopff.

10. Melvyn Read, David Marsh, and David Richards, "Why Did They Do It? Voting on Homosexuality and Capital Punishment in the House of Commons," *Parliamentary Affairs* 47 (July 1994): 384.

11. Gallup found that 70 per cent in 1985 and 63 per cent in 1991 favoured the death penalty for reasons of "Revenge: an 'eye for an eye,'" or "Acts as a deterrent" or "Murderers deserve punishment" (the third option was not asked in 1991). See Mary Ann E. Steger and Brent S. Steel, "Death Penalty: Crime Deterrent or Legalized Homicide?," Tatalovich and Daynes, *Moral Controversies in American Politics* 77.

12. Phoebe C. Ellsworth and Samuel R. Gross, "Hardening of the Attitudes: Americans' Views on the Death Penalty," *Journal of Social Issues* 50 (1994): 19-25.

13. Tom R. Tyler and Renee Weber, "Support for the Death Penalty: Instrumental Response to Crime, or Symbolic Attitude?," *Law and Society Review* 17 (1982): 43. Also see Phoebe C. Ellsworth and Lee Ross, "Public Opinion and Capital Punishment: A Close Examination of the Views of Abolitionists and Retentionists," *Crime & Delinquency* 29 (January 1983) 116-69; and E.A. Fattah, "Perceptions of Violence, Concern about Crime, Fear of Victimization and Attitudes to the Death Penalty," *Canadian Journal of Criminology* 21 (January 1979): 22-38.

14. Chandler, *Capital Punishment in Canada* 29-30.

15. Forst 115-16.

16. Mohrenschlager 512-13, 516.

17. Cowley, "Unbridled Passions" 75.

18. Cowley, "Unbridled Passions" 80.

19. Dalton, *Citizen Politics* 247.

20. Ronald Inglehart, "Postmaterialism in an Environment of Insecurity," *American Political Science Review* 75 (1981): 880-900.

21. Dalton, *Citizen Politics* 248. However there was no conventional Left-Right alignment on the issue of nuclear power (see 249-51).

22. James Kennedy, "The Moral State: How Much Do the Americans and the Dutch Differ?," *Regulating Morality: A Comparison of the Role of the States in Mastering the Mores in the Netherlands and the United States*, ed. Hans Krabbendam and Hans-Martien Ten Napel (Antwerpen-Apeldoorn, Netherlands: E.M. Meijers Institute en Maklu-Uitgevers, 2000) 9-22.

23. Nevitte 218.

24. John Griffiths, "Self-Regulation by the Dutch Medical Profession of Medical Behavior that Potentially Shortens Life," Krabbendam and Ten Napel 173, 174.

25. Griffiths 175-77.

26. Marlise Simons, "Dutch Becoming First Nation to Legalize Assisted Suicide," *New York Times* 29 November 2000: A3.

A.I

Attitudes Toward Capital Punishment in Five Western Democracies

United States (a): favouring death penalty for murder
(Gallup)

1936	1937	1953	1956	1957	1960	1965	1966	1967	1969	1971	1972	1972
61%	65%	68%	53%	47%	53%	45%	42%	54%	51%	49%	50%	57%

1976	1978	1981	1/85	11/85	1986	1988	1991	1994	1995	1999	2000	2001
66%	62%	66%	72%	75%	70%	79%	76%	80%	77%	71%	66%	67%

United States (b): favouring death penalty for murder
(NORC)

1972	1973	1974	1975	1976	1977	1978	1980	1982	1983	1984
57%	63%	66%	64%	70%	72%	71%	72%	78%	78%	76%

1985	1986	1987	1988	1989	1990	1991	1993	1994	1996	1998
79%	76%	74%	76%	78%	79%	76%	78%	80%	78%	73%

United States (c): favouring death penalty or life imprisonment for murder
(Gallup)

	1985	1986	1991	1992	1993	1994	1997	1999	2000
death penalty	56%	55%	53%	50%	59%	50%	61%	56%	52%
life imprisonment	34	35	35	37	29	32	29	38	37

Canada (d): supporting capital punishment or against its abolition
(Gallup)

1943	1953	1958	1960	1965	1966	1970	1971	1978	1982
73%	71%	52%	51%	55%	53%	70%	63%	68%	70%

1984	1985	1986	1987	1990	1994	1996	1997	1998
71%	68%	68%	61%	60%	59%	55%	63%	61%

Canada (e): supporting capital punishment for certain types of crimes
(Gallup)

	kill prison guard/policeman	kill any innocent person	murder by terrorists
11/81	72%	69%	74%
2/81	73	67	74
10/79	70	68	71

United Kingdom (f): against abolition of the death penalty (Gallup)

1938	1947	1953	1955	7/62	8/62	1964	1970	1999
55%	69%	73%	61%	70%	81%	79%	61%	68%

United Kingdom (g): favour reintroducing death penalty for types of crime
(Gallup)

	1978	1981	1982
army and police murder	73%	71%	75%
terrorist murders		75%	78%
murdering woman after sexual assault		72%	73%
murdering a man who breaks into premises		40%	47%
murder while under influence of alcohol		29%	29%
murder while suffering insanity/mental disease		17%	11%
murder after considerable provocation		20%	20%
murder just for the fun of it		75%	74%
child rape		64%	61%
rape		43%	41%

France (h): supporting the death penalty or opposing its abolition
(Gallup/SOFRES/IFRES)

1947	5/69	10/69	8/72	10/72	1976	1978	1981	1984
68%	39%	33%	53%	63%	72%	58%	62%	46%

Germany (i): for or against reinstating the death penalty
(Allensbach Institut)

	1948	1958	1960	1961
pro:	74%	70%	54%	49%
con:	21	14	26	26

Germany (j): fundamentally for or against the death penalty
(Allensbach Institut)

	1950	1952	1960	1961	1963	1964	1967	1971	1972	1973
pro:	55%	55%	54%	51%	52%	52%	50%	43%	33%	30%
con:	30	28	26	28	30	29	31	46	53	46

	1975	1976	1977	1979	1980	1983	1986	1992	1995	1996
pro:	35%	36%	44%	30%	28%	24%	22%	24%	30%	35%
con:	49	42	39	51	49	59	57	56	53	45

Germany (k): support for the death penalty for murder
(EMNID)

	1958	1973	1974	1977	1997
pro:	80%	53%	44%	60%	55%
con:	17	34	44	38	44

(a) The question was: "Are you in favour of the death penalty for a person convicted of murder?" Sources: *The Gallup Report* 232-33 (January/February, 1985): 4 (which included 1936 and 1937) and *The Gallup Poll Monthly* 417 (June 2000): 65 (for 1953-2000 series). 2001 is reported at http://www.gallup.com/poll/indicators/inddeath_pen.asp.

(b) The question was "Do you favour or oppose the death penalty for persons convicted of murder?" Source: National Opinion Research Center (NORC), General Social Survey, Chicago, IL: http://www.icpsr.umich.edu/GSS/rnd1998/merged/cdbk-trn/cappun2.htm (for 1972 and 1973 data); http://www.icpsr.umich.edu/GSS/rnd1998/merged/cappun.htm (since 1974).

(c) The question was: "What do you think should be the penalty for murder—the death penalty, or life imprisonment with absolutely no possibility of parole?" Source: *The Gallup Poll Monthly* 413 (February 2000): 50.

(d) Variable questions (polling organizations not identified before 1965) were used for the 1943-71 period, including these on the last four surveys. For 1965 Gallup asked: "Some people say we should do away with capital punishment, that is, executing people for murder. Do you think we should or should not abolish capital punishment?" For 1966 Gallup asked: "If a national referendum were held today on the question of capital punishment, that is, executing people for murder, would you vote for retaining the death penalty in Canada or abolishing it?" For 1970 Gallup asked: "The criminal code was recently changed to abolish the death penalty except for certain crimes such as killing a policeman or prison guard on duty, on a five-year trial basis. Do you or do you not think that the death penalty should be reinstated for the kidnapping of people in public or political life?" For 1971 Gallup asked: "As you may know, some years ago Canada suspended the death penalty except for the killing of prisons guards or policemen on duty on a five-year trial basis which comes to an end shortly. In your opinion, should the death penalty be brought back or not?" Sources: Solicitor General of Canada, *Capital Punishment: New Material 1965-1972*, 69 and Ronald Manzer, *Canada: A Socio-Political Report* (Toronto: McGraw Hill, 1974) 287, as reported in David B. Chandler, *Capital Punishment in Canada: A Sociological Study of Repressive Law* (Toronto: McClelland and Stewart, 1976) 41, 50.

For 1978-98, the question was: "If a national referendum were held today on the question of executing a person for murder, would you vote for reinstating the death penalty in Canada or would you vote against reinstating it?" Source: Elizabeth Hann Hastings and Philip K. Hastings, eds., *Index to International Public Opinion, 1998-1999* (Westport, CT: Greenwood Press, 2000) 42.

(e) The question asked once in 1979 and twice in 1981 was: "Do you favour or oppose capital punishment for the killing of a prison guard or an on-duty policeman, the killing of any innocent person, or for murders committed by terrorists?" Source: Elizabeth Hann Hastings and Philip K. Hastings, eds., *Index to International Public Opinion, 1980-1981* (Westport, CT: Greenwood Press, 1982) 28.

(f) In 1938 respondents were asked: "Should the death penalty be abolished?" but were asked the following in 1947, 1953, and 1955: "In this country most people convicted of murder are sentenced to death. Do you agree with this or do you think that the death penalty should be abolished?" The question asked in July 1962 was repeated (without the introductory phrase) in August 1962, 1964, and 1970: "Now turning to capital punishment, should the death penalty be abolished altogether, or not?" Source: George H. Gallup, *The Gallup International Public Opinion Polls: Great Britain 1937-1975*, Vols. 1 and 2 (London: Greenwood Press, 1976) 11, 156, 308, 361, 645, 774, 1087. The 1999 poll was cited in *Europe Magazine* 401 (November 2000): 8.

(g) The question asked was: "Do you think the death penalty should, or should not be introduced for: Murder of members of the army and police forces? Terrorist murders? Murdering a woman following a sexual assault? Murdering a man who surprises him breaking into premises? Murder by someone while under the influence of alcohol? Murder by someone while suffering from insanity, or some serious mental disease? Murdering someone as a result of considerable provocation? Murdering someone just for the fun of it? Child rape? Rape?" Source: Elizabeth Hann Hastings and Philip K. Hastings, eds., *Index to International Public Opinion, 1981-1982* (Westport, CT: Greenwood Press, 1983) 29; Elizabeth Hann Hastings and Philip K. Hastings, eds., *Index to International Public Opinion, 1982-1983* (Westport, CT: Greenwood Press, 1984) 30.

(h) The 1947 Gallup question was: "The Italian Parliament has recently decided to abolish the death penalty. Do you think the death penalty should be maintained or abolished in France?" The August, 1972 Gallup question was: "Do you think that, at the present time in France, the death penalty should or should not be abolished?" Source: George H. Gallup, ed., *The Gallup International Public Opinion Polls: France 1939, 1944-1975*, Vols. 1 and 2 (New York: Random House, 1976) 87, 865. The May and October 1969 polls (no organizations are cited), one taken in October of 1972 (no organization cited), the 1981 SOFRES poll, and the 1984 IFRES poll are reported in Michel Forst, "The Abolition of the Death Penalty in France," *The Death Penalty Abolition in Europe* (Germany: Council of Europe Publishing, May 1999) 109, 113, 115. The 1976 and 1978 SOFRES polls are reported in G. Picca, "La Peine De Mort: Un Probleme Politique Et Social," *Revue Internationale de Droit Penal* vol. 58: 449.

(i) In 1948 the Allensbach Institut asked: "If a new criminal code were to be introduced, would you be for the retention or abolition of the death penalty?" Source: M. Mohrenschlager, "The Abolition of Capital Punishment in the Federal Republic of Germany: German Experiences," *Revue Internationale de Droit Penale* vol. 58 (1987): 513.

Those persons who knew there was no death penalty in Germany (97% in 1958, 98% in 1960, and 95% in 1961) were asked: "Supposing it would be voted on whether we should reinstate the death penalty, would you be for or against it?" Source: Elisabeth Noelle and Erich Peter Neumann, *Jahrbuch Der Offentlichen Meinung, 1958-1964*, Vol. III (Allensbach and Bonn: Institut fur Demoskopie Allensbach, 1965) 341.

(j) The 1950-96 polls by Allensbach Institut asked: "Are you fundamentally for or against the death penalty?" Elisabeth Noelle-Neumann and Renate Kocher, *Allensbacher Jahrbuch der Demoskopie, 1993-1997*, Vol. 10 (Allensbach am Bodensee: Verlag fur Demoskopie, 1997) 767.

(k) This series by EMNID Institut asked: "Are you for or against a murderer for whom there are no mitigating circumstances being sentenced to death?" Source: M. Mohrenschlager, "The Abolition of Capital Punishment in the Federal Republic of Germany: German Experiences," *Revue Internationale de Droit Penal* vol. 58 (1987): 513.

For 1997 the EMNID Institut asked: "The death penalty should be re-introduced for the most severe crimes, e.g. sexual murder or the murder of children." This supporting percentage combines those who answered "agree very much" (37%) and "to some degree agree" (18%) while the opposing percentage combines "disagree very much" (28%) and "to some degree disagree" (16%). Source: Elizabeth Hann Hastings and Philip K. Hastings, eds., *Index to International Public Opinion, 1998-1999* (Westport, CT: Greenwood Press, 2000) 44.

A.2

Attitudes Toward Abortion in Five Western Democracies

United States (% supporting abortion): (a)

	any circumstance	certain circumstances	illegal in all circumstances
1975	21%	54%	22%
1977	22	55	19
1979	22	54	19
1980	25	53	18
1981	23	52	21
1983	23	58	16
1988	24	57	17
1989	29	51	17
1990	31	53	12
1991	33	49	14
1992	34	48	13
1993	32	51	13
1994	33	52	13
1995	31	54	12
1996	24	52	17
1997	26	55	17
1998	23	59	17
1999	27	55	16

Canada (% supporting abortion): (b)

	any circumstance	certain circumstances	illegal in all circumstances
1975	23%	60%	16%
1978	16	69	14
1983	23	59	17
1988 (Feb)	28	55	13
1988 (June)	25	59	15
1988 (Sept)	20	65	13
1989 (Feb)	27	59	13
1989 (Aug)	26	63	10
1989 (Dec)	27	59	12
1991	24	60	14
1992	31	57	10
1993	31	56	10
1995	35	49	13
1997	34	49	14
1998	30	55	12

United Kingdom (% supporting abortion): (c)

	1966	1967	1998
mother's health endangered	79%	86%	88%
child born deformed	71	76	74
family lacks money	33	36	45

	1975	1998
on demand	18%	26%
circumstances	62	63
never	12	10

	1995
agree with principle of abortion on request	66%
disagree with principle of abortion on request	24

	1980	1996	1998
change law to make abortions more difficult to get	29%	26%	41%
change law to make abortions easier to get	13	11	17
leave law as it is	37	55	35
no opinion	21	8	7

France (% supporting abortion): (d)

	1969		1973		1973
within 3 months		abnormal births	41%	sanction abortion	
favourable	43%	abn birth & psych*	21	in general	22%
opposed	47	freedom of choice	22	sanction abortion	
		maintain law	13	in liberal law	65

	1973 (in specified cases)	
	yes	no
mother's physical or mental condition	90%	5%
abnormal child	88	8
father or mother incapable	82	12
economic circumstances	76	20
mother alone without economic means	69	24
mother under 18 years	55	32
unmarried mother	44	42
happiness of mother/couple adversely affected	44	43

	1988
on principle anti-abortion	47%
on principle pro-abortion	43
don't know	10

* abnormal births and psychological reasons

Germany: Allensbach Institut — three opinions on abortion (e)

West Germany	1973	1979	1980	1983	1985	1988
elective within 3 months	38%	30%	35%	27%	29%	22%
only in special cases	41	50	47	55	54	61
should be outlawed	15	13	11	11	11	12

Germany: Allensbach Institut — three opinions on abortion in East and West Germany (f)

1990		1991		1992		1993		1994		1995		
West	East	West	East	West	East	West	East	West	East	West	East	Total
38%	58%	43%	70%	35%	64%	40%	64%	50%	75%	44%	75%	50%
42	30	37	22	38	25	40	25	32	18	39	20	35
10	7	14	3	16	6	14	6	12	4	11	2	10

Germany: Allensbach Institut—abortion under varied conditions in East and West Germany (g)

	1963 West	1983 West	1988 West	1992 West	1992 East	1995 West	1995 East	Total
during first 3 months				21%	38%	31%	48%	34%
after counselling				32	34	27	29	28
in specific instances				29	20	25	19	23
outlaw except medical				12	5	10	2	9
only rape	65%	74%	80%					

(a) The question was: "Do you think abortions should be legal under any circumstance, legal only under certain circumstances, or illegal in all circumstances?" Source: *The Gallup Poll Monthly* 404 (May 1999): 54.

(b) The question was: "Do you think abortions should be legal under any circumstance, legal only under certain circumstances, or illegal in all circumstances?" Source: Elizabeth Hann Hastings and Philip K. Hastings, eds., *Index to International Public Opinion, 1998-1999* (Westport, CT: Greenwood Press, 2000) 425.

(c) The 1966, 1967, and 1998 question was: "Do you think abortion operations should or should not be legal in cases where: The health of the mother is in danger? The child may be born deformed? The family does not have enough money to support another child?" The 1975 and 1998 question was: "Which of these statements best expresses your own feeling about abortion? Should be available on demand. Should be allowed only in particular circumstances. Should never be allowed." Some (8% in 1975 and 2% in 1998) didn't know or refused to respond. Sources: George H. Gallup, ed., *The Gallup International Public Opinion Polls: Great Britain 1937-1975*, Vol. 2 (New York: Random House, 1976) 854, 910, 1385; Elizabeth Hann Hastings and Philip K. Hastings, eds., *Index to International Public Opinion, 1998-1999* (Westport, CT: Greenwood Press, 2000) 428.

A more elaborate question was asked by MORI in June of 1995: "I would like to ask you a question on the issue of termination of pregnancy. On balance, do you agree or disagree with the principle of abortion on request, which means that a woman can have an abortion if she wants one, provided she has thought about the matter carefully and discussed it with her doctor? How strongly do you tend to agree/disagree?" We combined the "strongly agree" (34%) and "tend to agree" (32%) categories as well as the "strongly disagree" (15%) and "tend to disagree" (9%) categories. Another 6% said "neither agree nor disagree" and others either offered "no opinion" (3%) or "refused" (1%)

to respond. Source: Elizabeth Hann Hastings and Philip K. Hastings, eds., *Index to International Public Opinion, 1995-1996* (Westport, CT: Greenwood Press, 1997) 418-19.

Questions by MORI in 1980 and 1996 asked about changing the law on abortion: "Do you think Britain's abortion law should be changed to make it more difficult for women to obtain an abortion, changed to make it easier for women to obtain an abortion, or should it be left as it is?" Source: Elizabeth Hann Hastings and Philip K. Hastings, eds., *Index to International Public Opinion, 1996-1997* (Westport, CT: Greenwood Press, 1998) 442.

The 1998 question by Gallup was worded differently: "Which of the following statements do you agree with? The present laws on abortion are satisfactory. The present laws on abortion should be altered to make abortions more difficult to obtain. The present laws on abortion should be altered to make abortions easier to obtain." Elizabeth Hann Hastings and Philip K. Hastings, eds., *Index to International Public Opinion, 1998-1999* (Westport, CT: Greenwood Press, 2000) 428.

(d) The 1969 question was: "Would you be in favour of or opposed to a law allowing a pregnant woman of less than three months to terminate her pregnancy with the approval of her doctor?" The "very favourable" (18%) and "somewhat favourable" (25%) categories were combined as were the "somewhat opposed" (22%) and "very opposed" (25%). Ten per cent had no opinion. The March 1973 survey that questioned existing French law was: "French law sanctions abortion only in the event that the mother's health is endangered? Of the following, which do you favour? An extension of the law to include abortion in the event of abnormal births. An extension which includes the above and adds psychological trauma as another reason. Total freedom of choice. Maintaining the law as it stands." The September 1973 survey had a battery of questions on abortion. One asked simply: "In your opinion, what is the best legal solution to the abortion question? Sanction abortion in general. Sanction abortion in accordance with new and more liberal laws." It also asked this multiple-pronged question: "Do you consider that abortion should be authorized in the case in which: Pregnancy jeopardizes the mother's physical or mental condition? The child may be abnormal? The father or mother would be either physically or mentally incapable of raising the child? The household already contains as many children as economic circumstances permit? The future mother lives alone, without sufficient economic means? The future mother is less than 18 years old? The future mother is unmarried? The happiness of the future mother or of the couple will be adversely affected by the birth of another child?" Source: George H. Gallup, ed., *The*

Gallup International Public Opinion Polls: France 1939, 1944-1975 (New York: Random House, 1976) 761, 963, 1065-1066.

The 1988 question asking about principled support or opposition to abortion read: "On principle, are you for or against abortion?" Source: Elizabeth Hann Hastings and Philip K. Hastings, eds., *Index to International Public Opinion, 1988-1989* (Westport, CT: Greenwood Press, 1990) 425.

(e) In 1973, 1979, 1980, 1983, 1985, and 1988 Allensbach Institut asked some version of this question: "A question about termination of a pregnancy, which is illegal under paragraph 218. Here are three opinions. With which opinion would you agree? Opinion 1: The interruption of a pregnancy should be fundamentally allowed for every woman in the first three months. Opinion 2: An interruption of pregnancy should only be allowed in very specific instances, for example, when doctors suggest it or when bad social conditions exist or other compelling reasons. Opinion 3: The interruption of a pregnancy should remain forbidden as it has been. Paragraph 218 should not be changed." Sources: For 1973, Elisabeth Noelle and Erich Peter Neumann, *Jahrbuch Der Offentlichen Meinung*, Vol. 5 *1968-1973* (Allensbach und Bonn: Verlag Fur Demoskopie, 1974) 245-46; for 1979 and 1980, Elisabeth Noelle-Neumann and Edgar Piel, *Allensbacher Jahrbuch Der Demoskopie, 1978-1983*, Vol. 8 (New York: K.G. Saur, 1983) 310; for 1983, 1985, and 1988, Elizabeth Hann Hastings and Philip K. Hastings, eds., *Index to International Public Opinion, 1988-1989* (Westport, CT: Greenwood Press, 1990) 426.

(f) In the 1990-95 series the most restrictive option allowed abortion for medical reasons, unlike the earlier question: "A question about abortion. Here are three opinions. With which of the opinions would you agree? Opinion A: An Abortion should be fundamentally allowed for all women in the first three months; Opinion B: Abortion should only be allowed in very specific instances, for instance, if doctors recommend it, or if social conditions exist, or other urgent cases; Opinion C: Abortion should again be outlawed. Termination of a pregnancy should only be allowed for purely medical reasons." Source: Elisabeth Noelle-Neumann and Renate Kocher, *Allensbacher Jahrbuch der Demoskopie, 1993-1997*, Vol. 10 (Munchen: K.G. Saur; Allensbach am Bodensee: Verlag fur Demoskopie, 1997) 782.

(g) In June 1963 Allensbach Institut asked: "Under the new organization of punishment law, there is a discussion on whether abortion should be allowed for a woman or girl who was raped and now pregnant as a result. What is your opinion?" Source: Elisabeth Noelle and Erich Peter Neumann, *Jahrbuch Der*

Offentlichen Meinung, 1965-1967, Vol. 2 (Allensbach und Bonn: Verlag Fur Demoskopie, 1968) 172.

The 1983 and 1988 rape question was: "Allow me to sketch you a case: a woman was raped and is now pregnant. What do you think—should she have an abortion if she doesn't want the child, or should she not?" Source: Elizabeth Hann Hastings and Philip K. Hastings, eds., *Index to International Public Opinion, 1988-1989* (Westport, CT: Greenwood Press, 1990) 427.

In 1992 and 1995 Allensbach Institut added a counselling alternative to its three options on abortion: "A question about abortion. Here are four opinions. With which of these opinions would you most likely agree? 1. An abortion should be fundamentally allowed for all women in the first three months. 2. An abortion should be allowed for every woman, if she first has gone to pregnancy counseling. 3. Abortion should only be allowed in very specific instances, for instance, if doctors recommend it, or if social conditions exist, or other urgent cases. 4. Abortion should again be outlawed. Termination of a pregnancy should only be allowed for purely medical reasons." Source: Elisabeth Noelle-Neumann and Renate Kocher, *Allensbacher Jahrbuch der Demoskopie, 1993-1997,* Vol. 10 (Munchen: K.G. Saur; Allensbach am Bodensee: Verlag fur Demoskopie, 1997) 781.

A.3

Attitudes Toward Homosexuality in Five Western Democracies

United States (a)

	is adult same-sex wrong (percentage)		same-sex marriages (percentage)		adopting children (percentage)	
	yes	no	yes	no	yes	no
2001			44	52 (G)		
2000			42	54 (G)		
1998	59	35 (G)				
1998	48	45 (T)	29%	64 (T)	35	57 (T)
1996			(for men) 10	64 (H)	(for men) 15	65 (H)
			(for women) 11	63 (H)	(for women) 16	61 (H)
1996			27	68 (G)	36	47 (N)
1994					29	65 (N)
1988-91			12	73 (NORC)		
1978	53	38 (T)				

Note: Various surveys are coded as follows: Gallup (G), Harris (H), Time/CNN/Yank (T), and NEWS/PRIN (N), and National Opinion Research Center (NORC).

United States (b): Gallup—legalize consenting homosexual relations

	1977	1982	1985	1986	1987	1989	1992	1996	1999	2001
yes	43%	45%	44%	33%	33%	47%	48%	44%	50%	54%
no	43	39	47	54	55	36	44	47	43	42

(b) Gallup—equal job opportunities

	1977	1982	1989	1992	1993	1996	1999	2001
yes	56%	59%	71%	74%	80%	84%	83%	85%
no	33	28	18	18	14	12	13	11

United States: (b) Gallup—alternative lifestyle

	1982	1992	1996	1997	1999	2001
yes	34%	38%	44%	42%	50%	52%
no	51	57	50	52	46	43

(b) Gallup—homosexuality due to nature or nurture

	1977	1982	1989	1996	1999	2001
born with	13%	17%	19%	31%	34%	40%
upbringing/ environment	56	52	48	40	44	39
both	14	13	12	13	13	9
neither	3	2	2	3	1	3

(c) is same-sex wrong (NORC)

	always wrong	almost always wrong	sometimes wrong	not wrong at all
1998	59%	6%	7%	28%
1996	61	5	6	28
1994	68	4	6	23
1993	66	4	8	22
1991	77	4	4	15
1990	76	5	6	13
1989	74	4	6	15
1988	77	4	6	13
1987	78	4	6	13
1985	76	4	7	13
1984	75	5	7	13
1982	74	5	7	14
1980	74	6	6	14
1977	73	6	8	14
1976	70	6	8	16
1974	69	6	9	13
1973	73	7	8	11

Canada (d):

	as acceptable lifestyle		legalize relations		same-sex marriages		adopt children	
	yes	no	yes	no	yes	no	yes	no
1998					40%	52%	36%	57%
1996	60%	33%	64%	28%	34	58	34	58
1994					29	60	30	57
1992					24	61	31	56
1991							27	65
1988							25	67

United Kingdom (e):

	decriminalize homosexual behaviour	legalize homosexual relations					
	1966	1979	1981	1985	1986	1991	1993
should	39%	62%	63%	61%	55%	66%	65%
should not	44	23	25	27	33	24	24
don't know	17						

	allow to adopt children		an accepted lifestyle		causes of homosexuality			
	should	should not	yes	no	born	upbringing	both	neither
1979	24%	63%			39%	29%	19%	2%
1981	21	65			37	33	17	1
1985	19	69			34	27	22	2
1986	16	75	44%	47%	36	35	18	2
1991	20	67	53	36	35	33	19	2
1993	23	65	54	37	37	25	22	2

Germany (f): Allensbach Institut—punish homosexuality

	1963				1968	1987	
	between men		between women		between men	with minor	with adult
	male	female	male	female			
yes	61%	70%	51%	66%	45%	42%	11%
no	21	9	26	12	38		
no opinion/ undecided	18	21	23	22	17		

Germany (g): Allensbach Institut—same-sex marriages

	Unified Germany		West Germany	
	1996	1998	1998	1985
for	13%	27%	26%	13%
against		53	55	69

France (h)

	1986 custody rights	1986 adopt children
agree	40%	25%
against	42%	62%
don't know	18%	13%

(a) A Gallup poll in 1998 used this question: "Do you personally believe homosexual behaviour is morally wrong or is not morally wrong?" A Time/ CNN/Yank survey of 1998 and 1978 asked: "Are homosexual relationships between consenting adults morally wrong or not a moral issue?" Source:

Elizabeth Hann Hastings and Philip K. Hastings, eds., *Index to International Public Opinion, 1998-1999* (Westport, CT: Greenwood Press, 2000) 451-52.

In 1996 Harris Survey asked these gender-specific questions on same-sex marriages: "How do you feel about so-called single-sex marriages between two men or two women? Single-sex marriages between two men. Single-sex marriages between two women." Source: Elisabeth Hann Hastings and Philip K. Hastings, eds., *Index to International Public Opinion, 1996-1997* (Westport, CT: Greenwood Press, 1998) 474.

The 1998 question on same-sex marriages by Time/CNN/Yank was: "Should homosexual marriages be recognized as legal by the law?" Time/CNN/Yank also asked in 1998 this question on adoption: "Should homosexual couples be legally permitted to adopt children?" Source: Elizabeth Hann Hastings and Philip K. Hastings, eds., *Index to International Public Opinion, 1998-1999* (Westport, CT: Greenwood Press, 2000) 453.

Polls taken in 1996 and 1994 by NEWS/PRIN asked about gay adoption: "Do you think gay couples should have the right to adopt children, or not?" Harris Survey asked a similar question about adoption by female or by male couples in 1996: "What about adoption of children by two men or two women who live together as a couple, whether they are married or not?" Source: Elizabeth Hann Hastings and Philip K. Hastings, eds., *Index to International Public Opinion, 1996-1997* (Westport, CT: Greenwood Press, 1998) 474-75.

In 1996 Gallup asked this question on same-sex marriage: "Do you think marriages between homosexuals should or should not be recognized by the law as valid, with the same rights as traditional marriages?" Source: *The Gallup Poll Monthly* 367 (April 1996): 21. In 2000 and 2001 Gallup rephrased the question about same-sex marriage: "Would you favour or oppose a law that would allow homosexual couples to legally form civil unions, giving them some of the legal rights of married couples?" Source: *The Gallup Poll Monthly* (June 2001): 9. The NORC General Social Survey asked "Do you agree or disagree? Homosexual couples should have the right to marry one another." The responses were cumulated over the years 1988-91. Source: http://www.icpsr.umich.edu/GSS/rnd1998/merged/cdbk/marhomo.htm.

(b) In order here are the four questions asked by Gallup. "Do you think homosexual relations between consenting adults should or should not be legal?" Source: *The Gallup Poll Monthly* 375 (December 1996): 13 and 429 (June 2001): 5. The 1999 poll is reported in George Gallup, Jr., *The Gallup Poll 1999* (Wilmington, DE: Scholarly Resources, Inc., 2000) 168.

"As you may know, there has been considerable discussion in the news regarding the rights of homosexual men and women. In general, do you think homosexuals should or should not have equal rights in terms of job opportunities?" Source: *The Gallup Poll Monthly* 402 (March 1999): 30 and (June 2001): 6.

"Do you feel that homosexuality should be considered an acceptable alternative lifestyle or not?" Source: *The Gallup Poll Monthly* 402 (March 1999): 30 and 429 (June 2001): 8.

"In your view, is homosexuality something a person is born with or is homosexuality due to other factors such as upbringing or environment?" *The Gallup Poll Monthly* 429 (June 2001): 9.

(c) The NORC question on wrongfulness of same-sex was: "What about sexual relations between two adults of the same sex—Do you think it is: Always wrong, Almost always wrong, Wrong only sometimes, Not wrong at all." Source: National Opinion Research Center, Chicago, IL. Source: http://www.icpsr.umich.edu/GSS/rnd1998/merged/cdbk-trn/homosex.htm.

(d) The Gallup question on lifestyle was: "Do you feel that homosexuality should be considered an acceptable alternative lifestyle or not?" The Gallup question on legalization was: "Do you think homosexual relations between consenting adults should or should not be legal?" The Gallup question on same-sex marriage was: "Do you favour or oppose marriages between people of the same sex?" The Gallup question on adopting was: "In your opinion, should homosexuals be allowed to adopt children or not?" Sources: Elizabeth Hann Hastings and Philip K. Hastings, eds., *Index to International Public Opinion, 1996-1997* (Westport, CT: Greenwood Press, 1998) 470-71; Elizabeth Hann Hastings and Philip K. Hastings, eds., *Index to International Public Opinion, 1998-1999* (Westport, CT: Greenwood Press, 2000) 447.

(e) The Gallup question for 1966 was: "Do you think that homosexual behaviour, if it is conducted in private between men aged 21 and over, should or should not be a criminal act?"

Source: George H. Gallup, ed., *The Gallup International Public Opinion Polls: Great Britain 1937-1975*, Vol. 2 (London: Greenwood, 1976) 874.

The Gallup Social Survey question on homosexual relations was: "Do you think homosexual relations between consenting adults should or should not be legal?" The Gallup Social Survey question on adoption was: "Do you think homosexuals should or should not be allowed to adopt children?" The Gallup Social Survey question on lifestyle was: "Do you think that homosexuality should be considered as an accepted alternative lifestyle or not?" The Gallup Social Survey question on the cause of homosexuality was "In your opinion, is homosexuality something a person is born with or is it due to other factors such as upbringing or environment?" Source: Elizabeth Hann

Hastings and Philip K. Hastings, eds., *Index to International Public Opinion, 1993-1994* (Westport, CT: Greenwood Press, 1995) 489.

(f) In September 1963 Allensbach Institut posed this question to men and women: "In some countries homosexuality between men is punished, in others not. How should it be in West Germany: should homosexuality between men be punished or not punished? ... and between women?" Source: Elisabeth Noelle and Erich Peter Neumann, *Jahrbuch Der Offentlichen Meinung, 1958-1964*, Vol. 1 (Allensbach und Bonn: Verlag Fur Demoskopie, 1965) 591.

In December 1968 Allensbach Institut asked: "For a long time people here have talked about changing the penal laws. Now the German government has made new suggestions towards it. I would like to know your opinion on some important points. Among other things, the German government wants that homosexuality, or in other words, love relationships between two grown men, should no longer be punishable. Do you find the abolition of the punishment fundamentally correct or not correct?" Source: Elisabeth Noelle and Erich Peter Neumann, *Jahrbuch Der Offentlichen Meinung, 1968-1973*, Vol. 5 (Allensbach und Bonn: Verlag Fur Demoskopie, 1974) 244.

In February 1987 Allensbach Institut allowed respondents to choose among these 14 answers (percentages to the italicized answers are reported above): "What is your position on homosexuality between men? Perhaps you can tell me according to this list? *Homosexuality between men should be punished if underage youths are affected*; disgusts/sickens me; I can't understand it; people shouldn't make such a big deal of it; doesn't bother me; is a topic which makes me uneasy; one shouldn't make fun of it; is a sickness; damages your health; is something I don't want to talk about; is a very natural thing; one should resolutely combat it; *should be punished in adults*; nothing to say." Source: Elisabeth Noelle-Neumann and Renate Kocher, *Allensbacher Jahrbuch der Demoskopie, 1984-1992*, Vol. 9 (Allensbach am Bodensee: Verlag fur Demoskopie, 1993) 126.

(g) In October 1996 Allensbach Institut asked: "Here on this list different statements are written out. Which ones are particularly important to you, and which ones would you say definitely have to be put into place? That homosexual women or men marry, can enter into a same-sex marriage." Source: Elisabeth Noelle-Neumann and Renate Kocher, *Allensbacher Jahrbuch der Demoskopie, 1993-1997*, Vol. 10 (Allensbach am Bodensee: Verlag fur Demoskopie, 1997) 167.

The 1985 and 1998 question was: "There has been talk recently about permitting same-sex marriages, i.e., so that a woman may marry another woman, or a man another man. Do you think marriages to partners of the same sex should be permitted, or would you be opposed?" Source: Elizabeth Hann Hastings and Philip K. Hastings, eds., *Index to International Public Opinion, 1998-1999* (Westport, CT: Greenwood Press, 2000) 449.

(h) The question asked in October 1986 was: "Are you in agreement with or are you against each of the following proposals? Grant the same rights of custody to homosexuals that heterosexual parents have.... Permit homosexuals to adopt children." Source: Elizabeth Hann Hastings and Philip K. Hastings, eds., *Index to International Public Opinion, 1987-1988* (Westport, CT: Greenwood Press, 1989) 474.

Selected Bibliography

Abramowitz, Alan I. "Issue Evolution Reconsidered: Racial Attitudes and Partisanship in the US Electorate." *American Journal of Political Science* 38 (February, 1994): 1-24.

——. "It's Abortion, Stupid: Policy Voting in the 1992 Presidential Election." *Journal of Politics* 57 (February, 1995): 176-86.

Abramowitz, Alan I., and Kyle L. Saunders. "Ideological Realignment in the US Electorate." *Journal of Politics* 60 (August 1998): 634-52.

Ackerman, Bruce. *Social Justice in the Liberal State.* New Haven, CT: Yale University Press, 1980.

Adams, Greg D. "Abortion: Evidence of Issue Evolution." *American Journal of Political Science* 41 (July, 1997): 718-37.

Agresto, John. *The Supreme Court and Constitutional Democracy.* Ithaca, NY: Cornell University Press, 1984.

Almond, Gabriel A., and Sidney Verba. *The Civic Culture: Political Attitudes and Democracy in Five Nations.* Boston: Little, Brown and Company, 1963.

Anderson, James E. *Public Policymaking.* 4th ed. Boston: Houghton Mifflin, 2000.

Arendt, Hanna. *The Origins of Totalitarianism.* New York: Harcourt, Brace, 1951.

Arington, Michele. "English-Only Laws and Direct Legislation: the Battle in the States Over Language Minority Rights." *Journal of Law and Politics* 7 (1991): 325-52.

Badhwar, Neera Kapur. "Altruism versus Self-Interest: Sometimes a False Dichotomy," *Altruism*, ed. Ellen Frankel Paul, Fred Miller, Jr., and Jeffrey Paul. New York: Cambridge University Press, 1993.

Baum, Lawrence. *The Supreme Court.* 3rd ed. Washington, DC: CQ Press, 1989.

Bauman, Zygmunt. *Freedom.* Minneapolis, MN: University of Minnesota Press, 1988.

Baumgartner, Frank R., and Byron D. Jones. *Agendas and Instability in American Politics.* Chicago: University of Chicago Press, 1993.

Beck, Ulrich. "Beyond Status and Class: Will There Be an Individualized Class Society?" *Modern German Sociology.* Ed. Volker Meja, Dieter Misgeld, and Nico Stehr. New York: Columbia University Press, 1987. 340-55.

Beck, Ulrich. *Risk Society: Towards a New Modernity.* London: Sage, 1992.

Becker, Theodore. *The Impact of Supreme Court Decisions: Empirical Studies.* New York: Oxford University Press, 1969.

Bell, Daniel, ed. *The New American Right.* New York: Criterion Books, 1955.

Bell, Derrick A. Jr. "The Referendum: Democracy's Barrier to Racial Equality." *Washington Law Review* 54 (1978-79): 1-29.

Bentley, Arthur F. *The Process of Government*. Chicago: University of Chicago Press, 1908.

Berger, Peter L. "Identity as a Problem in the Sociology of Knowledge." *European Journal of Sociology* 7 (1966): 105-15.

Berger, Peter. *The Human Shape of Work*. New York: Macmillan, 1964.

Berger, Peter, Brigitte Berger, and Hansfried Kellner. *The Homeless Mind: Modernization and Consciousness*. New York: Random House, 1973.

Berger, Peter, and Thomas Luckmann. "Social Mobility and Personal Identity." *Life-World and Social Realities*. Ed. Thomas Luckmann. London: Heinemann Educational Books, 1983. 110-23.

Berger, Raoul. *Government by Judiciary: The Transformation of the Fourteenth Amendment*. Cambridge, MA: Harvard University Press, 1977.

Bernstein, Basil. *Pedagogy, Symbolic Control and Identity: Theory, Research, Critique*. London: Taylor and Francis, 1996.

Beyme, Klaus Von. *The Legislator: German Parliament as a Centre of Political Decision-making*. Aldershot, UK: Ashgate, 1998.

Bickel, Alexander M. *The Least Dangerous Branch*. New Haven, CT: Yale University Press, 1986.

Bindman, Stephen. "Door Opens: Supreme Court Lets Groups Intervene," *Ottawa Citizen* 9 March 1987: B8.

Bitensky, Susan H. "Spare the Rod, Embrace our Humanity: Toward a New Legal Regime Prohibiting Corporal Punishment of Children." *University of Michigan Journal of Law Reform* 31 (Winter 1998): 353-474.

Bogdanor, Vernon. *The People and the Party System: The Referendum and Electoral Reform in British Politics*. Cambridge: Cambridge University Press, 1981.

——, ed. *Representatives of the People? Parliamentarians and Constituents in Western Democracies*. Aldershot, UK: Gower, 1985.

——. "Western Europe." Butler and Ranney, *Referendums around the World*. Bork, Robert H. *The Tempting of America: The Political Seduction of the Law*. New York: Simon and Schuster, 1990.

Bourdieu, Pierre. *Distinction: A Social Critique of the Judgment of Taste*. Cambridge, MA: Harvard University Press, 1984.

Boyd, Monica, and Deirdre Gillieson. "Canadian Attitudes on Abortion: Results of the Gallup Polls." *Canadian Studies in Population* 2 (1975): 53-64.

Bradley, Robert C., and Paul Gardner. "Underdogs, Upperdogs and the Use of the Micus Brief: Trends and Explanations." *The Justice System Journal* 10 (1985): 78-96.

Braunstein, Richard, and Tricia Wempe. "The Best Custodians of Moral Principle: A Comparative Study of Legislative and Citizen Morality Policy Making." Annual Meeting, Western Political Science Association. Las Vegas, NV. 2001.

Brenner, Saul, and Harold J. Spaeth. *Stare Indecisis: The Alteration of Precedent on the Supreme Court, 1946-1992*. New York: Cambridge University Press, 1995.

Brodie, Janine, Shelley A.M. Gavigan, and Jane Jensen. *The Politics of Abortion*. Toronto: Oxford University Press, 1992.

Brown, Robert D., and Edward G. Carmines. "Materialists, Postmaterialists, and the Criteria for Political Choice in US Presidential Elections." *Journal of Politics* 57 (1995): 483-94.

Brown, Stephen P. "The New Christian Right, Religious Liberty, and the Supreme Court." Annual Meeting, Southern Political Science Association. Norfolk, VA. 1998.

Bullock, Charles S. III, and Charles M. Lamb, *Implementation of Civil Rights Policy*. Monterey, CA: Brooks/Cole Publishing, 1984.

Burke, Craig C. "Fencing Out Politically Unpopular Groups from the Normal Political Processes: The Equal Protection Concerns of Colorado Amendment Two." *Indiana Law Journal* 69 (1993-94): 275-98.

Burkett, Tony. "The West German Deputy." Bogdanor, *Representatives of the People*.

Butler, David, and Austin Ranney. *Referendums: A Comparative Study in Practice and Theory*. Washington, DC: American Enterprise Institute, 1978.

——, eds. *Referendums around the World*. Washington DC: AEI Press, 1994.

Butler, David, and Donald Stokes. *Political Change in Britain: Forces Shaping Electoral Choice*. New York: St. Martin's Press, 1969.

Button, James W., Barbara A. Rienzo, and Kenneth D. Wald. *Private Lives, Public Conflicts: Battles over Gay Rights in American Communities*. Washington, DC: CQ Press, 1997.

Cain, Bruce E. "Voting Rights and Democratic Theory: Toward a Color-Blind Society." *Controversies in Minority Voting*. Ed. Bernard Grofman and Chandler Davidson. Washington, DC: Brookings Institution, 1992.

Cairns, Alan C. "The Fragmentation of Canadian Citizenship." *Belonging: The Meaning and Future of Canadian Citizenship*. Ed. William Kaplan. Montreal and Kingston: McGill-Queens University Press, 1993.

Carmines, Edward G., and James A. Stimson. *Issue Evolution: Race and the Transformation of American Politics*. Princeton, NJ: Princeton University Press, 1987.

Carmines, Edward G., and Geoffrey C. Layman. "Value Priorities, Partisanship, and Electoral Choice: The Neglected Case of the United States." 19 *Political Behavior* (1997): 283-316.

Carson, Rachel. *Silent Spring*. Greenwich, CT: Fawcett Crest Books, 1962.

Carson, Rob. "Washington's I-119." *Hastings Center Report* (March-April, 1992).

Casper, Jonathan D. *Lawyers Before the Warren Court: Civil Liberties and Civil Rights, 1957-1966*. Urbana, IL: University of Illinois Press, 1972.

Caulfield, Henry P. "The Conservation and Environmental Movements: An Historical Analysis." Lester, *Environmental Politics and Policy*.

Chandler, David B. *Capital Punishment in Canada*. Toronto: McClelland and Stewart, 1976.

Choper, Jesse. *Judicial Review and the National Political Process: A Functional Reconsideration of the Role of the Supreme Court*. Chicago: University of Chicago Press, 1980.

Christoph, James B. "Capital Punishment and British Party Responsibility." *Political Science Quarterly* 77 (July 1962): 19-35.

——. *Capital Punishment and British Politics*. London: George Allen and Unwin, 1962.

Clark, Peter, and James Q. Wilson. "Incentive Systems: A Theory of Organizations." *Administrative Science Quarterly* 6 (1961): 129-66

Clark, Terry Nichols, and Ronald Inglehart. "The New Political Culture: Changing Dynamics of Support for the Welfare State and other Policies in Postindustrial Societies." Clark and Hoffmann-Matinot 1-12.

Clark, Terry Nichols, and Vincent Hoffmann-Martinot, eds. *The New Political Culture*. Boulder, CO: Westview Press, 1998.

Clarke, Harold D., Jane Jenson, Lawrence LeDuc, and Jon Pammett. *Absent Mandate: Canadian Electoral Politics in an Era of Restructuring*. Toronto: Gage, 1996.

Clotfelter, Charles T., and Philip J. Cook. *Selling Hope: State Lotteries in America*. Cambridge, MA: Harvard University Press, 1989.

Cobb Roger W., and Charles D. Elder. *Participation in American Politics: The Dynamics of Agenda-Building*. Baltimore, MD: Johns Hopkins University Press, 1972.

Cobb, Roger Jennie-Keith Ross, and March Ross. "Agenda Building as a Comparative Political Process." *American Political Science Review* 70 (March, 1976): 126-38.

Coleman, James S. *Community Conflict*. New York: The Free Press, 1957.

Conradt, David P. *The German Polity*. 6th ed. White Plains, NY: Longman, 1996.

Cook, Elizabeth Adell, Ted G. Jelen, and Clyde Wilcox. "Issue Voting in Gubernatorial Elections: Abortion and Post-Webster Politics." *Journal of Politics* 56 (February 1994): 187-99.

——. "Issue Voting in US Senate Elections: The Abortion Issue in 1990." *Congress and the Presidency* 21 (1994): 99-112.

Cook, Rebecca J., and Bernard M. Dickens. "A Decade of International Change in Abortion Law: 1967-1977." *American Journal of Public Health* 68 (July 1978): 637-44.

Cooter, R. "Expressive Law and Economics." *Journal of Legal Studies* 27 (1998): 585-607.

Cortner, Richard. "Strategies and Tactics of Litigants in Constitutional Cases." *Journal of Public Law* 36 (1968): 287-307.

Costain, A.N. *Inviting Women's Rebellion: A Political Process Interpretation of the Women's Movement*. Baltimore: Johns Hopkins University Press, 1992.

Costain, W.D., and J.P. Lester. "The Environmental Movement and Congress." *Social Movements and American Political Institutions*. Ed. A.N. Costain and A.S. McFarland. Lanham, MD: Rowman and Littlefield, 1998.

Cowley, Philip, ed. *Conscience and Parliament*. London: Frank Cass, 1998.

——. "Unbridled Passions? Free Votes, Issues of Conscience and the Accountability of British Members of Parliament." *Journal of Legislative Studies* 4 (Summer 1998).

Cowley, Philip, and Mark Stuart. "Sodomy, Slaughter, Sunday Shopping and Seatbelts: Free Votes in the House of Commons, 1979-1996." *Party Politics* 3 (1997): 119-30.

Dalton, Russell J. *Citizen Politics: Public Opinion and Political Parties in Advanced Industrial Democracies*. Chatham, NJ: Chatham House Publishers, 1996.

——. *The Green Rainbow: Environmental Groups in Western Europe*. New Haven, CT: Yale University Press, 1994.

Davies, J. Clarence. "How does the agenda get set?" *The Governance of Common Property Resources*. Ed. Edwin Haefele. Baltimore: Johns Hopkins University Press, 1974. 149-77.

Davis, James A. "Changeable Weather in a Cooling Climate Atop the Liberal Plateau." *Public Opinion Quarterly* 56 (1992): 261-306.

Davis, Nancy J., and Robert V. Robinson. "Are the Rumors of War Exaggerated? Religious Orthodoxy and Moral Progressivism in America." *American Journal of Sociology* 102 (November 1996): 756-87.

Daynes, Byron W. "Pornography: Freedom of Expression or Sexual Degradation?" Tatalovich and Daynes, *Moral Controversies in American Politics*.

——. "Pornography: Freedom of Expression or Societal Degradation?" Tatalovich and Daynes, *Social Regulatory Policy*.

Daynes, Byron W., and Raymond Tatalovich. "Presidential Politics and Abortion, 1972-1988." *Presidential Studies Quarterly* 22 (Summer 1992): 545-61.

den Dulk, Keven R. "Representing Christ in Court." Crossroads Conference. Jackson, TN. 1998.

Derthick, Martha A. *Up in Smoke: From Legislation to Litigation in Tobacco Politics*. Washington, DC: CQ Press, 2002.

Destro, Robert A. "Abortion and the Constitution: The Need for a Protective Amendment." *University of California Law Review* 63 (September 1975).

DiMaggio, Paul, John Evans, and Bethany Bryson. "Have American's Social Attitudes Become More Polarized?" *American Journal of Sociology* 102 (November 1996).

Dollard, John. *Caste and Class in a Southern Town*. New York: Harper, 1949.

Dolnick, Edward. "Deafness as Culture." *Atlantic Monthly* 272 (September 1993): 37-53.

Donovan, Todd, and Shaun Bowler. "An Overview of Direct Democracy in the American States." *Citizens as Legislators: Direct Democracy in the United States*. Ed. Shaun Bowler, Todd Donovan, and Caroline J. Tolbert. Columbus, OH: Ohio State University Press, 1998.

——. "Direct Democracy and Minority Rights: Opinions on Anti-Gay and Lesbian Ballot Initiatives." Witt and McCorkle.

Douglas, Mary, "Cultural Bias." *Occasional Paper* 34. London: Royal Anthropological Institute of Great Britain and Ireland, 1978.

——. "The Depoliticization of Risk." Ellis and Thompson, *Culture Matters*.

Douglas, Mary, and Baron Isherwood. *The World of Goods: Towards an Anthropology of Consumption*. London and New York: Routledge, 1979.

Duberman, Martin. *Stonewall*. New York: Dutton, 1993.

Dunlap, R.E. "Public Opinion and Environmental Policy." Lester, *Environmental Politics and Policy*.

Dunlap, Riley E., and Kent D. Van Liere. "The 'New Environmental Paradigm.'" *Journal of Environmental Education* 9 (1978): 10-19.

Dunsmuir, Mollie. "Abortion: Constitutional and Legal Developments." Current Issue Review, 89-10E. Ottawa: Library of Parliament, Research Branch, Law and Government Division. Rev. 3 September 1991.

Duverger, Maurice. *Political Parties*. New York: John Wiley and Sons, 1963.

Dworkin, Ronald. *Taking Rights Seriously*. London: Duckworth, 1977.

Easton, David. *The Political System*. New York: Alfred A. Knopf, 1953.

Eckstein, Harry. "A Culturalist Theory of Political Change." *American Political Science Review* 82 (1988): 789-804.

Elias, Norbert. *The Germans: Power Struggles and the Development of Habitus in the Nineteenth and Twentieth Centuries*. New York: Columbia University Press.

Elias, Norbert, and John L. Scotson. *The Established and the Outsiders: A Sociological Enquiry into Community Problems*. London: Frank Cass, 1965.

Ellis, Margaret. "Gay Rights: Lifestyle or Immorality?" Tatalovich and Daynes, *Moral Controversies in American Politics*.

Ellis, Richard J., and Fred Thompson, "Seeing Green: Cultural Biases and Environmental Preferences," Ellis and Thompson, *Culture Matters* 172.

Ellis, Richard J., and Michael Thompson, eds. *Culture Matters: Essays in Honor of Aaron Wildavsky*. Ed. Boulder, CO: Westview, 1997.

Ellsworth, Phoebe C., and Lee Ross. "Public Opinion and Capital Punishment: A Close Examination of the Views of Abolitionists and Retentionists." *Crime and Delinquency* 29 (January 1983): 116-69.

Ellsworth, Phoebe C., and Samuel R. Gross. "Hardening of the Attitudes: Americans' Views on the Death Penalty." *Journal of Social Issues* 50 (1994): 19-25.

Ely, John Hart. "The Wages of Crying Wolf: A Comment on *Roe v. Wade*." *Yale Law Journal* 82 (1973).

Epp, Charles. "Do Bills of Rights Matter?: The Canadian Charter of Rights and Freedoms." *American Political Science Review* 90 (December 1996): 765-79.

Epstein, Lee. *Conservatives in Court*. Knoxville, TN: University of Tennessee Press, 1985.

——. "Courts and Interest Groups." *The American Courts: A Critical Assessment.* Ed. John B. Gates and Charles A. Johnson. Washington, DC: CQ Press, 1991. 335-71.

Eule, Julian. "Crocodiles in the Bathtub: State Courts, Voter Initiatives and the Threat of Electoral Reprisal." *University of Colorado Law Review* 65 (1994): 733-740.

——. "Judicial Review of Direct Democracy." *Yale Law Journal* 99 (1990): 1503-1590.

Ezell, John Samuel. *Fortune's Merry Wheel: The Lottery in America.* Cambridge, MA: Harvard University Press, 1960.

Fattah, E.A. "Perceptions of Violence, Concern about Crime, Fear of Victimization and Attitudes to the Death Penalty." *Canadian Journal of Criminology* 21 (January 1979): 22-38.

Faux, Marian. *Roe v. Wade.* New York: New American Library, 1988.

Featherstone, Mike. *Undoing Culture: Globalization, Postmodernism and Identity.* London: Sage, 1995.

Fenno, Richard E., Jr. *Home Style: House Members in Their Districts.* Boston: Little, Brown and Company, 1978.

Fiorina, Morris P. *Congress: Keystone of the Washington Establishment.* New Haven, CT: Yale University Press, 1989.

Flanagan, Scott C. "Value Change in Industrial Societies." *American Political Science Review* 81 (1987): 1289-1319.

Flanagan, Tom. *Waiting for the Wave: The Reform Party and Preston Manning.* Toronto: Stoddart Publishing Company, 1995.

Fletcher, Joseph F., and Paul Howe. "Public Opinion and the Courts." *Choices* 6 (May 2000).

Fogelman, Eva. *Conscience and Courage: Rescuers of the Jews during the Holocaust.* New York: Anchor Books, 1994.

Forbes, H.D. *Ethnic Conflict: Commerce, Culture, and the Contact Hypothesis.* New Haven, CT: Yale University Press, 1997.

Forst, Michel. *The Death Penalty Abolition in Europe.* Germany: Council of Europe, May 1999.

Fountaine, Cynthia L. "Note: Lousy Lawmaking: Questioning the Desirability and Constitutionality of Legislating by Initiative." *Southern California Law Review* 61 (1988): 733-76.

Francione, Gary L. *Rain Without Thunder: The Ideology of the Animal Rights Movement.* Philadelphia, PA: Temple University Press, 1996.

Franklin, Charles, and Liane C. Kosaki. "Republican Schoolmaster: The US Supreme Court, Public Opinion, and Abortion." *American Political Science Review* 83 (September 1989).

Fraser, Blair. *The Search for Identity: Canada, 1945-1967.* Toronto: Doubleday Canada, 1967.

Freidan, Betty. *The Feminine Mystique.* New York: W.W. Norton, 1963.

Fromm, Erich. *Escape from Freedom.* New York: Farrar and Rinehart, 1941.

Furlong, Paul. *Modern Italy: Representation and Reform.* London: Routledge, 1994.

Gamble, Barbara S. "Putting Civil Rights to a Popular Vote." *American Journal of Political Science* (1997).

Gamson, William A. "The Fluoridation Dialogue: Is It an Ideological Conflict?" *Public Opinion Quarterly* XXV (Winter 1961): 526-37.

Gamson, William A., and Peter H. Irons. "Community Characteristics and Fluoridation Outcome." *Journal of Social Issues* 17 (1961): 66-74.

Garrow, David J. *Bearing the Cross: Martin Luther King, Jr., and the Southern Christian Leadership Conference.* New York: William Morrow and Company, 1986.

Geis, Sally B. "The Meaning of Death: Time to Talk." *Christianity and Crisis* (February 3, 1992).

Gehlen, Arnold. *Man in the Age of Technology.* New York: Columbia University Press, 1980.

George, Tracey E., and Lee Epstein. "On the Nature of Supreme Court Decision Making." *American Political Science Review* 86 (June, 1992): 323-37.

Gerber, Elisabeth. "Legislative Response to the Threat of Popular Initiatives." *American Journal of Political Science* 40 (1996): 101-02.

Gerson, Mark. *The Neoconservative Vision: From the Cold War to the Culture Wars.* Lanham, MD: Madison, 1996.

Girvin, Brian. "Ireland and the European Union: The Impact of Integration and Social Change on Abortion Policy." Githens and Stetson.

Githens, Marianne, and Dorothy McBride Stetson, eds. *Abortion Politics: Public Policy in Cross-Cultural Perspective.* New York: Routledge, 1996.

Glazer, Nathan. "Is Assimilation Dead?" Melzer, Weinberger, and Zinman.

Glendon, Mary Ann. *Abortion and Divorce in Western Law.* Cambridge, MA: Harvard University Press, 1987.

Glick, Henry R. *The Right to Die: Policy Innovation and Its Consequences.* New York: Columbia University Press, 1992.

Glick, Henry R., and Amy Hutchinson. "Physician Assisted Suicide: Agenda Setting and the Elements of Morality Policy." Mooney, *Symposium.*

Goblot, Edmond. "Class and Occupation." *Theories of Society: Foundations of Modern Sociological Theory.* Ed. Talcott Parsons, Edward Shils, Kasper D. Naegele, and Jesse R. Pitts. Glencoe, IL: Free Press, 1961.

Goguel, Francois. "Parliament Under the Fifth Republic: Difficulties in Adapting to a New Role." *Modern Parliaments: Change or Decline?* Ed. Gerhard Loewenberg. Chicago: Aldine Atherton, 1971.

Graber, Mark A. *Rethinking Abortion: Equal Choice, the Constitution, and Reproductive Politics.* Princeton, NJ: Princeton University Press, 1996.

Granberg, Donald. "The Abortion Activists." *Family Planning Perspectives* 13 (July/August 1981): 157-63.

——. "Pro-Life or Reflection of Conservative Ideology? An Analysis of Opposition to Legalized Abortion." *Sociology and Social Research* 62 (1978): 414-29.

Granberg, Donald, and Beth Wellman Granberg. "Social Bases of Support and Opposition to Legalized Abortion." *Perspectives on Abortion.* Ed. Paul Sachdev. Metuchen, NJ: The Scarecrow Press, 1985.

Granberg, Donald, and Donald Denney. "The Coathanger and the Rose." *Society* Magazine 19 (May/June 1982): 39-46.

Grasmick, H.G., and D.E. Green. "Legal Punishment, Social Disapproval and Internalization as Inhibitors of Illegal Behavior." *Journal of Criminal Law and Criminology* 71 (Fall, 1980): 325-35.

Green, John C., and James L. Guth. "The Christian Right in the Republican Party: The Case of Pat Robertson's Supporters." *Journal of Politics* 50 (February, 1988): 150-65.

Green, John C., James L. Guth, and Cleveland R. Fraser. "Apostles and Apostates? Religion and Politics Among Party Activists." Guth and Green *The Bible and the Ballot Box.* 113-36.

Greenberg, Jack, *Judicial Process and Social Change: Constitutional Litigation.* St. Paul, MN: West, 1977.

Grendstad, Gunnar, and Per Selle. "Cultural Theory, Postmaterialism, and Environmental Attitudes." Ellis and Thompson, *Culture Matters.* 151-68.

Griffiths, John. "Self-Regulation by the Dutch Medical Profession of Medical Behavior that Potentially Shortens Life." Krabbendam and Ten Napel.

Guinier, Lani. "Keeping the Faith: Black Voters in the Post-Reagan Era." *Harvard Civil Rights-Civil Liberties Law Review* 24 (1989).

——. *The Tyranny of the Majority: Fundamental Fairness in Representative Democracy.* New York: The Free Press, 1994.

Gusfield, Joseph R. "The Reflexivity of Social Movements: Collective Behavior and Mass Society Theory Revisited." Johnston, Larana, and Gusfield.

Gusfield, Joseph R. *Symbolic Crusade: Status Politics and the American Temperance Movement.* Urbana, IL: University of Illinois Press, 1963.

Guth, James L., and Cleveland Fraser. "Religion and Partisan Preference in Canada." *Journal for the Scientific Study of Religion* 40 (March 2001): 51-64.

Guth, James L., and John C. Green. "Faith and Politics: Religion and Ideology Among Political Contributors." *American Politics Quarterly* 14 (July, 1986): 186-99.

——. "The Moralizing Minority: Christian Right Support Among Political Contributors." *Social Science Quarterly* 68 (September, 1987): 598-610.

——., eds. *The Bible and the Ballot Box: Religion and Politics in the 1988 Election.* Boulder, CO: Westview Press, 1991.

Guttman, Amy. "Introduction." *Multiculturalism and "The Politics of Recognition:" An Essay by Charles Taylor.* Charles Taylor. Princeton, NJ: Princeton University Press, 1992.

Hahn, Harlan. "Voting in Canadian Communities: A Taxonomy of Referendum Issues." *Canadian Journal of Political Science* I (December 1968): 462-69.

Haider-Markel, Donald P., and Kenneth J. Meier. "The Politics of Gay and Lesbian Rights: Expanding the Scope of Conflict." *Journal of Politics* 58 (May 1996).

Hakman, Nathan. "Lobbying the Supreme Court: An Appraisal of Political Science 'Folklore.'" *Fordham Law Review* 35 (1966): 15-50.

Halimi, Gisèle. *The Right to Choose.* Trans. Rosemary Morgan. Brisbane: University of Queensland Press, 1977.

Hamilton, Howard D. "Direct Legislation: Some Implications of Open Housing Referenda." *American Political Science Review* 64 (March 1970): 124-37.

Harrison, Kathryn, and George Hoberg. "Setting the Environmental Agenda in Canada and the United States: The Cases of Dioxin and Radon." *Canadian Journal of Political Science* 24 (1991): 3-27.

Hartnagel, Timothy F., James J. Creechan, and Robert A. Silverman. "Public Opinion and the Legalization of Abortion." *Canadian Review of Sociology and Anthropology* 22 (1985).

Hausegger, Lori. "The Impact of Interest Groups on Judicial Decision Making: A Comparison of Women's Groups in the US and Canada." Annual Meeting, American Political Science Association. Boston. 1998.

Hegel. *The Phenomenology of Spirit.* Trans. A.V. Miller. Oxford: Oxford University Press, 1977.

Hein, Gregory. "Interest Group Litigation and Canadian Democracy." *Choices* 6 (March 2000).

Herman, Didi. *The Antigay Agenda: Orthodox Vision and the Christian Right.* Chicago: University of Chicago Press, 1997.

Hertzke, Allen D. *Representing God in Washington.* Knoxville, TN: University of Tennessee Press, 1988.

Hibbing, J.R., and D. Marsh. "Accounting for the Voting Patterns of British MPs on Free Votes." *Legislative Studies Quarterly* 12 (1987): 275-97.

Higham, John. "Another Look at Nativism." *Catholic Historical Review* 44 (July 1958): 151-52.

Hindell, Keith, and Madeleine Simms. *Abortion Law Reformed.* London: Peter Owen, 1971.

Hirsch, Fred. *The Social Limits of Growth.* Cambridge, MA: Harvard University Press, 1978.

Hoge, Dean R., and David A. Roozen. "Some Sociological Conclusions about Church Trends." *Understanding Church Growth and Decline: 1950-1978.* Ed. Dean R. Hoge and David A. Roozen. New York: Pilgrim, 1979. 315-33.

Holland, Kenneth M. "The Courts in the Federal Republic of Germany." *The Political Role of Law Courts in Modern Democracies.* Ed. Jerold L. Waltman and Kenneth M. Holland. New York: St. Martin's Press, 1988.

——. "Judicial Activism in Western Europe." *Handbook of Global Legal Policy.* Ed. Stuart S. Nagel. New York: Marcel Dekker, 2000.

——., ed. *Judicial Activism in Comparative Perspective.* New York: St. Martin's Press, 1991.

Holton, Robert J., and Bryan S. Turner. *Max Weber on Economy and Society.* London: Routledge, 1989.

Honneth, Axel. *The Struggle for Recognition: The Moral Grammar of Social Conflicts.* Trans. Joel Anderson. Cambridge, UK: Polity Press, 1995.

Hood, Roger. *The Death Penalty: A World-Wide Perspective.* New York: Clarendon Press, 1996.

Hoover, Dennis R. "The Christian Right Under Old Glory and the Maple Leaf." *Sojourners in the Wilderness: The Christian Right in Comparative Perspective.* Ed. Corwin E. Smidt and James M. Penning. Lanham, MD: Rowman and Littlefield, 1997.

——. "Conservative Religious Interest Groups and the Courts: Comparing Canada." Annual Meeting, Midwest Political Science Association. Chicago. April 1999.

Hoover, Dennis R., and Kevin R. den Dulk. "Christian Conservatives Go to Court: Religion and Legal Mobilization in the United States and Canada." *International Political Science Review* (forthcoming).

Horowitz, Irving Louis, ed. *Power, Politics, and People: The Collected Essays of C. Wright Mills.* New York: Ballantine, 1963.

Howlett, Michael. "Issue-Attention and Punctuated Equilibria Models Reconsidered: An Empirical Examination of the Dynamics of Agenda-Setting in Canada." *Canadian Journal of Political Science* 30 (March 1997).

Huckfeldt, Robert, and Carol Weitzel Kohfeld. *Race and the Decline of Class in American Politics.* Urbana, IL: University of Illinois Press, 1989.

Hughes, Colin A. "Australia and New Zealand." Butler and Ranney, *Referendums around the World.*

Hunter, James Davison. "Reflections on the Culture War Hypothesis." *The American Culture Wars: Current Contests and Future Protests.* Ed. James L. Nolan. Charlottesville, VA: University Press of Virginia, 1996.

Hunter, James Davison. *Before the Shooting Begins.* New York: The Free Press, 1994.

——. *Culture Wars.* New York: Basic Books, 1991.

——. "Response to Davis and Robinson: Remembering Durkeim." *Journal for the Scientific Study of Religion* 35 (1996): 246-48.

Hynes, H. Patricia. *The Recurring Silent Spring.* New York: Pergamon, 1989.

Hyson, Stewart. "Governments on a Gamble in the Canadian Federation: The Case of New Brunswick's Video Gambling Policy." Annual Conference, Atlantic Provinces Political Studies Association. Halifax, NS. 2000.

Inglehart, Ronald. *Culture Shift in Advanced Industrial Society.* Princeton, NJ: Princeton University Press, 1990.

——. "Postmaterialism in an Environment of Insecurity." *American Political Science Review* 75 (1981): 880-900.

Inglehart, Ronald, and Jacques-René Rabier. "Political Realignment in Advanced Industrial Society: From Class-Based Politics to Quality of Life Politics." *Government and Opposition* 21 (1986): 456-79.

Inglehart, Ronald, and Paul R. Abramson. "Economic Security and Value Change," *American Political Science Review* 88 (June, 1994): 336-54.

Ingram, David. *Group Rights: Reconciling Equality and Difference*. Lawrence, KS: University Press of Kansas, 2000.

Ivers, Gregg. "Please, God, Save This Honorable Court: The Emergence of the Conservative Religious Right." *The Interest Group Connection: Electioneering, Lobbying, and Policymaking in Washington*. Ed. Paul Hernson, et al. Chatham, NJ: Chatham House Publishers, 1998.

Jackson, Robert J., and Michael M. Atkinson. *The Canadian Legislative System*. 2nd ed. Toronto: Macmillan Canada, 1980.

Jacobs, James B., and Kimberly Potter. *Hate Crimes: Criminal Law and Identity Politics*. New York: Oxford University Press, 1998.

James J. Seeley, "The Public Referendum and Minority Group Legislation: Postscript to *Reitman v. Mulkey*." *Cornell Law Review* 55 (1970): 881-910.

Jasper, James M., and Dorothy Nelkin. *The Animal Rights Crusade: The Growth of a Moral Protest*. New York: The Free Press, 1992.

Jelen, Ted G. "God or Country: Debating Religion in Public Life." in Tatalovich and Daynes, *Moral Controversies in American Politics*.

Jensen, Eric L., Jurg Gerber, and Ginna M. Babcock. "The New War on Drugs: Grass Roots Movement or Political Construction" *Journal of Drug Issues* 21 (1991): 651-67.

Johnston, Hank, Enrique Laraña, and Joseph R. Gusfield, eds. *New Social Movements: From Ideology to Identity*. Philadelphia, PA: Temple University Press, 1994.

Johnston, Richard. *Public Opinion and Public Policy in Canada: Questions of Confidence*. Toronto: University of Toronto Press, 1986.

Jones, Bill, ed. *Political Issues in Britain Today*. New York: Manchester University Press, 1994.

Kellough, Gail. *Aborting Law: An Exploration of the Politics of Motherhood and Medicine*. Toronto: University of Toronto Press, 1996.

Kellstedt, Lyman A., Corwin E. Smidt, and Paul M. Kellstedt. "Religious Tradition, Denomination, and Commitment: White Protestants and the 1988 Election." Guth and Green, *The Bible and the Ballot Box* 139-58.

Kennedy, James. "The Moral State: How Much Do the Americans and the Dutch Differ?" Krabbendam and Ten Napel. 9-22.

Kinder, Donald R., and Lynn M. Sanders. *Divided by Color: Racial Politics and Democratic Ideals*. Chicago: University of Chicago Press, 1996.

Kingdon, John W. *Agendas, Alternatives, and Public Policies*. 2nd ed. New York: HarperCollins, 1995.

Kitschelt, Herbert P. "Political Opportunity Structures and Political Protest: Anti-Nuclear Movements in four Democracies." *British Journal of Political Science* 16 (January, 1986): 57-85.

Kluger, Richard. *Simple Justice: The History of Brown v. Board of Education and Black America's Struggle for Equality*. New York: Knopf, 1976.

Kniss, Fred. "Culture Wars (?): Remapping the Battleground." Williams, *Culture Wars in American Politics*.

Kobach, Kris W. "Recent Developments in Swiss Direct Democracy." *Electoral Studies* 12 (1993): 342-65.

——. "Switzerland." Butler and Ranney, *Referendums around the World*.

Koenig, René. "West Germany." *Contemporary Europe: Class, Status, and Power*. Ed. Margaret S. Archer and Salvador Giner. London: Weidenfeld and Nicholson, 1971.

Kornhauser, William. *The Politics of Mass Society*. Glencoe, II.: The Free Press, 1959.

Koshner, Andrew Jay. *Solving the Puzzle of Interest Group Litigation.* Westport, CT: Greenwood Press, 1998.

Krabbendam, Hans, and Hans-Martien Ten Napel, eds. *Regulating Morality: A Comparison of the Role of the States in Mastering the Mores in the Netherlands and the United States.* Antwerpen-Apeldoorn, Netherlands: E.M. Meijers Institute en Maklu-Uitgevers, 2000.

Krieger, Leonard. *The German Idea of Freedom.* Chicago: University of Chicago Press, 1957.

Krislov, Samuel. "The Amicus Curiae Brief: From Friendship to Advocacy." *Yale Law Journal* 72 (1963): 694-721.

Kymlicka, Will. *Liberalism, Community and Culture.* Oxford: Clarendon Press, 1989.

——. *Multicultural Citizenship: A Liberal Theory of Minority Rights.* Oxford: Clarendon Press, 1995.

Lachmann, Ludwig M. *Capital, Expectations, and the Market Process: Essays in the Theory of the Market Economy.* Ed. Walter E. Grinder. Kansas City, MO: Sheed Andrews and McMeel, 1977.

——. *Legacy of Max Weber.* Berkeley, CA: Glendessary Press, 1970.

Ladd, Everett Carll, Jr., with Charles D. Hadley. *Transformations of the American Party System.* New York: Norton, 1975.

Landfried, Christine. "Constitutional Review and Legislation in the Federal Republic of Germany." *Constitutional Review and Legislation: An International Comparison.* Ed. Christine Landfried. Baden-Baden: Nomos Verlagsgesellschaft, 1988.

Lane, Harlan L. *The Mask of Benevolence: Disabling the Deaf Community.* New York: Vintage Books, 1992.

Lash, Scott, and Scott Urry. *The End of Organized Capitalism.* Madison, WI: University of Wisconsin Press, 1987.

Lawless, Jill. "Britain Keeps Law that Allows Spanking." *Chicago Tribune* 9 November 2001: 27.

Layman, Geoffrey C. "Parties and Culture Wars: The Cultural Division of the Parties' Elites." Paper presented at the annual meeting, American Political Science Association, 1994, New York City.

Layman, Geoffrey C., and Edward G. Carmines. "Cultural Conflict in American Politics: Religious Traditionalism, Postmaterialism, and US Political Behavior." *Journal of Politics* 59 (August 1997).

Layman, Geoffrey C., and Thomas M. Carsey. "Why do Party Activists Convert? An Analysis of Individual-Level Change on the Abortion Issue." *Political Research Quarterly* 51 (September 1998): 723-49.

Lederer, Emil. *State of The Masses.* New York: W.W. Norton, 1940.

Lee, Eugene C. "California." *Referendums: A Comparative Study of Practice and Theory.* Ed. David Butler and Austin Ranney. Washington, DC: American Enterprise Institute for Public Policy Research, 1978.

Leites, Nathan. *On the Game of Politics in France.* Stanford, CA: Stanford University Press, 1959.

Lester, James P., ed. *Environmental Politics and Policy: Theories and Evidence.* Durham, NC: Duke University Press, 1989.

Lester, James P., and Joseph Stewart, Jr. *Public Policy: An Evolutionary Approach.* 2nd ed. Belmont, CA: Wadsworth Thompson Learning, 2000.

Lijphart, Arend. *The Politics of Accommodation: Pluralism and Democracy in the Netherlands.* Berkeley, CA: University of California Press, 1968.

Lipset, Seymour Martin. *American Exceptionalism: A Double-Edged Sword.* New York: W.W. Norton, 1996.

——. *Political Man.* Garden City, NY: Doubleday, 1960.

Lipset, Seymour M., and Earl Raab. *The Politics of Unreason: Right-Wing Extremism in America, 1790-1970.* New York: Harper and Row, 1970.

Lipset, Seymour Martin, and Stein Rokkan, eds. *Party Systems and Voter Alignments: Cross-National Perspectives*. New York: Free Press, 1967

Lo, Clarence Y.H. "Countermovements and Conservative Movements in the Contemporary US." *American Review of Sociology* 8 (1982): 111-12.

Lovenduski, Joni, and Joyce Outshoorn, eds. *The New Politics of Abortion*. London: SAGE Publications, 1986.

Lowi, Theodore J. "American Business, Public Policy, Case Studies, and Political Theory." *World Politics* 16 (July 1964): 677-715.

——. "Foreword: New Dimensions in Policy and Politics." Tatalovich and Daynes, *Moral Controversies in American Politics*. xiii-xxvii.

——. "The Welfare State, The New Regulation and the Rule of Law." *Distributional Conflicts in Environmental-Resource Policy*. Ed. Allan Schnaiberg, Nicholas Watts, and Klaus Zimmermann. New York: St. Martin's Press, 1986.

Luker, Kristin. *Abortion and the Politics of Motherhood*. Berkeley, CA: University of California Press, 1984.

MacMillan, C. Michael. *The Practice of Language Rights in Canada*. Toronto: University of Toronto Press, 1998.

MacMillan, C. Michael, and Raymond Tatalovich. "Judicial Activism vs. Restraint: The Role of the Courts in Official Language Policy in Canada and the United States." *American Review of Canadian Studies* (forthcoming).

Madison, James, Alexander Hamilton, and John Jay. *The Federalist Papers*. New York: The New American Library, Mentor Books, 1961.

Magleby, David B. "Direct Legislation in the American States." Butler and Ranney, *Referendums Around the World*.

——. "Let the Voters Decide? An Assessment of the Initiative and the Referendum Process." *University of Colorado Law Review* 66 (1995): 13-46.

Mandel, Michael. *The Charter of Rights and the Legalisation of Politics in Canada*. Toronto: Wall and Thompson, 1989.

Manning, E. Preston. "A 'B' for Prof. Russell." *Policy Options* 20 (April 1999).

Mansbridge, Jane J., ed. *Beyond Self-Interest*. Chicago: University of Chicago Press, 1990.

Manwaring, David. *Render Unto Caesar: The Flag Salute Controversy*. Chicago: University of Chicago Press, 1962.

Marcuse, Herbert. *Reason and Revolution: Hegel and the Rise of Social Theory*. New York: The Humanities Press, 1954.

Marsh, David, and Melvyn Read. *Private Members' Bills*. Cambridge: Cambridge University Press, 1988.

Mason, Thomas L. *Governing Oregon*. Dubuque, IA: Kendall/Hunt, 1994.

Mauser, Gary A. "The Case of the Missing Canadian Gun Owners." Annual Meeting, American Society of Criminology. Atlanta, GA. November 2001.

——. "The Politics of Firearms Registration in Canada." *Journal of Firearms and Public Policy* 10 (Fall 1998): 1-26.

Mauser, G.A., and M. Margolis. "The Politics of Gun Control: Comparing Canadian and American Patterns." *Government and Policy* 10 (1992).

Maxwell, Carol J.C. "'Where's the Land of Happy?' Individual Meaning and Collective Antiabortion Activism." *Abortion Politics in the United States and Canada*. Ed. Ted G. Jelen and Marthe A. Chandler. Westport, CT: Praeger, 1994.

McAdam, Doug, John D. McCarthy, and Mayer N. Zald, eds. *Comparative Perspectives on Social Movements: Political Opportunities, Mobilizing Structures, and Cultural Framing*. Cambridge: Cambridge University Press, 1996.

McKenzie, Robert T. *British Political Parties*. New York: St. Martin's Press, 1955.

McLauchlan, William P. "Supreme Court Abortion Policy: The Selection and Development of a Social Policy." Annual Meeting, Midwest Political Science Association. Chicago, IL, 1987.

McNaught, Kenneth. "Political Trials and the Canadian Political Tradition." *Courts and Trials*. Ed. Martin L. Friedland. Toronto: University of Toronto Press, 1975.

Mead, George Herbert. *Mind, Self and Society: From the Standpoint of a Social Behavioralist*. Chicago: University of Chicago Press, 1934.

Means, Cyril C. Jr. "The Phoenix of Abortional Freedom: Is a Penumbral or Ninth Amendment Right About to Arise from the Nineteenth-Century Legislative Ashes of a Fourteenth Century Common Law Liberty?" *New York Law Forum* 17 (1971): 335-410.

Meier, Kenneth J. *The Politics of Sin*. Armonk, NY: M.E. Sharpe, 1994.

Meja, Volker, Dieter Misgeld, and Nico Stehr, eds. *Modern German Sociology*. New York: Columbia University Press, 1987.

Melzer, Arthur M., Jerry Weinberger, and M. Richard Zinman, eds. *Multiculturalism and American Democracy*. Lawrence, KS: University Press of Kansas, 1998.

Menkel-Meadow, Carrie. "The Causes of Cause Lawyering: Toward an Understanding of the Motivation and Commitment of Social Justice Lawyers." *Cause Lawyering: Political Commitments and Professional Responsibilities*. Ed. Austin Sarat and Stuart Scheingold. New York: Oxford University Press, 1998. 31-68.

Meyer, David S., and Suzanne Staggenborg. "Countermovement Dynamics in Federal Systems: A Comparison of Abortion Politics in Canada and the United States." *Research in Political Sociology* 8 (1998): 209-40.

——. "Movements, Countermovements, and the Structure of Political Opportunity." *American Journal of Sociology* 101 (1996): 1628-60.

Mezey, Susan Gluck. "Civil Law and Common Law Traditions: Judicial Review and Legislative Supremacy in West Germany and Canada," *International and Comparative Law Quarterly* 32 (1983): 700, 704, 705.

Miller, Arthur H., and Martin P. Wattenberg. "Politics from the Pulpit: Religiosity and the 1980 Elections." *Public Opinion Quarterly* 48 (Spring, 1984): 301-17.

Miller, Hugh. "Weber's Action Theory and Lowi's Policy Types in Formulation, Enactment, and Implementation." *Policy Studies Journal* 18 (Summer, 1990.

Millett, Kate. *Sexual Politics*. Garden City, NY: Doubleday and Company, 1970.

Mills, C. Wright. "The Sociology of Stratification." *Power, Politics, and People: The Collected Essays of C. Wright Mills*. Ed. Irving Louis Horowitz. New York: Ballantine, 1963. 305-23.

Mises, Ludwig von. *Human Action: A Treatise on Economics*. Chicago: Regnery, 1966.

Moen, Matthew C. *The Christian Right and Congress*. Tuscaloosa, AL: University of Alabama Press, 1989.

——. "School Prayer and the Politics of Life-Style Concern." *Social Science Quarterly* (December 1984): 1065-71.

Mohrenschlager, M. "The Abolition of Capital Punishment in the Federal Republic of Germany: German Experiences." *Revue Internationale de Droit Penal* 58 (1987).

Monroe, Kristin R. "John Donne's People: Explaining Differences between Rational Actors and Altruists through Cognitive Frameworks." *Journal of Politics* 53 (1991): 394-433.

Monroe, Kristen R., Michael C. Barton, and Ute Klingemann. "Altruism and the Theory of Rational Action: Rescuers of Jews in Nazi Europe." *Ethics* 101 (October 1990): 103-22.

Mooney, Christopher Z., ed. *The Public Clash of Private Values: The Politics of Morality Policy*. New York: Seven Bridges Press, 2000.

——., ed. *Symposium: The Politics of Morality Policy. Policy Studies Journal* 27/4 (1999).

Mooney, Christopher Z. and Mei-Hsien Lee. "The Influence of Values on Consensus and the Contentious Morality Policy: U.S. Death Penalty Reform, 1956-1982." *Journal of Politics* 62 (2000): 223-39.

Morton, F.L. *Morgentaler v. Borowski: Abortion, The Charter, and The Courts*. Toronto: McClelland and Stewart, 1992.

——. *Pro-Choice vs. Pro-Life: Abortion and the Courts in Canada*. Norman, OK: University of Oklahoma Press, 1992.

Morton, F.L., and Rainer Knopff. *The Charter Revolution and The Court Party*. Peterborough, ON: Broadview Press, 2000.

Mossuz-Lavau, Janine. "Abortion Policy in France under Governments of the Right and Left (1973-84)." Lovenduski and Outshoorn.

Mueller, John E. "The Politics of Fluoridation in Seven California Cities." *Western Political Quarterly* 19 (March 1966): 54-67.

Murley, John A. "School Prayer: Free Exercise of Religion or Establishment of Religion?" Tatalovich and Daynes, *Social Regulatory Policy*.

Nader, Ralph. *Unsafe at Any Speed*. New York: Grossman, 1965.

Nelson, Barbara J. *Making an Issue of Child Abuse*. Chicago: University of Chicago Press, 1984.

Nevitte, Neil. *The Decline of Deference*. Peterborough, Ontario: Broadview Press, 1996.

Nevitte, Neil, William P. Brandon, and Lori Davis. "The American Abortion Controversy: Lessons from Cross-National Evidence." *Politics and the Life Sciences* (February 1993).

Newman, Tim. "Physician Assisted Suicide and Voluntary Euthanasia: the Links between Ethics and Policy." Paper presented to the Annual Meeting, Midwest Political Association.

Niblock, John F. "Anti-Gay Initiatives: A Call for Heightened Judicial Scrutiny." *UCLA Law Review* 41 (1993).

Noelle-Neumann, Elisabeth, ed. *The Germans: Public Opinion Polls, 1967-1980*. Westport, CT: Greenwood Press, 1981.

Nolan, James L., ed. *The American Culture Wars: Current Contests and Future Protests*. Charlottesville, VA: University Press of Virginia, 1996.

Noonan, John T. Jr. "Raw Judicial Power." *National Review* (March 2, 1973).

O'Connor, Karen. *Women's Organizations' Use of the Courts*. Lexington, MA: Lexington Press, 1980.

O'Connor, Karen, and Lee Epstein. "The Rise of Conservative Interest Group Litigation." *Journal of Politics* 45 (May, 1983): 478-89.

Offe, Claus. "Reflections on the Institutional Self-transformation of Movement Politics: A Tentative Stage Model." *Challenging the Political Order: New Social and Political Movements in Western Democracies*. Ed. Russell J. Dalton and Manfred Kuechler. New York: Oxford University Press, 1990. 232-50.

O'Neill, Timothy. *Bakke and the Politics of Equality: Friends and Foes in the Classroom of Litigation*. Middletown, CT: Wesleyan University Press, 1985.

Oliner, Samuel P., and Pearl Oliner. *The Altruistic Personality: Rescuers of Jews in Nazi Europe*. New York: Free Press, 1988.

Olson, Mancur, Jr. *The Logic of Collective Action: Public Goods and the Theory of Groups*. Cambridge, MA: Harvard University Press, 1965.

Olson, Susan M. "Interest Group Litigation in Federal District Court: Beyond the Political Disadvantage Theory." *Journal of Politics* 52 (August, 1990).

Orey, Byron D'Andra. "Racial Threat, Republicanism and the Rebel Flag." Annual Meeting, Midwest Political Science Association. Chicago, IL. 2000.

Outshoorn, Joyce. "The Stability of Compromise: Abortion Politics in Western Europe." Githens and Stetson. 145-64.

Overby, L. Marvin, Raymond Tatalovich, and Donley T. Studlar. "Party and Free Votes in Canada: Abortion in the House of Commons." *Party Politics* 4 (July 1998): 381-92.

Page, Ann L., and Donald Clelland. "The Kanawha County Textbook Controversy: A Study of the Politics of Life Style Concern." *Social Forces* 57 (September 1978): 265-81.

Pal, Leslie A. "Advocacy Organizations and Legislative Politics: The Effect of the Charter of Rights and Freedoms on Interest Lobbying of Federal Legislation, 1989-91." *Equity and Community: The Charter, Interest Advocacy and Representation.* Ed. F. Leslie Seidle. Montreal: Institute for Research on Public Policy, 1994.

——. "Gun Control: US and Canada." Pal and Weaver.

Pal, Leslie A., and R. Kent Weaver, eds. *The Politics of Pain: Political Institutions and Loss Imposition in the United States and Canada.* Washington, DC: Georgetown University Press, forthcoming.

Pfeffer, Leo. "Amici in Church-State Litigation." *Law and Contemporary Problems* 44 (1981): 83-110.

Phillips, Anne. *The Politics of Presence.* Oxford: Clarendon Press, 1995.

Pierce, Patrick A., and Donald E. Miller. "Variations in the Diffusion of State Lottery Adoptions: How Revenue Dedication Changes Morality Policy." Mooney, *Symposium* 696-706.

Pinard, Maurice. "Structural Attachments and Political Support in Urban Politics: The Case of Fluoridation Referendums." *American Journal of Sociology* LXVIII (March 1963): 513-26.

Pitkin, Hanna. *The Concept of Representation.* Berkeley, CA: University of California Press, 1967.

Piven, Frances Fox, and Richard Cloward. *Regulating the Poor.* New York: Vintage Books, 1971.

Plaut, T.F.A. "Analysis of Voting Behavior on a Fluoridation Referendum." *Public Opinion Quarterly* 23 (1959): 213-22.

Pothier, Diane. "Parties and Free Votes in the Canadian House of Commons." *Journal of Canadian Studies* 14 (Summer 1979): 80-96.

Price, Charles M. "The Initiative: A Comparative State Analysis and Reassessment of a Western Phenomenon." *Western Political Quarterly* 28 (June, 1975): 243-62.

Pross, A. Paul. "Pressure Groups: Adaptive Instruments of Political Communication." *Pressure Group Behaviour in Canadian Politics.* Ed. A. Paul Pross. Toronto: McGraw-Hill Ryerson, 1975.

Pym, Bridget. *Pressure Groups and the Permissive Society.* Newton Abbot, G.B.: David and Charles, 1974.

Radwanski, George. *Trudeau.* Toronto: Macmillan, 1978.

Ram, Christopher D. "Living Next to the United States: Recent Developments in Canadian Gun Control Policy, Politics, and Law." *New York Law School Journal of International and Comparative Law* 15 (1995): 279-313.

Ranney, Austin. "United States of America." Butler and Ranney, *Referendums: A Comparative Study of Practice and Theory.*

Rawls, John. *A Theory of Justice.* Cambridge, MA: Harvard University Press, 1971.

——. "Justice as Fairness: Political Not Metaphysical." *Philosophy and Public Affairs* 14 (1985): 223-51.

Rayside, David. *On the Fringe: Gays and Lesbians in Politics.* Ithaca, NY: Cornell University Press, 1998.

Rayside, David, and Scott Bowler. "Research Note: Public Opinion and Gay Rights." *The Canadian Review of Sociology and Anthropology* 25 (November 1988).

Raz, Joseph. "Multiculturalism: A Liberal Perspective." *Dissent* 41 (Winter 1994): 67-79.

Read, Melvyn D., and David Marsh. "Homosexuality." Cowley, *Conscience and Parliament.*

Read, Melvyn, David Marsh, and David Richards. "Why Did They Do It? Voting on Homosexuality and Capital Punishment in the House of Commons." *Parliamentary Affairs* 47 (July 1994).

Rhode, Deborah L., and Martha Minow. "Reforming the Questions, Questioning the Reforms: Feminist Perspectives on Divorce Law," *Divorce Reform at the Crossroads*. Ed. Stephen D. Sugarman and Herma Hill Kay. New Haven, CT: Yale University Press, 1990. 191-210.

Richards, Peter G. *Parliament and Conscience*. London: George Allen and Unwin, 1970.

Richmond, Keith. "Daylight Savings in New South Wales: A Case of Emotive Symbolic Politics." *Australian Journal of Public Administration* 37 (1978): 374-85.

Ripley, Randall B., and Grace A. Franklin, *Congress, the Bureaucracy, and Public Policy*. Pacific Grove, CA: Brooks/Cole, 1991.

Rivera, Rhonda R. "Our Straight-Laced Judges: The Legal Position of Homosexual Persons In The United States." *The Hastings Law Journal* 30 (March 1979).

Robinson, P.H., and J.M. Darley. *Justice, Liability, and Blame*. Boulder, CO: Westview Press, 1997.

——. "The Utility of Desert." *Northwestern University Law Review* 91 (1997): 453-99.

Roepke, Wilhelm. *Welfare, Freedom and Inflation*. Tuscaloosa, AL: University of Alabama Press, 1960.

Rogers, Everett M., and James W. Dearing. "Agenda-Setting Research: Where Has It Been, Where Is It Going?" *Communication Yearbook* 11: 555-94.

Roof, Wade Clark. *Community and Commitment: Religious Plausibility in a Liberal Protestant Church* (New York: Elsevier, 1978).

Rose, Arnold M., ed. *Human Behavior and Social Processes*. Boston: Houghton Mifflin, 1962.

Rossotti, Jack E., Laura Natelson, and Raymond Tatalovich. "Nonlegal Advice: The *Amicus* Briefs in *Webster v. Reproductive Health Services*." *Judicature* 81 (November-December, 1997): 118-21.

Rozell, Mark, and Clyde Wilcox. *Second Coming: The New Christian Right in Virginia Politics*. Baltimore, MD: Johns Hopkins University Press, 1996.

Russell, Peter H. "Prof. Russell Replies." *Policy Options* 20 (April 1999).

——. "Reform's Judicial Agenda." *Policy Options* 20 (April 1999).

Samar, Vincent J. *The Right to Privacy: Gays, Lesbians, and the Constitution*. Philadelphia, PA: Temple University Press, 1991.

Santoro, Wayne A. "Conventional Politics Takes Center Stage: The Latino Struggle against English-Only Laws." *Social Forces* 77 (1999): 887-909.

Sarat, Austin, and Stuart Scheingold, eds. *Cause Lawyering: Political Commitments and Professional Responsibilities*. New York: Oxford University Press, 1998.

Savage, James. "Postmaterialism of the Left and Right: Political Conflict in Postindustrial Society." *Comparative Political Studies* 17 (January 1985): 431-51.

Schattschneider, E.E. *The Semi-Sovereign People*. New York: Holt, Rinehart and Winston, 1960.

Scheingold, Stuart A. *The Politics of Rights: Lawyers, Public Policy, and Political Change*. New Haven, CT: Yale University Press, 1974.

Scheppele, Kim Lane. "Constitutionalizing Abortion." Githens and Stetson.

Schildkraut, Deborah J. "Official-English and the States: Influences on Declaring English the Official Language in the United States." *Political Research Quarterly* 54 (June 2001): 454-55.

Schmidt, Ronald, Sr. *Language Policy and Identity Politics in the United States*. Philadelphia, PA: Temple University Press, 2000.

Schriwer, Tania. "Establishing an Affirmative Governmental Duty to Protect Children's Rights: The European Court of Human Rights as a Model for the United States Supreme Court." *University of San Francisco Law Review* 34 (Winter 2000): 379-408.

Schumaker, Paul. "Moral Principles of Local Officials and the Resolution of Culture War Issues," Sharp, *Culture Wars and Local Politics*.

Schuman, Howard, and Stanley Presser. "The Attitude-Action Connection and the Issue of Gun Control." *Gun Control*. Ed. Philip J. Cook *The Annals of the American Academy of Political and Social Science* 455 (May 1981): 40-47.

Schutz, Alfred. "Tiresias, or Our Knowledge of Future Events." *Collected Papers: Studies in Social Theory*. Ed. Arid Brodersen. The Hague, Netherlands: Martinus Nijhoff, 1971. 277-293.

Schwartz, Mildred A. *Public Opinion and Canadian Identity*. Berkeley, CA: University of California Press, 1967.

Schweisguth, Etienne. "The Myth of Neoconservatism." *How France Votes*. Ed. Michael S. Lewis-Beck. New York: Chatham House Publishers, 2000.

Scott, Wilbur J. "The Equal Rights Amendment as Status Politics." *Social Forces* 64 (December 1985): 499-506.

Segal, Jeffrey, and Harold J. Spaeth. *The Supreme Court and the Attitudinal Model*. Cambridge, UK: Cambridge University Press, 1993.

Setala, Maija. *Referendums and Democratic Government: Normative Theory and the Analysis of Institutions*. New York: St. Martin's Press, 1999.

Shafer, Byron E. "The New Cultural Politics." *Political Science and Politics* 18 (Spring, 1985): 221-31.

Shafer, Byron E., and William J. Clagget. *The Two Majorities: The Issue Context of Modern American Politics*. Baltimore, MD: Johns Hopkins University Press, 1995.

Sharp, Elaine B. "Agenda-Setting and Policy Results: Lessons from Three Drug Policy Episodes." *Policy Studies Journal* 20 (1992): 538-51.

——., ed. *Culture Wars and Local Politics*. Lawrence, KS: University Press of Kansas, 1999.

——. "Culture Wars and City Politics: Local Government's Role in Social Conflict." *Urban Affairs Review* 31 (July 1996): 738-58.

——. "Paradoxes of National Antidrug Policymaking." *The Politics of Problem Definition: Shaping the Policy Agenda*. Ed. D.A. Rochefort and R.W. Cobb. Lawrence, KS: University Press of Kansas, 1994.

Shaw, Steven. "No Longer a Sleeping Giant: The Re-Awakening of Religious Conservatives in American Politics." Witt and McCorkle.

Shils, Edward A. *The Torment of Secrecy*. Glencoe, IL: The Free Press, 1956.

Silverman, M. "Toward a Theory of Criminal Deterrence." *American Sociological Review* 41 (June, 1976): 442-61.

Simmel, Arnold. "A Signpost for Research on Fluoridation Conflicts: The Concept of Relative Deprivation." *Journal of Social Issues* 17 (1961): 26-36.

Simpson, John H., and Henry G. MacLeod, "The Politics of Morality in Canada." *Religious Movements*. Ed. Rodney Stark. New York: Paragon, 1985.

Singer, Peter. *Animal Liberation*. New York: Avon, 1977.

Skerry, Peter. "The Class Conflict over Abortion." *Public Interest* (Summer 1978).

Slonin, Marc, and James H. Lowe. "Comment: Judicial Review of Laws Enacted by Popular Vote." *Washington Law Review* 55 (1979): 175-209.

Smith, Gordon. "The Functional Properties of the Referendum." *European Journal of Political Research* 4 (1976): 1-23.

Smith, Kevin B. "Clean Thoughts and Dirty Minds: The Politics of Porn." Mooney, "Symposium" 723-34.

Smith, Miriam. *Lesbian and Gay Rights in Canada*. Toronto: University of Toronto Press, 1999.

Smith, T. Alexander. *The Comparative Policy Process*. Santa Barbara, CA: CLIO Press, 1975.

——. "A Phenomenology of the Policy Process." *International Journal of Comparative Sociology* 23 (1982): 1-5.

——. *Time and Public Policy*. Knoxville, TN: University of Tennessee Press, 1988.

Smith, T. Alexander, and Lenahan O'Connell. *Black Anxiety, White Guilt, and the Politics of Status Frustration*. Westport, CT: Praeger, 1997.

Smith, Tom W. "Atop a Liberal Plateau? A Summary of Trends since World War II." *Research in Urban Policy: Coping with Urban Austerity*. Vol. 1. Ed. Terry Nichols Clark. Greenwich, CT: JAI Press, 1985. 245-57.

——. "Liberal and Conservative Trends in the United States since World War II." *Public Opinion Quarterly* 54 (1990): 479-507.

Smith, Tom W., and Paul B. Sheatsley. "American Attitudes toward Race Relations." *Public Opinion* 14-15 (October/November, 1984): 50-53.

Sniderman, Paul M., Joseph F. Fletcher, Peter H. Russell, and Philip E. Tetlock, *The Clash of Rights*. New Haven, CT: Yale University Press, 1996.

——. "Political Culture and The Problem of Double Standards: Mass and Elite Attitudes Toward Language Rights in the Canadian Charter of Rights." *Canadian Journal of Political Science* 22 (1989): 259-84.

Sniderman, Paul M., Richard A. Brody, and Philip E. Tetlock. *Reasoning and Choice*. Cambridge, UK: Cambridge University Press, 1991.

Sniderman, Paul, and Thomas Piazza. *The Scar of Race*. Cambridge, MA: Harvard University Press, 1993.

Soper, J. Christopher. "Political Structures and Interest Group Activism: A Comparison of the British and American Pro-Life Movements." *Social Science Journal* 31 (1994): 319-34.

Sorauf, Frank J. *The Wall of Separation: The Constitutional Politics of Church and State*. Princeton, NJ: Princeton University Press, 1976.

Spiro, Herbert J. *Government by Constitution: The Political Systems of Democracy*. New York: Random House, 1959.

Spitzer, Robert J. "Gun Control: Constitutional Mandate or Myth?" Tatalovich and Daynes, *Moral Controversies in American Politics*. 172-174.

——. *The Politics of Gun Control*. Chatham, NJ: Chatham House Publishers, 1995.

Steger, Mary Ann E., and Brent S. Steel. "Death Penalty: Crime Deterrent or Legalized Homicide?" Tatalovich and Daynes, *Moral Controversies in American Politics*.

Stetson, Dorothy McBride. "Abortion Law Reform in France." *Journal of Comparative Family Studies* 17 (Autumn 1986).

——. "Abortion Policy Triads and Women's Rights in Russia, the United States, and France." Githens and Stetson.

Stone, Alex. "Abstract Constitutional Review and Policy Making in Western Europe." *Comparative Judicial Review and Public Policy*. Ed. Donald W. Jackson and C. Neal Tate. Westport, CT: Greenwood Press, 1992.

——. *The Birth of Judicial Politics in France: The Constitutional Court in Comparative Perspective*. New York: Oxford University Press, 1992.

Stone, Gregory P. "Appearance and the Self." *Human Behavior and Social Processes*. Ed. Arnold M. Rose. Boston: Houghton Mifflin, 1962. 87-95.

Strickland, Ruth Ann. "Abortion: Prochoice versus Prolife," Tatalovich and Daynes, *Moral Controversies in American Politics.* 16-22.

Strossen, Nadine. *Defending Pornography: Free Speech, Sex, and the Fight for Women's Rights.* New York: Scribner, 1995.

Studlar, Donley T. "Elite Responsiveness or Elite Autonomy: British Immigration Policy Reconsidered." *Ethnic and Racial Studies* 3 (April 1980): 207-23.

——. *Great Britain: Decline or Renewal?* Boulder, CO: Westview Press, 1996.

——. "What Constitutes Morality Policy? A Cross-National Analysis." Mooney, *The Public Clash of Private Values.*

Studlar, Donley T., and Ian McAllister. "A Changing Political Agenda? The Structure of Political Attitudes in Britain, 1974-87." *International Journal of Public Opinion Research* 4 (1992).

Sunstein, C.R. "Social Norms and Social Roles." *Columbia Law Review* 96 (1997): 903-68.

Sussman, Glen, and Byron W. Daynes. "Party Promises and Presidential Performance: Social Policies of the Modern Presidents, FDR-Clinton." *Southeastern Political Review* 28 (March 2000): 125-26.

Swan, Kenneth. "Intervention and Amicus Curiae Status in Charter Litigation." *Charter Cases 1986-1987.* Colloquium of the Canadian Bar Association. Ed. Gerald Beaudoin. Montreal: Les Editions Yvon Blais, 1987.

Szarka, Joseph. "Green Politics in France: The Impasse of Non-Alignment." *Parliamentary Affairs* 47 (July 1994).

Tarrow, Sidney. *Power in Movement: Social Movements, Collective Action and Politics.* Cambridge, UK: Cambridge University Press, 1994.

Tatalovich, Raymond. *Nativism Reborn?: The Official English Language Movement and the American States.* Lexington, KY: University Press of Kentucky, 1995.

Tatalovich, Raymond, and Byron W. Daynes. "The Lowi Paradigm, Moral Conflict, and Coalition Building: Pro-Choice Versus Pro-Life." *Women & Politics* 13 (1993): 39-66.

——. *Moral Controversies in American Politics.* Armonk, NY: M.E. Sharpe, 1998.

——. *The Politics of Abortion.* New York: Praeger, 1981.

——. *Social Regulatory Policy: Moral Controversies in American Politics.* Boulder, CO: Westview Press, 1988.

Tatalovich, Raymond, and Melissa A. Haussman. "Provincial Policies on Abortion Since *Morgentaler.*" Annual Meeting, Canadian Political Science Association. Quebec City. 2000.

Tatchell, Peter. *Out in Europe: A Guide to Lesbian and Gay Rights in 30 European Countries.* London: Published by Channel 4 Television, 1990.

Taylor, Charles. *Multiculturalism and "The Politics of Recognition:" An Essay by Charles Taylor.* Princeton, NJ: Princeton University Press, 1992.

Thompson, Michael. "The Dynamics of Cultural Theory and their Implications for the Enterprise Culture." *Understanding the Enterprise Culture.* Ed. Shaun Hargreaves Heap and Angus Ross. Edinburgh: Edinburgh University Press, 1992.

Thompson, Michael, Richard Ellis, and Aaron Wildavsky. *Cultural Theory.* Boulder, CO: Westview Press, 1990.

Thorne, Susan. "Private Member's Bill: Success Stories in Canada's Parliament." *The New Federation* (February/March, 1990): 21-23.

Tocqueville, Alexis de. *Democracy in America.* Vol. 1. Ed. J.P. Mayer. Trans. George Lawrence. New York, Perennial Library, Harper and Row, 1988 (c1969).

Tribe, Laurence. *American Constitutional Law.* Mineola, NY: Foundation Press, 1988.

Truman, David B. *The Governmental Process.* New York: Alfred A. Knopf, 1960.

Tushnet, Mark. *The NAACP's Legal Strategy Against Segregation, 1925-50.* Chapel Hill, NC: University of North Carolina Press, 1987.

Tyler, Tom R. *Why People Obey the Law.* New Haven, CT: Yale University Press, 1990.

Tyler, Tom R., and Renee Weber. "Support for the Death Penalty: Instrumental Response to Crime, or Symbolic Attitude?" *Law and Society Review* 17 (1982): 21-46.

Vaid, Urvashi. *Virtual Equality: The Mainstreaming of Gay and Lesbian Liberation.* New York: Doubleday, Anchor Books, 1995.

Vose, Clement E. *Caucasians Only: The Supreme Court, The NAACP, and The Restrictive Covenant Cases.* Berkeley, CA: University of California Press, 1959.

Wagner, Robert A. "Evans v. Romer: Colorado Amendment 2 and the Search for a Fundamental Right for Groups to Participate Equally in the Political Process." *St. Louis University Law Journal* 38 (Winter, 1993-94): 523-51.

Wald, Kenneth D., Dennis E. Owen, and Samuel S. Hill, Jr. "Evangelical Politics and Status Issues." *Journal for the Scientific Study of Religion* 28 (1989).

Walker, Clive, and Russell L. Weaver. "The United Kingdom Bill of Rights 1998: The Modernisation of Rights in the Old World." *University of Michigan Journal of Law Reform* 33 (Summer 2000).

Wasby, Stephen L. *The Impact of the United States Supreme Court: Some Perspectives.* Homewood, IL: The Dorsey Press, 1970.

Wattier, Mark J., and Raymond Tatalovich. "Issue Publics, Mass Publics, and Agenda-Setting: Environmentalism and Economics in Presidential Elections." *Government and Policy* 18 (2000).

Wattier, Mark J., Byron W. Daynes, and Raymond Tatalovich. "Abortion Attitudes, Gender, and Candidate Choice in Presidential Elections: 1972 to 1992." *Women and Politics* 17 (1997): 55-72.

Weaver, R. Kent. "The Politics of Blame Avoidance." *Journal of Public Policy* 6 (1986): 371-78.

Webb, Marilyn. *The Good Death.* New York: Bantam, 1997.

Weber, Max. *Economy and Society.* New York: Bedminister, 1968.

Wechsler, Herbert. "Toward Neutral Principles of Constitutional Law." *Harvard Law Review* 73 (November, 1959): 1-35.

Weir, Lorna. "Social Movement Activism in the Formation of Ontario New Democratic Policy on Abortion, 1982-1984." *Labour/Le Travail* 35 (Spring 1995): 163-93.

Wilcox, Clyde. *Onward Christian Soldiers: The Religious Right in American Politics.* Boulder, CO: Westview Press, 1996.

Wildavsky, Aaron. "A Cultural Theory of Preference Formation." *American Political Science Review* 81 (March 1987): 7-21.

———. *The Rise of Radical Egalitarianism.* Washington, DC: The American University Press, 1991.

Williams, Philip M. *The French Parliament: Politics in the Fifth Republic.* New York: F.A. Praeger, 1968.

———. *Politics in Post-War France: Parties and the Constitution in the Fourth Republic.* New York: Longmans, Green, 1958.

Williams, Rhys H., ed. *Cultural Wars in American Politics: Critical Reviews of a Popular Myth.* New York: Aldine De Gruyter, 1997.

Wintemute, Robert. *Sexual Orientation and Human Rights.* New York: Oxford University Press, 1995.

Witt, Stephanie L., and Suzanne McCorkle. eds. *Anti-Gay Rights: Assessing Voter Initiatives.* Westport, CT: Praeger, 1997.

Witt, Stephanie L., W. David Patton, and Jacque Amoureux. "Morality Politics: The Use of Local Initiatives in the Backlash Against Local Gay-Rights Ordinances." Annual Meeting, Western Political Science Association. Seattle, WA. 1999.

Wolfinger, Raymond E., and Fred I. Greenstein. "The Repeal of Fair Housing in California: An Analysis of Referendum Voting." *American Political Science Review* 62 (September, 1968): 753-69.

Woliver, Laura R., Angela D. Ledford, and Chris J. Dolan. "The South Carolina Confederate Flag: The Politics of Race and Citizenship." *Politics and Policy* 29 (December 2001): 707-30.

Women's Legal Education and Action Fund. *Equality and the Charter: Ten Years of Feminist Advocacy Before the Supreme Court of Canada*. Toronto: Edmund Montgomery Publications, 1996.

Wouters, Cas. "On Status Competition and Emotion Management." *Journal of Social History* 24 (1991).

Wuthnow, Robert. *The Restructuring of American Religion: Society and Faith Since World War II*. Berkeley, CA: University of California Press, 1988.

Young, Iris M. *Justice and the Politics of Difference*. Princeton, NJ: Princeton University Press, 1990.

Young, Lisa. *Feminists and Party Politics*. Vancouver, Canada: University of British Columbia Press, 2000.

Zurcher, Louis A. Jr., R. George Kirkpatrick, Robert G. Cushing, and Charles K. Bowman. "The Anti-Pornography Campaign: A Symbolic Crusade." *Social Problems* 19 (Fall 1971): 217-38.

Zurcher, Louis A., Jr., and R. George Kirkpatrick. *Citizens for Decency: Antipornography Crusades as Status Defense*. Austin TX: University of Texas Press, 1976.

Zwier, Robert. "Coalition Strategies of Religious Interest Groups." *Religion and Political Behavior in the United States*. Ed. Ted G. Jelen. New York: Praeger, 1989. 171-86.

Index

abortion, 111, 129, 165, 187, 188, 189-90, 191
  Canada, 74, 79, 81-82, 97, 114, 115, 116-17, 151-52, 165, 204-05, 208, 210, 218-19, 231, 232, 241, 244, 260
  France, 72-73, 80, 87-88, 124, 129-30, 160, 208, 210, 220-22, 231, 261
  Germany, 158-59, 165, 208, 210, 222-24, 232, 233, 261-62
  United Kingdom, 80-81, 73, 97, 126, 129, 208, 210, 219-20, 231, 233, 260
  United States, 11, 30, 70, 72, 81, 87, 92, 97, 112, 165, 175, 176, 205, 208, 210, 218-19, 232, 241, 242, 244, 259
agenda-setting
  cause célèbre, 87
  environmentalism, 67-68, 70, 73, 86-87, 92-93
  litigation strategy, 69, 139, 141-44, 145, 150-51
  mass media, 68-69, 91-93
  policy venues, 96, 144, 146, 181

  political opportunity structure, 97, 139, 247
  political parties, 70-75, 79-80, 173, 191, 247-48
  private member's bills, 68
  single-issue groups, 76-77, 79-83
  social movements (new), 75-76
  theory of, 65-66, 91-92, 93, 96-98
  triggering events, 83-91
American Sign Language, as culture, 35-36
animal rights, 35, 79, 85-86, 176, 191
Arington, Michele, 193

Baumgartner, Frank R., 96
Beck, Ulrich, 49-50
Bell, Daniel, 29
Bell, Derrick, 193
Bernstein, Basil, 50-51, 57
Bogdanor, Vernon, 173, 189, 190, 192
Bowler, Scott, 226
Bowler, Shaun, 180, 192
Brandon, William P., 219
Brodie, Janine, 115
Bullock, Charles S. III, 203

Cain, Bruce E., 193
Cairns, Alan, 149

capital punishment
  Canada, 11, 74, 114, 117, 119, 212, 214-15, 233, 239, 242, 243, 253-54
  France, 72, 90-91, 123-24, 130, 202, 212, 215-17, 233, 239, 242, 243, 254
  Germany, 217-18, 233, 242, 243, 254-55
  United Kingdom, 13, 73, 80, 89-90, 126-27, 212-14, 233, 239, 242, 254
  United States, 16, 174, 175, 214, 232, 239, 242, 253
Carmines, Edward G., 71
children's rights (UK), 161-62
Christian Right
  Canada, 19, 40-41, 72, 185
  United States, 19, 30, 39-40, 72, 145, 180, 181
Christoph, James B., 13, 89, 90, 127, 213
church-state relations, 81, 82, 145-46, 153, 159, 186, 187, 189, 191, 204
civil rights (US), 33, 83, 84, 139-40, 174, 175, 176, 179-80, 185, 193, 203
Clark, Terry Nichols, 36-37
class conflict, 15, 18, 30, 31, 33, 36-37, 42, 47, 50, 60, 70-71, 73, 245
Clotfelter, Charles T., 177
Cobb, Roger W., 66, 76, 91
Coleman, James, 185
compliance, 140, 202-08
confederate flag debate (US), 183-84
Conradt, David P., 123
Cook, Philip J., 177
Cowley, Philip, 82, 114, 119, 121, 132, 239, 240, 245, 246
critical social philosophy, 31-32
cultural theory, 11, 19, 42, 52-60, 240

grid-group analysis, 53-55
  moral conflict as cultural hierarchism vs. cultural egalitarianism, 57-60
culture wars, 17, 19, 38-41, 57-58, 77, 181

Dalton, Russell J., 70, 71, 247, 248
Davis, James A., 208
Davis, Lori, 219
daylight savings time, 185, 187
Daynes, Byron W., 14, 78
de Tocqueville, Alexis, 17
deaf, 35-36
den Dulk, Kevin R., 150
Derthick, Martha, 165
disabled, 35
divorce, 187, 188, 189, 190, 211
Donovan, Todd, 180, 192
Douglas, Mary, 52, 54, 56, 57, 58
drugs, 14, 16, 69-70, 148, 176, 178, 187, 188, 208, 210

egalitarianism, as cultural value, 12, 37, 53-60, 110, 111, 112, 139
Elder, Charles D., 76, 91
Ely, John Hart, 141
English-Only laws. *See* language laws
environmentalism, 38, 175, 188. *See also* agenda-setting
Epp, Charles, 151
Epstein, Lee, 144
equal rights (Canada), 153
Eule, Julian, 193
European Commission of Human Rights, 156, 158, 163
European Court of Human Rights, 20, 131, 156-57, 161-64
European Court of Justice, 157, 159

euthanasia, 20, 82, 91, 92, 93, 148, 152-53, 176, 180, 208, 209, 210, 212, 230, 232, 248-50
    Netherlands, 248-50

Featherstone, Mike, 47, 50
feminism, 31, 32, 33, 68, 74, 75, 159
flag debate (Canada), 73-74, 78, 114-15, 127-28, 184, 230, 241-42
Flanagan, Scott, 37-38, 201, 247-48
Flanagan, Tom, 186
fluoridation, of water supplies, 185, 240, 246
Forbes, H.D., 32
fox-hunting (UK), 15, 60, 120, 230, 232
Franklin, Grace, 14
French Constitutional Council, 132, 137-38, 157, 159-60, 164-65

Gamble, Barbara S., 193
gambling, 68, 175, 176-78, 185-86, 187, 191, 230, 231-32
gender equity (Canada), 154, 159.
    See also feminism
Gerber, Elisabeth, 192
German Constitutional Court, 132, 137-38, 157-59, 164, 222-23, 232
Glazer, Nathan, 33
Glendon, Mary Ann, 165
Glick, Henry R., 209
Granberg, Donald, 241
Griffiths, John, 249-50
Guinier, Lani, 33
gun control, 72, 74-75, 79, 88-89, 93, 176, 202, 205-07, 230, 231, 232, 240, 244
Gusfield, Joseph, 76
Guttmann, Amy, 31, 32

Haider-Markel, Donald P., 180

hate crimes, 34
hate speech, 155-56
Hein, Gregory, 150
hierarchism, as cultural value, 12, 30, 37, 52-59, 110, 111, 112, 131, 245
Holland, Kenneth, 138, 156, 157, 158, 160, 164
homosexuality, 157, 191
    Canada, 85, 114, 116, 117-18, 128, 139, 153-54, 208, 210, 225-27, 230, 232, 242, 268
    France 11, 208, 210, 228, 229-30, 233, 251, 269
    Germany, 69, 208, 210, 228-29, 231, 233, 269
    United Kingdom, 82, 118-19, 161, 162-64, 208, 210, 227, 230, 232, 233, 242, 269
    United States, 39-40, 82, 84-85, 146-48, 176, 180-83, 193, 208, 210, 224-25, 232, 242, 267-68
Hoover, Dennis R., 41, 72, 150
Hunter, James Davison, 39-41
Hutchinson, Amy, 209

identity (or identity politics), 19, 25-28, 30-35, 50, 75, 240
    postmodern identities, 50-51, 57-58, 60
individualism
    as cultural value, 12, 53-57, 59, 110, 111, 112, 139
    modernity, 11, 48-50
Inglehart, Ronald, 36-38, 71, 201, 208, 247-48
Ingram, David, 32, 34

Johnston, Richard, 215
Jones, Byron D., 96
judicial review, 98, 137-41, 156-57, 160-61, 164-65, 193, 251

Kinder, Donald R., 203
Kingdon, John, 83
Kniss, Fred, 40, 41
Knopff, Rainer, 69, 149, 151, 154, 242, 247
Kobach, Kris, 190, 191
Kymlicka, Will, 32

Lachmann, Ludwig M., 94
Lamb, Charles M., 203
Landfried, Christine, 164
language laws, 82-83, 154-55, 176, 179-80, 193, 230, 232, 242
Layman, Geoffrey C., 71
legislative process. *See* morality policy, legislative process
Lipset, Seymour Martin, 29-30, 70, 112, 173, 241
    working-class authoritarianism, 241
litigation strategy. *See also* agenda-setting
    cause lawyering, 142-43
    Court Challenges Program (Canada), 150
Lowi, Theodore J., 13-15, 67, 77-79, 96, 234
Luker, Kristin, 30

MacKinnon, Catherine A., 155
MacMillan, C. Michael, 154
Madison, James, 192
Magleby, David, 174, 175, 192, 193
Mandel, Michael, 149
Margolis, M., 206
marijuana, medical use of, 148, 176, 178
Marsh, David, 113, 162, 242
mass society thesis, 18, 28, 29
Mauser, Gary A., 206, 207, 244
McNaught, Kenneth, 149

Meier, Kenneth J., 14, 16, 66, 177, 180, 201, 242
Meyer, David S., 97
Mezey, Susan Gluck, 151
Miller, Hugh, 78
Millett, Kate, 31, 75
Mills, C. Wright, 26
Mooney, Christopher Z., 41
Moral Majority, 39, 40, 41, 82
morality policy
    anti-majoritarianism, 165, 222, 231, 232, 233, 241-44, 247, 251
    attributes of, 239-40
    elitism, 11, 17, 20, 194, 212-13, 230, 232, 234, 240, 241, 243, 244, 245, 247
    depolitization, avoidance, post-ponement strategies, 111
    frequency of, 239
    implementation (*see* compliance)
    juridicization of, 20, 137-38, 165
    one-sided versus two-sided, 16, 66-67, 69, 177, 201, 242
    plebiscite, 173-94, 246 (*see also* referendum)
    political motivations, 16, 76-77, 78-79, 180-81, 202
    redistribution of values, 14-16, 20, 76, 194, 201-04, 209, 217, 230, 231, 241-42
    rise of, 11-12, 25-28, 47-48
morality policy, legislative process
    collective responsibility, 108, 109, 112-14, 121-23, 125, 127, 245
    unwhipped (free) votes, 114, 115, 116, 118, 119, 246-47
    comparing the 4th and 5th French Republics, 107-10
    parliamentary timetables, 108, 109, 112, 116, 125-27, 128-29

political parties, 69, 108, 109, 112, 113, 114, 121, 124, 129-31, 158, 188, 245
political unaccountability, 132, 241, 241, 247, 251
private member's bills, 109, 113, 114, 118, 119, 120-21
Morton, F.L. (Ted), 69, 116, 149, 151, 154, 242, 247
multiculturalism, 28, 32, 33-34

Nevitte, Neil, 36, 59, 208, 209, 219
New Political Culture (NPC), 36-38
Niblock, John F., 193
nuclear (anti-), 97

obscenity, 72, 82, 144-45, 155, 176
Olson, Mancur, 76
Olson, Susan, 145
Outshoorn, Joyce, 111, 129, 222, 248

Pal, Leslie A., 81-82, 149, 206
Phillips, Anne, 33
physician-assisted suicide (PAS). *See* euthanasia
political opportunity structure. *See* agenda-setting
political parties. *See* agenda-setting; morality policy, legislative process
pornography. *See* obscenity
postmaterialism, 11, 17, 19, 20, 25, 57, 59, 191, 192, 208-09, 230-31, 242, 248
political realignment, 36-38, 70-72, 201, 247-48
postmodern. *See* identity
Pothier, Dianne, 114
prohibition, of alcoholic beverages, 184, 185, 186, 239
Pross, Paul, 149

public opinion, 208-09, 210-11
abortion, 205, 208, 218-24, 232, 233, 241, 244, 259-65
anti-majoritarianism (*see* morality policy)
capital punishment, 73, 130, 212, 213-18, 233, 242-43, 244, 253-58
environmentalism, 92-93
euthanasia (or physician-assisted suicide), 93, 209, 211, 212, 232, 249, 250
flag debate (Canada), 230, 241-42
fox-hunting (UK), 120
gun control, 206-07, 244
homosexuality, 224-30, 230, 233, 242, 267-73
legal change, impact on, 230-34
school prayer, 232
public policy
distribution, regulation, redistribution, 13, 14-15, 77-78, 96, 140, 201-04, 234
emotive symbolic, 13
as purposive plan, 94, 95, 96
social regulation, 14, 76

race relations (US). *See* civil rights (US)
Ranney, Austin, 173, 175
Rayside, David, 116, 118, 128, 226
Raz, Joseph, 32
Read, Melvyn D., 113, 162, 242
referendum, 184, 186-91. *See also* morality policy
Canada, 98, 184-86
France, 98, 187-88
Germany, 98, 187
United Kingdom, 98, 187
United States, 98, 174-84, 185, 192-93
Ripley, Randall, 14

Russell, Peter, 149, 152, 153

Sanders, Lynn M ., 203
Sarat, Austin, 142
Schattschneider, E.E., 14, 95, 96, 138
    socialization of conflict, 95-96
Scheingold, Stuart, 139-40, 142
Scheppele, Kim Lane, 165
school prayer (US), 72, 204, 230, 232
Sharp, Elaine, 15, 17, 69, 70,
Shaw, Steven, 181
Sheatsley, Paul B., 203
single-issue groups. *See* agenda-set-
    ting
Smith, Miriam, 85, 139
Smith, T. Alexander, 13, 115
Smith, Tom W., 203
social movements (new). *See* agen-
    da-setting
Soper, J. Christopher, 97
Spaeth, Harold, 145
Spitzer, Robert J., 206
Staggenborg, Suzanne, 97
status
    left-wing extremism, 35-36
    in moral conflicts, 11, 17-19, 25-28,
        30, 31, 42, 47-50, 58, 60, 75, 240
    moral conflict as status differ-
        entiation vs. status equaliza-
        tion, 58, 60, 240
    right-wing extremism, 28-30

Stetson, Dorothy McBride, 80, 88,
    124, 221
Stone, Alex, 137, 156, 165
Stone, Gregory, 27
Studlar, Donley T., 73, 119, 239-40

Tarrow, Sidney, 97
Tatalovich, Raymond, 14, 78, 154,
    218
Taylor, Charles, 31-32, 33
terrorism (UK), 164
Thorne, Susan, 114
Tyler, Tom R., 204

video lottery terminals
    (VLTs)(Canada), 185-86

Wald, Kenneth D., 84
Weber, Max, 17-18, 78-79
Wildavsky, Aaron, 52, 53, 56, 57, 112
Women's Legal Education and Ac-
    tion Fund (LEAF)(Canada),
    150, 151, 155
women's rights. *See* feminism

Young, Iris Marion, 32